I0004784

Denise Gengatharen

Government Sponsored Online Platforms for SMEs

Denise Gengatharen

Government Sponsored Online Platforms for SMEs

Assessing Success and Evaluating Benefits

VDM Verlag Dr. Müller

Imprint

Bibliographic information by the German National Library: The German National Library lists this publication at the German National Bibliography; detailed bibliographic information is available on the Internet at http://dnb.d-nb.de.

Cover image: www.purestockx.com

Publisher:
VDM Verlag Dr. Müller Aktiengesellschaft & Co. KG , Dudweiler Landstr. 125 a, 66123 Saarbrücken, Germany,
Phone +49 681 9100-698, Fax +49 681 9100-988,
Email: info@vdm-verlag.de

Zugl.: Western Australia, Edith Cowan University, Diss., 2006

Produced in USA and UK by:
Lightning Source Inc., La Vergne, Tennessee, USA
Lightning Source UK Ltd., Milton Keynes, UK
BookSurge LLC, 5341 Dorchester Road, Suite 16, North Charleston, SC 29418, USA

ISBN: 978-3-639-05866-6

ACKNOWLEDGEMENTS

I would like to thank my supervisor Professor Craig Standing for his gentle guidance, patience, perseverance and understanding throughout this journey. Your encouragement, knowledge-sharing and dedicated mentoring are greatly appreciated.

To Professor Janice Burn, my associate supervisor, thank you for your contributions.

To all the participants in this study, I thank you for your valuable time and assistance. Thanks especially to the participants from regional WA; your willingness to share and your collaboration are exemplary.

Thanks also to my fellow travellers in the PhD Suite at 2.149 in Joondalup. The bumpy ride is bearable when there's someone to share it with.

I would also like to thank all those in administration at ECU who have helped in one way or another to smoothen the journey.

To my wonderful family, my husband Genga and my children Rohan and Sonia, this work could not have happened without your unfailing love, support and sacrifice. Guys, I'm back!!!!

Last but not least, to the one constant in my life, my heavenly Father – All glory and honour is Yours.

TABLE OF CONTENTS

CHAPTER 1

INTRODUCTION

1.1   BACKGROUND

Small and medium enterprises (SMEs) are an integral part of many economies. They contribute half of private non-farm gross domestic product (GDP) and employment in the USA (Office of the Advocacy United States Small Business Association, n.d), roughly half of GDP in Canada (Canadian Federation of Independent Business, 2003) and account for between 60 to 70 percent of total employment in some countries (OECD, 2000). In Australia, small businesses alone (those with less than 20 full time employees) contribute 30 percent of GDP (Australian Government Department of Foreign Affairs and Trade, 2005), while SMEs create 40 percent of Australia's GDP, represent 48 percent of the workforce and make up 96 percent of all businesses in Australia (CPA Australia cited in Australian Centre for Co-operative Research and Development, n.d). Given their importance, many countries pay specific attention to stimulating the business development of their SME sectors.

In the last decade, the Internet has been viewed as a way for SMEs to overcome the disadvantages of distance and size and compete with large companies, both locally and internationally. However, although research on the uptake of Internet e-commerce by SMEs indicated growing levels of awareness and enthusiasm for e-commerce (Bode & Burn, 2001; Daniel, Wilson & Myers, 2002; Poon & Swatman, 1997; Walczuch, Van Braven & Lundgren, 2000), these studies also showed that in the late 1990s and early 2000s only a small proportion of SMEs were realising substantial benefits from the Internet. Some studies showed that the majority of SMEs used the Internet mainly for communication and research, and that e-commerce was not integrated with their business processes (Stansfield & Grant, 2003; Walczuch et al., 2000). The major challenges faced by SMEs in adopting e-commerce stemmed from a lack of technological expertise, uncertainty about the benefits offered by e-commerce and a lack of advice on Internet strategy (van Akkeren & Cavaye, 1999b).

In an effort to ensure that SMEs did not fall on the wrong side of a digital divide, governments at both the national and regional levels introduced a number of measures to encourage increased uptake of e-commerce by SMEs. Some of these were broad-based measures like providing suitable telecommunications and regulatory environments. Others were more targeted and include websites containing advice for SMEs on the benefits of e-commerce (see for example Western Australia's

Small Business Development Corporation's 'e-com entry point' at http://www.sbdc.com.au/index2.asp) and case studies of successful SME e-commerce ventures (at http://www.noie.gov.au/projects/ebusiness/Advancing/case_studies.htm#casestudy).

Some governments at the national, state and local levels attempted to stimulate SME adoption of e-commerce by creating or sponsoring Internet-based trading platforms designed specifically for this sector. Examples of these trading platforms are MySouthWest in Western Australia, Korean Marketplace, Nextr@de of Japan, Taiwantrade, Thailand.com and Hong Kong's HKenterprise. The use of government-sponsored regional Internet trading platforms to encourage SME participation in e-commerce was also an approach taken in Europe (E-Business Policy Group, 2002). The Electronic Mall Bodensee, Europe's first regional e-marketplace (REM) covering the Lake Constance area bounded by Switzerland, Austria and Germany, was launched in 1995.

These platforms were established to introduce SMEs to Internet-trading in a trusted environment without the need for high costs or compliance with complex technology. The platforms have differing business models (online shopping malls, procurement hubs, regional e-marketplaces, online catalogues) as well as varied sponsorship or ownership structures (federal government agencies; state governments; single local governments; local chambers of commerce; public/private consortia comprising local governments, local business associations, higher education institutes and private investors). At the regional level, these platforms were viewed as vehicles to promote regional economic development by balancing out geographical disadvantages (Zimmerman, 1998).

Some platforms like the Lonxanet (Dans & Freire, 2002) and Regional Electronic Trade Facilitation Centre (Wilkins, Swatman & Castleman, 2003a; 2003b) were developed as stand-alone business-to-business (B2B) vertical e-marketplaces within specific industry sectors. Others like Bizewest (Tatnall & Burgess, 2002), were designed as broader-based horizontal B2B portals catering for e-commerce across different sectors. There were also government-sponsored regional Internet trading platforms for SMEs that were part of wider regional online community portals (the Electronic Mall Bodensee in Europe). These catered for both B2B and B2C (business to consumer) online trading and was the model favoured by local governments and other regional consortia in Western Australia (WA).

The owners of one such WA regional online community portal (the research industry partner, a consortium comprising the local governments of two neighbouring towns, their business associations and Edith Cowan University [ECU]) originally partly funded this research, the other research funding body being the Australian Research Council (ARC). The trading arm of the portal was a horizontal REM which was expected to be the electronic gateway to trade with SME

2

businesses in the region. The funding was to enable research into the evaluation of the benefits of REMs for SMEs. However, the portal was discontinued midway through the research.

When the research first began in early 2003, little was available in either the business or academic literature on government-sponsored regional Internet trading platforms for SMEs. Although some of these types of platforms had been in existence for a few years, information was scarce on their performance and whether or not they were meeting their objectives of encouraging SME participation in e-commerce and contributing to regional economic development.

The portal owned by the research industry partner had become operational a few months earlier (December 2002), but had difficulty attracting the participation of local buyers and sellers on the REM. Anecdotal evidence also indicated that while some of the regional community portals in WA were up and running, their e-commerce platforms were either faltering or could not get off the ground. Therefore, while the research was required to fulfil the funding criteria of the ARC by evaluating the benefits of REMs for SMEs, there was an even greater need to determine the factors that facilitated or inhibited the successful implementation of such platforms.

In examining the literature available then, there was a strand of literature that focused on critical success factors for e-marketplaces (Brunn, Jensen & Skovgaard, 2002; Fong, Fowler & Swatman, 1998; Kollmann, 2000; Le, 2002) and inter-organisational information systems (Grover, 1993). This helped in developing an initial understanding of the possible facilitators and inhibitors of successful implementation of government-sponsored regional Internet trading platforms for SMEs. However, these studies did not provide a complete view of the development and management of such platforms and participation in them, especially where the platforms were developed as part of regional online community portals. Some studies (Fong et al., 1998; Kollmann, 2000) viewed e-marketplaces only in terms of specific industries, while others examined e-marketplaces from a value proposition perspective (Le, 2002). Although some studies proposed guidelines for successful deployment of e-marketplaces (Brunn et al., 2002; Kambil & Van Heck, 1998; Khalifa, Banerjee & Ma, 2003), inter-organisational information systems (Kurnia & Johnston, 2000) and portals (Damsgaard, 2002), they could not be used on their own for an holistic examination of government-supported regional Internet trading platforms for SMEs, due to the different motivation behind the creation of this type of platform and the presence of additional stakeholder groups. Furthermore these studies did not provide any insight into how the supposed benefits of e-marketplaces, inter-organisational information systems (IOIS) and portals were to be evaluated. Given that government-supported regional Internet trading platforms for SMEs encompass a complex interplay between technical, economic, social, political and cultural factors, it was imperative to determine the direct

3

and indirect costs and tangible and intangible benefits for all stakeholder groups concerned and to develop the metrics to measure them.

There was also a need to determine if the target participants of these sorts of platforms had any special characteristics or needs that could affect the success of the platforms and the realisation of benefits from participating in them. The then extant literature on the adoption of information technology by SMEs (Caldeira & Ward, 2002; Cragg & King, 1993; Fink, 1998; Thong, 1999) and SME adoption of e-commerce (Ba, Whinston & Zhang, 2001; Brown & Lockett, 2001; Chau, 2001; Cloete, Courtney & Fintz, 2002; Levy & Powell, 2003) could provide some theoretical insights into how SMEs could possibly respond to adopting Internet e-commerce via a portal. However, participation in government-sponsored regional Internet trading platforms would add new dimensions to this area of research because of the community, economic development and non-profit motives underlying the creation of such platforms.

This research therefore took an exploratory approach to assessing the success and evaluating the benefits of government-sponsored regional Internet trading platforms for SMEs. An examination was first undertaken of the SME sector in Australia. Next, the Internet and e-commerce were examined in the light of the role that they were expected to play in bridging a digital divide that was perceived to exist at the turn of the century between regional and suburban Australia and between SMEs and large companies. This was followed by an examination of Internet trading platforms to determine their evolution, the benefits that they could provide to participating SMEs and the existing 'state of play' of government-supported platforms. Existing theoretical perspectives on SME adoption of ICT (information communication technologies) and e-commerce were then reviewed to determine which constructs of these theories could be used to provide an initial understanding of the factors that could possibly influence SME participation in government-sponsored regional Internet trading platforms.

Constructs from the literature in these two major areas were then synthesised into a conceptual framework of the factors that could facilitate or inhibit the successful implementation of government-supported regional Internet trading platforms for SMEs. To derive an appropriate conceptual framework against which to evaluate the benefits, costs and ultimately the success of such platforms, the research then turned to an examination of the literature on evaluation, particularly the evaluation of information systems (IS) and of policies/programmes/regional development. Existing economics-based evaluation models of IS were extended by constructs from evaluation studies of policies/programmes/regional development to consider the "conceptualization of local or regional e-commerce as a form of commerce which is embedded in the social, political, cultural, technical and economic structures [of a region]" (Steinfield & Klein, 1999, p.49) and the context of the evaluation over time.

The usefulness of the conceptual frameworks was empirically examined in a structured longitudinal multiple case study of three government-supported regional Internet trading platforms for SMEs in WA. These platforms were developed as part of regional online community portals. The first case, the portal owned by the research industry partner, was the subject of an in-depth case study and a participant-observation action research approach, given the access to artefacts, documents and personnel that the funding arrangements made available. Subsequent cases were mini-cases chosen for theoretical replication (Yin, 2003, p.47) and analytical generalisation (Darke, Shanks & Broadbent, 1998, p.278). The conceptual frameworks were refined by comparing the data from each case with themes that emerged, insights gained from the research and the extant literature.

The research culminates in the proposal of refined empirically-based theoretical frameworks which can be used to assess the success and evaluate the benefits of other government-supported regional trading platforms for SMEs. A process model is also proposed to guide the planning, implementation and management of these types of platforms where they are developed as part of regional online community portals.

1.2   RESEARCH QUESTIONS

The research project has both theoretical and practical objectives. The theory relates to examining appropriate strategies, frameworks and models for the adoption and use of information systems that involve community, social, economic and technical objectives. However, in order to be relevant, the implications of the research have to be 'implementable' or prescribed in a manner that could be put to use to exploit an opportunity or solve a problem (Benbasat & Zmud, 1999). The relevance and practical nature of this study is demonstrated by the need for theoretical (and practical) guidance in formulating strategies for the successful development and evaluation of government-sponsored regional Internet trading platforms for SMEs. The relevance of the project is further highlighted by the decision of the regional governments in one of the cases to sponsor an Australian Research Council Linkage grant in order to obtain direct support and guidance.

When research is funded, the research design and scope of the questions that the research seeks to address are influenced by the expectations of the funding bodies and other stakeholders (Darke et al., 1998). The application for funding for this research was made on the basis that its main focus would be a) the evaluation of benefits that government-supported REMs can provide SMEs, local government sponsors and the region, and b) the provision of information and recommendations to help SMEs in the decision making processes related to e-marketplace selection and adoption. A subsidiary focus of the research was to be an examination of the issues relating to the creation and management of e-marketplaces by regional governments, with an emphasis on the stimulation of business development. The research questions arising from these foci were to be answered by an in-depth case study with an embedded design (Yin, 2003, p.40) of the portal owned by the research industry partner, the units of analysis being SME participants, the local governments supporting the portal and the region.

However, by the time funding approval was obtained and the research could officially commence, the portal owned by the research industry partner was in difficulties with low participation rates, no trade transactions, and problems with the REM technology and with the overall management of the portal. It became imperative that the research had to have a balanced focus between determining the facilitators and inhibitors of successful implementation of government-supported REMs for SMEs and on the evaluation of the benefits that these platforms could provide for SMEs, government sponsors and the region. There was also a need to find a balance between the contributions that the research could make to theory and the practical outcomes that could be used to advise the development and management of such platforms. While the initial research approach was to be one of an in-depth case study and participant-observation action research of the portal owned by the research industry partner, the low participation rates and the threats to the continued existence of the portal meant that the research had to look at other Internet trading platforms for SMEs in order to be both rigorous and relevant and also fulfil the funding requirements of the ARC. The research approach thus evolved into a structured multiple case study of three such portals in Western Australia.

The three main research questions and their subsidiary questions were therefore as follows:

Research Question 1 - What are the factors that facilitate and inhibit the successful implementation of government-sponsored regional Internet trading platforms for SMEs?

Subsidiary Questions:

RQ1i. How do existing theoretical frameworks explain these facilitators and inhibitors?

RQ1ii. Why are these factors significant?

Research Question 2 – How and where can existing theories of IT adoption be used to explain the adoption and use of Internet trading platforms by governments in promoting SME uptake of e-commerce and regional economic development?

Subsidiary Questions:

RQ2i.   What are the strengths of existing IT adoption theories?

RQ2ii.   What are the limitations of these theories?

Research Question 3 - What are the costs and the benefits (for SME participants, government sponsors and the region) of government-sponsored regional Internet trading platforms for SMEs?

Subsidiary Questions:

RQ3i.   How can these costs and benefits be measured?

RQ3ii.   How can this type of platform be effectively evaluated?

To address Research Questions 1 and 2, the research looked to the existing body of knowledge in related areas (RQ1i, RQ2i and RQ2ii) to help build the initial conceptual theoretical framework for the study. The theory-based framework was refined and tailored to the specific context of the study through the collection and analysis of empirical evidence from the multiple cases (RQ1ii).

Research Question 3 then sought to determine the metrics with which the costs and benefits for all stakeholders of these sorts of platforms could be evaluated (RQ3i) and the process by which this evaluation could be effectively conducted (RQ3ii). This was to enable consideration of the different costs and benefits that the stakeholders could experience at different stages of platform development and to measure the outcomes that are achieved against the objectives behind the creation of the platforms and thus determine their success.

1.3   ETHICAL CONSIDERATIONS

In Australia, this research falls under the ambit of The National Statement on Ethical Conduct in Research Involving Humans (1999). This entailed the approval of the Information Letters to Participants, Participant Informed Consent forms and the Interview Schedules by the Human Research Ethics Committee (HREC) of the researcher's university prior to the collection of any primary data. The forms and interview schedules were submitted for approval in November 2003, after the research industry partner decided then that the portal would continue to operate. Approval was obtained in early 2004. Primary data collection from Case 1 proceeded in February 2004 but portal operations were halted two months later and the portal was officially wound up in October that same year.

All participants (platform owners and SMEs) in face-to-face interviews in this study were given an Information Letter stating the purpose of the research and informing them of their rights. They were given Informed Consent forms to sign, which stated their understanding of their role and their rights as participants. The Informed Consent forms also recorded the participants' agreement that the research data gathered for this study may be published provided anonymity was preserved or alternatively that such agreement was given with the full understanding that the participants may be identified. This option was offered to interview participants who may have chosen to be identified because they were willing to share their experiences or act as mentors or advisors to existing or potential platform participants or owners. With telephone interviews, approval was obtained for the recorded agreement to be used to clearly establish participants' consent. All participants in this study chose to remain anonymous. Pseudonyms were therefore used to identify the portals and each interview respondent was allocated a research code by which they were referred to throughout the study.

1.4   CONTRIBUTION OF THIS BOOK

Although government-supported regional Internet trading platforms for SMEs had been in existence for almost a decade when this research commenced, it was an area of nascent research where theory and understanding were not well developed. The absence of comprehensive or definitive theoretical frameworks meant that researchers and practitioners in this area had to pick and choose relevant constructs of existing best practices, theories and models from related areas to examine the facilitators and inhibitors of successful implementation of such platforms and to evaluate their costs and benefits. Although these platforms were set up for benefits like lower transaction costs and access to wider markets that they could provide to SMEs and for regional development purposes, empirical evidence to support or disprove the realisation of these benefits was not readily available. There were also no benefits-evaluation frameworks that considered holistically the economic, social, political and cultural factors that could affect the realisation of benefits and influence the costs of these sorts of platforms.

This book contributes to both the research and practice communities in the area of government-supported regional Internet trading platforms for SMEs by providing three interrelated theory-based and empirically refined frameworks to guide the planning, development, management and evaluation of such platforms. These frameworks are:

1. An integrated definitive conceptual theoretical framework or model that can be used to provide a holistic view of the facilitators and inhibitors of the successful implementation of these types of platforms. The initial conceptual framework considered previous knowledge as a scaffolding for the research design and data collection (Walsham, 1995, p. 76) by drawing on existing theories and best practices in the areas of a) the creation and management of Internet trading platforms and participation in them and b) SME adoption of ICT and e-commerce. A structured longitudinal multiple case study (Carroll & Swatman, 2000) with an embedded design was used to refine the initial theoretical frameworks through an iterative process of empirical data collection, analysis and comparison to extant literature and developments in the field. In this way, an understanding was developed of the significant facilitators and inhibitors of successful implementation of these types of platforms and of any moderating factors. This research therefore allows practitioners and researchers in this field to have an empirically derived theory-based frame of reference with which to begin the assessment of the facilitators and inhibitors of other government-supported Internet trading platforms for SMEs.

2. A benefits-evaluation framework which can be used to evaluate the tangible and intangible benefits and the direct and indirect costs of this type of regional Internet trading platform for various stakeholders, viz SMEs, government sponsors and the region over time. This is necessary given the large investments outlaid on some regional trading platforms and the fact that some benefits could materialise only at later stages of platform development. The West Midlands Commerce Collaborative Marketplace involved total costs of £3.1 million (Government Office for The West Midlands, 2002, April 23) and this was to upgrade the already existing 'go4gain' SME portal in the West Midlands into a collaborative e-marketplace. Public funds of AU$360,000 were expended on the portal owned by the research industry partner before it could even be aggressively marketed to the inhabitants of the region. The opportunity costs of these funds and the frequent calls on the public purse for economic development expenditure make it necessary to determine how government-supported regional Internet trading platforms for SMEs can be properly evaluated to measure their effectiveness as regional economic development tools and to determine whether or not they are meeting the objective of increasing Internet e-commerce uptake by SMEs. This can be used to guide other regional authorities in Australia and in other countries, who may be tempted to view the ubiquitousness of the Internet as a quick,

9

inexpensive and easy way to bridge the digital divide that may exist between regional or rural and suburban areas and between SMEs and larger companies.

3. A process model to guide the effective implementation of government-supported regional Internet trading platforms for SMEs that are developed as part of regional online community portals. The model incorporates the principles of managing the development and implementation of large imprecise information systems. It allows for a structured approach to realistic goal setting and allows iterative application of both the aforementioned frameworks to determine the facilitators and inhibitors, costs and the economic and social benefits of these types of Internet trading platforms for all stakeholders at every stage of development.

The approach taken during this research was to disseminate the findings as early as possible to inform the academic research community and provide information for trading platform stakeholders and the wider practitioner community interested in regional trading platforms and e-marketplaces. The research study resulted in a number of refereed papers in conferences and journals as per the list appended after the References section.

1.5   LAYOUT OF THIS BOOK

A graphical representation of the layout of this book is presented in figure 1.1:

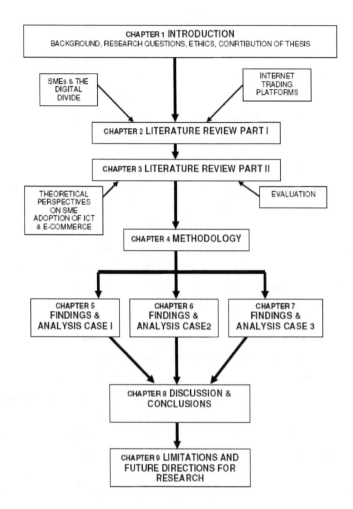

Figure 1.1 Graphical Representation of Book Layout

Following the introduction to the study in this chapter, **Chapter 2** contains the first part of a comprehensive literature review which begins with definitions of SMEs, an overview of the SME sector in the Australian economy and the antecedents to government intervention in stimulating Internet e-commerce adoption by this sector. The literature in the related research area of Internet trading platforms is then reviewed in terms of theoretical contributions, models and critical success factors.

Chapter 3 contains the second part of the literature review, in which SME adoption of ICT and e-commerce, and the research area of evaluation are reviewed. The knowledge gleaned from the sources in chapters 2 and 3 is synthesised to create the initial conceptual frameworks for the study. The literature reviewed in these 2 chapters was thus published prior to 2004. The literature published after this date is reviewed in subsequent chapters, as part of the iterative process of comparing the data collected from each case to the extant literature and insights that emerged during the course of the study.

Chapter 4 discusses the underlying philosophical perspectives influencing the research approach and shows how the most suitable research method was selected to answer the research questions. A research model is then presented. The context of the research is set with a discussion of the Western Australian perspective on government-supported regional Internet trading platforms for SMEs and descriptions of the three cases in the study. A description is provided of the research design which contains the data collection and analysis techniques and the protocols used. The chapter continues with a discussion on the issues of reliability, validity, generalisability and triangulation and concludes with a discussion of the view of the researcher.

The results from the action research part of the study provided insights which were used in developing the conceptual framework for the multiple case study design. The results are presented in **Chapter 5.** The findings from the in-depth study of Case 1 are also presented in this chapter, categorised according to the constructs in the conceptual frameworks. The broad constructs are the Owner or Sponsor context, the Technology (or trading platform) context, the Organisational (SME participant) context and the Environmental context. The results from Case 1 are discussed and compared with emergent themes and insights and the extant literature, which are then used to advise the conceptual theoretical framework for the next case, Case 2. The findings from Case 2 are presented in **Chapter 6.** The process of analysis, recognition of emergent themes and insights and comparison of the results to the extant literature is repeated to further refine the conceptual frameworks for Case 3, the findings of which are discussed in **Chapter 7.**

In **Chapter 8**, some of the major findings across the three cases are discussed collectively and are related back to the research questions. A refined theoretical framework of *significant* facilitators and inhibitors to the successful implementation of government-supported regional Internet trading platforms for SMEs is presented. This chapter also proposes a refined benefits-evaluation framework that considers the direct and indirect costs and the tangible and intangible benefits of such platforms for all stakeholders. An integrated stage model is proposed for the development, implementation and management of government-supported regional Internet trading platforms for

SMEs where they are developed as part of regional online community portals. Finally, conclusions that are drawn from the research are discussed. An acknowledgement of the limitations to the study and recommendations for future research are presented in **Chapter 9**.

This is followed by the **References** section which lists all references used in this book and a list of the **Refereed Publications** that arose out of this study. Five **Appendices** are then provided on terms and definitions, interview schedules and consent forms and finally two lists are included of tables and figures that can be found in the book.

CHAPTER 2
LITERATURE REVIEW PART I

2.1 INTRODUCTION

The literature reviewed in this chapter (and the subsequent chapter) was published prior to 2004. The literature was used as scaffolding in the construction of the initial conceptual frameworks for the study which, according to Miles and Huberman (1994, p. 18), explain "either graphically or in narrative form, the main things to be studied – the key factors, constructs or variables - and the presumed relationships between them".

The chapter starts with the literature reviewed on definitions of SMEs. The problems relating to a universal and Australian definition of SME are highlighted, necessitating a definition of Australian SME in the context of this research. Next, the role of the SME sector in the Australian economy and the antecedents to government intervention in stimulating the uptake of e-commerce in this sector are reviewed exposing gaps which this research strives to fill. The review then discusses literature in the area of Internet trading platforms. Two other major areas of research are reviewed in the subsequent chapter. They are the various theoretical perspectives on SME adoption of ICT and e-commerce and the literature relating to evaluation of IS and policy/programme evaluation. The use of multiple theoretical perspectives in building the initial conceptual frameworks is influenced by Walsham's belief that "research on micro phenomena of IS development and use can, and should, be informed by more general macro theories on the nature of organizations and social processes within them" (1995, p. 77). This approach is also proposed by Dobson (2001a, p. 295), especially for longitudinal studies as "different theories can be critically applied [over the duration of the study] dependent on the organizational situation". The use of multiple theoretical perspectives as scaffolding for the initial conceptual framework of the study was also mitigated by the fact that government-sponsored Internet trading platforms for SMEs was a research area that was complex, was poorly understood and on which not much was available in the literature at the beginning of 2003 when the research began.

The literature review included the extant research in the abovementioned areas in journals, conference proceedings, monographs, university working papers, reports and web sites of local, interstate and international government and SME bodies. The websites of other regional trading platforms that had some form of government support were also examined, as were the internal documents of the research industry partner and the websites and other published and unpublished documents on the two regional portals in this study. As the research areas on Internet trading platforms (e-marketplaces and portals) were relatively new and evolving, the 'grey' literature comprising business and press publications was also reviewed to obtain a deeper understanding of the phenomena from all possible angles. The insights and knowledge gleaned from all these sources were synthesised to form the initial conceptual frameworks of the study which are summarised at the end of chapter 3.

2.2   SMALL AND MEDIUM ENTERPRISES (SMEs)

2.2.1   Definition of SMEs

The definition of SMEs varies from country to country. In the United States, small businesses are generally defined as independent businesses having fewer than 500 employees (Office of the Advocacy United States Small Business Association, n.d.), but are further classified according to varying industry standards on employment size, sales and annual turnover for government programmes such as contracting (U. S. Small Business Administration, 2002). In Japan, SMEs are generally businesses employing between 4 and 299 people but definitions vary according to sectors and capital invested (see http://www.chusho.meti.go.jp/sme_english/outline/03/01.html).

In the European Union, effective 1st January 2005, the category of micro, small and medium-sized enterprises (SMEs) is made up of enterprises which employ fewer than 250 persons and which have an annual turnover not exceeding € 50 million, and/or an annual balance sheet total not exceeding € 43 million. Within the SME category, a small enterprise is defined as an enterprise with fewer than 50 persons and an annual turnover and/or annual balance sheet total that does not exceed € 10 million, while a micro enterprise is one which employs fewer than 10 persons and whose annual turnover and/or annual balance sheet total does not exceed € 2 million (European Union, 2003).

Within Australia, the definition of SMEs is also problematic. The Australian Bureau of Statistics (ABS) (1999a) defined non-agricultural SMEs according to employment size. The categories of SMEs include:

- Micro businesses - businesses employing less than 5 people.

- Other small businesses - businesses employing 5 or more people, but less than 20 people; and

- Medium business - businesses employing 20 or more people, but less than 200.

In the same publication, the ABS warned that their other publications "including Small Business in Australia (Cat. No. 1321.0), define a small business as all manufacturing businesses with less than 100 employees and all other non-agricultural businesses with less than 20 employees".

The ABS (2000b) in its catalogue 1321.0 defined *agricultural small businesses* not by the number of employees but by Estimated Value of Agricultural Operations (EVAO) which is based on the area of crops sown; the number of livestock; and crops produced and livestock turn-off (mainly sales) during the year. A small agricultural business is defined as one having an EVAO of between AU$22,500 and AU$400,000. In addition, small businesses are also defined as having the following management or organisational characteristics:

- independent ownership and operations;

- close control by owners/managers who also contribute most, if not all the operating capital; and

- principal decision-making by the owners/managers.

Other popular reports on SME uptake of technology in Australia (see for example Sensis Pty Ltd, 2003) defined SMEs only by number of employees i.e. less than 200 employees. In the light of the inconsistencies in the definitions of SMEs both within Australia and overseas, it was important to determine at the outset a standardised definition of Australian SMEs in the context this study. This has been done using the qualitative definitions of the ABS regarding managerial and organisational characteristics, but the quantitative criteria are based on staffing levels only. The quantitative definition of Australian SME in this study is presented in Table 2.1 below:

Table 2.1 Definition of Australian SMEs used in this Study

Business Type	Number of Employees
Micro Enterprise (including non-employing owner-operated businesses)	Less than 5
Small Enterprise	Less than 20
Medium Enterprise	Less than 200

2.2.2 The Role of SMEs in the Australian Economy

In examining the literature to determine the importance of the SME sector to the Australian economy the following sources were identified:

- In 1997-1998, there were approximately 948,000 private sector non-agricultural SMEs in Australia accounting for one third of GDP, 50 percent of total private sector non-agricultural employment and about 40 percent of total public and private sector employment (OECD, 2000, p. 87);

- It was estimated that there were 1,233,200 private sector small businesses (those with less than 20 employees) in Australia during 2000–2001 which represented 97 percent of all private sector businesses and employed almost 49 percent of all private sector employment (Australian Bureau of Statistics, 2002b, p. 1);

- In 2000-2001, all businesses which employed less than 200 persons and did not have assets worth more than AU$200million, (excluding those in the agriculture, forestry, fishing, finance and insurance industries), contributed 49 percent of total industry value added (IVA) to the Australian economy (Australian Bureau of Statistics, 2002a) (The sum of gross value added across all industries plus taxes less subsidies on products equals GDP which is valued at purchases' prices);

- Australia's healthy small business sector accounted for 70 per cent of jobs growth over the past decade and contributed about 30 per cent to GDP (Department of Industry Tourism and Resources, 2003, p. 61).

- SMEs "are vitally important to Australia's economic and social prosperity" (National Office for the Information Economy (NOIE), 2002).

From these sources we can conclude that in Australia, as in other countries, the SME sector plays an important role in the national economy warranting close scrutiny in terms of economic development programs.

2.2.3 SMEs and the Digital Divide in Australia

During the hubris surrounding the dot.com boom and the spread of the Internet, there was a fear in the late 1990s that a digital divide was developing in Australia. This divide was perceived to be between rural/regional and metropolitan Australia in terms of the percentage of population having access to computers and the Internet (figure 2.1), and between SMEs and their larger counterparts (figure 2.2).

	Access to Computer (at home)			Access to Internet (at home)		
	City	Country	Gap	City	Country	Gap
Nov 1998	50	43	7	22	13	7
Nov 1999	53	44	9	30	17	13
Nov 2000	59	52	7	40	32	8

*City refers to capital city statistical divisions.
Source: Australian Bureau Statistics 8147.0 February 2001

Figure 2.1 Computer and Internet Access in City/Country areas* (Source: Curtin, 2001, p. 4)

	Micro businesses	Other small businesses	Total small businesses	Medium businesses	Large businesses	All businesses
	%	%	%	%	%	%
Businesses with access to Internet	17	24	19	49	85	21
Businesses with web site/home page	2	7	3	18	50	5
Major uses of the Internet						
Email	15	23	18	48	79	20
Gathering information	14	20	16	43	79	18
Data transfer	8	9	8	17	44	9
Marketing	2	7	4	16	33	5
Selling	1	2	1	3	2	1
Purchasing	1	0	1	1	3	1
Voice/video communication	0	0	0	0	1	0

Source: Small and Medium Enterprises, Business Growth and Performance Survey, Australia (8141.0).

Figure 2.2 Proportion of Businesses using Computers and Internet, by Size of Business as at 30th June 1997 (Source: Australian Bureau of Statistics, 1999b, p. 588)

In response, a range of government funding opportunities was made available to address the problem, among them being programs like Networking the Nation (NTN). The NTN programme was launched in June 1997 to assist the economic and social development of rural Australia by funding projects to enhance not only telecommunications infrastructure and services in these regions, but also to promote the use of such services and reduce disparities in access to them.

There was also the Information Technology Online (ITOL) programme (launched in 1996 and administered by NOIE) which was designed to accelerate the national adoption of e-business solutions, especially by SMEs. ITOL provided funding up to AU$200,000 (50 per cent of the total eligible project cost) each to industry based projects that accelerated the adoption of collaborative innovative B2B e-commerce solutions, across a wide range of industry sectors, especially by clusters of SMEs. Applications had to be consortium-based, with at least three separate organisations which could include companies, tertiary institutions, industry or business associations, government agencies, educational institutions and other not for profit organisations. This reflected the Australian government's belief that these groups were best placed to know the needs of their local business communities. Projects had to begin as soon as the funding agreement was signed and had to be completed within 12 months. Since its launch in 1996, ITOL has funded more than a hundred projects across diverse sectors.

Funding was also made available under the Department of Employment, Workplace Relations and Small Business (DEWRSB) Regional Assistance Programme (RAP) to not-for-profit organisations for innovative, quality projects with community value to boost business growth and create sustainable jobs. Some of these projects involved promoting the uptake of e-commerce among small businesses in places like Wangaratta in North East Victoria (National Office for the Information Economy (NOIE), 2003).

In 1998, a report by AUSe.NET and the Department of Communications Information Technology and the Arts (DCITA) entitled *Taking the Plunge* (National Office for the Information Economy (NOIE), 2000, p. 1) found that there was still "resistance to and a low level of engagement with e-commerce amongst SMEs". This was due partly to the fact that few SMEs appreciated the potential of e-commerce to enhance business efficiency. This resulted in a greater push for increased involvement of SMEs in e-commerce, and the funding opportunities provided by the NTN, ITOL and RAP programs provided the impetus for many collaborative community and SME online ventures between 1998 and 2000, including the three regional community portals researched in this study.

However, despite the efforts of the government, a follow-up report in 2000 showed that while enormous strides had been made by SMEs in adopting technology and the Internet, still only a fraction were actively engaged in Internet e-commerce, evidenced by the relatively low levels of online orders and payments made and received, as shown in table 2.2. There was also a slight gap in the uptake of e-commerce between capital cities and other areas (Australian Bureau of Statistics, 2000a, p. 11).

Table 2.2 SME Internet E-Commerce Activity 1998 and 2000 (Source: National Office for the Information Economy (NOIE), 2000, p. 8)*

	Buying Over the Internet				Selling over the Internet			
	Place Orders		Pay		Take Orders		Receive Payment	
	1998	2000	1998	2000	1998	2000	1998	2000
Small Business	16%	17%	8%	11%	NA	14%	NA	7%
Medium Business	NA	28%	NA	17%	NA	23%	NA	15%

*Note: These figures were based on the Yellow Pages® Index Survey, June 2000 and May 1998: E-Commerce and Computer Technology in Australian SMEs.

Reasons cited by respondents in the ABS survey as barriers to the use of IT (whether a computer, the Internet or a Web page) were the perception that the technology was not suited to the nature of the business and a lack of skills or appropriate training. For businesses with web sites, the factors that most limited the further development of their web sites or home pages were the cost of further development, the low rate of use of Internet commerce by customers or suppliers, and lack of skills (Australian Bureau of Statistics, 2000a, pp. 16-17).

The response of the Australian government to the gap between small and large businesses online was to commit further funding to reduce it, and in September 2001, a AU$6.5 million assistance package specifically for small businesses was announced. The package was to encourage SME uptake of e-business and to promote e-trading between SMEs and Commonwealth agencies. In 2001, the Australian government also extended the ITOL programme to 2006 (National Office for the Information Economy (NOIE), 2001, p. 41), providing it with an additional AU$13 million in funding.

A review of the literature published after 2001 indicated that e-commerce levels had risen as per table 2.3.

Table 2.3 Business Use of the Internet as at 30th June 2002 (Source: Australian Bureau of Statistics, 2003, p. 14)

	Size of Business (Number of Employees)			
	0-4	5-19	20-99	100 or more
Internet Access	65%	81%	91%	99%
Web Presence	15%	33%	51%	80%
Placing Orders	20%	30%	42%	57%
Receiving Orders	5%	8%	10%	17%

Although the statistics by then indicated an increase in e-commerce uptake rates by SMEs, there was still insufficient evidence to directly link this increase to the efficacy of specific types of government-funded collaborative e-commerce projects under programmes like the NTN, ITOL and RAP. An exploratory study was conducted by McGrath and More (2002) of the 67 projects carried out under the first five rounds of ITOL funding to determine the following: a) if any categories of ITOL projects were more successful than others; b) what the ITOL projects revealed about critical success factors for e-commerce projects and c) the extent to which the ITOL projects supported the then current views relating to e-commerce and the new organisational forms enabled by the same.

The research comprised a survey (35 respondents) substantiated by in-depth interviews with 27 project managers of completed, ongoing, successful and failed projects. Findings of the study were:

- 22 of the 35 survey respondents felt their projects were successful in terms of achieving desired outcomes.

- Underestimation of amount of effort, time, awareness-raising and training required.

- Lack of funding and resources for project management and lack of time to devote to project due to heavy workloads.

- Most of the portal projects had plans then to provide full online e-commerce capabilities at a later date but respondents expressed the fear that funding constraints could limit the full realisation of future plans for their projects.

It was not evident that any particular category of project was more successful than others and in cases where the project objectives were altered or not met, success was claimed in so far as learning

21

and knowledge gained from the experience were concerned. Some of the critical success factors uncovered by the research were:

- The importance of managing people, relationships and business processes rather than concentrating only on managing the technology.

- Choice of project manager; the importance of preparation, the need for effective communication and personal representation and the need for the project to be driven hard.

- The need to overcome the lack of appreciation of the potential benefits of e-commerce.

Although the McGrath and More (2002) report provided some valuable insights into some of the success factors and problems experienced generally by the funding participants of the first five rounds of ITOL, there was still a need for further empirical studies of particular types of government-funded collaborative e-commerce projects. This was necessary to determine the factors contributing to the success or failure of specific categories of projects and their actual costs and benefits to determine which were more effective in promoting e-commerce among SMEs.

2.2.4 Summary

This section provided the background to the issues surrounding government intervention in the uptake of Internet e-commerce by SMEs in Australia. A range of funding opportunities enabled a number of initiatives specifically targeted at this group, among them the government-sponsored regional Internet trading platforms for SMEs that were the subjects of this study. However, while Internet e-commerce uptake by SMEs increased after the intervention, there was scant empirical evidence in the literature to enable in-depth evaluations of the initial and continuing costs, benefits and problems relating to the initiatives. There was also little in the government reports to indicate if indeed government-sponsored regional Internet trading platforms for SMEs were effective in bridging the digital divide between SMEs and larger companies and between regional SMEs and their suburban counterparts. Of even more importance was the gap in the literature on the actual metrics with which to measure the outcomes and evaluate the costs and benefits of these platforms. This research strives to fill that gap.

To build the conceptual frameworks to assess the success and evaluate the benefits of the three government-sponsored regional Internet trading platforms for SMEs in this study, it was necessary to draw on the literature in the related areas of Internet trading platforms, SME adoption of ICT and e-commerce, and evaluation. The review is presented in the following sections and the next chapter.

2.3   INTERNET TRADING PLATFORMS

This research originally set out to determine the benefits that government-sponsored regional e-marketplaces could provide to participating SMEs and the region. However, a review of the extant literature on Internet e-commerce revealed that there were a number of e-commerce business models that were not termed e-marketplaces but did bring together buyers and sellers at some centralised point on the Internet for the purpose of trade. These models were referred to as portals, virtual trading communities, exchanges, virtual platforms etc. While some definitions of e-marketplaces encompassed some of these models, others did not. To further complicate matters, many of these models appeared to only consider B2B e-commerce while the models adopted by the consortia in this research included B2C and B2G (business to government) e-commerce.

In an effort to include the salient features of all types of Internet e-commerce models relevant to this study, preference has been given to the term 'Internet trading platform' to describe the type of phenomenon examined in this research.

According to the Commission of the European Communities' Expert Group on B2B Internet Trading Platforms (Commission of the European Communities, 2003b), B2B Internet trading platforms could take many different forms. These are: company web sites; pin boards (announcements of intentions to buy or sell where price negotiation and eventual transactions usually take place outside the platform); product supply and procurement exchanges; specialised or vertical industry portals; web-Electronic Data Interchange (EDI) systems; e-marketplaces; catalogue-based Internet platforms and collaboration platforms.

While these types of platforms are primarily B2B, some of them could easily encompass B2C and B2G trading as well. Therefore, in this research, the term Internet trading platform will refer to a central point on the Internet where a number of sellers are present to provide price and product information to a number of buyers, be they consumers, other businesses or the government, in an effort to secure sales. The conclusion of the transactions of such sales could be executed either on the platform or outside the platform, but the primary matching of buyer and seller is done on the platform.

Although there were many different models of Internet trading platforms prior to 2004, a review of the literature revealed that these could be subsumed under two major categories: e-marketplaces and portals/virtual trading communities.

2.3.1 Electronic Marketplaces (E-Marketplaces)

2.3.1.1 The Role of the Marketplace

Marketplaces and markets have been part of civilization since ancient times. From the ancient Greek Agora at the foot of the Acropolis to the Forum in Rome, the suks and bazaars of the Middle East to fairs and markets organised by individuals under franchises from the king during the Middle Ages in England, marketplaces have fulfilled two basic functions: trade exchange and a meeting place. Indeed the ancient marketplaces were the seats of commercial, political and administrative power in their respective countries. Through the ages, despite changes in structure, the fundamental commercial functions of marketplaces remain the same: to match buyers and sellers, to disseminate information about features and prices of products and services and to facilitate exchange.

2.3.1.2 Definitions of E-marketplaces

It would stand to reason that in essence an e-marketplace will still fulfil the basic functions of a marketplace but will do so using technology to bring together buyers and sellers at a central point in cyberspace. In examining the definitions of e-marketplaces in the literature, it became obvious that the basic functions of marketplaces are maintained in the electronic environment.

An e-marketplace has been defined as 'an inter-organizational information system that allows the participating buyers and sellers in some market to exchange information about prices and product offerings" (Bakos, 1997). This definition of e-marketplace carries the connotation of a system or an entity whose boundaries in space are delineated according to the provision of common mechanisms by which buyers and sellers can be brought together and exchange can be facilitated. It allows for the presence of markets (for example buyers and sellers of particular types of goods and services) within the marketplace. According to Bakos (1998), e-marketplaces serve the following functions: matching buyers and sellers; facilitating the exchange of information, goods, services and payments associated with market transactions; and providing an institutional infrastructure, such as a legal and regulatory framework, that enables the efficient functioning of the market.

While there has been widespread consensus about the basic attributes of e-marketplaces, a single widely accepted definition of an e-marketplace has been problematic. It is also pertinent to note that the term e-marketplace is often used interchangeably with the term e-market. In a literature review of e-marketplaces, Grieger (2003) highlighted the problem of e-marketplace definitions by identifying a number of other definitions as per table 2.4:

Table 2.4 Selected Definitions of e-marketplaces (Source: Grieger, 2003, p. 282)

Source	Definition of e-marketplace
McCoy and Sarhan (1988)	"An EM separates the negotiating function from the physical transfer of the product or commodity in which the market trades. It can manage buyers' and sellers' offers and bids, as well as moving products directly from sellers to buyers. The system is open to all buyers and sellers, regardless of their location and can provide instant market information to all traders"
Bradley and Peters (1997)	"can be viewed as a public listing of products and their attributes from all suppliers in an industry segment, and available to all potential buyers"
Schmid et al. (1998)	"is a media which foster market based exchanges between agents in all transaction phases"
Segev et al. (1999)	"Compared to many other electronic procurement solutions, EMs represent a relatively neutral position between buyer and seller, providing services to both sides of a transaction. An EM represents a virtual place where buyers and sellers meet to exchange goods and services"
Dai and Kauffman (2000)	"function as digital intermediaries that focus on industry verticals or specific business functions. They set up marketplaces where firms participate in buying and selling activities after they obtain membership"
Mueller (2000)	"Electronic markets allow buyers and sellers to exchange information about product offerings and prices bid and asked"
Ariba (2000)	"are commerce sites on the public Internet that allow large communities of buyers and suppliers to "meet" and trade with each other. They present ideal structures for commercial exchange, achieving new levels of market efficiency by tightening and automating the relationship between supplier and buyer"
Kaplan and Sawhney (2000)	"is a meeting-point where suppliers and buyers can interact online"
Lipis et al. (2000)	"is an Internet-based solution that links businesses interested in buying and selling related goods or services from one another. It can be distinguished from a procurement or distribution system insofar as it must be neutral, taking into account the interests of both buyers and sellers in its governance"

According to Grieger (2003, p. 282), the unique feature of an e-marketplace that distinguished it from other types of e-commerce models was the bringing together of *multiple* buyers and sellers in one central virtual market space. He further stated that if "it also enables them to buy and sell from each other at a dynamic price which is determined in accordance with the rules of the exchange, [it is] called an electronic exchange; otherwise it is called a portal". Thus Grieger considered trading portals and exchanges with multiple buyers and sellers to be e-marketplaces. Raisch (2001, p. 51) considered procurement portals to be examples of B2B e-marketplaces. In contrast, although the

Commission of the European Communities' Expert Group on B2B Internet trading platforms (2003b, p. 4) defined an e-marketplace as an "online service run by a third party where several buyers and sellers meet to buy and/or sell products and/or services – the famous 'butterfly' model", it classified e-marketplaces as a type of Internet trading platform, alongside product supply and procurement exchanges and specialised or vertical industry portals.

eMarket Services (2002), a not for profit project funded by the trade promotion organisations of eight European countries and Australia and New Zealand, defined an e-marketplace as a web site with trading functions (like auctions or a catalogue of products that allow placement of online orders or request for quotes) for several buying and selling companies who are members of the e-marketplace and pay a membership fee. The definition further stated that the provider of the e-marketplace has no control over prices of products and e-marketplaces are sometimes called exchanges but exchanges are only considered e-marketplaces if they are public many-to-many exchanges and are not one-to-many private exchanges.

From the various definitions above, apart from bringing together multiple buyers and sellers online, disseminating price and product information and facilitating exchange, an e-marketplace is also a neutral digital intermediary which focuses on specific business functions or specific industries and is open only to members. However, this definition does not appear to cover multi-industry non specific business function e-marketplaces like Alibaba.com (www.alibaba.com), GlobalSources (www.globalsources.com) or Ariba Inc (www.ariba.com) which were considered to be among the significant e-marketplaces in November 2003 (Lauren, 2003). Neither does the definition cover private exchanges (which, in a report on B2B e-marketplaces for the European Commission, Popovic (2002) considered to be private e-marketplaces). Popovic (2002) regarded Dell Computer Corporation's private exchange as "one of the most visible success stories from all existing e-marketplaces". Le (2002, p. 113) considered a private e-marketplace (or private trading network) like that owned by Cisco Inc. to be a one-to-many vertical e-marketplace that was set up to meet specific supply chain requirements. According to Standing and Stockdale (2003), government procurement e-marketplaces in Australia tend to favour this one-to-many hierarchical private e-marketplace structure.

The review on definitions of e-marketplaces shows that an all encompassing definition of an e-marketplace would be 'an information system that brings together buyers and suppliers online to exchange information about prices and products or services for the purpose of exchange'. This is the definition that will be adopted in this study. Beyond this parsimonious definition of the basic purpose of an e-marketplace, any other definition appears to have been attempts to segment e-marketplaces on the basis of the underlying focus or function, exchange mechanism and ownership.

2.3.1.3 A Short History of E-marketplaces

E-marketplaces existed long before the advent of the Internet. The agricultural industry was one of the first to introduce e-marketplace trading. According to Cassidy (cited in Henderson, 1984, p. 848) the first evidence of an electronic market was 'Selevision' for citrus fruits in Florida in the mid 1940s which used telephone communications. However, it was much later in the 1960s that interest in e-marketplaces grew with the introduction of a teletype auction for butcher hogs in Ontario (Peer cited in Henderson, 1984, p. 848) and the proposal for a computerised egg exchange in 1968; but it was only in 1978 that the Egg Clearing House Inc. (ECI) eventually became computerised (prior to that it was operated as a manual telephone clearinghouse). TELCOT, an electronic cotton trading mechanism was established in 1975 in the United States of America by the Plains Cotton Cooperative Association (PCCA) to promote transparent cotton pricing among its members (Lindsey, Cheney, Kasper & Ives, 1990). Both ECI and TELCOT were developed commercially and the TELCOT system effectively transformed the PCCA from a cotton merchant (buying from its members and selling to buyers) into a broker, mediating electronically between cotton buyers and sellers. However, apart from a few e-marketplaces in the agriculture (Fong et al., 1998), finance, airline, healthcare (Grover & Ramanlal, 1999) and automobile industries (Lee, 1998) many attempts at creating e-marketplaces in the mid 1970s to 1980s failed for a number of reasons.

In some cases, there was active resistance to the formation of e-marketplaces because of the threat to incumbent market intermediaries (Hess & Kemerer, 1994). In the agricultural markets, although the benefits of e-markets were well documented, most attempts at e-markets failed due to "inadequacies or immaturity of the technologies, inertia resulting from the large investments in existing physical infrastructures, the reluctance by actors to embark on a new round of organisational learning and the absence of a leader" (Lundvall, 1989 cited in Clarke & Jenkins, 1993). Other factors affecting early failures of e-marketplaces in the agricultural sector were over-developed systems, lack of sufficient and active market participants, dual marketing, free-riders and the impersonal nature of an electronic market system (Fong et al., 1998).

While e-marketplace successes were few and far between, the late 1970s to the early 1990s saw the rise of many inter-organisational electronic trading systems which were restricted to transactions between a single firm and its suppliers, agents or buyers over dedicated communication lines or extranets. This rise was fuelled by the development of IOISs and standards like EDI (electronic data interchange) which provided a structured form of electronic transfer of information in purchase orders, sales invoice, shipping, billing, and other tasks between firms (Premkumar, Ramamurthy & Nilakanta, 1994). Most of these IOISs were attempts at automating the supply chain but some did evolve into many-to-many e-marketplaces (Malone, Yates & Benjamin, 1989) and others became private e-marketplaces. However, membership to these e-marketplaces was still constrained by costs of proprietary software, technology and access costs.

It was the advent of the Internet with its open standards and the possibility of ubiquitous access and low communications costs that saw a rise in interest in e-marketplaces between the mid 1990s and mid 2000. During this time there were predictions of an e-business revolution that would see trade over the Internet reaching trillions of dollars (Downes & Mui, 1998). Companies like the Gartner Group predicted that organisations that developed e-marketplaces in specific industries would propel Internet e-commerce to US$7.29 trillion by 2004 (Brunelli, 2000).

According to Coltman, Devinney, Latukefu and Midgley (2001, p. 59), the B2C sector was expected to be the driver of the Internet e-commerce revolution, lowering prices, reducing search costs, increasing convenience for buyers, and offering firms the opportunity to build personalised relationships with their customers. B2C sites were established to follow in the footsteps of companies like eBay and Amazon.com which were established in 1995 but experienced renewed interest during the late 1990s. These B2C sites were 'pure-play start-ups', new entrants into the industry who attempted to create new services or products based on the perceived changes that the Internet would bring to buying behaviour.

In terms of B2B e-commerce, it was believed that the Internet would revolutionise business because it was "driving a global market-place transformation and paradigm shift in how companies get things done, how they compete and how they serve their customers" (Booz-Allen & Hamilton cited in Coltman et al., pp. 75-76). The opportunities that the Internet offered spelt the deconstruction of supply chains and there were dire warnings to some types of incumbent brick and mortar companies that if they did not review their operations in the light of the Internet, "new competitors on the Internet will be able to come from nowhere to steal customers" (Evans & Wurster, 1997). These new entrants would not be weighed down by expensive liabilities such as physical sales forces, branches and stores or constrained by management traditions, organisational structures and longstanding but sub-optimal profit-generating supplier and customer relationships. These beliefs and predictions spawned the first wave of Internet e-marketplaces between 1995 and 1999 (Soh & Markus, 2002a), which were mostly B2B exchanges, many of which were independent venture capital-funded dot.com third party exchanges (Le, 2002), otherwise known as B2B pure-plays, like MetalSite, Chemdex and Neoforma (Day, Fein & Ruppersberger, 2003, p. 132).

In mid 2000 when public independent e-marketplaces began to falter (Soh & Markus, 2002a), industry incumbents in many industries joined forces to create the birth of the second wave of e-marketplaces that were industry-sponsored (Le, 2002) and often owned by industry consortia. Examples of these e-marketplaces were Enerva in chemicals, Covisint in the motor vehicle industry, e2open in electronics and Transora in consumer products (Day et al., 2003). According to Deloitte Research (cited in Le, 2002, p. 112) 1,501 independent and 287 industry sponsored public e-marketplaces were created between 1998 and mid 2000.

The third wave of e-marketplaces comprised private e-marketplaces like those created by Cisco Inc, Wal-Mart and Dell Computers that followed close on the heels of industry-sponsored e-marketplaces. Private e-marketplaces were designed to re-intermediate existing trading arrangements by bringing already functioning business relationships online (Le, 2002). In some cases like General Motors and the U.S. arm of Daimler in the automotive industry, they were to overcome governance problems in industry-supported consortia e-marketplaces like Covisint (Day et al., 2003). Industry-supported consortia and private e-marketplaces comprised only a small proportion of exchanges in early 2001, with independent third-party e-marketplaces comprising 92 percent of the total number of exchanges (Day et al., p. 133). Nevertheless, according to PRIME Faraday Technology Watch (2001, p. 14), almost 90 percent of the B2B commerce in 2000 was through private e-marketplaces.

Some of the predictions made during the dot.com boom about the effect of the Internet on business were the demise of brands and middlemen, economies of scale that would flatten the competitive landscape and make size less important to online firms, falling prices that would lead to more efficient markets, and first mover advantages in terms of reaping rewards and capturing the lion's share of the market. Most of these predictions failed to materialise (Booker, 2000; Coltman et al., 2001). Venture capital for pure-plays and independent start-ups began to dry up in 2000 (Day et al., 2003), precipitating a rush to exit the e-marketplace landscape in early 2001 as financial backers began to realise that promised predictions were not being realised (Doyle & Melanson, 2001, p. 10).

The reality in the B2B e-marketplace arena was that while the Internet itself could be considered a revolution, in most industries Internet-enabled B2B e-business was evolutionary and not revolutionary (Dickinson Waters, 2001). It favoured re-formed markets where industry incumbents used the technology to reduce costs and improve existing business processes and trading relationships. The start-ups in the breakthrough markets (independent third party e-marketplaces) counted on the rapid customer acceptance of the new ways of doing business (for example scouring the Internet to look for the best deals thereby driving prices down). Incumbents in the re-formed markets (industry-sponsored and private e-marketplaces) however, had for the previous decade been looking at improving supply chain efficiencies by consolidating supply contracts and reducing suppliers. Therefore there was a preference for suppliers that could lower the customers' total acquisition costs (which included elements of reliability, trust, interoperable standards) and not just suppliers who could offer the lowest price (Day et al., 2003). According to Miller (2001), some industry analysts attributed the failure of B2B third party e-marketplaces to insufficient integration of buyers and sellers, incomplete service offerings, difficulty in attracting suppliers and low margins.

The abruptness of the rise and fall of e-marketplaces was attributed to a delusional departure from sound basic theories and rules of business (Coltman et al., 2001). "[M]any B2B exchanges were launched because they were possible, not because there was a compelling customer problem that they could solve" (Day et al., 2003, p. 143). According to Sawhney (2002), B2B exchanges should have begun by solving focused business problems and the real problem faced by enterprises was not in finding new buyers or suppliers but in improving the efficiencies of existing buyer-supplier relationships. Warnings from past research on e-marketplaces showed that regardless of any new facilities proffered, the e-market system should fulfil a real need and complement or be integrated into the existing sales value chain (Fong et al., 1998, pp. 46-47). Many of the e-marketplaces created during 1998 to 2000 were built on unrealistic expectations about the market share they could garner that would be needed to cover the venture-capital that funded them. Their success also depended upon users changing their way of doing business, a process that was slow at best (Brunn et al., 2002).

By 2002, many independent third-party e-marketplaces were struggling because they could not attract the necessary critical mass as a result of competition from the more financially resilient and better-placed consortia-led and private e-marketplaces. Many either closed down completely, merged with consortia-led e-marketplaces or changed their business models to become software providers (Mello, 2002). However, consortia-led e-marketplaces were not spared as they faced proprietary issues and huge integration barriers. There were predictions that there would be a severe shake-out in digital markets and industry researchers like Forrester Research (cited in Steele Brown, 2001) predicted that the number of e-marketplace companies in the U.S. could be reduced to fewer than 200 by 2003.

However, by 2003, although a consolidation did actually take place in B2B e-marketplaces, the contraction was not as severe as earlier predictions had projected. According to a report by the Commission of the European Communities (2003b), Berlecon Research reported that in April 2002, the number of active B2B e-marketplaces in Europe, North America and the World were 381, 669 and 1060 respectively, while the figures for February 2003 were 381 in Europe, 556 in North America and 889 worldwide. The report also stated that eMarket Services placed the number of e-marketplaces in Europe, North America and the World at 540, 619 and 1189 respectively in April 2002, while the figures for June 2003 stood at 516 in Europe, 447 in North America and 1008 worldwide.

The e-marketplace landscape in 2003 was one that favoured consortia-led and private B2B e-marketplaces where industry incumbents capitalised on their positions to maintain and develop their existing relationships in the supply chains. There was also a move towards e-marketplaces providing more than just sourcing or transaction services. They began to add logistic services, line-item dispute resolution, auction, and business process expertise as part of the overall e-marketplace offerings (Ordanini, 2003; Tao, 2003).

2.3.1.4 Theoretical Approaches to E-marketplaces

E-marketplaces in the agricultural, finance and travel industries were computerised in the mid 1970s to mid 1980s to gain a sustainable competitive advantage by using IT. The move to computerise operations was to bring transparency to pricing and make the e-marketplaces more efficient by reducing costs, improving productivity and also for marketing purposes. These economic benefits were typical incentives for participation in IOISs (Barrett & Konsynski, 1982) and were achieved by reducing the time and cost of communicating information about prices and products, thereby reducing overall transaction costs. It was therefore not surprising that early theoretical approaches to e-marketplaces were built on *Transaction Cost Economics (TCE)* of which Coase (1937) was an early pioneer and Williamson (1971; 1975; 1979) extended upon.

TCE was part of the New Institutional Economics which viewed the firm as a governance structure and not as a production function in transforming inputs into outputs. According to Coase (1937), the main reason for the existence of firms (instead of only production units in market exchanges) is the cost of using the price mechanism to organise production, the most obvious cost of which is price discovery. According to TCE, when the market coordination costs of transactions are high, instead of having stand-alone units of production which depend on the market mechanism to allocate the resources for production, buyers and sellers of production inputs integrate vertically to form firms or hierarchies and coordination of transaction costs are handled internally by fiat.

Williamson (1985) extended Coase's arguments to conclude that market exchanges suffer whenever increasing transaction costs are present. Transaction costs are positively correlated to asset-specific investments to carry out the transactions, the uncertainty surrounding the transactions and the frequency of occurrences of the transactions. According to Williamson (1985), this is because the greater the asset-specificity, uncertainty and frequency of the transactions, the greater the scope for opportunism by agents. Highly specific assets are more likely to be acquired through hierarchical rather than market coordination because of the complex issues (for example time and relationship building) that are involved in enabling the supplier to satisfactorily meet the specific needs of the procurer.

Because IT was viewed as a way of reducing coordination costs, it was a common view in the late 1980s and 1990s that increasing use of IT would lead to the deconstruction of tightly coupled supply chains (large firms or hierarchies) in favour of small companies loosely bound in a technology-coordinated market economy (Johnston & Lawrence, 1988; Miles & Snow, 1986). Malone, Yates and Benjamin (1987) developed the *Electronic Market Hypothesis (EMH)*, building on the work of Malone and Smith (cited in Malone et al., 1987) who summarised the relationships between organisation structure and production and coordination costs by stating that markets had low production costs and high coordination costs, while hierarchies had high production costs and low coordination costs.

The EMH stated that "By reducing the cost of coordination, information technology will lead to an overall shift toward proportionately more use of markets – rather than hierarchies – to coordinate economic activity". Malone et al. (1987) gave the example of online reservations in the airline industry to support the EMH. In examining the factors that affect production and coordination costs, Malone et al. also focused on other factors that are susceptible to change by IT. These were asset specificity and complexity of production.

Malone et al. (1987) further stated that IT and electronic coordination could also be used to take advantage of the 'electronic brokerage' and 'electronic integration' effects. The electronic brokerage effect would see the electronic market mechanism playing the role of a traditional broker between suppliers and procurers by providing price and product information quickly, conveniently and inexpensively. The EMH predicted an evolutionary path that industries would follow in the transformation towards electronic markets suggesting that the end-point would be attempts to garner a slice of the consumer surplus that e-markets are expected to deliver.

Bakos (1991) also used an economics perspective to demonstrate that e-marketplaces held great promise for improving inter-organisational coordination in market settings and were likely to eventually become strategic necessities and part of industry infrastructure. According to Bakos (1991), e-marketplaces would lower search costs for buyers and ultimately reduce prices. Others like Sculley and Woods (2001) and Downes and Mui (1998) predicted that the Internet would favour the proliferation of B2B e-marketplaces and Kaplan and Sawhney (2000) further predicted that public B2B exchanges would predominate.

Empirical tests of the EMH and reduced price hypothesis have produced mixed results. In the home mortgage industry, while financial intermediaries were threatened by the electronic market coordination offered by computerised loan origination systems, the structure of the industry had not fundamentally changed from hierarchies to e-marketplaces in the ten years that the systems were introduced (Hess & Kemerer, 1994). Daniel and Klimis (1999) in a study of the retail financial services and music industries found that some elements of the EMH were observed in the two industries. While there was evidence of electronic brokerage, there was at the time no evidence of unbiased e-marketplaces in both industries. In the retail financial services sector, trust and regulation were important factors that could see personalised markets regionalised instead of globalised. They also suggested that buyer power would ultimately result in the evolutionary path from e-hierarchies to e-markets having an end point of reverse markets (where buyers electronically publish their requirements and suppliers bid for their business).

Choudhury, Hartzel and Konsynski (1998) in an empirical study of an e-market in the airline parts industry showed that while in some cases the e-market helped buyers find a better price, in others it helped suppliers extract an extra premium by providing more information about parts availability. Grover and Ramanlal (1999) used fundamental economic arguments to challenge the notion that ubiquitous IT networks and e-commerce would ultimately be biased in favour of buyers. They demonstrated that IT could also facilitate supplier strategies like customisation by versioning, leveraging of the supply chain monopoly, bundling or creating subnets, restricting information across markets, leveraging network externalities and implicit price fixing, scenarios which would not be in the best interest of consumers. Lee (1998) found that contrary to the reduced price hypothesis proffered by Bakos (1991), to minimise the potential for risks in quality as buyers would not be able to physically inspect the cars before bidding, the average contract price for cars sold through an e-marketplace for used cars was higher than that of traditional markets.

Clemons and Row (1992) suggested that transaction costs comprised not only coordination costs but transaction risks as well. Because IT could lower the cost of coordination without necessarily increasing the risk associated with a greater level of explicit coordination, a greater degree of outsourcing could be experienced. Clemons, Reddi and Row (1993), extended the argument of the move towards greater outsourcing (away from ownership and vertical integration). They also concluded, however, that firms would rely on fewer suppliers than before and engage in close and

33

long-term closely coordinated and cooperative relationships with these suppliers. This prediction of a move away from the market to intermediate governance structures for outsourcing was termed the *Move to the Middle Hypothesis*.

Gurbaxani and Whang (1991), used a combined *agency theory-TCE* approach to demonstrate that while IT could reduce the coordination costs in a market setting, it could also reduce internal coordination costs. They concluded that the size of a firm is determined by the trade off between external coordination costs and internal coordination and operational costs. The ability of IT to reduce coordination costs is thus not guaranteed to favour markets over hierarchies. Rosenthal, Shah and Xiao (1993) in investigating the effect of corporate purchasing policy on the feasibility of e-markets arrived at the same conclusion.

Using a *synthesis of TCE, organisational, network and marketing theories* and empirical case studies, Holland and Lockett (1997) demonstrated that rather than a general move towards e-marketplaces or e-hierarchies (as proposed by Malone et al., 1987), or a move towards intermediate governance structures for outsourcing (as proposed by Clemons et al. (1993)), IT would enable industries to develop mixed-mode network structures in which elements of both hierarchies and markets co-exist. Ho, Au and Newton (2002) supported the mixed-mode theory and concluded that virtual trade communities would comprise some business relationships that were short-term and loose (i.e. market-based relationships) and some that were long-term and close (i.e. hierarchy-based relationships).

Although Kumar, van Dissel and Bielli (1998) examined the failure of a large IOIS and not an e-marketplace per se, their research is also pertinent as the SPRINTEL system in the textile industry in Prato, Italy had all the hallmarks of a regional e-marketplace. Kumar et al. (1998) used a synthesis of three complementary theoretical bases (*industrial networks in organisational theory*, trust as an alternative to opportunism in understanding *inter-organisational relationships* and the *cultural context* of the textile industry in Prato) to explain the failure of SPRINTEL. While SPRINTEL was designed to reduce transaction costs, Kumar et al. surmised that given the relationship and trust basis of the textile industry in Prato, those costs were low to begin with. While one of the services of SRINTEL was to offer the sale of redundant stock, use of the service was low because 'culturally' its use by suppliers would be an admission that their forecasting was erroneous in the first instance. The findings from the SPRINTEL study held three important lessons for IOIS implementation. Firstly, caution is needed when applying economic theories and their predictions to societies that are different from those in which the theories were developed. Secondly, traditional development and implementation approaches (techno-economic rationalisation) to IS need to be augmented by considering existing patterns of culture, relationships and trust. Finally, recognition of the existence of trust and relationships can lead to cooperative strategies and a view of IT as a collaborative advantage. Kumar et al. refer to their approach as a *'trust-based rationalism'* for examining the role of IT in organisations and networks.

With the downturn in the proliferation of e-marketplaces, researchers in the field began to look at factors beyond just transaction costs to examine e-marketplaces. Soh and Markus (2002a) used Porter's *Strategic Positioning Theory* to examine the success and failure of a pair of independent B2B e-marketplaces. They found that the success of one e-marketplace and the lack thereof in the other were well explained by the concepts of value proposition (types of benefits offered), product market forces and value activities of strategic positioning theory.

Koch (2002) used *Public Good Theory* (Monge et al., 1998) as an umbrella to integrate *Resource Dependence Theory* (Pfeffer & Salancik, 1978), *TCE* and Oliver's (1990) *determinants of inter-organisational relationships* (an integration of resource dependence and institutional theories) to examine why companies form alliances to create B2B e-marketplaces and why participants join these e-marketplaces. The transaction cost perspective and stability and efficiency contingencies explain why initial organisations form B2B e-marketplaces while the resource dependency perspective and reciprocity, asymmetry, and legitimacy contingencies explain how participants can be attracted to form a critical mass on the e-marketplace.

Lenz, Zimmerman and Heitman (2002), used the theoretical foundations of *organisational strategy* and the *resource-based view of the firm* (and the core competencies approach that it is derived from) as a basis to examine the implications of strategic partnering on the competitiveness of B2B e-marketplaces. They found that "partnering in various forms seems to be a crucial element in the strategy of B2B marketplaces".

Grewal, Comer and Mehta (2001), in examining firms' motives for joining a third-party independent unbiased e-market, used a *motivation-ability framework* which drew on Oliver's (1990) determinants of inter-organisational relationships, *TCE*'s economic efficiency motives and the legitimacy motive of *institutional theory*. Their study found that both motivation and ability are important in determining the nature of participation.

A *relational or network perspective* views an e-marketplace as a mechanism to foster inter-organisational relationships (Koch, 2002) which can be developed into more sophisticated communities of practice (Braun, 2002; Brown & Lockett, 2001). Christiaanse and Markus (2003) in studying adoption of collaboration e-marketplaces, found that each of four theoretical areas (transaction cost theory, the motivation-ability framework, EDI adoption research and *Rational Exchange Theory*) had something to offer but that there was also considerable overlap among them.

Ordanini (2003) in a study of 32 European B2B e-marketplaces, used a *resource-based approach* to determine the potential competitive effect of a firm participating in a B2B exchange. His study found that e-marketplaces that survived the shakeout of the dot.com bust integrated more services in their offerings beyond just the ability to affect transaction costs. They included services focused on other functional processes, which ended up within the firms, and services dedicated to strategic partnerships, cooperation, and knowledge sharing which were embedded in the value-chain networks.

Apart from the theoretical approaches mentioned above, some authors developed frameworks to guide deployment of e-marketplaces and Internet trading platforms. Raisch (2001) predicted that e-marketplaces would develop along an evolutionary curve, from simple matchmaking services focused on transactions and e-commerce to value trust networks that would integrate the transaction exchange with value-added services and knowledge services. Tapscott, Ticoll and Lowy (2000) provided a taxonomy of business-web models (agoras, aggregations, value chains, alliances and distributive networks) and strategy concepts for each model.

Brunn et al. (2002) developed a framework for the creation of successful public e-marketplaces. The model comprised five elements (focus, governance, functionality, technology and partnerships) which combine to make up the strategic position of the e-marketplace and provide the foundation of success. However the model developed by Brunn et al. does not consider other aspects of e-marketplaces like financing, marketing, organisation and management team which they considered were not among the most important issues of e-marketplace development.

Kurnia and Johnston's (2000) model to study EDI adoption in the Australian grocery industry uses the constructs of external factors (e.g. demand, competition), the nature of the technology (e.g. relative advantage, compatibility), capability of the organisation (top management commitment, IT infrastructure) and the supply chain or industry structures (relationships in terms of power, economics, etc.). Their model, however, only looks at a vertical e-marketplace.

Kambil and van Heck (1998) developed a *Process-Stakeholder Framework* of trade processes (search, valuation, logistics, payments and settlements, authentication) and trade context processes (product representation, legitimisation, influence and dispute resolution) that was used to evaluate the successes and failures of e-markets in the Dutch flower auction marketplace. In examining e-markets in China, Khalifa et al. (2003) extended the Kambil and van Heck (1998) model to include a socio-political context (government support and environmental factors like the political and cultural scenario, infrastructural adequacy, technical sophistication of e-market providers) and strategic processes (financial backing, support services like training and consultancy, alliances) in a framework for the successful deployment of e-markets.

In a study of the relatively low rate of adoption of a B2B e-marketplace in the Australian beef industry, Driedonks, Gregor and Wassenaar (2003) used a combination of the Kambil and van Heck (1998) *Process-Stakeholder Framework* and Rogers' (1995) *Diffusion of Innovation Theory (DOI)*. The Kambil and van Heck (1998) framework was used to examine the economic perspective of adoption at the level of key stakeholders, while Rogers' DOI was used to examine the social aspects of adoption at the level of individual stakeholders. The process-stakeholder framework broke down when adoption was not mandatory and it required a combination of social, technical, economic and political perspectives to understand the low adoption rates.

Wassenaar and Gregor (2003) provided a theoretical foundation for a more integrated model that could be developed to study e-marketplaces. The model comprised four views: the coordination system view (the TCE approach), the strategic choice view (the stakeholder and resource dependence approaches), the ecological natural selection view (perspectives of institutional economics and dynamic markets) and network action view (network cluster concept, virtual organisations, social capital and community concepts).

The literature on the theoretical approaches to e-marketplaces and IOIS reveals that techno-economic approaches alone are not sufficient to provide a holistic understanding of the issues surrounding the creation, participation and success of e-marketplaces. This is especially so in the light of the number of e-marketplace failures at the start of this century. Techno-economic theories like TCE need to be augmented with other theoretical perspectives like organisation theory, resource-based dependency and the resource-based view of the firm, institutional theory, determinants of inter-organisational relationships and cultural issues in order to better explain the e-marketplace phenomenon. The need for a broader theoretical basis for examining e-marketplaces is even more pronounced when e-marketplaces are used as part of regional economic development strategies, as local or regional e-commerce has to be conceptualised "as a form of commerce which is embedded in the social, political, cultural, technical and economic structures [of a region]" (Steinfield & Klein, 1999, p. 49). This view of regional e-commerce is borne out by findings of Kumar et al. (1998) Driedonks et al. (2003), Wassenaar and Gregor (2003), and is a view that has been adopted in this study.

37

2.3.1.5 E-marketplace Models and Structures

The broadest general classifications of e-marketplaces have been according to either ownership (public, private, industry consortia-owned) or function (vertical e-marketplaces serving specific industries or horizontal non industry-specific e-marketplaces). However, as the e-marketplace landscape evolved, shaped by the dot.com fall out, e-marketplace owners/operators sought to acquire market share by product differentiation and strategic positioning. This led to the blurring of the traditional categories of e-marketplaces and spawned new ones as e-marketplaces also began to be categorised according to price and exchange mechanisms, type of products traded and types of trading activities (see table 2.5).

Table 2.5 Taxonomy of E-Marketplace Models and Structures

Basis of Classification	Model	Features	Examples	Source
Stakeholder or Governance Focused (Can be private, consortia-owned, or public) (Baldi & Borgman, 2001; Day et al., 2003; Grieger, 2003; Krammer, Browning, Rozwell & Shu, 2001; Le, 2002; Popovic, 2002; Segev, Gebauer & Farber, 1999)	Buyer-Oriented e-marketplace	Aggregates buyers and creates efficiencies for corporate buyers. Concentrate primarily on creating efficiencies for the corporate buyer	Covisint (consortia) Walmart (private)	(Day et al., 2003) (Popovic, 2002)
	Seller-Oriented e-marketplace	Brings together sellers to aggregate their product offerings in a single platform	Transora	(Skjott-Larsen, Kotzab & Grieger, 2003)
	Neutral (3rd party) e-marketplace	Third-party driven independent e-marketplaces that try to attract both buyers and sellers.	BuildOnline	(Popovic, 2002)
Industry-focused or function-focused (Skjott-Larsen et al., 2003)	Vertical e-marketplace	Industry-Specific. Focus on automating vertical supply chains in order to make the market more efficient.	Digital Exchange	(Segev et al., 1999)
	Horizontal e-marketplace	Non Industry-Specific. Can be function-specific (maintenance, repair and operating goods [MRO], procurement, Human Resources) or non function specific catering for various types of goods across industries.	Freemarkets (procurement) Gatetrade.net (non function specific) Global Sources	(Skjott-Larsen et al., 2003) (Brunn et al., 2002) (Markus, Banerjee & Ma, 2002)

Table 2.5   Taxonomy of E-Marketplace Models and Structures (continued)

Basis of Classification	Model	Features	Examples	Source
Focused on what and how businesses purchase (Kaplan & Sawhney, 2000)	MRO Hubs	Systematic sourcing of operating inputs	W.W.Grainger	(Kaplan & Sawhney, 2000)
	Yield managers	Spot sourcing of operating inputs	Capacityweb.com	(Kaplan & Sawhney, 2000)
	Catalogue Hubs	Systematic sourcing of manufacturing inputs	Chemdex	(Kaplan & Sawhney, 2000)
	Exchanges	Spot sourcing of manufacturing inputs	e-Steel	(Kaplan & Sawhney, 2000)
Market mechanism (price or transaction) focus (Popovic, 2002; PRIME Faraday Technology Watch, 2001; Skjott-Larsen et al., 2003)	Aggregation	A value-adding intermediary between buyers and sellers	Ariba	(Tapscott et al., 2000)
	Negotiation/ Matching	Portals where requests for quotes (RFQs) or request for bids (RFBs) are posted. Deals could be closed off-line. Often no price mechanism	Alibaba.com	(Ming Zeng, 2001)
	Auctions	Dynamic Price-building by Standard [English] Auction, Dutch Auction, other types of auction (Lucking-Reiley, 2000), Reverse Auction	USBid Farmbid, FreeMarkets	(Grieger, 2003) (Popovic, 2002)
	Exchanges	Dynamic Price-building	ChemConnect.com	(Skjott-Larsen et al., 2003)
	Catalogues	Fixed Price	Papersite	(Grieger, 2003)
	Collaboration Platform	Provides technology and information for collaboration between enterprises.	Cisco Elemica	(Popovic, 2002) (Christiaanse & Markus, 2003)

Table 2.5   Taxonomy of E-Marketplace Models and Structures (continued)

Basis of Classification	Model	Features	Examples	Source
Region focused (Zimmerman, 1998) (Standing, Sims, Stockdale, & Wassenaar, 2003)	Consortia-owned Third party Horizontal Regional e-marketplace (Agora-type)	Non-industry specific. Many buyers and sellers across industries and functions. May be part of a regional community portal. Often not profit-driven.	Electronic mall Bodensee (Emb.net) 2Cities.com	(Zimmerman, 1998) (Standing et al., 2003)
	Vertical Regional e-marketplace	Industry specific. Caters to participants in regional value chains.	Regional Electronic Trade Facilitation Centre Lonxanet	(Wilkins et al., 2003a; 2003b) (Dans & Freire, 2002)
	Private Regional e-marketplace (government-owned)	Procurement hubs of national, state and local governments created for efficiency	GEM	(Standing et al., 2003)
	Private Regional e-marketplace (non-government owned)	Non-industry specific. Many-to-many platform which seeks to act as intermediary for buyers and sellers in a region.	SME Online Marketplaceitaly.com	(Hsiao, 2003) (Ordanini & Pol, 2001)

(Note: These were e-marketplaces in existence prior to 2004. Some may have ceased to operate, have amalgamated with others or have changed business models).

Raisch (2001, p. 186) also used types of products and services to differentiate e-marketplaces, while Lennstrand, Frey and Johansen (cited in Soh & Markus, 2002b) classified e-marketplaces based on value added contributions and sources of revenue. Dai and Kauffman (2002) used the roles played by e-marketplaces to classify them: basic market functions, fulfilment of management needs and technology adapters.

It is also possible to classify e-marketplaces according to the motivations of the market-makers (Standing et al., 2003). The motives underlying e-marketplace creation can be economic (reducing costs, improving productivity, marketing strategy), service (providing better services to customers), community (development of a community), a network view (for purposes of inter-organisational alliances) or hybrid arrangements. According to Standing et al., e-marketplaces with local community development motives are usually created, owned or operated by local or state governments to raise awareness and uptake of e-commerce by businesses in the community. Standing and Stockdale (2003, p. 20) also stated that these e-marketplaces with their simple requests for quotes negotiation mechanisms, are well suited to SMEs' first foray into e-marketplace participation.

The review of the literature on e-marketplace models and structures shows that there are many areas of overlap and inconsistencies in the classifications. This can create difficulties for researchers as they try to determine how the attributes are related and which ones are most suitable to their research (Soh & Markus, 2002b). It can also be confusing for market-makers to decide which models would give them the greatest returns. Nevertheless, a good starting point for both researchers and practitioners alike would be to first determine the underlying motive for the creation of the e-marketplace and to then evaluate the relationship between the motivation, structure, costs, benefits and institutional factors that could affect the success (or lack thereof) of the e-marketplace in question.

2.3.1.6 Benefits of E-marketplaces

The literature review revealed that there are many purported and real benefits to be obtained from the creation of e-marketplaces and participation in them. Standing and Stockdale (2001) identified and collated a list of benefits from 150 articles from the business literature and categorised them according to IS success measures of system quality, information quality, information use, user satisfaction, individual impact and organisational impact. Another useful way of categorising these benefits would be the Standing et al. (2003, p. 343) classification according to whether the benefits produce economic, network, service or community advantages.

Economic benefits of e-marketplaces can be categorised according to benefits for market-makers and participants. Benefits for market-makers are typically sources of revenue generated from participation, transaction, advertising fees, software sales and licenses, gain sharing (Popovic, 2002), professional service charges/referral fees in areas like human resources, logistics, finance (Bakos, 1998; Ordanini, 2003). According to Euromonitor (cited in PRIME Faraday Technology Watch, 2001, p. 23), the top sources of revenues in B2B marketplaces are seller transaction fees, marketing fees, buyer transaction fees, seller subscription fees, storefronts for suppliers, buyer subscription fees, revenue from other sites and fees for market data and analysis. For buyers (or owners of buyer-owned e-marketplaces), benefits from e-marketplaces are from reduced costs in procurement, communication, inventory holding and search activities which lead to lower prices

(Bakos, 1991, 1997; Benjamin & Wigand, 1995). Sellers in an e-marketplace (or owners of seller-owned e-marketplaces) can expect benefits in the form of lower selling and transaction costs and access to wider markets (Porter, 2001; Raisch, 2001). In some cases, sellers have been able to charge a premium on e-marketplaces (Choudhury et al., 1998; Lee, 1998). There are also productivity benefits for both buyers and sellers like process cost reduction, time saving, better information flows that arise from automation and outsourcing of internal procedures and complementary activities (Goldsby & Eckert, 2003; Ordanini, 2003).

E-marketplaces can also provide *network benefits* in the form of new levels of innovation arising from network externalities and knowledge sharing (Bakos, 1991; Braun, 2002; Ordanini, 2003; Raisch, 2001). According to Brunn et al. (2002) e-marketplaces can leverage network externalities by creating alliances with technology providers, logistic or financial service providers or even complementary e-marketplaces. Ordanini (2003) cites the example of 1city.biz, Italy's largest B2B online auctioneer which in addition to transactions, offers a virtual knowledge network on its exchange where purchase managers, academics and consultants can share knowledge without having to transact financially.

Service benefits from e-marketplaces include improved quality of products and customer service (Standing et al., 2003). This can be achieved through streamlined workflows and by reducing communication times (Le, 2002) as well as offering greater service and product scopes via partnering (Lenz et al., 2002). According to Standing et al. (2003) while the service benefits are closely aligned to the economic benefits, there is a need to differentiate between the two as improved service and quality may sometimes come at a cost to sellers who may choose to deliver the higher level of services despite the extra costs. Dai and Kauffman (2001) point out that this role of marketplaces as infomediaries is not solely focused on lowering communications and search costs, but also in providing procurement and industry specific expertise in a value chain.

With the community motive, the main objective of the e-marketplace owner or sponsor is to encourage adoption of e-marketplace trading. This is most common in regional e-marketplaces where *community benefits* that are expected to be realised are raised levels of e-business knowledge, skills and technology within the community (Standing et al., 2003; Zimmerman, 1998). These community benefits can lead to the community or region becoming an attractive location for business and for skilled labour. A regional e-marketplace can also provide the benefits of efficient show-casing of regional offerings.

In some cases where the motives of e-marketplace makers become blurred there will be a mix of benefits to be realised from e-marketplace creation and participation. For example, some

43

government e-marketplaces like GEM (the procurement e-marketplace of the Western Australian state government), have been established to streamline the procurement processes and lower the costs for participating government departments but at the same time hope to be a catalyst for e-marketplace participation by their SME suppliers. Additionally, according to Standing et al. (2003, p. 345), while a community-motivated e-marketplace may be for the common good of the community, it may still need to be economically viable.

2.3.1.7 Critical Success Factors for E-marketplaces

The critical success factors for e-marketplaces identified in both the business and academic literature are critical mass or liquidity (Brunn et al., 2002; Driedonks et al., 2003; Raisch, 2001), providing participants with a competitive advantage (Ordanini & Pol, 2001), strategic partnering in B2B marketplaces (Lenz et al., 2002), identification and recruitment of experts or key players who will motivate others to join (Grewal et al., 2001). Also critical to success are the provision of value-added services (Ordanini, 2003), provision of revenue streams (Brunn et al., 2002; Standing, 2001), large capital investments (Bakos, 1991), open software standards, effective contract handling and relationship management (Standing, 2001), complementing existing value chains for sales and fulfilling a real need (Fong et al., 1998), privacy and trust.

As a critical success factor of e-marketplaces, trust has received much attention in the academic literature. Given the impersonal nature of the online environment, trust in online transactions is even more crucial than in traditional exchange transactions (Ba & Pavlou, 2002; Bakos, 1998). Pavlou (2002) examined how institution-based trust can be developed in online B2B marketplaces to facilitate inter-organisational trust between buyers and sellers. He proposed five specific institution-based mechanisms: perceived monitoring, perceived legal bonds, perceived accreditation, perceived feedback, and perceived cooperative norms. Pavlou and Gefen (2002) showed that the presence alone of structural assurances in a B2B marketplace does not necessarily engender trust, unless buyers perceive these mechanisms as reliable and credible. According to Hsiao (2003), distrust as a barrier to e-marketplace adoption can be in the forms of reliability-related and value oriented distrust. While the former can be reduced by technical remedies, the latter may be rooted in the cultural beliefs of the would-be adopters targeted by the e-marketplace. As such, there is a need to be sensitive to value-oriented fears in order to break down the distrust barriers to e-marketplace participation. This is especially so in dealing with regional e-marketplaces, regional e-commerce and SMEs, which may require Kumar et al.'s (1998) trust-based rationalism and Steinfield and Whitten's (1999) trust-and-embeddedness views.

2.3.1.8 Summary on E-Marketplaces

The literature on e-marketplaces showed that beyond a basic definition of an e-marketplace as 'an information system that brings together buyers and suppliers online to exchange information about prices and products or services for the purpose of exchange', other definitions are problematic. This is because they appear to segment e-marketplaces on the basis of the underlying focus or function, exchange mechanism and ownership. Classification of e-marketplace models is also problematic as some e-marketplaces demonstrate attributes across different classifications, while other e-marketplaces have evolved to blur the boundaries of classifications. This study will adopt the basic definition of an e-marketplace to ensure that all relevant attributes and issues associated with the different e-marketplace models that are pertinent to this research are considered.

Although e-marketplaces existed in some industries before the Internet, a short and acute Internet-triggered hype pattern that began in the late 1990s saw the proliferation of many venture capital-funded pure play start-up e-marketplaces. They were created simply because the ubiquitousness of the Internet was perceived to promise a revolution in the way consumers purchased and businesses traded, as search and coordination costs were predicted to fall. New web-based entities were predicted to flourish, unfettered by the constraints of existing infrastructure, large operating costs and existing buyer and supplier relationships. The e-marketplace hype-cycle began its downturn in late 2000/early 2001 when a contraction in e-marketplace numbers occurred. Far from breaking new ground in business applications and business relationships, the Internet held more promise for improving existing processes and relationships thus favouring industry incumbents over new entrants. In 2003 the e-marketplace landscape favoured consortia-led and private e-marketplaces, while B2B exchanges that survived the shakeout began to widen their service offerings to include more than just transaction cost savings.

In a sense, the theoretical approaches to e-marketplaces (and to some extent the various classification schemas) mirror the history of e-marketplace development. This supports the view of some authors that "experience is the major means by which theorists ground their writings" (Shadish Jr., Cook & Leviton, 1991, p. 33). In the early years the theoretical focus was on the transaction cost view of what was termed 'the new institutional economics'. It was mainly during and after the fallout in digital exchanges that researchers started to view e-marketplaces from a broader theoretical base. Institutional and resource-based views of e-marketplaces began to emerge and e-marketplaces, especially when they were regional in nature, were seen to be bound up not just in technological and economic structures but also in the cultural and socio-political environments in which they operated. This view of e-marketplaces will prevail in this study.

Finally, the classification of benefits that can be derived from e-marketplace creation and participation, and the critical success factors of e-marketplaces can also be traced to the history of e-marketplaces. As the e-marketplace landscape evolved, benefits have enlarged from just transaction cost savings and productivity benefits to strategic benefits like network externalities and improved market shares through improved service levels. In the early days of e-marketplaces, critical success factors like building liquidity through pricing and the ability to offer participants advantages in the form of lower coordination costs predominated. Today, other critical success factors like offering more value-added services, strategic partnering and issues of trust have begun to play an important role in the success of e-marketplaces.

2.3.2 *Portals/Virtual Trading Communities*

As indicated in section 2.3.1.2 above, certain types of portals are considered to be e-marketplaces by some authors (Grieger, 2003; Raisch, 2001) but not by others (Commission of the European Communities, 2003b). Portals can also exist within an e-marketplace (PRIME Faraday Technology Watch, 2001) and some authors consider e-marketplaces to be a type of portal (Chaffey, 2002), albeit a multi-buyer, multi-seller portal (Kalakota, Oliva & Donath, 1999, p.29). According to Warkentin, Bapna and Sugumaran (2001) B2B e-commerce activity falls under the sphere of 'vortals', vertically integrated portals serving a given industry. Buy-side (e.g. Ford Suppliers Network) and sell-side (e.g. Cisco) enterprise portals (Kalakota et al., 1999, p. 28) are sometimes referred to as private e-marketplaces (Le, 2002).

Armstrong and Hagel (1996) in categorising virtual communities, considered 'communities of transaction' (which primarily facilitate the buying and selling of products and services and deliver information related to those transactions) as one type of virtual community. Swatman (Swatman, Bytheway, Cavill, Cooper & Wilde, 1996) believed that e-markets were a form of virtual community.

Thus, the terms portals and/or virtual trading communities have sometimes been used interchangeably with the term e-marketplaces (and may sometimes exhibit similar characteristics and constructs). In this research, the preference is to differentiate between portals, virtual communities and e-marketplaces for the following reasons: a) the Internet trading platforms in this study were developed as part of regional community portals catering for B2C, B2B and B2G e-business; b) of the three Internet trading platforms in this study, one was labelled a regional e-marketplace, one an e-shopping mall and the third a hybrid shopping-cart e-shop/RFQ-enabled portal.

46

2.3.2.1 Definitions of Portals/Virtual Trading Communities

Portals

Saha (1999) viewed a portal as a single integrated point of comprehensive, ubiquitous, and useful access to information (data), applications, and people. According to Clarke and Flaherty (2003), web-based portals were the entry points which directed the Internet user to the ultimate location of their choice, while Donegan (2000) defined a portal as an entry point or homepage for accessing Internet content and services such as local news, weather and chat rooms. According to Robles (2002, p. 30) "[the] modern portal can be defined as a network leader that provides content, commerce and community, and orchestrates value creation among users, partners, service providers, and a myriad of other participants". These broad definitions of portals allow a variation of portal models based on their functions and the markets they serve.

Virtual Trading Communities

One of the earliest definitions of virtual communities was "social aggregations that emerge from the [Internet] when enough people carry on those public discussions long enough with sufficient human feeling, to form webs of personal relationships in cyberspace" (Rheingold, 1993). Hagel and Armstrong (1997) considered virtual communities to be groups of consumers united by a common interest, while Williams and Cothrel (2000) referred to them as groups of people engaged in many-to-many interactions online.

Armstrong and Hagel (1996) coined the term 'communities of transaction' to describe virtual communities which primarily facilitated online trade, and were not communities in the traditional social sense. Participants in communities of transaction were encouraged to interact with one another to engage in a specific transaction that could be informed by the input of other members of the communities. Ho, Au and Newton (2003) in describing the virtual trading community of the Hong Kong textile industry considered it to be the overarching virtual network comprising infomediary portals, e-hubs or e-marketplaces and strategic alliances (in areas like logistics and finance) that facilitate online trade along the supply chain.

Lee, Vogel and Limayem (2003, p. 49) synthesised the definitions of virtual community from a number of authors to arrive at four common constructs in the definitions. The constructs are: cyberspace (all definitions agreed that the community should be on the Internet); computer-based information technology (to support the activities of the virtual communities); communication and interaction are the main focus, and content and topics of virtual communities are driven by the participants; and successful virtual community relationships that culminate after a certain period of time communicating together. These constructs were used to arrive at a working definition of a virtual community which is: "a cyber space supported by communication technology, centered [sic] upon communication and interaction of participants to generate member-driven contents, resulting in a relationship being built up" (Lee et al., 2003, p. 51)

2.3.2.2 Models and Structures of Portals/Virtual Trading Communities

Portals

The first Internet portals were search engines, starting points for web consumers to explore and access information on the Internet, which reflected the traditional meaning of the term portal as an entry way or access point (Clarke & Flaherty, 2003). According to Winkler (2001), when search engines like Yahoo, Infoseek and MSN expanded the breadth of their offerings to include a structured navigable interface, they were considered to be Internet portals. Since then portals have evolved and are today classified according to functionality and infrastructure. A synthesis of portal classifications by Chaffey (2002), Davison, Burgess and Tatnall (2003) and Winkler (2001) resulted in the following types:

- Horizontal, mega or general portals like Yahoo, MSN, and AOL that target the entire Internet community

- Horizontal industry portals that target a broad base of users across a horizontal market (can also be a B2B or B2C e-marketplace)

- Vertical portals that offer information and services customised to niche audiences about a particular area of interest, for example health portals

- Vertical industry portals (vortals) are sites that provide a gateway to information (and other services) related to a particular industry (can also be a B2B or B2C e-marketplace)

- Enterprise information portals (EIPs) which are gateways to extranets of specific companies

- Geographic portals which cater for specific regions and can be vertical or horizontal, commercial (they can be e-marketplaces) or non commercial (sometimes called community portals, like the Blacksburg Electronic Village)

- Specialised/niche/information portals which provide information to niche markets

- Knowledge portals (which can be collaborative portals) which cater to workers in specific industries by providing easy access to information and other services to help them in one or more specific roles.

These types are not mutually exclusive and some types can be subsumed under others allowing for hybrid portals with a variety of offerings. Clarke and Flaherty (2003) chose to classify B2B web portals according to broad categories of function or mission (transactional versus informational portals), depth of portal content (horizontal versus vertical portals) and target users (private versus public portals).

Virtual Trading Communities

Lee, Vogel and Limayem (2003), used the literature on virtual communities to provide a classification based on basic needs and use (interest, fantasy, transaction), social structure (e.g. virtual voluntary organisations), and technology base (e.g. Usenet or chat groups). These broad classifications can be considered non-mutually exclusive because it is possible for a virtual trading community to be a transactional, interest and relationship community at the same time. Indeed in describing the components that make up the virtual trading community of the Hong Textile Industry supply chain, Ho et al. (2003) included non-transactional informational/knowledge portals and trade and industry associations (relationship communities). Within the sub-classification of virtual trading communities however, there is also a need to differentiate between B2C and B2B (or hybrid) trading communities as each community type has different needs and may require different technical and educational support by the convenor of the community.

Kozinets (1999, p. 254) defined a sub-classification of commercial virtual communities as communities of consumption, "affiliate groups whose online interactions are based upon shared enthusiasm for, and knowledge of, a specific consumption activity or related group of activities". This sub-group presented value propositions for Internet marketing.

2.3.2.3 Theoretical Approaches to Portals/Virtual Trading Communities

As some authors consider portals and virtual trading communities to be e-marketplaces, theoretical approaches that have been used in portal and virtual trading community research which have already been reviewed in section 2.3.1.4 above will not be included in this section.

Portals

In using *Actor-Network Theory* (ANT) to study Bizewest, a B2B portal for SMEs in Melbourne, Australia, Tatnall and Burgess (2002) concluded that such an approach could offer a much better explanation of the complexities involved in the technical, human and social interactions and negotiations inherent in such platforms.

Robles (2002) used the combined theoretical areas of **Internationalisation Theory, Theory of International Business** and the **Integration-Responsiveness Framework,** three streams of **International Theory,** to examine the strategies of regional versus global positioning of general horizontal portals like Yahoo, AOL and MSN. He termed his model **the global portal evolution framework** and identified four stages of internationalisation of portals. They are: provision of foreign language content on domestic-hosted portals; partnering with local media or telecommunications companies in other countries; extensive localisation and consolidation.

Sieber and Sabatier (2003) discussed theoretical business models that could be used to produce superior returns and sustainability in horizontal portals. They looked at *'stickiness'* (Zott, Amit & Donlevy, 2000), the value of user-developed content and *product bundling* (Bakos & Brynjolfsson, 1999) as strategies that could be considered by horizontal portals.

Clarke and Flaherty (2003) in examining B2B portals, used a *5 Ds process* for effective portal development. The five D's were *defining* measurable business objectives, business processes and the size and scope of the portal; *designing* suitable systems and applications, information content and appearance/navigation of the portal; *developing* a pilot portal to obtain feedback from users; *delivering* the finished product and *defending* the market position of the portal by continuous benchmarking, strategic partnering and by defending against cyber-attacks.

Damsgaard (2002) used *network economics* to propose a sequential four-stage portal life cycle model for the management of B2C portals. The stages were: *attraction* (the portal is launched and visitors are attracted to the site), *contagion* (repeat visits and bandwagon effect causing critical mass to be achieved), *entrenchment* (services of the portal are adopted by the users) and *defence* (the portal is nurtured).

Virtual Trading Communities

In developing their **Virtual Communities and Society Model,** Romm, Pliskin and Clarke (1997) used a synthesis of the literature and theories on three types of variables which characterise the major stages in the life cycle of virtual communities. The types of variables were: variables that affect individuals' decision to join virtual communities (technological; motivational; task and system level explanations); variables that explain how members of virtual communities affect their immediate environment (linguistic; performance; social and political variables) and variables that describe how virtual communities are transforming society (integration of production systems;

integration of national identities; community integration/fragmentation and redefinition of personal relationships). According to Romm et al. (1997), the three elements of the proposed model can be seen as reflecting not just phases in the history of the research on virtual communities, but also as actual developmental stages of the virtual community itself.

Lee et al. (2003) proposed five stages for classifying growth in research on virtual communities. They were: fundamental understanding of concepts, principles, definitions and models; technology development for sustained growth; protocols for applications development, relationship building and knowledge sharing; evaluation of implementation and outcome assessments; institutionalisation and enlargement of benefits. An extensive review of the literature (almost forty sources) on virtual communities was conducted and the literature was classified according to the stages above. Lee et al. concluded that research on virtual communities was still immature and there was still room for further research in many areas.

In examining the shift of virtual communities from being purely social phenomena to becoming actual business models, Lechner and Hummel (2002) reviewed developments in the music industry. They looked at how virtual communities in the music industry were challenging the strong positions of the music industry incumbents with "novel architectures that follow the community paradigm - that is, with self-organization and symmetrical positioning of the actors involved in the creation and consumption of contents".

Hagel and Armstrong (1997) surmised that profit could be generated from Internet communities by controlling access; aggregating content; profiting from side payments like the goodwill of the community; increased customer retention rate or advertising revenue (Krieger & Muller, 2003). Bughin and Hagel (2000), viewed online communities as important business models, which by combining unique reach and selectivity, should show strong promise to create value in the medium-term. They showed that online B2C communities tended to show superior performance (compared to other B2C models like transaction and content aggregation sites) in terms of their efficiency to transform online traffic into revenue-generating members. However, Bughin and Hagel (2000) indicated that there was also evidence that online communities, like any other B2C model, were still far from being cost-effective at that time.

In a study of stickiness of Commercial Virtual Communities (CVCs), Walczuch, Verkiujlen, Geus and Ronnen (2001) surveyed 'experts' from thirty four companies which had introduced such communities or consulted in the field of CVCs to rank the importance of drivers of stickiness. Some of their findings were that in terms of content, community content ranked as the stickiest, followed by information, e-mail, storage space, entertainment and finally commercial services. In terms of dimension of content, frequent updates were considered the stickiest followed by depth and then breadth. In ranking the stickiness of sources of content, experts were found to be the stickiest, followed by members, celebrities and finally editors. A ranking of community drivers (factors that needed to be taken into account when building a community) revealed that user-friendliness was the most important, followed by a virtual identity, motivation, multiple tools of interaction, privacy, social control and finally off-line events.

2.3.2.4 Critical Success Factors for Portals/ Virtual Trading Communities

Portals

According to Damsgaard (2002) the difference between success and failure of a portal lies in managing the portal community and in timing the taxation of the community for accessing the portal's services. Lock-in strategies need to be deliberately incorporated into the design and development of the portal so that switching costs will be high, not only in terms of personal lock-in but also from the point of view of network externalities. Services that exhibit high network externalities (chat, discussion forums, instant messaging) need to be offered.

Robles (2002) found that the key success factors for portals were partnering, innovation, delivery of the online experience through multiple platforms, and the maintenance and creation of dynamic communities that attracted and retained membership. The user online experience was critical to a portal's long-term success and would be evaluated based on the organisation of the information and interface, the effectiveness of the presentation, the range and depth of choice (selection), the usability and the relevance of the information provided.

Portal success was found by Clarke and Flaherty (2003) to be a function of content, flexibility and customisation. They surmised that the primary measures of portal success were high levels of user acquisition and retention. According to Spitzer (2000), the "trick to building an effective vortal lies in getting the correct mix of content, dialog, services and transaction processing that reflects the target industry's business practices". He recommended that the first lesson to be learned in vortal development was to get individuals with extensive domain experience to determine the service mix.

Virtual Trading Communities

Williams and Cothrel (2000) concluded that three activities that were central to the success of every online community were member development, asset management and community relations. Member development involved getting and maintaining a critical mass of active members by having a clearly defined focus, working with influential members within the community and one-on-one promotional and training activities. Management of community assets (which range from content, to alliances, knowledge and opinions of experts, community infrastructure and community commitment) would mean maintaining and cultivating the assets by way of member feedback, shared asset management efforts with the community and by harnessing the voluntary power of participants. In maintaining community relations, explicit rules and guidelines need to be drawn up for moderators of virtual community groups.

The critical success factors for regional community networks according to Cavill (Swatman et al., 1996) are: vision, leadership, broad community engagement, relevance, access, education and training, open technological base, support infrastructure, funding and collaboration.

2.3.2.5 Summary on Portals/Virtual Trading Communities

The literature on portals and virtual trading communities showed that apart from being considered e-marketplaces in some cases, there are different definitions and models of portals and virtual trading communities that can create confusion for both researchers and practitioners. As with e-marketplaces, the differing definitions, models and structures of portals and virtual trading communities are based on the market they target and the function that they seek to perform. Other than the transactional mechanisms (which could be e-marketplaces), the commercial aspects of portals and virtual trading communities appear to centre on stickiness of the platforms, and interaction and knowledge sharing among participants.

The theoretical approaches to portals and virtual trading communities reviewed excluded those already considered under the section on e-marketplaces. As such, most of the literature centred on attracting and maintaining a vibrant community of users and the value propositions of these platforms. Finally some of the more significant critical success factors of portals and virtual trading communities appear to be relevance, engagement and retention of users, having a clear focus and building relationships.

2.3.3   SME Participation in E-Marketplaces and Portals/Virtual Trading Communities

In this section, the literature reviewed is in relation to SME participation in non-Government owned or supported e-marketplaces and Portals/Virtual Trading Communities. While some of the advantages of and barriers to e-marketplace participation by SMEs are those that are applicable to SME e-commerce uptake in general, there are others that need to be treated separately.

Most of the literature on SME participation in e-marketplaces and portals/virtual trading communities deals with the negative i.e. the barriers to participation and how to overcome them. Gulledge (2001) in investigating incentives for SMEs to participate in supply-chain e-marketplaces, spoke of the supply squeeze (economic issues) and technology squeeze (different standards required by multiple exchange partners) faced by SMEs. He concluded that at the time, the implementation of such e-marketplaces was not attractive to suppliers especially SMEs, as most emphasis was on the buyer-side. According to Gulledge (2001), what was needed was for such e-marketplaces to emphasise the collaboration aspects of supply relationship management.

Trust was a major issue in SME participation in e-marketplaces. Ba, Whinston and Zhang (2001) looked at the role of trust on two levels in enabling SMEs to successfully grow and compete in e-marketplaces. Firstly, asymmetric information available in e-marketplaces meant that SMEs faced the risk of misinterpretation of information due to a lack of trust in web-based sites. Secondly, given their lack of size and resources for brand-building, it was difficult for SMEs to get the trust of buyers. Ba et al. (2001) proposed digital intermediaries and trusted third parties as one way to overcome these trust issues. Brown and Lockett (2001) also considered the role of trusted intermediaries within eClusters of SMEs. They viewed eClusters as a future type of digital enterprise community which could be interconnected e-marketplaces, guaranteed e-markets, Internet business communities or community-centric application service providers. Underpinning eClusters would be a Trust Platform which will comprise structure, services and governance provided by three kinds of intermediaries: technology, enterprise and community. The primary role of the trust platform would be to "facilitate the formation and development of eClusters from 'natural' communities of SMEs" (Brown & Lockett, 2001, p. 54). Hsiao (2003) viewed the failure of Chinese SMEs in Singapore to adopt e-marketplace trading from a perspective of distrust through a socio-cultural analysis at the societal level. He showed that such value-oriented distrust could precipitate fear and rejection of technology.

Anderson (2000) related how SMEs in the engineering and manufacturing sectors within the East Midlands region of the United Kingdom acquired knowledge and access to knowledge diffusion networks via the Internet through a vortal.

The Lonxanet, an e-marketplace in Galatia, Spain was created to address issues of fragmentation, inefficiencies, income inequalities and economic and biological sustainability in the Galacian artisanal fisheries industry (Dans & Freire, 2002). The exchange mechanism was an 'anticipated auction' or an 'electronic implementation of a sealed envelope, first-price auction with multiple items', where buyers submit their orders via the Internet (or a call centre) before fishermen leave the ports and on their return bidders are allotted the lots according to the previously established orders. The Lonxanet began commercial activities in December 2001. As at 2002, the amount invested in the Lonxanet was €510,000 and although at that time the sponsors were not yet calling it a success, the early indications were encouraging. The successful implementation of Lonxanet could be attributed to trust in the system, the strong partnering strategy, commitment of the stakeholders by having user representatives involved in the governance and adequate resources (financial, technical and management resources).

Ordanini and Pol (2001) in demonstrating how competitive infomediation worked in B2B digital marketplaces, used the example of Marketplaceitaly.com, a B2B trading portal targeted specifically at SMEs. The Marketplaceitaly.com portal comprised three functional areas: Exchangeitaly, the dynamic trading platform with a classifieds bulletin board, auctions and an exchange; Business Services which provide value-added services like logistics, insurance, financing to SME participants; and a Business Community comprising different vertical B2B trade communities acting as knowledge portals or collaborative platforms for SMEs.

According to the Commission of the European Communities' Expert Group on B2B Internet trading platforms (Commission of the European Communities, 2003b), despite new possibilities to reduce operational costs and raise productivity, the use of B2B Internet trading platforms was still relatively low and their acceptance by SMEs was not widespread. Simple catalogue-based transactions were more popular with SMEs compared to the more sophisticated auctions. The report also showed that smaller companies preferred e-marketplaces that were operated by a single buyer/seller or by an independent third party, the latter also being the most preferred among medium-sized enterprises. According to the report, the barriers to e-marketplace trading by SMEs were: lack of awareness of the risks and benefits; difficulties in identifying the most relevant B2B Internet trading platforms; insufficient clarity of product definitions and incompatible technical standards; new commercial risks resulting from incomplete information about market rules; financial barriers and lack of qualified personnel.

The literature on SME involvement in e-marketplaces, portals and virtual trading communities thus appears to have emphasised the need to look beyond transactional issues and encompass a wider range of issues like culture and relationship building. There was also a broader vision of the support that can be provided by such trading platforms to encompass areas like online knowledge management and collaborative benefits for SMEs.

2.3.4   *Government-sponsored Regional Internet Trading Platforms for SMEs*

In government-sponsored regional Internet trading platforms for SMEs, it is important that the sponsors possess good IS project management skills to properly manage the contractors of the technical development of the platform and the various resources and relationships within the platforms. A resource-based view of the project would determine the need to ensure IT/IS core capabilities like leadership, business systems thinking and vendor development (Feeny & Willcocks, 1998) are present in the platform sponsors. Although one of the success factors for the government-funded ITOL projects in the McGrath and More (2002) study was the importance of managing people, relationships and business processes rather than concentrating only on managing the technology, the choice of project manager and the need for the project to be driven hard were also viewed by the operating officers of the projects concerned as critical to success. Based on the observations made of the management of the project by the research industry partner, it appeared that this was one of the weak areas.

Most of the literature on government-sponsored e-marketplaces and portals/virtual trading platforms deals with regional models. According to Tatnall and Burgess (2002) early results of Bizewest, a government-sponsored horizontal B2B portal for SMEs in Melbourne, Australia, indicated that the participants had no clear perception of benefits from participation; rather they were encouraged to join by mimetic peer pressure.

Wilkins et al.(2003a; 2003b) used critical social theory to study two B2B portals in the agricultural industry in Victoria and New South Wales, Australia. The portals were the Regional Electronic Trade Facilitation Centre (RETFC, a vertical B2B portal in horticulture which became a showcase collaborative project) and Food Connect Australia (FCA, a B2B marketplace which was designed to assist Australian fresh food exporters, particularly those who exported to the Asian region. FCA failed within a year of being launched). In RETFC, the trust engendered in the project by the broad consultative governance style ensured commitment of all stakeholders to the project whereas FCA was viewed as a top-down model, with the sponsor imposing its model on the users. Wilkins et al. found that the processes developed in implementing an electronic market were as important as products; governance procedures required to implement an electronic market were not well understood and differed significantly from those used for developing tangible products; e-markets were attractive to users only if they added value to their business and extended standard ways of operating and finally, the ability to establish a sense of community could play an important part in establishing some electronic markets.

According to Thompson (2003), a taxonomy developed by Denison, Hardy, Johanson, Stillman and Schauder (2002), which differentiated between various types of ICT and community networking initiatives, proved to be useful when applied to a cluster of community informatics initiatives originating from the Central Highlands region of Victoria, Australia. A case study was conducted of GrowExport.com (one of the online communities within that cluster) which was designed to specifically promote and support further networking amongst exporters and potential exporters in the Central Highlands region. GrowExport.com was a two-way communication tool which acted as a conduit for information flow between regional development agencies and industry representatives and their stakeholders, with communication being equally initiated at both ends. It also served as an information 'hub' for exporters and potential exporters to find further information on government and non-government organisations, networks and groups with the ability for all organisations to post information. The results of the case study showed that important factors in the initial success of the project were: the active involvement of community members in designing, implementing and sustaining the services; access to a comprehensive toolset specifically designed to meet the skills and infrastructure gaps of the region; the ability of multiple users to contribute, publish and maintain the web-based information, and, finally, the degree to which web-based applications were tailored to meet the particular business, organisation or community purpose.

The Electronic Mall Bodensee or emb.net which was established in 1995 was Europe's first regional e-marketplace (Zimmerman, 1998). It was based on the concept of the ancient Agora which fulfilled both commercial (supply, demand and pricing mechanisms) and communication functions, and was created in an attempt to accelerate diffusion and acceptance of modern telematic services and applications among participants in the Lake Constance region of Germany, Switzerland and Austria. Emb.net catered for C2C, G2C, B2G, B2C and B2B relationships. The Shopping Centre within Emb.net was the trading centre, but the whole portal was considered to be the regional e-marketplace. In examining the socio-economic aspects of e-marketplaces using emb.net as a case study, Schubert (n.d.) made the following conclusions:

- An e-market is framed in a socio-economic context and its related social interaction patterns and cannot be analysed from a technical point of view alone

- E-business transactions require trust in the trading partner and the supporting technology

- The factors affecting the participant's degree of confidence in the offerings of an e-market are: integration of logistics services; matching of payment preferences; reliability; customer-vendor relationship; image (e.g. brand name, well-known company) and exclusivity (e.g. closed user group).

Among the preliminary findings from the emb.net study was that although consumers from the region used the regional e-marketplace to look for information about the offerings of local suppliers, they actually visited the store in person to make the purchase. According to Steinfield, Mahler and Bauer (1999b) local merchants who are offering products that are readily obtainable elsewhere, may need a web strategy that emphasises the synergy between their physical presence in a local market and their web storefront. This could be done by mentioning their website in their traditional store, in their advertisements, or in the telephone directory, and by offering a few featured special services for local customers, or highlighting local information as a way of building trust on their website.

One of the policies under the eEurope Go Digital programme to increase uptake of e-commerce among SMEs was the facilitation of effective participation of SMEs in e-business networks. The objectives under this policy were the promotion of the participation of SMEs in B2B e-marketplaces and public electronic procurement and the promotion of virtual collaborative SME networks (E-Business Policy Group, 2002). Under this policy, public-funded trading platforms like Rakat in Denmark, Achatville in France and Empower.ie in Ireland were established to give SMEs the opportunity to participate in e-marketplace trading in a trusted environment. Some of the recommendations of the report by the Commission of the European Communities' Expert Group on B2B Internet trading platforms (Commission of the European Communities, 2003b) were that the main role of enterprise policy should be to reduce economic risks due to the lack of information and interoperable solutions, and to prepare SMEs for participating effectively in the new forms of electronic trading. SMEs should be made aware that benefits from participation in B2B Internet trading platforms extended beyond the benefits from buying and selling online, to include co-operation, collaboration and information exchange, improving relations with suppliers and customers and increasing the efficiency of internal business processes.

Standing et al. (2003), in studying a government-sponsored local consortium-owned regional e-marketplace in Western Australia noted that although it was viewed as a way of building a local online community, it did not emphasise or include the provision for a strong network model through e-collaboration and knowledge sharing. Instead, the regional e-marketplace had a transaction-cost/market expansion focus. According to Standing et al. a broader vision (than just a techno-economic view) for government-sponsored regional e-marketplaces should be considered to harness the full benefits of online business for the local economy.

At the end of 2003, there were various models of government-sponsored regional Internet platforms for SMEs [for example whole-of-country B2B regional e-marketplaces (Nextr@de); government procurement regional e-marketplaces at the country level (MERX of Canada), state level (GEM of Western Australia, Smartbuy of New South Wales) and local/borough/municipality level (Roses Marketplace and London Marketplace in the United Kingdom, RAKAT in Denmark); vertical regional e-marketplaces (Agribazaar in Malaysia); online shopping malls (Wisconsin

Common Market)]. However, while some of these models may prove to be profitable or at least sustainable in the longer term, others could be only transitory. According to the E-Business Policy Group of the European Commission (2002, p. 34) "specific actions in support of e-business for SMEs are designed to deal with situations where the market has failed to address the specific needs of SMEs, and therefore, they should be limited in time and not perpetuated endlessly. Once the policy objectives are met, or the specific SME needs that a policy addresses have disappeared, or the market starts responding successfully to the SMEs needs, these policy initiatives should stop." There is therefore a need to determine which models of trading platforms fall under this category of e-business policies for SMEs and plan accordingly for them.

The review of the literature on SME participation in e-marketplaces and portals/virtual trading communities suggests that prior to 2004, there were still large gaps in the research area. There was uncertainty about which models could successfully engage the SME community in online trading; most of the research was exploratory in nature and only preliminary results were available. It was also unclear whether government-sponsored trading platforms for SMEs were in fact suitable vehicles to promote e-commerce uptake in this sector and if they were, then which models would better achieve this objective. There was also not much empirical evidence in the literature to indicate the actual costs of these initiatives and the problems related to specific models of government-sponsored trading platforms for SMEs, nor the actual benefits that could be derived from them.

2.3.5 Summary on Internet Trading Platforms

The literature reviewed on Internet trading platforms like e-marketplaces and portals or virtual trading communities showed that it was an area that was still evolving, with a myriad of definitions, models and structures. The initial view of the phenomenon was basically an economic one, with the Internet-enabled reduced cost of coordination expecting to favour the move towards such platforms over hierarchies. However, the reality was that lower coordination costs alone were not sufficient to create a revolution in the way business was conducted or to forge totally new cyber-based trading relationships. Instead, although there were some successes among pure plays and break through applications like Amazon.com and eBay, the greatest advantages were experienced when the new technology was used to strengthen existing trading relationships in supply chains.

In so far as regional Internet trading platforms are concerned, the literature has indicated that e-marketplaces and portals/virtual trading communities are complex phenomena that need to be examined not only from technical and economic perspectives but also from a social, cultural and political view. The literature has also shown that it was during the e-marketplace hype cycle that the fear began to surface of SMEs being marginalised in the move towards e-marketplace trading. This resulted in a number of experiments by governments at the federal, state and local levels (and sometimes in collaboration with community groups) to develop or fund trading platforms specifically for SMEs. There were a number of models and structures of such platforms initiated. However, not much was available empirically in the literature on the actual costs, benefits, problems and outcomes of such initiatives. This research sets out to evaluate one such type of platform: horizontal government-sponsored regional Internet trading platforms for SMEs which were developed as part of community portals in Western Australia.

2.4   CHAPTER SUMMARY

The advent of the Internet and e-commerce were viewed as opportunities for SMEs to compete with their larger counterparts by overcoming distance and size. However, in the mid 1990s, statistics began to show that certain sectors could be marginalised in the move to the digital economy and there was a fear of a growing digital divide between SMEs and big business and between regional areas and cities. A number of interventions were designed to narrow this divide, among them collaborative initiatives that promoted e-commerce among SMEs at the regional levels. In Australia, a number of funding opportunities at the federal, state and regional levels were available to fund these initiatives. In Western Australia, one response to the funding opportunities available was the creation of regional Internet trading platforms for SMEs that were created as part of community portals. Although such platforms and portals had been introduced in 1999, there was not much in the literature to indicate how these platforms were performing and whether or not they were meeting the objectives behind their creation. There were few sources in the academic literature to guide academics and practitioners alike in the development and evaluation of such platforms.

Complex phenomena such as government-sponsored regional Internet trading platforms for SMEs need to be viewed in the context of the social, political, cultural, technical and economic structures of the region. To construct the conceptual frameworks of this study, the existing literature prior to 2004 in the area of e-marketplaces, portals and virtual trading communities was reviewed to identify relevant theoretical approaches and constructs that could be used in the study. The literature review revealed that the development pattern of research (theoretical approaches, structures and models, critical success factors and benefits of e-marketplaces, portals and virtual communities) was practice-driven. The early focus was on areas like transaction costs, productivity benefits, independent third-party trading exchanges and liquidity as the belief prior to mid-2000 was that e-commerce would lead to more e-marketplaces than hierarchies. It was during this dot.com boom that the idea for many of the government-sponsored regional Internet trading platforms for SMEs was conceived. When the bottom fell out of the dot.com boom and the world woke up to the reality that the Internet would not create a revolution in the way business was conducted but rather an evolution in the way the technology was used to improve existing practices, research in the area took a different focus. Resource based views, institutional perspectives and inter-organisational relationships were the lenses used to research Internet trading platforms. Socio-political views were integrated with the techno-economic approaches in attempts to obtain a holistic understanding of Internet trading platforms. Critical success factors and benefits that grew in prominence were strategic partnering, provision of value added services and knowledge building rather than merely critical mass or transaction cost reductions. Horizontal government-supported Internet trading platforms for SMEs that were predicated on the belief that 'if you build it they will come' began to falter as they struggled to demonstrate economic benefits for their participants and self sustainability. This was the climate within which this research was undertaken.

The literature reviewed on e-marketplaces and portals/virtual trading communities in this chapter will serve as scaffolding for the conceptual frameworks to be developed for this study. Constructs and success factors from the literature have been identified that will help in understanding the development and management of government-supported regional Internet trading platforms for SMEs and the benefits that these platforms can offer stakeholders. However, the literature in this area alone does not provide a sufficient basis for the frameworks as the target participants of such platforms, SMEs, could exhibit particular characteristics that could specifically impact on their uptake of Internet trading. It is therefore necessary to examine the related research area of SME adoption of ICT and e-commerce to identify these characteristics. There is also a need to review the literature in the area of evaluation to determine how best to conduct evaluation of government-supported regional Internet trading platforms for SMEs. The review of the literature in these two areas of research is done in the following chapter.

CHAPTER 3
LITERATURE REVIEW PART II

3.1 INTRODUCTION

This chapter continues the review of related literature published prior to 2004. The review first examines the literature on the various theoretical perspectives of SME adoption of ICT and e-commerce. This is done to determine if there are any constructs from existing theories and research that can be applied to this study. The chapter then turns to the review of the literature on evaluation to identify approaches and metrics that can be used in the effective evaluation of government-sponsored regional Internet trading platforms for SMEs. The chapter culminates in the conceptual frameworks that have been constructed for this research.

3.2 THEORETICAL PERSPECTIVES OF SME ADOPTION OF ICT AND E-COMMERCE

While there is a large body of literature on IT/IS and e-commerce adoption in general, a relatively smaller, but nonetheless significant body of literature deals with how SMEs perform in these areas. Research on SME adoption of IT/IS and e-commerce use as their basis, the popular theories and models of IT adoption like the diffusion-of-innovation theory, resource-based theory, the technology acceptance model, the theory of planned behaviour and stage theory. Given the inter-organisational aspect of Internet trading platforms, SME adoption of trading on Internet platforms should also be examined through the lens of institutional theory and inter-organisational relationships.

3.2.1 Diffusion of Innovation (DOI) Theory

Rogers' DOI theory, first postulated in 1962 and subsequently updated and enhanced in 1971, 1983 and 1995, identifies five broad factors that can affect the adoption of an innovation. These factors are innovation factors, individual factors, task factors, environmental factors and organisational factors (Rogers, 1995). In terms of innovation factors, Rogers' DOI theory states that potential users' perception of the relative advantage, compatibility, complexity, trialability and observability of an innovation will determine not only their decision to adopt the innovation but the extent of the adoption as well. In a meta-analysis of the literature on the relationship between characteristics of innovation and adoption, Tornatzky and Klein (cited in Premkumar et al., 1994) found that compatibility, relative advantage and complexity were the most significant factors affecting the adoption of an innovation. The process-based innovation adoption model developed by Tornatzky and Fleischer (1990) includes three broad factors or contexts affecting adoption and implementation. They are the organisational context, the technological context and the external environmental context.

Most studies having DOI as their theoretical basis use derivatives of the Tornatzky and Fleischer or Rogers' models or combine them with other factors to form hybrid models. For example Premkumar et al. (1994) in studying the implementation of electronic data interchange (EDI) from an innovation-diffusion perspective, examined the relationship between innovation characteristics (some of which were from the Rogers' model), and diffusion variables identified in the stage models of diffusion and traditional IS success literature. The results of their study suggest that relative advantage, technical compatibility and costs were the major predictors of adoption.

DOI studies of SME adoption of IT also tend to be based on hybrid models. Iacovou, Benbasat and Dexter's (1995) study of the adoption and impact of EDI in small organisations used innovation characteristics such as relative advantage (in the form of perceived benefits) and trialability, but included other factors affecting IT adoption such as external pressure and organisational readiness. Cragg and King's (1993) longitudinal study of motivators and inhibitors of small firm computing used relative advantage as one of the four motivator categories, the others being consultant support, competitive pressure and managerial enthusiasm. Thong and Yap (1995) in their study of small business adoption of IT in Singapore classified factors affecting adoption into individual characteristics (like top management attitude towards IT adoption) and organisational characteristics (like business size and information intensity). Scupola (2003) found that an adapted version of the Tornatzky and Fleischer (1990) model was very useful in investigating facilitators of SME Internet e-commerce adoption in Southern Italy. Her study indicated that while organisational and technological contexts are important, the major factor affecting adoption and implementation of e-commerce is the external context in the form of government intervention, public administration and pressure from customers, suppliers and competitors.

A major critique of these studies is that they do not specifically consider economic factors like resources and return on investment (van Akkeren & Cavaye, 1999a).

3.2.2 Resource-Based Theory (RBT)

RBT involves taking a knowledge-based perspective of the assets and resources of a firm that are used to attain sustainable competitive business advantage. In RBT core-competencies or unique attributes of a firm, which are difficult or costly to copy, need to be exploited. RBT views IT/IS as one of the resources that can be used to achieve competitive advantage depending on how it is managed. Feeny and Willcocks (1998) concentrate on the capability of the IT function and define nine core IT/IS capabilities, some of which are IT/IS leadership, business systems thinking and vendor development. In a study of attributes of IT, Mata, Fuerst and Barney (1995) concluded that managerial IT skills can provide sustainable advantage.

Caldeira and Ward (2003) used RBT to interpret the successful adoption and use of IT/IS in Portuguese manufacturing SMEs. They found that the firms that were more successful in adopting IT/IS had managements that viewed IT/IS as an important determining capability and developed internal IT/IS competencies. In contrast, Thong's (2001) resource-based study of 114 small businesses in Singapore showed that while adequate IS investment, high IS knowledge level among users, high CEO support and user involvement were positively correlated with successful IS, the most significant factor was found to be highly effective external expertise (vendor development in the Feeny and Willcocks (1998) model). This could have been due to the fact that the subjects in the study were small businesses that did not have the requisite resources to develop in-house IT competencies.

Competence development in SMEs was the object of the ADAPT research programme launched by the European Union in 1994 (Löfstedt, 2001). In terms of e-commerce and SMEs, the building of SME e-business competencies is considered a high priority area by the European Union (Commission of the European Communities, 2003a) and the OECD (DSTI (Directorate for Science Technology and Industry) OECD, 2002). Duhan, Levy and Powell (2001) in an empirical investigation of the role of IS as firm resources in knowledge-based SMEs found that systemic, knowledge-based resources are likely to be the prime competitive tools of this type of firm. They concluded that the competence-based view of strategy was vital to strategic information systems planning and that business objectives were realised through exercising competence leveraging and building, while core competencies become the locus of competitive advantage.

3.2.3 Stage Theory

Understanding how IT/IS is adopted can have policy implications for the creation of Internet trading platforms for SMEs as far as development and delivery of benefits are concerned. Gibson and Nolan's (1974) stages of growth theory to describe the process by which IT/IS evolves in an organisation has been criticised as lacking an empirical basis (Benbasat, Dexter, Drury & Goldstein, 1984). Nevertheless, variations of the stage model have been developed and continue to be used to explain the growth of technology adoption (Drazin & Kazanjian, 1990), information systems planning (King & Teo, 1997) and the internationalisation of SMEs (Gankema, Snuif & Zwart, 2000).

In recent times, the stage approach has proved a popular framework to chart the phases that companies go through to reach e-commerce maturity (DTI, 2001; McKay, Prananto & Marshall, 2000; Prananto, Marshall & McKay, 2002). A popular model to describe e-commerce adoption is the United Kingdom DTI e-commerce adoption ladder. It describes business use of the Internet according to six stages: messaging, online marketing, online ordering, online payment, order progress/online sales support and e-business. There is also evidence to suggest that SMEs are adopting e-commerce in stages and that their progression along the e-commerce maturity curve can be characterised according to distinct phases or levels (Daniel et al., 2002; Poon & Swatman, 1997; Prananto, Marshall & McKay, 2003; Subba Rao, Metts & Mora Monge, 2003). These studies identified certain characteristics that are typically found in organisations at different stages of e-commerce maturity and provided some empirical validation for the stages of growth theory. Prananto et al. (2003) also showed in their study that SMEs which have adopted e-commerce, could actually describe this adoption as progressing in stages.

An underlying assumption of e-commerce participation is that it allows SMEs to access international markets. While this may be the case, SMEs still need to understand about the legal and trust implications of international trading. In a longitudinal study of 144 firms in Europe, Gankema et al. (2000), found that stage theory was still valid to describe the internationalisation of SMEs.

A major criticism levelled at these and other stage models is that adoption need not be evolutionary or necessarily progress in hierarchical or sequential steps. This is particularly true as the technology becomes more pervasive. Proponents of the stages of growth theory however, point to the descriptive and prescriptive qualities of the model, where benchmark variables can be used to position adopters on the adoption curve. Levy and Powell (2003) found that rather than staged adoption of Internet use (among 12 SMEs studied), adoption was contingent upon their attitude to growth and the owners' recognition of the business value of the Internet. Nevertheless, stage theory still remains an attractive lens through which to view adoption of technology, especially in the early stages where applications are novel and adopters need to learn as they adopt these technologies.

3.2.4 *The Theory of Planned Behaviour (TPB) and the Technology Acceptance Model (TAM)*

TPB is an updated and more general form of the theory of reasoned action (TRA). It is an intention model that deals with behavioural actions describing an "active, deliberate decision process within the constraints of social expectations and limited resources" (Harrison, Mykytyn Jr & Riemenschneider, 1997, p. 172). The factors determining the decision (or behavioural intention) are attitude towards adoption, subjective norm or social expectations and perceived behavioural control. Attitude is determined by behavioural beliefs and evaluations of the consequences of adoption.

Subjective norm is determined by social pressure to adopt, while perceived behavioural control is determined by potential adopters' beliefs about the ease or difficulty of adoption and their ability to deal with potential obstacles. In studying the executive decision about adoption of IT in 162 small businesses, Harrison et al. (1997) chose TPB over DOI as they took the view that not all ITs are innovative and that there was a difference between initial IT adoption and diffusion of innovation. Their study gave strong support to TPB as a description of small business executives' decision to adopt IT.

Like TPB, the TAM which was first put forward by Davis in 1986 (Davis, Bagozzi & Warshaw, 1989), had its roots in the theory of reasoned action. However, unlike the preceding theories, the TAM deals specifically with computer use. In the TAM, a user's voluntary intention to adopt an IT/IS is determined by the perceived usefulness of using the new IT/IS and its perceived ease of use. The TAM was designed to determine the impact of external factors on internal beliefs, attitudes and intentions towards adoption. It is widely used and has been tested under a variety of contexts, including e-commerce (Gefen, Karahanna & Straub, 2003; Lu, Yu, Liu & Yao, 2003), proving it is robust and parsimonious. While the TAM is a model that deals with a personal user perspective of technology adoption, its inclusion as a lens to study technology adoption in the SME context is valid in cases where the adoption decision is one that is made by owners/proprietors in their personal capacity. In a study of 203 manufacturing and engineering SMEs in New Zealand, Igabria, Zinatelli, Cragg and Cavaye (1997) found that perceived ease of use was a strong determinant of personal computing acceptance. However, some researchers like Agarwal and Prasad (1998), Hu, Chau, Sheng, and Tam (1999) and Mathieson (1991) felt that the TAM is too general and that it needs to either consider other factors or be integrated with other IT acceptance models. An extension of TAM (Venkatesh & Davis, 2000) includes social norms which however, are likely to have a greater effect on perception and behaviour when a user does not have first hand experience of an IT. Both TPB and the TAM have been criticised for not specifically addressing economic factors (van Akkeren & Cavaye, 1999a).

Venkatesh, Morris, Davis and Davis (2003) developed and empirically tested a unified model of technology acceptance called the Unified Theory of Acceptance and Use of Technology (UTAUT). The UTAUT integrates acceptance determinants from eight existing models i.e. TRA, TAM, TPB, combined TPB/TAM, DOI theory, model of PC utilisation, motivational model and social cognitive theory. The motivation behind development of the UTAUT was the weakness of existing models in providing prescriptive guidance to designers. The UTAUT resulted in a model that contained four main effects (performance expectancy, effort expectancy, social influence and facilitating conditions) and four moderators (gender, age, experience and voluntariness of use) of determinants of intention and behaviour towards adoption. Empirical tests indicated that the UTAUT performed better than any of the eight models individually. However, as the UTAUT is a model based on individual user behaviour, Venkatesh et al. (2003) called for further research to extend and enhance their model especially in areas like the link between user acceptance and organisational usage outcomes.

3.2.5 Inter-organisational Relationships and Institutional Theory

By using existing theories on IT/IS adoption in relation to participation in Internet platforms by SMEs, the trading platform is viewed as an IT/IS. However, in the B2B and B2G contexts, such platforms are inter-organisational information systems (IOIS) and therefore the network aspect needs to be examined to determine its effect on the decision by SMEs to participate in them.

The network view of e-marketplaces focuses on the motivation for inter-organisational relationships (Oliver, 1990). A digital knowledge network can potentially enable SMEs to compete with their larger counterparts that have larger internal networks and communities of practice (Braun, 2002). For the sponsor or owner of a government-sponsored Internet trading platform for SMEs, the network motive is intertwined with the community motive, which is to stimulate community development by encouraging adoption of Internet trading to ultimately raise the levels of e-business knowledge, skills and technology within the community (Standing et al., 2003).

The effect of inter-organisational networks on Internet trading platforms for SMEs can be examined using the constructs of institutional theory and inter-organisational relationships (IORs). Institutional theory posits that in an institutional environment, where shared norms exist about organisational forms and behaviours, organisations face coercive, normative and mimetic pressure to conform to these norms. Coercive pressure to participate in an Internet trading platform could stem from suppliers or buyers. Potential participants in an Internet trading platform for SMEs could face normative pressure from not only buyers and sellers, but also from the business, trade or professional networks to which they belong, if these networks are already participants themselves. Mimetic pressure may cause the competitors of a participant in an Internet trading platform to also participate. Teo, Wei and Benbasat (2003), examined the decisions of organisations in Singapore to adopt financial EDI, and found that all three institutional pressures were significant in influencing the decision.

Oliver's (1990), six determinants of the formation of IORs (necessity, asymmetry, reciprocity, efficiency, stability and legitimacy) can be used to examine not only the creation or development of Internet platforms, but also the decisions to participate in them. Necessity and asymmetry could be viewed as coercive pressure. Reciprocity carries connotations of cooperation, collaboration and coordination among organisations, which in an Internet trading platform for SMEs can help participants overcome size disadvantages by aggregation and knowledge sharing. Internet trading platforms for SMEs could provide stability to prospective participants, for example in the form of access to trusted value-added service providers. Finally, legitimacy in IORs can be equated with normative pressure, which in Internet trading platforms for SMEs can be used to build critical mass.

3.2.6 Partial, Hybrid and Integrated Models of ICT and E-Commerce Adoption by SMEs

Theoretical frameworks and models used in the research area of SME adoption of IT/IS and e-commerce are also quite often partial models, hybrid models or integrated models using the constructs from the preceding theoretical frameworks. For example, Evans (2002) examined the impact of the external context (local and regional governance intervention) on SME e-commerce adoption in the Greater Manchester and Merseyside regions of the United Kingdom. His findings indicate that despite the intervention, e-commerce had not fundamentally changed the relative economic status of the two cities. He also found that a firm's potential to develop e-commerce services in the technology, business management and design/creative industry sectors was to a large extent dependent on higher order knowledge skills (competencies in RBT).

Poon and Swatman (1997) developed a four-stage model, which reflected how the Internet had been used by SMEs during the different stages of business relationship development. They found that the key drivers of Internet use were perceived benefits (relative advantage in DOI theory) and management involvement in adopting e-business (organisational context of DOI theory or managerial IT skills in RBT). In examining the inhibitors to EDI adoption by SMEs in Hong Kong, Chau (2001) used 12 factors classified under three broad constructs of perceived benefits and costs, organisational context and environmental context (DOI theory). His study suggested that the most significant inhibitors were related to organisational readiness, which included factors like knowledge skills about technology, attitude, internal IT support and support provided by vendors (constructs of RBT). Riemenschneider, Harrison and Mykytyn Jr. (2003) in integrating TPB and TAM found that the resultant collected model better explained IT adoption decisions of small business executives in the USA regarding having a web presence. Their collected model showed that improved social contact with customers, vendors etc. that the Internet provided, was the major factor affecting decision to adopt web sites. However it could also be argued that this factor could be viewed as a perceived benefit (relative advantage in DOI theory). Van Akkeren and Cavaye (1999a) in reviewing the theoretical frameworks of many studies on SME adoption of IT/IS, concluded that not enough importance was assigned to economic factors. Their integrated model of

SME IT/IS adoption uses the constructs of owner-manager characteristics, firm characteristics and return on investment (ROI) as the factors affecting adoption.

3.2.7 Summary on Theoretical Perspectives of SME Adoption of ICT and E-Commerce

It can be seen that not only do the different theories on IT/IS/e-commerce adoption have areas of overlap; in the SME context most studies are not based on any one framework in its entirety or in its pure form. Furthermore, the community and economic development motives underlying the creation of Internet trading platforms for SMEs introduce additional significant constructs (like the not-for-profit motive of the market maker, ownership structure of the platform and competencies of the market-maker), which cannot be explained or satisfactorily dealt with by existing theoretical frameworks or adoption models individually. This suggests a need to synthesise or integrate existing theories on SME adoption of IT/IS/e-commerce in order to apply them to study SME participation in government-supported regional Internet trading platforms.

While the literature in this section adds another significant dimension to the conceptual frameworks of this study, the evaluation of the benefits that can be realised from government-sponsored Internet trading platform for SMEs requires a review of the literature in yet another area of research, viz. evaluation.

3.3   EVALUATION

"Evaluation is endemic to human existence" (Smithson & Hirschheim, 1998) and everything can be evaluated including evaluation itself (Shadish Jr. et al., 1991), but it can have different meanings and outcomes depending on the content, context and process of the evaluation (Symons, 1991). The content-context-process (CCP) approach to information systems evaluation developed by Symons (1991) was based on Pettigrew's (1985a; 1985b) work in evaluating organisational change. In the CCP approach, content refers to what is being evaluated and the relevant measures, values and metrics of the evaluation. Process of the evaluation relates to the way in which the evaluation is done, its timing and frequency, and the manner in which the results will be made available. The context of the evaluation is concerned with why the evaluation is being done and who is doing it (Smithson & Hirschheim, 1998, p. 169). In view of the multiple motivations behind the creation of government-sponsored regional Internet trading platforms for SMEs and the number of stakeholders involved, evaluation of such initiatives would require the application of the CCP approach on a number of levels at different stages in the development of such platforms. In attempting to provide an evaluation framework that is holistic but at the same time robust and practical, the CCP approach will be used as the overarching evaluation approach in this research and will be incorporated in a benefits-evaluation framework that will be developed specifically for government-sponsored regional Internet trading platforms for SMEs.

According to Bakos (1991), e-marketplaces are socially desirable when net welfare gains are greater than development and operating costs. While a substantial body of literature exists on the evaluation of IS, there have been few attempts to develop evaluation models with a holistic view of the benefits of e-marketplaces or Internet trading platforms for all stakeholders at various levels, which is a prerequisite for the measurement or evaluation of net welfare gain. This is partly due to the fact that Internet trading platform models are themselves evolving and while there are benefits that are common to all types of Internet trading platforms, there are some benefits that can be differentiated on the basis of structure and ownership and some benefits that only evolve over time. When Internet trading platforms are created to promote e-commerce uptake among SMEs and for regional economic development purposes, the issue of evaluation is further complicated, given the absence of the profit motive of the owner/sponsor and the economic development/community motive behind creation. There is therefore a need to not only view evaluation of government-sponsored regional Internet trading platforms for SMEs from an IS perspective, but also from the perspectives of evaluation of policy/social programmes and regional development.

3.3.1 A Short History of Evaluation

Although evaluation existed in areas like physics and chemistry, it was only in the late 19th century and early 20th century that evaluation research began to be formally published in non-mainstream scientific areas like education (Guba & Lincoln, 1989). Even so, the early years of evaluation in education were concerned more with testing and measurement as researchers attempted to apply the 'scientific' approach to the study of social phenomena. According to Guba and Lincoln (1989), this first generation of evaluation (which they refer to as the measurement generation) viewed the role of the evaluator in a technical light. Evaluators were expected to have knowledge of (or else be able to develop) instruments which could measure or test any given variable to be investigated.

One of the greatest shortcomings of first generation evaluation was the targeting of students as the objects of evaluation, as student profiles altered dramatically after the interruption caused by World War 1. This deficiency was addressed by the second generation of evaluation, which was characterised by description of patterns of strengths and weaknesses of outcomes against predefined curriculum objectives. These descriptions were then used to refine and revise the curricula (formative evaluation). Measurement was not equated with evaluation but was seen as one of the many instruments which could be used in the evaluation of outcomes against objectives and the role of the evaluator was extended to include that of describer (Guba & Lincoln, 1989, p. 28). There was thus a shift in focus from evaluation of students to evaluation of policies or programmes.

The third generation of evaluation incorporated a call to include judgement in the act of evaluation and evaluators assumed the role of judge in addition to their technical and descriptor roles. The call for judgement as the other basic act of evaluation (description being the first) by Stake and echoed by Scriven (cited in Guba & Lincoln, 1989, p. 30) stemmed from the fact that objectives themselves needed to be evaluated. Third generation evaluation was marked by a dearth of evaluation theories and models which were established to cater especially for the growth in social programmes introduced after the Second World War. It was also during this period that investments in IT burgeoned, giving rise to the need to evaluate these investments.

According to Guba and Lincoln (1989), the first three generations of evaluation suffered three major flaws: a tendency towards managerialism; a failure to accommodate value-pluralism and an over commitment to the scientific paradigm of enquiry.

They proposed a fourth generation of evaluation based on the interpretive paradigm (although they called it a constructivist approach), where evaluation outcomes need to be negotiated among the different constructions of 'value' ascribed by different stakeholders in a given situation. The role of the evaluator would not be one of controller, investigator or discoverer but as collaborator, learner/teacher, reality-shaper and change agent (Walsham, 1993, p. 166). Thus fourth generation evaluation centres on the concerns, values and issues faced by all stakeholders, who together with the evaluator play an enlarged role in the evaluation process. This approach to evaluation is especially attractive to multi-stakeholder programmes and evaluations of investments in innovations where the benefits (and downsides) extend beyond the techno-economic to encompass the realm of the socio-political as well.

3.3.2 Policy/Programme/Regional Development Evaluation

Due to the interventionist roles played by federal governments after the Second World War, social programme and policy evaluation played a major role in shaping the history of evaluation. Shadish Jr. et al. (1991) demonstrated how programme evaluation evolved from borrowed concepts and practices in fields from which the practitioners and scholars were trained (like education) to become a theory-based practice-driven field in its own right. Programme evaluation theory progressed from a first stage of rigorous scientific search for the truth about effective solutions to social problems, to a second stage of alternative approaches predicated on detailed knowledge of the operation of organisations in the public sector, and finally to approaches that attempted to integrate the alternatives in the first two stages. According to Shadish Jr. et al. (p. 36) "the fundamental purpose of programme evaluation theory is to specify feasible practices that evaluators can use to construct knowledge of the value of social programs that can be used to ameliorate the social problems to which programs are relevant".

In integrating the work of past theorists in programme evaluation, Rossi and Freeman (1989) highlighted the importance of programme conceptualisation, monitoring and utility or impact. However, they acknowledged that political and social factors can play a more important role than evidence about impact of a programme in a decision on whether or not to continue with the programme. Rossi and Freeman (1989) also advocated for an even-handed treatment of each stakeholder's perspective in the evaluation.

Stake (cited in Walsham, 1993, p. 166) advocated a responsive approach to programme evaluation, which emphasised the usefulness of the findings of the evaluation to the stakeholders in the programme, instead of a preordinate approach which emphasised the statement of goals, the use of objective tests and the production of research type reports. The responsive approach meant that more attention had to be paid to identifying the various stakeholders or users of each evaluation and working closely with them.

The W.K. Kellogg Foundation (1998) believed that evaluation should be supportive and responsive to projects, rather than become an end in itself. Guiding principles for effective and meaningful evaluation of social programmes are:

- Evaluation should strengthen projects i.e. leave an organisation stronger and more able to use such an evaluation when outside support ends

- Use of multi-disciplinary approaches

- Evaluation should be designed to address real issues and should be community-based and contextual

- Evaluations should create a participatory process, value multiple perspectives and involve a representation of people who care about the project

- Allow for flexibility by taking an emergent approach, adapting and adjusting to the needs of an evolving and complex project

- Build capacity by encouraging ongoing self reflection and dialogue on the part of every person involved with evaluation in order to reach increasingly sophisticated understandings of the projects being evaluated

To the W.K. Kellogg Foundation (1998, p. 3), effective evaluation is "not an 'event' that occurs at the end of a project, but an ongoing process which helps decision makers better understand the project; how it is impacting participants, partner agencies and the community; and how it is being influenced/impacted by both internal and external factors". Evaluation should thus not be viewed only as an accountability measuring stick imposed on projects, but rather as a management and learning tool for all stakeholders and for practitioners and researchers in the field who can benefit from the experiences of other projects. According to the W.K. Kellogg Foundation, the hypothetic-deductive natural science model, which drove much of the early programme evaluation, is ill-equipped to help understand complex, comprehensive, and collaborative community initiatives. Other paradigms and methods need to be considered, among which are: the interpretivist or constructivist paradigm (Guba & Lincoln, 1989); participatory evaluation (Clarke, 1999; Guba & Lincoln, 1989; Remenyi & Sherwood-Smith, 1999); theory-based evaluation (Chen & Rossi, 1987; Weiss, 1995 cited in Diez, 2002, p. 288).

Theory-based evaluations involve ex-ante construction of models that describe the logic, context and impact of the programme and guide evaluators in selection of research methods for data collection and data analysis (Torvatn, 1999). The models also enable the evaluator to check on programme progress and impact during the programme and to evaluate the programme ex-post to refine the models for future applications. The W.K. Kellogg Foundation (1998, p. 35), advocates the use of programme logic models in evaluation. A programme logic model links outcomes with programme activities/processes and the theoretical assumptions/principles of the programme and provides a roadmap of the programme, highlighting how it is expected to work, what activities need to come before others, and how desired outcomes are to be achieved. Programme logic models can be outcomes-based models, activities-based models, theory-based models or hybrid-models (which combine the preceding types of models). According to the W.K. Kellogg Foundation (1998, p. 37), "the theory-based programme logic model is also particularly appropriate for complex, multi-faceted initiatives aimed at impacting multiple target populations".

In evaluating a regional innovation programme for SMEs in Norway, the evaluation was based on a theoretical understanding of the innovation process from evolutionary economics (Isaksen, 1999). The emphasis is on innovation as a broader concept than just technological innovations, and innovation activity was understood as an interactive process within firms and with external actors.

Diez (2002) also viewed embeddedness or the cultural and political context of a programme as being an intrinsic part of the evaluation. Evaluation is seen as a socio-political process and socio-economic elements of the policy must be wholly integrated in the evaluation.

Given the number of stakeholders and the complexity of government-supported regional Internet trading platforms for SMEs that are developed as part of community portals, a qualitative interpretivist theory-based approach would thus appear to be a good starting point in the evaluation of this type of phenomenon. Nevertheless, given that such initiatives are often innovative and novel projects, it would also be beneficial to attempt to determine some of the quantifiable costs involved in implementing them.

3.3.3 IS Evaluation Studies

In attempting to understand the complexities underlying IS evaluation, Willcocks and Lester (1999) point to the value of examining the technology shifts that have occurred in shaping the history of IS evaluation studies. According to Moschella (cited in Willcocks & Lester, 1999), IT adoption and use can be demarcated into four distinct eras. They are:

- The Systems-Centric Era (1964-1981), which initially favoured large transaction-based systems where IT investment decisions centred on centralised data centres and were thus relatively simple. Dissatisfaction with centralised control of IT, a move towards time sharing arrangements with non-financial functions, outsourcing to independent service suppliers, small-scale or mini computers and falling costs in software and peripherals, led to a shift around 1975 from centralised to business unit IT spending. The monitoring of IT costs became difficult as it led to growth in computing IT costs outside official central budgets.

- The Personal Computer or PC-Centric Era (1981-1994) provided increased access to cheap processing for business unit users and resulted in IT demand and expenditure coming from multiple areas in organisations. This caused a tendency towards a loosening of justification of IT costs coupled with difficulties in rigorously verifying the claimed benefits from IT spending. Although equipment and software costs fell during this era, constant upgrades, support and training costs, user demands for rapid database access times etc. put additional pressure on organisational IT budgets.

- The Network-Centric Era (1994-2005), seen as the integration of worldwide communications infrastructure and general-propose computing, marked a shift from local area networks (LANs) to wide area networks (WANs), intranets, and extranets; from individual productivity to virtual communities. Further investments in IT were undertaken as organisations attempted to leverage the ubiquitousness of the Internet to garner the benefits from e-commerce and inter connected networks.

- The Content-Centric Era (2005 to?) predicted to be one of virtual businesses and individualised services which will see a shift from specific technological capabilities to software, content and services. Information economics will be the driver of the IT industry and this era will make describing and quantifying the full IT value chain even more fraught with difficulties.

When viewing IS evaluation in the light of these four different eras, it is not surprising that dissatisfaction arose with early evaluation methods that concentrated mainly on traditional transaction systems and technical aspects of IT. It was in the 1980s that the IT productivity paradox was born when studies began to show that it was difficult to find a positive correlation between investment in IT and productivity (Roach cited in Brynjolfsson & Hitt, 1998). However, according to Brynjolfsson and Hitt (1998), while productivity was a simple concept, it was notoriously difficult to measure especially in the modern economy where value increasingly depended upon a number of intangibles. They also pointed out that IT investments need to be coupled with or complemented by large and time consuming organisational changes in order to produce maximum benefits. Authors like Willcocks and Lester (1999) have shown that the IT productivity debate continued largely because of disagreement about measurement of the net IT contribution and the reliability, usefulness and relevance of the data employed in that assessment. As IT became more pervasive and began to contribute significantly to overall budgets, the mid 1980s gave rise to the need for evaluation methods that addressed the question of strategic information systems and which encompassed wider aspects of an IS like user satisfaction (Bailey & Pearson, 1983; Doll & Torkzadeh, 1988).

Many methods were proffered and in 1992, DeLone and McLean (1992) synthesised the approaches to IS evaluation to propose an IS Success Model. However, according to DeLone and McLean (1992, p. 88) while their IS Success Model served to consolidate "a rich but confusing body of research into a more understandable and coherent whole...creating the long awaited 'cumulative tradition' much work [was] still needed, particularly in assessing the impact of information systems on organizational performance". Nevertheless, many subsequent studies were still concerned with economic/financial aspects and consequently financial measures like return on investment (ROI) and cost benefit analyses (CBA) prevailed (Serafeimidis & Smithson, 1999). Hirschheim and Smithson (1988) also noted that although many approaches to IS evaluation were based on quantification and used mostly technical or financial metrics, the results of those studies still appeared to gain organisational credibility. Walsham (1993) explained this paradox as resulting from ritualistic formal evaluation, where the evaluation was a symbolic belief in rational management rather than a trusted aid to decision-making. He cautioned that ritualistic evaluation could be a way of supporting powerful interests within an organisation and in some cases could be a hindrance to innovative organisational change, as evidenced from research findings by authors like Currie (1989).

The majority of IS evaluation studies till the late 1980s failed to consider the importance of the social context of an IS (Hirschheim & Smithson, 1988) or the intangible benefits that could accrue from it (Willcocks, 1994). Irani, Ezingeard and Grieve (1998) found that intangible costs were often omitted from project evaluations because they were not quantifiable. These shortcomings of a purely techno-economic/financial view of IS evaluation gave rise to a call for a more qualitative and holistic approach which would recognise a) the socio-political underpinnings of the evaluation of IS; b) the need for a dynamic iterative approach as benefits and users' constructions of them changed over time; c) a multi-stakeholder view and d) the need to view evaluation as learning. A number of interpretive approaches to IS evaluation were proposed (Hirschheim & Smithson, 1988; Symons, 1991; Walsham, 1993).

Farbey, Land and Targett (1999) described evaluation as "[a] process, or group of parallel processes, which take place at different points in time or continuously, for searching and for making explicit, quantitatively or qualitatively, all the impacts of an IT project and the programme and strategy of which it is a part ". Remenyi and Sherwood-Smith (1999) called for a continuous participative IS evaluation process built on the formative evaluation paradigm where all the primary or core stakeholders affected by the IS participate in the evaluation and the subsequent decision making associated with the project. These arguments echo the tenets of Guba and Lincoln's (1989) fourth generation evaluation and the guidelines of policy/programme evaluation (W.K. Kellogg Foundation, 1998).

The literature review has shown that there are pressing arguments for interpretive or non-solely techno-economic approaches to IS evaluation and there are overarching principles and frameworks that can be used to guide such evaluations [such as Symon's (1991) CCP approach, Palvia, Sharma and Conrath's (2001) socio-technical quality framework, Lincoln and Guba's (1989) 12-step fourth generation evaluation methodology, Rose and Haynes' (1999) Soft System Methodology approach]. However, there is also a need to design evaluation frameworks or tools for each case (or collection of like cases) as each one would be content, context and process specific. This research seeks to provide such an evaluation framework for government-sponsored regional Internet trading portals for SMEs which are created as part of community portals.

3.3.4 Evaluating E-Commerce Information Systems

While the review of the literature on IS evaluation yielded frameworks, models and metrics for evaluating different types of IS under varying contexts and at different levels, there was a lack of models and frameworks that could be used to evaluate e-commerce systems. Most of the literature dealt with the extension or re-specification of existing IS success or evaluation models to cater for e-commerce.

Chircu and Kauffman (2000) extended the Davern and Kauffman (2000) limits-to-value model (which explores market and process-level factors impacting on the value flows of IT investments) to a case study of Internet-based travel reservation systems in e-commerce. They found that the conversion of potential IT value was a lengthy process, fraught with valuation barriers (at the industry and organisational levels) and conversion barriers (in the form of resource, knowledge and usage barriers) which could limit the realised value of these e-commerce systems. They surmised that companies interested in investing in any new technology should identify not only organisation and industry IT value flows but also limits to value, in order to build realistic expectations about potential costs and benefits of the technology.

Standing and Stockdale (2001) in proposing a general model to evaluate the benefits of e-marketplaces, found that although the benefits of e-marketplaces mapped comfortably on to the success dimensions of the 1992 DeLone and McLean IS Success Model, further aspects like a longitudinal approach and the process of the evaluation need to be considered. Stockdale and Standing (2002) extended their earlier model to consider the role of the evaluator, the purpose of the evaluation, the recognition of stakeholders and stakeholder conflict and the need for informal evaluation to complement the formal evaluation process.

In attempting to respecify the DeLone and McLean 1992 IS Success Model (henceforth referred to as the D & M 1992 Model) for evaluation of e-commerce systems, Molla & Licker (2001) used customer e-commerce satisfaction as the dependent variable. Their e-commerce success model replaced the systems and information quality components of the D& M 1992 Model with measures of e-commerce system and content quality. Trust and support/service were incorporated to consider important issues like security and privacy and the need to build loyalty and make the site sticky. The success metrics used by Molla & Licker (2001) include hits and visits, website configuration and customer satisfaction, which could be important in a B2C e-commerce context or a community portal.

Torkzadeh and Dhillon (2002) developed two instruments to measure the 'means fundamental objectives' for B2C Internet commerce. By using a 5-factor 21-item scale they found that product choice and online payment were relatively strong in the means objectives category. A 4-factor, 16-item scale found that shopping convenience and ecological issues were relatively strong in the fundamental objectives category.

In applying the resource-based theory to net-enabled organisations, Zhu and Kraemer (2002) found that there was an important role for resource complementarity in the business value of e-commerce. Traditional companies needed enhanced alignment between e-commerce capability and their existing IT infrastructure to reap the benefits of e-commerce.

The preceding two sources on evaluation of e-commerce systems were part of two special editions of Information Systems Research that dealt with metrics for net-enabled organisations (Straub, Hoffman, Weber & Steinfield, 2002a). While some of the contributions in those issues indicated that existing theory, frameworks and approaches to IS evaluation could be extended and applied to e-commerce settings, in some cases new metrics were needed especially in evaluating Internet-enabled break through systems or applications. Straub, Hoffman, Weber and Steinfield (2002b) provided a taxonomy of metrics that could be mapped against research questions about e-commerce evaluation and provided sources in the literature which dealt with those metrics. According to Straub et al. (2002b) the work in the special editions "represent some old and new ways of looking at [net-enabled organisations], which, to a greater or lesser extent, have been validated for scientific use. They should serve as a sourcebook for future studies".

In developing an instrument to assess the benefits of retail e-commerce Zhuang and Lederer (2003) produced a 27-item instrument which was then reduced to five factors specific to B2C e-commerce. The factors were back-end efficiency, market expansion, inventory management, cost reduction and customer service benefits. According to the authors, their instrument provides B2C e-commerce researchers with a common measure of independent and dependent variables with which to evaluate the antecedents and outcomes of e-commerce.

DeLone and McLean updated their 1992 IS Success Model (DeLone & McLean, 2003) in the light of the "advent and explosive growth of e-commerce".

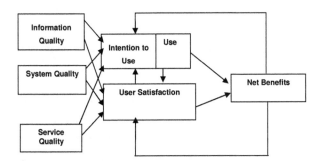

Figure 3.1 The Updated DeLone and McLean IS Success Model (Source: DeLone & McLean, 2003)

The updated model is a useful starting point in evaluating the benefits of e-commerce systems. The inclusion of the service quality dimension recognises the user support services of the IS function especially as e-commerce systems become more pervasive. Individual and organisational impact is replaced by net benefits (which could be synonymous with net welfare gain in e-marketplaces or Internet trading platforms) in an attempt to avoid complicating the model with the increasing number of entities on which the IS has an impact. In terms of e-commerce success, net benefits will measure the net impact of e-commerce on players like customers, suppliers, markets and even entire economies (or regions).

The success metrics developed in the Updated DeLone and McLean IS Success Model (DeLone & McLean, 2003) are as per table 3.1.

Table 3.1 E-Commerce Success Metrics (Source: DeLone & McLean, 2003, p. 26)

Systems Quality	Information Quality	Service Quality
Adaptability	Completeness	Assurance
Availability	Ease of Understanding	Empathy
Reliability	Personalisation	Responsiveness
Response Time	Relevance	
Usability	Security	
Use	**User Satisfaction**	**Net Benefits**
Nature of use	Repeat purchases	Cost savings
Navigation patterns	Repeat visits	Expanded markets
Number of site visits	User surveys	Incremental additional
Number of transactions		sales
executed		Reduced search costs
		Time savings

However, while DeLone and McLean (2003, p. 27) demonstrated that their updated model "is a useful model for developing comprehensive e-commerce success measures", they acknowledge that the context of the evaluation will determine the choice of IS success dimensions to be used in the evaluation.

Boon, Wilkin and Corbitt (2003) integrated the DeLone and McLean IS Success Model (1992; 2003) with Somers and Nelson's (cited in Boon et al., 2003) critical success factors (CSFs) for enterprise resource planning implementation (ERP). They found that the levels of IS success are influenced at the macro level by specific attributes of the CSFs like top management support, project champions and vendor support.

While there have been few attempts to create frameworks and instruments to evaluate e-commerce systems and e-marketplaces, even fewer models exist for evaluating virtual trading communities and portals. Bughin and Hagel (2000) cite the McKinsey & Company 'e-performance' line, aimed at measuring detailed effectiveness of mainly B2C sites. The 'e-performance' line uses indicators of visitor acquisition costs and new visitors momentum to evaluate visitor acquisition. Customer conversion is evaluated by indicators of new customer acquisition costs, new customer conversion rates, new customer revenue momentum, repeat visitor acquisition costs and repeat visitor conversion rate. Indicators for customer maintenance evaluation are repeat customer member maintenance costs, repeat customer member revenue momentum, repeat customer conversion rate and customer churn rate.

Data from the use of the McKinsey & Co e-performance line was used to demonstrate that B2C online communities seem to have developed better operational performance than other B2C models in their early stage of development.

The literature on the evaluation of e-commerce systems prior to 2004 dealt mainly with B2C systems and metrics for evaluating these systems. They represent a starting point to assist researchers in the development of context-specific instruments for the evaluation of e-commerce systems.

3.3.5 *Evaluating Government-Sponsored Regional Internet Trading Platforms for SMEs*

In government-sponsored regional Internet trading platforms for SMEs (especially where they are horizontal models catering for B2B, B2C and B2G e-commerce and part of community portals), the context of the evaluation is represented in the platform structure as well as in the stakeholder view of the benefits. These contexts are in turn determined by ownership model, motivation behind creation and profile of SMEs and the region. In applying a theory-based evaluation framework to government-sponsored regional Internet trading platforms for SMEs, this research will attempt to link together theoretical constructs underlying the contexts to determine what factors can inhibit or facilitate successful implementation of these platforms and determine the benefits that can be derived from them. An attempt will also be made to quantify some of the costs involved. The Updated DeLone and McLean IS Success model will be extended to consider these contexts, their underlying theory and the costs and benefits of the platforms. As some of the benefits of the platforms may take time to materialise, the evaluation in this study will also consider a longitudinal approach. The approach to evaluation taken in this research aims to provide an evaluation model which can be used by academia to examine similar initiatives, as well as by the practice community for ex-ante and ex-post evaluation of such initiatives. The theory-based evaluation frameworks for this research will be presented at the conclusion of this chapter.

3.3.6   Summary on Evaluation

In examining the literature on evaluation in general and on IS evaluation and policy/programme/regional development evaluation in particular, a common pattern can be observed. Although evaluation in non-mainstream scientific areas started in the late 19th and early 20th centuries, the hypothetic-deductive natural science model still prevailed until after World War 2. The dearth of social programmes implemented then and the realisation that there were competing demands for resources to implement such programmes, forced a review of evaluation methods. Conventional methodologies, such as the superiority of objective versus subjective knowing, the distancing of the researcher/evaluator from participants, and the assumptions of value-free, unbiased research/evaluations were found to have been seriously flawed (Guba & Lincoln, 1989; W.K. Kellogg Foundation, 1998, p. 10). There was a call to consider other paradigms, especially a qualitative naturalistic participative approach which would consider the views, concerns and issues faced by the various stakeholders involved in and affected by the evaluation. In the 1960s, the field of programme/policy evaluation began to move away from solely demonstrating effectiveness and measuring impact to include attempts to understand the richness and complexity of the collaborative community-based programmes that were being recommended and implemented.

This pattern was mirrored in the field of IS evaluation, with the 1980s seeing a move from techno-economic and transaction-processing based evaluation approaches to a more holistic approach. The new approach was one that considered the socio-political, institutional and external or environmental contexts of the IS in addition to the techno-economic, as IT began to be more pervasive. The advent of the Internet and e-commerce saw a move to even more distributed information systems with ICT becoming more entrenched in society. In many cases, extensions of existing IS evaluation approaches and models were proposed to satisfactorily evaluate these e-commerce systems. In the case of break-through applications, new metrics and measurement instruments needed to be designed as part of the evaluation process, to consider the novel features introduced by these new applications.

In evaluating government-sponsored regional Internet trading platforms for SMEs, the evaluation needs to be viewed from both policy/programme/regional development and IS evaluation perspectives. A theory-based evaluation that considers the context, content and process of the evaluation in attempting to identify the costs and benefits of such initiatives for all stakeholders is necessary to cater for cultural, technical, social and economic influences.

3.4   CHAPTER SUMMARY AND CONCEPTUAL FRAMEWORKS

While the literature on Internet trading platforms in the previous chapter provided the technology context to examine government-supported Internet trading platforms for SMEs, there was a need to also review the literature on SME adoption of ICT and e-commerce. This was necessary to determine the effects of the organisational (participants') context. Existing theoretical approaches to ICT and e-commerce adoption like diffusion of innovation, the technology acceptance model, the theory of planned behaviour, the uniform theory of acceptance and use of technology, stage theory and institutional theory/inter-organisational relationships were reviewed to determine their strengths and limitations in explaining the adoption and use of government-supported Internet trading platforms for SMEs. The literature revealed overlaps in the constructs of the different theories and that no one theory could be used solely and in its entirety to satisfactorily explain the adoption and use of such platforms, given the not-for-profit and economic development motives underlying their creation. It would thus be necessary to synthesise these theoretical approaches to SME adoption of ICT and e-commerce by removing duplicate constructs. By combining the resultant synthesised constructs with those from the theoretical approaches to Internet trading platforms, their critical success factors and findings from dealings with the research industry partner (market maker constructs), it was possible to construct a theory-based conceptual framework of facilitators and inhibitors to the implementation and use of such platforms by governments to promote e-commerce uptake by SMEs for regional economic development purposes. The conceptual framework is represented by figures 3.2 and table 3.2 respectively.

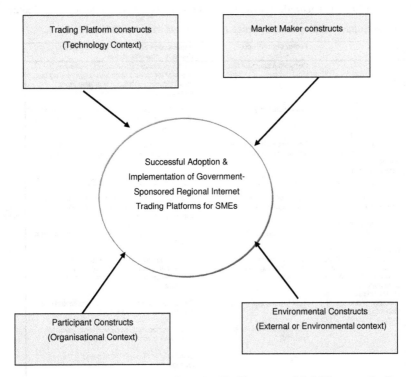

Figure 3.2 Conceptual Framework to Examine Facilitators and Inhibitors to the Successful Implementation and Use of Government-Supported Regional Internet Trading Platforms for SMEs.

Table 3.2 Integrated Theoretical Framework of Factors Affecting Success or Failure of Government-Supported Regional Internet Trading Platforms for SMEs

Category	Factors/constructs	Implications and effect on SME Trading Platform implementation
Market Maker Constructs (constructs in this category are based on e-marketplace literature, resource-based theory (RBT) and observations from dealings with the portal owned by the research industry partner)	Ownership structure and Governance	Single vs multiple stakeholders. Latter has potential for collaboration and larger funding but also for conflict. Community or user input necessary to ensure a sense of 'ownership'
	Motivation/focus	Motive affects market mechanism and services offered, benefits and success and the time taken to achieve it
	Competencies (IS/project management skills)	Has implications for issues like proper needs analysis, level of funding, ongoing support, which can directly affect success.
	Financial resources	Research shows large investments needed
Trading Platform Constructs (Nature of technology or innovation characteristics. Constructs are based on e-marketplace literature, diffusion of innovation theory, RBT, technology acceptance model (TAM), unified theory of acceptance and use of technology and stage theory)	Perceived benefits, relative advantage and usefulness	Need to convince participants of benefits to facilitate adoption. May require one-on-one consultation
	Critical mass/liquidity	Critical factor. Low entry fees alone not sufficient to guarantee success
	Value-added services/Strategic partnering (e.g. logistics, financial)	Value-added services provide convenience and/or trusted services and knowledge networks, which can enhance attractiveness of participation and therefore success
	REM training and technical support	Can be critical if technology is complicated or if SMEs do not use the Internet
	Compatibility (with users' systems)	Promotes participation by improving efficiency and lowering costs for participants
	Trust	Critical factor. Trust in owners and in the technology
	REM development and timing of features offered	Need to match sophistication/e-readiness of SMEs to ensure liquidity
	Perceived ease of use	A system perceived to be difficult will have negative effect on participation
	Good marketing plan	Creates awareness of platform within/outside region
Participant (owner/manager /firm) Constructs (constructs of RBT and TAM)	Top management commitment/innovativeness	Direct effect on decision to participate. May need to target SMEs with strong owner-innovativeness
	Internal IT/IS/e-business (readiness)	Greater proportion of e-ready SMEs can lead to quicker liquidity but they may need to be provided with more sophisticated offerings
	Size of firm	May need to target larger SMEs first. Need for clear idea of returns. May need demonstration or one-on-one consulting
Environmental Constructs (constructs of Institutional theory, inter-organisational relationships and RBT)	Regional SME profile. Local consumer needs and behaviour. Regional profile	Determines exchange mechanism and type of benefits. Geographical location of a region (e.g. are competitors to local SMEs within relatively easy reach of buyers?). Are there strong off-line relationships in the region or strong community ties?
	Government support and incentives	Depending on e-readiness of SMEs, there may be a need to provide one-on-one low cost consultancy on e-business process re-engineering to ensure liquidity. Tax breaks for participation/e-business training and consultation could positively affect uptake
	Normative, coercive and mimetic pressure/ existing trading relationships	Can positively affect participation via bandwagon effect. Can have a negative effect if market is created purely for legitimacy reasons and other factors are not given proper consideration

While figure 3.2 and table 3.2 were to be used as the conceptual framework to guide the research in investigating the factors affecting success or failure in implementation and use of government-supported regional Internet trading platforms for SMEs, there was also a need to construct a model to assess or measure the costs and benefits of such platforms. This is necessary for the study to be relevant especially to practitioners in the field. Given that the platforms were not merely information systems but were also interventions on the part of governments, evaluation of the costs and benefits of the platforms had to be viewed from the perspectives of IS evaluation and the evaluation of policy/programme/regional development. The literature on evaluation revealed a shift from the scientific hypothetic-deductive natural science approach to an interpretive naturalistic approach post World War 2. This shift was driven by the need to evaluate the vast number of social programmes that were being implemented, which often had multiple stakeholders. There was a need to adopt evaluation approaches that would go beyond solely demonstrating effectiveness and measuring impact to consider the views, concerns and issues faced by the various stakeholders affected by the evaluation so that stakeholders, evaluators and practitioners alike could learn from the evaluation and improve on the programme and on the evaluation process. Theory-based evaluations were proposed that involved ex-ante construction of models describing the logic, context and impact of the programme but which also enabled the evaluator to check on programme progress and impact during the programme (and make modifications if necessary) and to evaluate the programme ex-post so as to refine the models for future applications.

In the field of IS evaluation, as ICT and IS became more pervasive and moved out of the traditional transaction-processing domain, there were calls in the late 1980s for evaluation approaches that went beyond the techno-economic focus. This resulted in a shift from evaluation approaches that were based solely on quantification and that used mostly technical or financial metrics, to more holistic approaches that also considered the social, political and cultural nuances embedded in the context in which the IS was either introduced or existed. Evaluation approaches needed to recognise benefits that were uncertain, subjective and difficult to quantify and costs or constraints that could either impede the application of the IS or be a result of it. The holistic approach to IS evaluation needed to be a dynamic process that considered the different perspectives of multiple stakeholders at multiple levels of analysis. An overarching framework for such an evaluation approach would be the content-context-process (CCP) approach (Symons, 1991), or the 'what', 'why' and 'how' of evaluation, where managing or understanding the linkages between the content, context and process can lead to successfully managing the evaluation by drawing in the social and qualitative aspects of an IS. The CCP approach was identified as suitable for the overarching framework to guide the evaluation of government-sponsored regional Internet trading platforms for SMEs. The context of the evaluation would be addressed by the integrated theoretical framework of facilitators and inhibitors in figure 3.2 and table 3.2. To address the content of the evaluation, the literature on IS evaluation and the evaluation of e-commerce systems was reviewed for possible models and metrics. The Updated DeLone & McLean IS Success Model (a parsimonious model based on theoretical and empirical IS research from multiple sources which was updated to consider the effects of e-commerce) was found to be suitable. As government-sponsored regional Internet trading platforms for SMEs could involve different costs and benefits to different stakeholders at different points in the lifecycle of the project, a longitudinal approach to the process of evaluation would enable a holistic evaluation of the phenomenon. By synthesising the literature on IS evaluation with that of policy/programme and regional development evaluation, a theory-based evaluation framework for the study was derived as per figure 3.3 below.

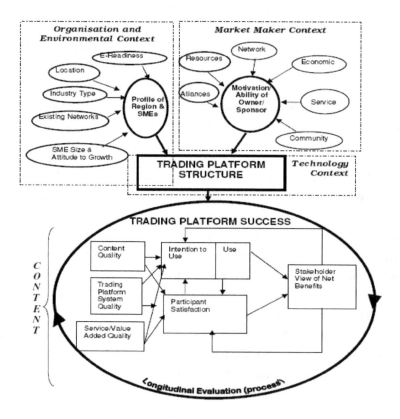

Figure 3.3   Trading Platform Success Model (Adapted from the DeLone and McLean (2003) Updated IS Success Model)

86

In the Trading Platform Success Model, ex-ante evaluation of the initiative will involve theory-based evaluation of the organisational, external and market-maker contexts that would affect and be affected by the introduction of the platform. The actual structure of the platform should be guided by the outcome of this theory-based evaluation. The trading platform structure will determine the costs and benefits of the initiative for all stakeholders concerned. The metrics to determine these costs and benefits (content of the evaluation) are presented in tables 3.3 and 3.4. The evaluation should be a longitudinal iterative process in order to cater for different costs and benefits throughout the lifecycle of the project and to allow for flexibility to improve outcomes of the initiative and modify processes where necessary.

Table 3.3 Stakeholder Costs

	Owners	Sellers	Buyers	Intermediaries
Direct Costs	Hardware/Software/ Network set-up & maintenance costs User Training & advice costs Marketing & Administration Overheads Provision of value added/ trust/ security services Maintaining parallel systems	Participation fee Transaction fee Flyer fee Hardware/software/ network & maintenance costs Administration costs Integration costs (business processes) Training costs	Hardware/software/ network & maintenance costs Administration costs Integration costs (business processes) Training costs	Advertising Hardware/ software/ network costs Training costs
Indirect Costs	Opportunity cost	Time	Time	Time

The list of possible stakeholder costs in table 3.3 were derived from the literature on e-marketplaces, portals and virtual trading communities, SME participation in e-marketplaces and Internet trading platforms, IS and e-commerce evaluation and from dealings with the research industry partner.

The list of success metrics in table 3.4 were derived by extending the success metrics in the Updated DeLone & McLean IS Success Model to consider benefits to all stakeholders and the region.

Table 3.4 Success Metrics

Content Quality	REM System Quality	Service/Value Added Quality
Quality of content Accuracy & currency of content Security, Privacy, Authenticity Comprehensiveness Timeliness Relevance Completeness *Quality of content presentation* Effective/meaningful organisation of content Navigation techniques Logical structure of content Personalisation	Reliability of software/network Accuracy of system Flexibility/Adaptability Ease of Use Online response time & page loading speed System architecture Visual Appearance Convenience of accessibility Market reach Integration with participants' systems	Trust Neutrality of market-maker Site intelligence (CRM) Feedback mechanisms Relevant search facilities Calculators Tracking capabilities Helpdesk/Set-up help/Advice Account maintenance Training (in conversion to e-business & system use) FAQ's

Use	REM Participant Satisfaction	
Informational Number of Hits/Visits *Transactional* Number of Transactions *Community* Presence of & participation in networks	*Overall satisfaction* Satisfaction with REM Offerings (Repeat visits, repeat transactions, use of networks and use of feedback mechanisms) Satisfaction with governance structure	

	Stakeholder Net Benefits	
Industry/Organisational/ Individual Impact	*Transactional Benefits* Lower transaction, staff, communication, search, marketing/advertising, inventory-holding costs Cheaper prices Lower inventory holdings *Productivity gains* Time savings Process efficiencies Wider market reach	*Strategic Benefits* Gains from Network Externalities & Collaboration Image/Legitimacy Improved market share Improved communications with customers (CRM), suppliers & employees Improved decision making process
Regional Impact	*Economic Benefits* Attractive location for business Attractive to skilled labour Efficient show-casing of regional offerings Reduced communication costs Increased productivity	*Community/Strategic Benefits* Collaboration/Partnerships Cooperation Increased level of online participation Become a knowledge region Narrow/Close digital divide Relationships with other markets

The integrated theoretical framework and the Trading Platform Success Model (together with its tables of costs and success metrics) were then empirically tested in a structured case study of the three platforms. The next chapter describes in detail the research approach used in this study.

CHAPTER 4

METHODOLOGY

4.1   INTRODUCTION

The selection of a research approach and the methodologies employed to undertake the research are influenced by the phenomenon being investigated (Leonard-Barton, 1990), the place of the research in the context of theory development (Galliers, 1992) and the various institutional contexts within which the researcher is trained and works (Orlikowski & Baroudi, 1991). The background to the wider context of the phenomenon investigated in this research (the purported promises of the e-commerce 'revolution', government intervention to bridge a perceived digital divide) has been discussed in previous chapters, as has been the conceptual framework for the study and the place of this research in relation to theory development. Within the conceptual framework of the study, the internal (stakeholder), technology and environmental contexts to be examined were identified.

In this chapter the effect of the institutional contexts of the research (in terms of the effect of funding on the research objective and approach) will be examined. The underlying philosophy of the research approach is then presented and this leads to a discussion of a suitable research methodology that will be aligned with the research problem, objective, philosophical stance, theoretical perspectives and conditions of funding. A suitable research method is identified and a research model is presented. The local context of the research is then described and the chapter culminates in a discussion of a suitable research design that covers data collection and analysis and addresses issues of reliability, validity, generalisability, triangulation, relevance, rigour and the role of the researcher in the study.

According to Orlikowski and Baroudi (1991), among the institutional contexts that could influence the choice of research approach and methodology are the research-funding policies of agencies. While funded research can offer advantages like raising the profile of the University and allowing easier access to empirical data, there could be a number of pitfalls or issues associated with funded qualitative research. Cheek (2000) categorises the issues into three broad groups: those pertaining to ethics, those that deal with the question of who controls the research and issues relating to the effect on the relationships among the various players in the research project. This research was jointly funded by the Australian Research Council (ARC) and the research industry partner under the title of 'Evaluating the Benefits of Regional e-Marketplaces for SMEs'. The aims of the research were as follows:

- To determine the benefits associated with introduction of a regional e-marketplace for SMEs and the regional government sponsor.

- To examine the issues in relation to the creation and management of e-marketplaces by regional governments, with a focus on the stimulation of business development.

- To determine the relevance of existing benefits evaluation frameworks for e-marketplaces.

The application for ARC funding detailed the approach and methodology of the study as an interpretive multi-case study approach with information to be gathered by extensive face-to-face interviews with companies participating in the e-marketplace. Interviews were also to be conducted with key employees of the regional government involved in the development and management of the e-marketplace. These were to be supplemented with telephone interviews, e-mail communication, access to company documentation and attending company meetings. Information was also to be gathered from strategic plans, job descriptions, and company reports. While the ARC was to provide the stipend for the research scholarship, the industry partner would contribute AU$8000 a year towards research expenses. The research was to span a three year period and comprise stages as follows:

Stage 1 - An investigation of the benefits associated with e-marketplace adoption and participation for SMEs. It would involve a literature review and preliminary discussions with early e-marketplace adopters. The findings would provide a basis for the further development of the conceptual framework for the study.

Stage 2 - This stage would involve the detailed interviewing across the e-marketplace sponsors, the regional/local government, and SMEs in the region to determine reasons for adoption or non adoption and the benefits associated with participation in the e-marketplace. It would involve preliminary and intermediate presentations and reports of the findings to the stakeholders.

Stage 3 - The thorough analysis of the data gathered and the interview transcripts would form the main tasks of the third stage.

Stage 4 - The evaluation of the findings would provide basis for the assessment of the impact of e-marketplace participation on the SMEs and government stakeholders. In addition, critical success factors, principles of best practice and barriers to adoption in the area would be presented.

It was on this basis that the researcher was offered the scholarship approved under the ARC funding and upon accepting the offer in early 2003 was advised that the project was in trouble and the 'rug could be pulled out from under the funding at any time'. In March 2003, the researcher was asked to make a presentation to the board of the non-profit organisation (henceforth known as NFPO) that was formed to own TwinTowns.com (the portal owned by the research industry partner). The NFPO comprised representatives from local governments 1 and 2, the business associations of Towns 1 and 2 and ECU. A presentation was made based on the original role as outlined in the ARC application. The researcher was verbally informed by the NFPO Board that in addition to the role detailed in the ARC application, the researcher was also expected to be a qualified reviewer of the e-marketplace's service in relation to its objectives- i.e. a) how well the web site worked both internally and externally, in terms of content, take up rate, design, features for improvement, etc. and b) how well the existing administration issues were handled (subscriber management, general project management, marketing, financial management, sales team etc.). This meant that in addition to the interpretive multiple case studies approved under the ARC funding, action research was also required. The additional role expected of the researcher was not disputed by ECU and the researcher for a number of reasons. These were:

- ECU had an ongoing relationship with the local governments of the two towns and other research projects were either being funded by them or were in the pipeline

- The prevailing climate of research funding constraints facing the tertiary sector in Australia meant that every 'external' funding opportunity had to be taken advantage of

- There was a real problem to be investigated as similar tax-payer-funded projects were in existence (without much empirical evidence about their performance and whether they were fulfilling the purposes for which they were intended) and it was an opportunity to contribute to a better understanding of the phenomenon for both academia and practice alike.

Although the research approach and methodology were dictated by the terms of the funding arrangements, an assessment still had to be conducted by the researcher as to their suitability to the phenomenon to be investigated. The sections to follow will deal with that assessment.

4.2   PHILOSOPHICAL PERSPECTIVES OF THE RESEARCH APPROACH

In a study of the research perspectives employed in the IS discipline between 1983 and 1988, Orlikowski and Baroudi (1991) classified the underlying research epistemologies of 155 articles from the four leading IS journals at the time according to positivist, interpretivist and critical studies. They found that the predominant philosophy was positivism which accounted for 98.6 percent of the studies while interpretive studies comprised only 3.2 percent and critical studies were not represented at all. In calling for IS researchers to be open to the possibilities of paradigms other than positivism, Orlikowski and Baroudi demonstrated that interpretive and critical perspectives could also offer valuable insights into phenomena in IS research.

Although progress has been made in the IS research community in terms of research diversity and methodological pluralism since then, Chen and Hirschheim (2004) found that a decade later the predominant paradigm was still positivism. They also found that in particular US journals (as opposed to European) tended to be more positivist, quantitative, cross-sectional and survey oriented. At the same time, however, their study showed that in terms of research design, although surveys still remained the most widely used method, case studies and qualitative methods were gaining recognition. The research approach adopted in this study will be appraised in terms of positivism, interpretivism and critical realism.

4.2.1 *Positivism and Interpretivism*

The debate on positivist versus interpretivist approaches in the field of IS research has traditionally been argued on the basis of the difference in their epistemological, ontological and methodological stances. Chen and Hirschheim's (2004) discussion of these differences to compare the two paradigms and categorise IS research articles is presented in table 4.1:

Table 4.1 The Epistemological, Ontological and Methodological Differences between Positivism and Interpretivism (Source: Chen & Hirschheim, 2004, p. 201)

Paradigm	Epistemology	Ontology	Methodology
Positivist	Reality exists objectively and independently from human experiences	Hypothetic-deductive testability of theories. Scientific knowledge should allow verification or falsification and seek generalisable results. Causal relationships are usually presented and a tight coupling among explanation, prediction and control is expected	Value-free position and employs objective measurement to collect research evidence. Surveys and case studies.
	Criteria for categorising positivist articles: indications of hypotheses, propositions, model formation, quantifiable measures of variables and the inferences drawn from samples to populations		
Interpretivist	Emphasises the subjective meaning of the reality constructed and reconstructed through a human and social interaction process	Scientific knowledge should be obtained through the understanding of human and social interaction by which the subjective meaning of the reality is constructed	Researchers need to engage in the social setting investigated and learn how the interaction takes place from participants' perspectives. Field studies and case studies
	Criteria for categorising interpretive articles: Should not involve any positivist indicators as described above (no deterministic perspectives imposed by researchers). Participants' perspectives are taken as the primary sources of understanding and investigating the phenomena. The phenomena are examined with respect to cultural or contextual circumstances.		

The previous chapter has demonstrated the need for a holistic approach to the evaluation of the benefits for all stakeholders from government-sponsored regional Internet trading platforms for SMEs. Such an approach would need to include both the interpretive evaluation of the costs and benefits as well as their quantification where ever possible, in order to provide as rich a picture as possible of the phenomenon not only from an academic perspective but also from the perspective of relevance to practice. The phenomenon to be evaluated is not merely an IS phenomenon but one that encompasses the evaluation of regional social and economic development policy as well. A parallel that can be drawn in terms of evaluating public policy is the existing approach favoured by regulatory policy-makers in the United Kingdom for the cost-benefit analysis of social legislation, which is "to quantify only what is genuinely quantifiable by reliable data and simply 'describe' other effects. The ultimate decision is then based not on a precise arithmetical comparison of costs and benefit, but rather on an impressionable balancing of the information on impact, both quantified and unquantified" (Ogus, 1994, p. 161).

The use of the Trading Platform Success Model and its accompanying tables of Costs and Success Metrics (section 3.4 of the previous chapter) in this research, if assessed against Chen and Hirschheim's (2004) criteria (table 4.1 above) may be viewed as a positivist approach. However, the overarching CCP (content-context-process) approach in this study is interpretivist. Thus while this research philosophy is predominantly interpretivist, the approach incorporates elements of positivism in an attempt to 'measure' costs and benefits that are quantifiable, while seeking to uncover, describe and understand those that are not. The research is also an attempt to demonstrate the methods, constructs and metrics which could be used to perform a holistic theory-based evaluation of government-sponsored regional Internet trading platforms for SMEs during the entire life-cycle of the initiative.

Although most authors argue for a purist or a singular approach and maintain that positivist and interpretivist approaches are opposed and irreconcilable, there are those who believe that in some circumstances (especially in organisational and policy research), the two approaches can be mutually supportive in a single study (Gable, 1994; Lee, 1991). Weber (2004) believes that both approaches have substantial value and argues that many, if not all, of the alleged metatheoretical differences between positivism and interpretivism are spurious. Landry and Banville (1992) are of the opinion that a disciplined methodological pluralism for the IS field is tenable (they define methodological pluralism as a position that favours a diversity of methods, theories and even philosophies in scientific enquiry). They provide a framework to dispel the notion that such an approach would imply anarchism. Mingers and Brocklesby (1997, p. 491) also present frameworks for multi-methodology, which they define as the "use of more than one methodology, or part thereof, possibly from different paradigms, within a single intervention". Lin (1998) demonstrates how the bridging of positivist and interpretivist approaches in an interdisciplinary area like public policy can lead to richer and more meaningful research. Taket and White (1998) describe the use of a 'pragmatic pluralism' approach to multi-methodology in public community health development programmes to demonstrate the advantages of such an approach in public policy practice.

While on a broader level, the original quantitative versus qualitative debate appears to have waned (indeed the mixed quantitative-qualitative approach in single studies appears to have been embraced by the Australian IS community, as evidenced by the criteria used to judge the best IS theses in

Australia in the past few years), the use of mixed interpretivist-positivist approaches in single studies (or an acknowledgement of use) is still difficult to find in the IS discipline. This lack appears to be the result of the continuing debate on paradigmatic pluralism as opposed to pluralism in methods within a given paradigm. Nevertheless, the call has been issued for an end to the paradigm wars in a number of disciplines, among which are IS (Goles & Hirschheim, 2000; Lee, 1991; Mingers, 2001; Weber, 2004), organisational studies (Silverman, 1998), policy research (Lin, 1998), theory building (Gioia & Pitre, 1990) and consumer research (Hunt, 1991).

4.2.2   Critical Research and Critical Realism

"Critical studies aim to critique the status quo, through the exposure of what are believed to be deep-seated, structural contradictions within social systems, and thereby to transform these alienating and restrictive social conditions" (Orlikowski & Baroudi, 1991). Critical studies are contextual and grounded in social and historical practices and therefore tend to be longitudinal as they take a processual view of a phenomenon. Generalisation in critical research "seeks to illuminate the forces at work in society as a totality…[an] extension from the micro context to the totality that shapes it" (Burawoy, 1985, p. 18 cited in Orlikowski & Baroudi, 1991). Epistemologically critical research differs from interpretivism in the belief that interpretation of the social world is not sufficient as actors (stakeholders) may not be able to interpret the wider circumstances that dominate or constrain them. Orlikowski and Baroudi's (1991) criticism of a purely interpretive approach is summarised as such:

> First, the interpretive perspective does not examine the conditions, often external, which give rise to certain meanings and experiences. Second, research in this perspective omits to explain the unintended consequences of action, which by definition cannot be explained by reference to the intentions of the humans concerned…Third, the interpretive perspective does not address structural conflicts within society and organizations and ignores contradictions which may be endemic to social systems…Finally, the interpretive perspective neglects to explain historical change; that is, how a particular social order came to be what it is, and how it is likely to vary over time. (p. 18)

Studies in IS adopting a critical approach include longitudinal historical and ethnographic studies, action research (Orlikowski & Baroudi, 1991) and case studies (Avgerou, 2002, cited in McGrath, 2005).

Critical realism assumes a realist ontology which posits "the existence of elements of the social world which exist despite or regardless of our current state of knowledge" (Mutch, 1999). While realism is traditionally placed alongside positivism, critical realism recognises the subjective and social nature of knowledge acquisition (Dobson, 2001a). In critical realism, one cannot break social investigation into the study of society, group and individual. It argues for a relational perspective by examining both structures and agencies (or micro and macro contexts) of a social situation and, specifically, brings time dependency into account (Dobson, 2001b). Critical realism seeks to go beyond the description of phenomena to understand and explain the 'why' behind them by hypothesising the structures and mechanisms that shape these phenomena (Mingers, 2002). Thus using critical realism would enable a consideration of the structural constraints of the wider contexts within which individual actors operate and which they may not be able to interpret at their individual levels. Mutch (1999) and Dobson (2001b) draw on the work of Archer (1995) to call for research in IS to consider a tri-partite look at the nature of agency, the inter-relationship between structure and agency and the incorporation of the temporal dimension.

Including critical research and critical realism in the philosophical underpinnings of this research is an attempt to overcome the weaknesses of a predominantly interpretive approach. This is done by examining the initiative and the way it is developed, implemented and governed in the context of the wider social, political and economic structures within which it is undertaken. From an organisational perspective, a critical approach to the evaluation of the initiative would seek to determine the effect of the initiative on the local government sponsor (in the case of the research industry partner) in the internal and external contexts.

4.3   THE SELECTION OF A SUITABLE METHODOLOGY

The research approach in this study has been determined as a predominantly interpretivist approach incorporating elements of positivism, critical research and critical realism. Selection of a method (or methods) to conduct the research was guided by the literature on research methods, their suitability to the research objectives and underlying philosophies of the research approach as well as the conditions of funding.

The funding conditions of this research determined the need for both case study and action research which, according to Cavaye (1996), possess some common characteristics. These are:

- Use of the case method

- Aimed at an understanding of the context

- Do not (though may) define a priori constructs

- Attempt to contribute to knowledge

- Relate findings to generalisable theory

- Use interpretation from a researcher's point of view

The general points that differentiate the two research strategies are that action research seeks to interfere in the phenomenon and the research topic is not determined by the researcher. The suitability of these two research strategies to the research problem and underlying philosophies are examined in subsequent sections.

4.3.1 Action Research

The action research method had its roots in participatory programme development after the Second World War. It was a method pioneered by Lewin (1946, cited in Susman & Evered, 1978, p. 586) that combined theory generation with changing the social system through the researcher acting on or in the social system. It is defined as a method that "aims to contribute both to the practical concerns of people in an immediate problematic situation and to the goals of social science by joint collaboration within a mutually acceptable ethical framework" (Rapoport, 1970, p. 499). In its simplest form, action research comprises a two-stage process. The first stage is a collaborative diagnosis of the social problem by the researcher and the subjects of the research, during which hypotheses are developed. The second stage is therapeutic, in which the hypotheses are tested by consciously directed change experiments in a real social setting (Blum, 1955). In the late 1970s and early 1980s, action research was linked to systems theory through the work of Susman and Evered (1978) who described the ideal action research method as an iterative five phase model that occurs after the research environment is determined. The five phases are diagnosis, action planning, action taking, evaluating and specifying learning (identifying general findings). It was Checkland's (1981) use of action research in systems development that legitimised its use as a method in IS research.

Action research may be considered a subset of case study research (Galliers, 1992) and is widely cited as a research method suitable for the study of technology in its human context as it is empirical yet interpretive, experimental yet multivariate and observational yet interventionist (Baskerville & Wood-Harper, 1996). In arguing for the wider use of the action research method in IS research, Baskerville and Wood-Harper (1998, p. 96) provide a taxonomy of action research forms according to the characteristics of process, structure, involvement of the researcher (collaborative, facilitative or expert), and primary goals. They identify nine forms of action research used from the IS literature. These are: canonical action research, IS prototyping, soft systems, action science, participant observation, action learning, multiview, ETHICS, clinical field work and process consultation.

The action research method selected for this study was participant observation (the reasons for selecting this method will become clearer when the local context of the research is discussed in greater detail in later sections of this chapter). According to Baskerville & Wood-Harper (1998, p. 101) participatory observation can be a research method in itself or a data collection technique in other types of research designs like case studies. Participant observation in action research requires the researcher to become an insider to gain access to the interior or subjective aspects of the organisation in order to intervene to precipitate change. It is a method with a fluid structure where activities are loosely defined, may be performed simultaneously and are not specific in terms of when they are to be undertaken. It is characterised by the reflective process model which seeks to discover the differences between espoused theory and theory-in-use in a given organisational/community situation. Generally, the objective in participatory observation within action research is the 'scientific knowledge' gained from the study and the researcher's role is normally one of expert (where the researcher's decisions will determine what interventions will be created). In this research however, the role of the researcher was as a facilitator to help subjects with expert advice, technical knowledge or an independent viewpoint but where the subjects were responsible for determining the interventions to be created (Baskerville & Wood-Harper, 1998).

Galliers (1992) views ethics as an important consideration in action research and cautions that researchers need to be aware that in certain circumstances they could align themselves with a particular grouping whose objectives are at odds with other groupings. Other acknowledged problems with action research include the conflict between practical problems and the research endeavour; clients' need for quick action versus the researcher's belief in the need for careful reflection and analysis (Rapoport, 1970); the problem of establishing rigour according to traditional positivist norms, and organisational problem solving that can come at the expense of transferable theoretical understandings (Susman & Evered, 1978).

Following Cavaye's (1996) classification of case study as a method in action research, Galliers' (1992) view of action research as a subset of case study and Yin's (2003) consideration of non-interventionist participant observation as a case study data collection technique (the researcher had doubts from the start about the extent to which any suggested interventions would be enacted), the participant observation in this study was considered part of the in-depth longitudinal case study of the initiative that was being undertaken by the research industry partner.

4.3.2 Case Study Research

Case study research is appropriate in situations where the research question involves a 'how', 'why', or exploratory 'what' question and the investigator has no control over actual behavioural events. A case study is an empirical inquiry that involves data collection from multiple sources to investigate a contemporary (as opposed to historical) phenomenon in a real life setting where the boundaries between phenomenon and context are blurred (Yin, 2003). It is particularly suitable for areas where research and theory are at their early formative stages (Benbasat, Goldstein & Mead, 1987). The research presented in this paper fits all the above criteria.

Cavaye's (1996) overview of case study research in IS showed that it was highly versatile and can be used in the positivist and interpretivist traditions, for testing or building theory, with a single or multiple design and using qualitative or mixed methods. Case studies can be used to investigate a complex phenomenon at a point in time or they may be longitudinal. Lee (1991) and Gable (1994) demonstrated how positivist and interpretivist epistemologies can be combined in single case studies. Lin (1998) described comparative case study as a way of reconciling the ends of positivist and interpretivist approaches in public policy research. Leonard-Barton (1990) combined a single longitudinal case study with replicated multiple cases to demonstrate mixed-methods within case research. Case studies have a distinctive place in evaluation studies where they have been used to describe, explore and explain the causal links in real-life interventions that are too complex for survey or experimental strategies (Yin, 2003, p. 15).

The common criticisms of the case study approach are the lack of generalisability and rigour (especially if they are interpretive and single cases) and the excessive amounts of data to be collected (Yin, 2003). The lack of generalisability has been defended by Stake (2000, p. 437) who gives the example of intrinsic case study where the researcher wants a better understanding of the particular case and instrumental case study to provide insight into an issue to redraw a generalisation. Multiple case studies can be used to generalise to theory (Yin, 2003) and structured case protocols and principles can be used to guide both positivist (Benbasat et al., 1987; Eisenhardt, 1989; Yin, 2003) and interpretivist (Carroll & Swatman, 2000; Klein & Myers, 1999; Walsham, 1995) case research to address rigour.

Traditionally the use of theory in case studies has been associated with the positivist or deductive approach where specific theoretical propositions are constructed based on a theoretical model. Data collection consists of gathering information on the individual variables indicated by the model and analysis would entail testing the conditions and relationships from the data against that of the theoretical model. Thus the initial theoretical model is tested against the empirical data and may be modified according to the findings. This approach is evidenced in the work of Yin (2003), Lee (1989) and Benbasat et al. (1987). Eisenhardt (1989; 1991) used an inductive approach to theory building using case studies by starting with a grounded theory approach that had no a priori hypotheses. In Eisenhardt's approach, opportunistic data collection is used to generate concepts, a conceptual framework, propositions or mid-range theory. However, her use of structured methods, her view that mid-range theory should be formally tested using positivist approaches and the acknowledgement of her epistemological stance as positivism, has resulted in her approach to theory-building from multiple case studies being branded as positivist.

The researcher has acknowledged that the Trading Platform Success Model (figure 3.3) and its accompanying tables of Stakeholder Costs (table 3.3) and Success Metrics (table 3.4) have positivist nuances, given the need to discover actual costs and benefits associated with the sort of intervention investigated in this research. However, theoretical constructs were used from existing theories in the field (to create the initial conceptual theoretical framework for the research i.e. figure 3.2 and table 3.2) as a guide to design and data collection. An openness was maintained to the empirical data as was a willingness to modify initial assumptions and theories by an iterative process of data collection, analysis and comparison to the theoretical frameworks and extant literature. This approach to the use of theory in case study is in keeping with the interpretive approach (Walsham, 1995). It is an attempt to use and expand the constructs from the cumulative richness of theory that has already been built up in the IS field to understand a complex under-researched area. The research model used to implement this approach is based on structured-case methodology discussed in the next section.

4.3.3 Structured-Case Study Methodology

Carroll and Swatman (2000) developed the structured-case methodological framework for theory building. It extended existing research frameworks for building theory from case study (Eisenhardt, 1989; Yin, 2003) by specifically addressing theory-building within the interpretive paradigm.

Structured-case uses a formal process method comprising a conceptual framework, a pre-defined research cycle and a literature-based scrutiny of the findings. The case may be a person, group of people, organisation, and process or information system. The conceptual framework in structured-case is the researcher's representation of the conceptual structure to be used in the research process. It is formed by broad research themes; existing knowledge from the literature in terms of current knowledge and theories in the area of interest including the gaps in the literature; researcher's insights gained from experience, experts and practitioners (from informal and unpublished sources); and from the researcher's theoretical foundations (world view comprising beliefs, assumptions and expectations). The conceptual framework represents the researcher's current understanding of the research themes and the areas of inquiry to be explored and depicts the key concepts and relationships to be examined. The conceptual framework goes through a series of refinements through research cycles during which it is critically examined against understanding obtained from the data and from the extant literature.

Each research cycle comprises four stages (partially adapted from the problem-solving cycle of action research (Susman & Evered, 1978)) as follows:

- Plan: selecting a research design or case; determining methods for data collection, processing, analysis and for reporting outcomes. The research design will be 'open' or responsive to any events from the field.

- Collect data

- Analyse data: although data collection and analysis have been modelled as separate stages, Carroll and Swatman (2000) acknowledge that these two activities may overlap so that analysis of data collected will allow adjustments in the data collected to respond to opportunities, unexpected outcomes and emergent themes. While there is some area of overlap, data analysis will continue after data collection ceases. The initial research themes according to which the data is coded could change or new themes could emerge from the coding process that would need further analysis and backtracking over previously examined artefacts.

- Reflect: in each cycle the researcher needs to reflect introspectively not only on the outcomes of the analysis and the emergent themes and extant literature, but also on the research process and the conceptual framework. When new themes emerge, it may be necessary to return to transcripts and artefacts previously examined in a continuing process of constructing meaning and understanding. The researcher then needs to look beyond the data to build theory (across-case analysis) and revise the conceptual framework to incorporate the additional knowledge built.

Theory building in structured-case is aimed at the middle-range i.e. to discover and discuss relationships between abstract concepts by creating a web of meaning out of the research themes (Carroll & Swatman, 2000, p. 239). Multiple iterations of research cycles allow a spiral towards understanding and each conceptual framework represents the latest version of the theory developed. Structured-case thus builds theory from multiple cases which are used to sequentially enrich and revise the conceptual framework. The entire process of theory building using structured-case is represented in figure 4.1.

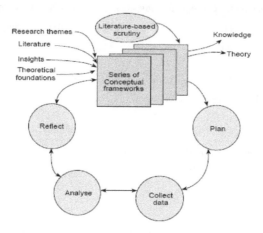

Figure 4.1 The Structured-Case Research Method (Source: Carroll & Swatman, 2000, p. 241)

4.3.4 A Research Model

This research involved assessing the success and evaluating the benefits (for all stakeholders) of government-sponsored regional Internet trading platforms for SMEs by using an overarching content-context-process (CCP) interpretive approach (Pettigrew, 1987, 1990; Symons, 1991). Within the CCP approach, an in-depth longitudinal case study was done of the initiative undertaken by the research industry partner. It involved participant observation as the action research part of the study. As the project undertaken by the research industry partner was under threat of termination from the moment the research commenced, a flexible research design had to be created in order to achieve relevance. This involved using mini cases of similar initiatives at two other sites for theoretical replication thus creating a multiple-case study design. Given the various stakeholders in these initiatives (SME participants, local governments and the region), an embedded design was incorporated to study the research problem at these different levels of analysis.

The research model for this study is presented in figure 4.2. The research design will be discussed in greater depth in later sections in this chapter.

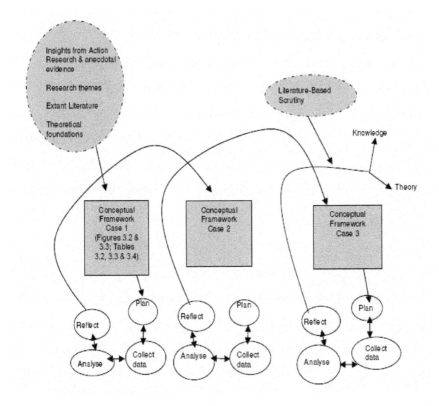

Figure 4.2 Research Model: Multiple-case study (1 in-depth longitudinal case study and 2 mini cases) with Embedded Design using Structured-Case Methodology (Adapted from Carroll & Swatman, 2000, p. 240)

The research model developed for this study is thus in alignment with the research problem, objective, philosophical stance, theoretical perspectives, conditions of funding and research methods.

4.4   LOCAL CONTEXT OF THE RESEARCH

Before a discussion can proceed on the research design used in this study, it is important to consider the local context of the research in greater detail. Government-supported regional Internet trading platforms for SMEs were only one response to bridging the digital divide. The collaborative projects that were undertaken to develop and implement such platforms around Australia were varied in terms of ownership, models, focus and development processes.

4.4.1 Government-Supported Regional E-Marketplaces and Internet Trading Platforms for SMEs in Western Australia

In Western Australia (WA), collaboratively-developed government-supported e-marketplaces and trading platforms for SMEs tend to be part of wider community models. There are a number of reasons for this, the main ones being:

- The need to try and get as much 'mileage' as possible out of federal government funds as it is difficult to find local sponsors for such projects.

- According to the terms of funding, the community portal projects needed to demonstrate the ability to be self sustainable and some of their owners/sponsors viewed taking a business focus as one way to generate income.

- It was a way to leverage local community networks and promote a 'buy local online' campaign in response to the perceived new threats of online competition from outside the region as the Internet threatened to break down physical distance barriers.

There were also a number of 'hidden agendas' behind some of these endeavours in WA which were uncovered during the research and will be discussed in subsequent chapters. The majority of these portals were conceived during the height of the dot.com boom when the 'build it and they will come' philosophy dominated many private sector e-commerce trading platform endeavours. At the time the research commenced, the government-supported portals in WA were struggling in terms of the e-commerce side, although some 'appeared' to be performing better than others.

While the general model of portals in WA is a combined community/business portal, there are also variances in the ownership structures, development and governance processes and even the profile of the regions, which could account for the different impacts of the portals in encouraging e-commerce adoption by local SMEs. There was thus a need to examine these variances to determine if they could account for the differing outcomes of the portals. In addition to the portal owned by the research industry partner (the portal will henceforth be known as TwinTowns.com, a pseudonym), two other WA community/business portals (henceforth referred to as RegWA.net and CountryWa.com, also pseudonyms) were selected for this study. The selection of RegWa.net and CountryWa.com as cases for the study was made on the basis of theoretical replication but they were also convenience samples. Both were in regional WA; ECU was involved in the development of CountryWA.com while in the case of RegWa.net, the local chamber of commerce (which was the original driving force behind the portal) was chaired by the original project manager of TwinTowns.com. In the following section a comparative overview is provided of selected features of the three cases. This will be followed by further pertinent details of TwinTowns.com, the subject of the in-depth longitudinal case study.

4.4.2 Overview of the Three Portals in This Study

In the CCP approach to evaluation, context refers not only to the internal contexts of the projects evaluated (participants, stakeholders and the technology or intervention) but the external or environmental context as well. This would include the profile of the region in terms of culture, economic and political structures as well as its physical location.

Table 4.2 below summarises a comparison of selected constructs of the internal and external contexts of the three portals studied.

Table 4.2 Selected Characteristics of the three portals in this Study.

	TwinTowns.com	RegWa.net	CountryWA.com
Year Initiative First Conceived & by Whom	1999. Mooted by the Business Enterprise Centre of one of the towns, supported by some people in the two local governments (LG1 and LG2).	1999. Committee of a few people in the chamber of commerce of the largest town in the region, resident web site developers and Internet Service Providers, a couple of the larger businesses in the region.	1999. Consortium of representatives from IBM, the Office of Information and Communication of the State Government, the regional development commission, the Business Enterprise Centre of the largest local town in the region, ECU and two major IT companies.
Ownership Structure	Not for Profit Organisation (NFPO) comprising Local Governments of 2 neighbouring towns, their Business Associations and ECU	The Camber of Commerce (CoC) of the largest town. In June 2003, purchased by the Regional Development Commission. Not-for-profit organisation formed to own it.	In 2001, the portal became a cooperative under the West Australian Cooperatives Board with locals owning shares, overseen by a Board of community representatives.
Details of the area served by the Community Portal	Two neighbouring towns in metropolitan Western Australia covering 900 km^2, having about 220,000 residents and 7000 small businesses. Major industries: manufacturing, agriculture, retail trade, services, tourism.	A regional area of Western Australia covering 24,000 km^2, having a population of 132,000 and 10,500 small businesses. Major industries: manufacturing, mining, agriculture, retail trade, services, tourism.	A regional area of Western Australia covering 44,000 km^2, having a population of 53,000 and approximately 4800 small businesses. Major industries: agriculture & livestock farming, viticulture, horticulture, timber plantations, retail, manufacturing, wholesaling, construction, services, tourism.
Funding 1999/2000	AU$ 20,000 (State government) AU$ 90,660 (Federal government - [RAP])	AU$6,000 (regional development corp.) AU$20,000 (State government)	AU$75,000 (ITOL)
2001/2002	AU$ 108,000 (Local governments of the two towns & ECU) AU$ 92,000 (State government-for training SMEs)	AU$90,000 (ITOL) AU$126,000 (State government)	AU$100,000 (Federal Government under the Networking the Nation Programme)

	TwinTowns.com	RegWa.net	CountryWA.com
2003/2004	AU$50,000 (Local governments of the towns). *Request for further federal & state government funding declined in 2001/2002.	AU$2,200,000 (State government, only a portion of this will be directly for the portal; other use will be for training SMEs etc.)	AU$68,500 (ITOL - part of AU$174,000 awarded to a joint consortia to develop an intelligent e-business search system for SMEs in the region)
TOTAL	AU$360,660	AU$2,442,000	AU$243,500 (An ITOL application for AU$50,000 for SME e-business training and use of the portal is pending. If approved, a regional consortium will inject AU$71,000 of its own)
Technical development	Outsourced for AU$70,000	The portal developer was a local IT company who hosted RegWa.net without any charge. Exact amount paid for the initial development of the portal not available. Development of Regional e-marketplace (REM) about AU$30,000. AU$200,000 paid for upgrade in 2004.	Total estimated amount spent on technical development to date AU$100,000
Portal and E-Commerce Features	• Internet based community portal catering for B2B, B2C, B2G (business to government) and C2C (consumer to consumer) activity • REM with business directory. Request-for-quote (RFQ) mechanism. Quotes can only be received by registered users. Notification of quote by e-mail, fax or SMS but user has to log onto system to retrieve quote and reply. • Community groups can have information listed for free. • Businesses listed for free but pay AU$199 p.a. for RFQ-enabled REM link and an additional AU$99 for a flyer page. Live links to user's websites if registered & paying. • Corporate	• Internet based community portal catering for B2B, B2C, B2G and C2C activity • REM with business directory. RFQ mechanism. Quotes can only be received by registered users. Notification and RFQ sent by e-mail, fax or SMS. User does not have to log onto the system to retrieve the quote. • Community groups can have information listed for free. • Businesses listed for free but members pay AU$22 p.a. for an e-mail link AU$66 p.a. for e-mail/web link AU$149 p.a. for preferential listing (shuffled up the page in a search) AU$199 p.a. for e-mail, web and 5 page website template (additional AU$11 p.a. to be listed in more than one business category). AU$250 p.a. for e-commerce solution (shopping cart) • Corporate sponsorship of site is available.	• Internet based community portal catering for B2B, B2C, B2G and C2C activity • Business Listings (Members and non members) and Members Listing (businesses and other organisations like schools etc.). No RFQs • Community groups can have information listed for free. • Businesses listed (via free link to the online directory of the Chamber of Commerce of the largest town in the region) but participants pay: (with discounts for shareholders) AU$77 p.a. for a premium listing (with live e-mail & web link, listing under both business and member listings, listing under up to 3 product/service categories and one town or topic category. AU$198 p.a. for premium listing and 1 fully editable web page (AU$220 p.a. to include shopping cart /Order Form) AU$605 p.a. for premium listing and 5 fully editable web

	TwinTowns.com	RegWa.net	CountryWA.com
	sponsorship of site is available.	• Monthly e-newsletter with community & business information, competitions etc.	pages (AU$880 p.a. to include shopping cart/Order Form). AU$990 p.a. for premium listing and 10 fully editable web pages (AU$1650 p.a. to include shopping cart /Order Form). • Corporate sponsorship of site is available. • Regular e-newsletter.
Date portal/ E-Commerce Features launched	December 2002 portal & REM (with business directory) launched simultaneously (soft launch due to prevailing technical issues). December 2003 development on the social community and B2C part of the portal abandoned to concentrate on B2G, B2B.	Regional portal & Business directory launched March 2000. REM page launched November 2002 (business listings with the ability to send RFQs to participants who have the facility). Technical Upgrade & shopping cart facility in November 2004. REM page removed. Instead, the shopping-cart link lists goods from participants with shopping cart facilities provided by the portal. RFQ forms now appear under some business categories where participants have signed up for this facility.	Regional portal launched May 2000. Shopping Mall page (collection of businesses with shopping cart facilities provided by the portal) launched in 2003. At the end of 2003, there were 4 merchants on the Mall. In 2004, the Shopping Mall page was removed.
Marketing Efforts	A few seminars prior to development; a handful of newspaper write-ups in local community newspapers, employment of a marketing manager only in late 2003 (previous marketing efforts were by the project manager)	It was (and still is) promoted to the community via television and newspaper advertising. Sales personnel were hired when it was launched. Seminars and talks given to both the business and social communities.	Promoted to the community via television (for free in exchange for a live link on the portal to the television station's daily programming page), seminars and talks. One of the board members is currently the part-time sales consultant for participation and advertising space on the portal

The selected characteristics provide some background information to the individual cases in the study. They had implications on the research design in terms of determining data collection and analysis methods.

4.4.3 Additional Details on TwinTowns.com

Town 2 was originally part of Town 1 which was carved up when the region (the second fastest growing region in Australia in terms of population and housing) became too big for one council to manage. The idea behind the creation of the TwinTowns.com portal originated in 1999 (at the height of the dot.com boom), in an attempt to emulate e-Brisbane, one of the first major community portals in Australia which was developed by Brisbane City Council (Queensland) in partnership with Dow Digital. The coordinator of the Local Government Town 2 (LG 2) Internet project developed the regional web concept – (including an implementation plan from a technical/logistical point of view) and the economic development manager of the Local Government Town 1 (LG 1) and the manager of the Business Enterprise Centre were coopted to form the TwinTowns Regional Online Steering Group (Internal Project History Document, TwinTowns.com, January 2003).

At the time the research began in early 2003, TwinTowns.com had gone through three changes in project manager and one change in representatives of the local government partners. Of the original local government members who had initially committed to the project, only the economic development manager of LG 1 remained (henceforth Local Governments of Towns 1 and 2 will be referred to as LG 1 and LG 2 respectively). He was the person responsible for obtaining the RAP funding for the project.

A timeline of a few significant events in the development of TwinTowns.com leading up to the commencement of the research is shown in table 4.3 below:

Table 4.3 Significant events in the development of TwinTowns.com February 2002 to February 2003.

Date	Events
Feb 2002	Portal designer wins contract. Original project manager becomes part time consultant. Technical development of portal begins
May 2002	Original project manager resigns. New project manager appointed. Training manager appointed to utilise training grant for SMEs (received from the State government). REM technology cannot be integrated with purchasing systems of LG1 and LG2 and is not ready for SMEs to be trained in hands-on use.
August 2002	Portal in test phase. Second project manager appointment withdrawn. Third project manager appointed (officer from within LG1). Training manager resigns. SMEs still not trained to use the REM.
Dec 2002	Portal completed (6 months overdue) with 60 users. Some participants are non-financial members (pilot group). Soft launch of REM.
Feb 2003	Intended official launch delayed as new business plan has been developed. AU$ 50,000 additional revenue sought from LG1 and LG2. Application for further Federal Government funding (ITOL) declined. Many technical issues arise with the REM technology.

It is significant to note that from project commencement there has only been 1 full time team member on the project. This person was the project manager who was expected to do everything from administration, to business development and user-testing. The project office was situated in the premises of LG 1 and all overheads (project manager's salary, rent, stationery, administration costs etc.) were paid out of project funds. The board of TwinTowns.com met once a month and apart from things like grant applications, stakeholders had no other hands-on input into the project. There was no attempt to garner voluntary hands-on participation from members of the general communities of the two towns.

It is also pertinent that the economic development manager of LG 1 had begun his professional doctoral studies at ECU in 2001 and was using the TwinTowns.com project as a case study to investigate if B2G portals could be used effectively to stimulate business in SMEs. His primary data collection (comprising interviews and focus groups with SMEs in the region) started in September 2002 and his thesis was submitted in April 2004. This had implications in so far as 'interview subject fatigue' was concerned when it came to selection of SME interview participants for the TwinTown.com case in this study.

4.5 RESEARCH DESIGN

4.5.1 Introduction

The research design is the architectural blueprint for how the research is to progress. It is here that the data collection and analysis procedures are determined and the research plan is developed. The research design should address the suitability or alignment of the data collection and analysis techniques with the research problem, objective, epistemology and research methodology. This is also where the researcher needs to address how reliability, validity, generalisability, triangulation, relevance and rigour will be addressed by the data collection and analysis.

4.5.2 Data Collection and Analysis

All artefacts collected from the research (minutes of meetings, financial and other project documents, press releases, web pages, interview transcripts) and researcher's journal and other notes were maintained in an N*Vivo project database. N*Vivo is a code-based theory-building computer programme based on a code-and-retrieve model (Weitzman, 2000, p. 809). It allows storage and coding of text-based files (text format files without any specific formatting or diagrams were found to be the most suitable for coding). It also allows other file formats (web pages, PDF documents, photos, etc.) to be stored and allows the creation of hyperlinks between passages of text in coded documents and between coded text and stored files in other formats. It has a hierarchical parent-child code structure with text coded according to nodes (constructs, themes, variables). Coded text can also be linked to short internal memos made by the researcher. N*Vivo allows search results to be saved as nodes for further coding, which is helpful when new themes emerge during the analysis of documents. The N*Vivo project pad for node functions is reproduced in figure 4.3 below:

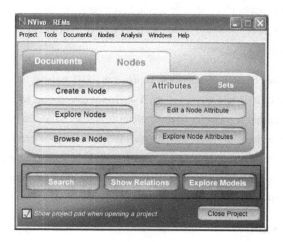

Figure 4.3 N*Vivo Project Pad for Nodes.

In keeping with the structured-case methodology, data collection and analysis were not performed sequentially. There was much back-tracking over documents/interview transcripts as new themes emerged from the analysis.

The data collection and analysis for this research occurred in two major phases. Phase 1 is depicted in figure 4.4.

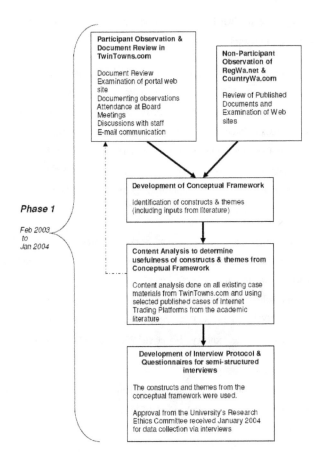

Figure 4.4 Phase 1 of Data Collection and Analysis

Phase 1 involved documenting observations from the participant-observation and reviewing documents as part of the in-depth case study of TwinTowns.com. This involved meetings, telephone conservations and e-mail communication with the project manager of TwinTowns.com and the economic development manager of LG 1. The researcher also had access to selected project documentation and attended some board meetings of the not-for-profit organisation (NFPO) which owned TwinTowns.com.

As the threat of project termination loomed over the research, the researcher identified RegWa.net and CountryWa.net as possible mini cases for theoretical replication in a later phase of the research as part of a flexible research design should TwinTowns.com close. This meant that secondary data was collected on these two portals during 2003.

Official interviews could not be undertaken without approval of ECU's Human Research Ethics Committee and approval was dependent upon provision of the research proposal with an outline of the types of questions that would be asked. The better part of 2003 was spent on the action research in TwinTowns.com and secondary data collection as the NFPO which owned the portal vacillated alternatively between closing down and continuing the project. In late 2003, a firm decision was made to continue the project and appoint a marketing manager. At this point, all the data that had been collected from the action research was used as an input into the development of the integrated theoretical framework of the study (table 3.2 in chapter 3).

In order to test the usefulness of the integrated theoretical framework, a qualitative content analysis was done by coding the existing documents in the N*Vivo database and selected published case studies on Internet trading platforms in the academic literature according to the constructs and themes of the framework. The published case studies used were the Lonxanet (Dans & Freire, 2002), Gatetrade.net (Brunn et al., 2002; Hunter & Doz, 2002), trading platforms in the virtual trading community of the Hong Kong textile industry (Ho et al., 2003), RETFC (Wilkins et al., 2003a; 2003b) and Polygon (Grewal et al., 2001).

Content analysis is a systematic examination of a particular body of material (in this instance the published case studies and TwinTowns.com documents) to identify patterns or themes. Qualitative content analysis seeks to categorise latent content (Silverman, 2001) and in this case differs from the standard literature review in the sense that the published case studies were used as data to uncover predetermined themes or constructs (the constructs from the integrated theoretical framework). The choice of published case studies for the content analysis was subject to availability in the academic literature of relevant in-depth information on Internet trading platforms. The coding was checked by another academic researcher to address researcher bias. The results of the content analysis showed that many of the constructs synthesised in the framework had been discussed in the published case studies. The factors that had not been discussed were considered contextual (for example effective external expertise for participants may not be a factor for profit-driven e-marketplaces like Gatetrade.net and Polygon but was important in the context of government-supported regional Internet trading platforms for SMEs).

The integrated theoretical framework together with the trading platform success model and cost/success metrics (figures 3.2 and 3.3 and tables 3.2, 3.3 and 3.4) were used to design a case protocol for the next phase of data gathering and analysis. Approval to proceed with collection of data by interviews was received in January 2004 from the HREC of ECU on the basis of the information letters to participants, interview questionnaires and informed consent forms as per Appendices 2 to 5. (These were amended with HREC approval as circumstances of the research changed). Phase 2 involved data collection and analysis as per figure 4.5.

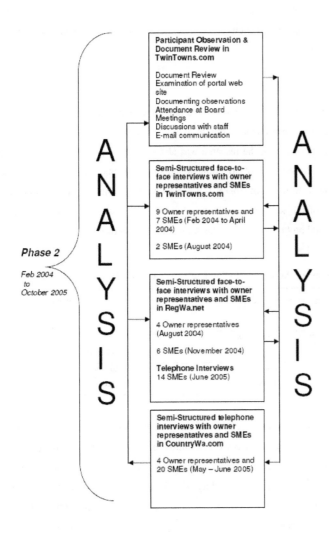

Figure 4.5 Phase 2 of Data Collection and Analysis

While participant observation continued, collection and analysis of primary data was the main focus in this phase. There was an overlap in the data collection and analysis and much recursive analysis of previously analysed documents as the conceptual frameworks evolved and were refined when new themes emerged. Interviews were conducted in different stages as the researcher had to respond to changes in circumstances (in the case of TwinTowns.com, operations on the portal were suspended in April 2004) and opportunities that arose (in RegWa.net, shopping cart facilities were introduced in late 2004). The following sections summarise the data collection and analysis process employed in Phase 2 of this study

Data Collection

Primary data in Phase 2 was mainly from semi-structured interviews which were identified as being the most suitable data collection instrument in this research. While there were specific facts and figures to be gathered from participants, the research was also seeking to uncover facilitators and barriers to the successful implementation of government-supported regional trading platforms and the benefits to be obtained from them for various stakeholders. This required examining stakeholders' interpretation of subjective issues like benefits and success and interviews were ideal for this as the researcher could probe further as to the reasons for the interpretation. The duration of interviews varied as per table 4.4.

Table 4.4 Duration of Interview According to Type of Interview and Role of Participant

Participant	Interview Type	Duration
Principal Operating Officer of Trading Platform	Face-to-face and telephone	>1.5 hours
Other owner representatives	Face-to-face	1 to 1.5 hours
	Telephone	1/2 hour to 1 hour
SMEs	Face-to-face	3/4 hour to 1 hour
	Telephone	1/2 hour maximum

Originally SME non-participants and intermediaries (those providing value-added services) on the trading platforms were also to be units of analysis (in addition to owners and SME participants). A decision was made not to pursue these groups for a number of reasons. Firstly there was a constraint on the funding budget for research expenses (funding of AU$8000 for research expenses ceased after the first year). In the case of TwinTowns.com, the portal had not been actively promoted and few non-SME participants even knew of its existence (as confirmed by a quick ask around of random SMEs in the region). The economic development manager of LG 1 had already been interviewing SMEs in the region as part of his research which could be used as secondary data for this research (and would eliminate 'interview subject fatigue'). In the case of the regional portals,

ECU had conducted research for the Rural Industries Research and Development Commission (Standing & Stockdale, 2003) which aimed to assist rural SMEs in the selection of e-marketplaces. This research entailed seminars for regional SMEs (which included the areas serviced by RegWa.net and CountryWa.com) during which reasons for SME lack of participation in e-marketplaces were identified. The results of the research were also used as secondary data for this study. The low levels of trading activities on the platforms also meant that there were no SME intermediaries providing value-added services registered as participants yet.

Owner interview participants were identified and selected in a combination of ways. In the case of TwinTowns.com, in addition to the project manager and the economic development manager of LG 1, NFPO board members representing each stakeholder (LG 1 and LG 2, their business associations) were chosen for the formal interview process. Other representatives from the local governments were identified via a snowball effect from interviews that had occurred earlier. SMEs in TwinTown.com selected were based firstly on purposive sampling, then availability. The participants selected for the interviews were identified from the directory of participants and were those who were relying on different target audiences (B2C, B2B, B2G); paying and non-paying participants and SMEs offering goods and services. As the researcher had access to the platform database, SMEs who had received RFQs were also selected.

For the regional portals, owner interview participants were identified both with the help of the principal operating officers of the platform and from the web sites. SME participants were identified by browsing the business directory on the portal and the selection process was similar to the one in TwinTowns.com except that participants who had received quotes or business via the platform were identified by the portal owners. Participant profiles are provided in later chapters.

For the face-to-face interviews, the information letters together with a list of preliminary questions mostly relating to demographics (where applicable) were e-mailed to the participants first and answers to preliminary questions were e-mailed back to the researcher before the interview (in some cases, the participant prepared the answers but only produced them during the interview). This allowed the researcher to analyse the answers to determine if further discussion was needed to clarify the answers. It also provided an opportunity to gather background information in addition to that obtained from the company and portal websites. Having as much background information as possible served a number of purposes. To SMEs, time is an important commodity. Participation in the research was voluntary and there were no pecuniary benefits for them. Background information on the participants saved time as they had the answers ready (where answers were provided prior to the interview, there was also an opportunity for clarifications or pre-identifying further questions).

SME participants also appreciated that the researcher had taken the time to know as much as possible about their business and this served as an ice-breaker. For telephone interviews, a different protocol was developed as participants' rights and formal consent were not in writing. Background information on identified potential telephone-interview participants was also gathered from the company websites and portal to reduce interview time and be used as ice-breakers. In all, a total of 68 potential participants were approached (for owner and SME face-to-face and telephone interviews) and interviews were conducted with 66 participants.

All interviews were tape-recorded (except two where the interviewees refused permission) and additional written notes were taken by the researcher during the interview. As the interview questions were structured according to the constructs in the conceptual frameworks, the researcher was able to control the direction and pace of the interview according to the demeanour of the participants. However, the open ended nature of the discussion questions (second half of the interview schedule) allowed flexibility in the interview structure where new opportunities or directions that opened up could be pursued. Field notes were written up about each interview immediately after the interview and all interviews were transcribed within 24 hours. Transcripts were e-mailed to participants for their confirmations and when these were obtained, they were coded in N*Vivo and analysed as soon as possible so that any anomalies or new themes that emerged could be followed up, or pursued in subsequent interviews. Informal post interview communication with some of the participants (telephone conversations and e-mails) was maintained to clarify some of the results of the analysis.

In preparing the interview protocol, schedules and understanding other issues pertaining to interviews as a data collection method, literature in the area was reviewed (see for example Burns, 1994; Leedy, 1993; Marshall & Rossman, 1995; Silverman, 2001; Yin, 2003)

Data Analysis

Interview transcripts were coded in N*Vivo according to the constructs in the conceptual frameworks (and their refined versions). The constructs were used as nodes but free nodes were used for emergent themes. Models of the conceptual frameworks were constructed from the nodes. Graphical depictions of the coding system and models in N*Vivo are presented in the next few pages to provide a clearer understanding of the analysis:

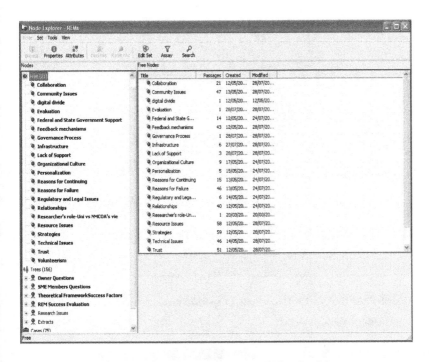

Figure 4.6 Coding Structure for Documents in the N*Vivo database

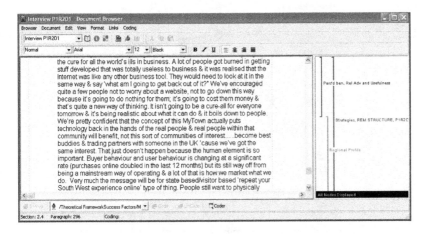

Figure 4.7 Coded Transcript with coding stripes

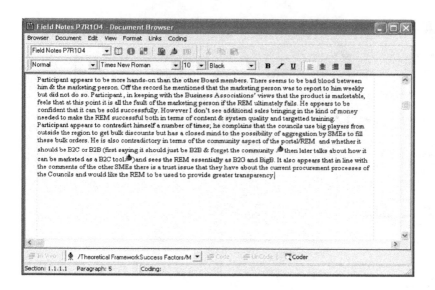

Figure 4.8 Coded Field Notes with Hyperlinks to specific passages of texts in the interview transcripts to provide chain of evidence

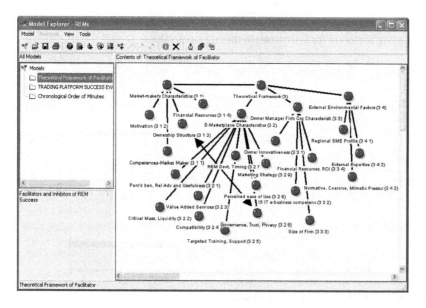

Figure 4.9 Modelling of Nodes according to Integrated Theoretical Framework (Table 3.2) in N*Vivo

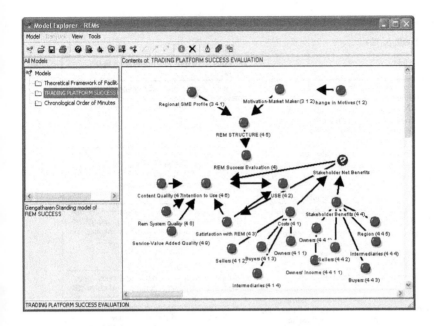

Figure 4.10 Modelling of Nodes according to Trading Platform Success Model (figure 3.3) and costs/success metrics (tables 3.3 and 3.4 respectively) in N*Vivo

The data and analysis was checked by another researcher. Given the small sample size of participants and the objective of the research (understanding a hitherto under-researched area from a number of different levels in a number of contexts), statistical methods (even simple descriptive ones like frequencies and averages) were avoided as most responses to particular questions were context dependent. The recursive analysis of data and refection on the analysis, allowed a refinement of the initial conceptual frameworks of the study not just at the case level but also at the participant level.

4.5.3 *Reliability, Validity, Generalisability, Triangulation, Relevance and Rigour*

The predominant underlying philosophy in this research has been identified as interpretive, with nuances of positivism and a critical stance. In attempting to address issues relating to reliability, validity, generalisability, triangulation, relevance and rigour in this study, principles identified in the literature for conducting and evaluating both positivist and interpretivist case or field studies were reviewed and were used to guide the research. These principles and how they were addressed in the research are presented in tables 4.5 and 4.6.

Table 4.5 Seven Principles of Interpretivist Research applied to this Research (Source: Klein & Myers, 1999, p. 72)

Principle	How this principle was addressed in this study
The Fundamental Principle of the Hermeneutic Circle All human understanding is achieved by iterating between considering the interdependent meaning of parts and the whole that they form	By the iterative nature of data collection and analysis, the movement between examination of the micro and macro contexts and the embedded design
The Principle of Contextualisation Requires critical reflection of the social and historical background of the research setting, so that the intended audience can see how the current situation under investigation emerged.	This has been provided by the discussion of the wider context within which the research phenomenon was situated (the perceived digital divide and e-commerce revolution)
The Principle of Interaction Between the Researcher and the Subjects Requires critical reflection on how the research materials (or "data") were socially constructed through the interaction between the researcher and participants.	The semi-structured interviews and iterative data collection and analysis allowed for probing behind the interpretations of the participants and those of the researcher
The Principle of Abstraction and Generalisation Requires relating the idiographic details revealed by the data interpretation through the application of principles one and two to theoretical, general concepts that describe the nature of human understanding and social action.	The conceptual frameworks for the study were based on a synthesis of constructs of empirically tested theories in the field and related areas as well as insights from the participant observation. The data was coded and analysed according to these constructs and themes allowing a deeper understanding of their role in the phenomenon
The Principle of Dialogical Reasoning Requires sensitivity to possible contradictions between the theoretical preconceptions guiding the research design and actual findings ("the story which the data tell") with subsequent cycles of revision.	This was addressed by taking a critical stance during the reflection stages of the research and allowing the frameworks to be refined as understanding developed
The Principle of Multiple Interpretations Requires sensitivity to possible differences in interpretations among the participants as are typically expressed in multiple narratives or stories of the same sequence of events under study. Similar to multiple witness accounts even if all tell it as they saw it	Multiple sources of information were sought using a multiple case design. Perceived anomalies were referred back to participants for further discussion and clarification. The data and analysis were reviewed by another academic
The Principle of Suspicion Requires sensitivity to possible" biases" and systematic "distortions" in the narratives collected from the participants.	Once again the recursive data analysis as new themes emerged, the clarification sought on anomalies, the checking between different sources enabled the biases and distortions to be identified and accounted for.

The seven principles of Klein and Myers (1999) were constantly referred to in each reflective stage. This helped avoid the interpretive problem of accepting participants' comments at face value as did the different units of analysis and consideration of the micro and macro contexts of the research phenomenon.

Table 4.6 Selected Guidelines for Conducting Rigorous Positivist Case Studies and how these were addressed in this Research (Source: Dubé & Paré, 2003, pp. 621-625)

Guideline	How this guideline was addressed in this study
Clear Research Questions Enable readers to understand the focus of the study and how it relates to a larger domain area	Addressed by three major research questions and their sub questions
A priori specification of constructs and adoption of clean theoretical slate Exploratory case researchers must continue to define a priori constructs to make sense of occurrences, guide interpretation and focus for theory-building	A priori constructs stated in terms of the Trading platform Success Model (figure 3.3 and tables 3.3 and 3.4). In the Integrated theoretical Framework (table 3.2) the relationships were loosely stated with tentative reasons as to why they needed to be investigated. Although constructs from existing theories were identified, there was no application of any formal theory on its own and in its entirety
Theory of Interest, predictions from theory and rival theories Explanatory case study researchers are encouraged to seek alternatives that most seriously challenge the design of the study to increase internal validity	This was done through the iterative cycles of data collection, analysis and reflection and by looking for anomalies and the reasons behind them
Multiple-case design More studies with multiple cases are needed to develop and test more robust theories. Multiple cases also have the potential to yield more compelling evidence	This research uses a multiple-case design
Nature of single case design and replication logic in multiple-case design Case selection must have clear rationales. Researchers must state whether cases are chosen for substantive significance or theoretical relevance	The rationale for the selection for the cases was given in section 4.3.4 and 4.4.1
Unit of analysis Researchers must state the unit of analysis to allow readers to understand how the case study relates to a broader body of knowledge	This has been done by placing participants in the context of stakeholders and the cases in the wider context of government-supported e-commerce initiatives for SMEs
Pilot Case Pilot cases must be used more widely because they may reveal inadequacies in initial design and may refine design and data collection plans. They provide insights into the issues being studied.	In a sense TwinTowns.com was the pilot but the iterative cycles of the structured case methodology also serve this purpose.
Context of the study More information about context is needed to increase credibility of results and to determine whether they are generalisable. Contextual information helps the external observer get a better sense of the 'big picture'	This has been done extensively throughout the preceding chapters and sections
Elucidation of the data collection process A clear description of the data sources and they way they contribute to the findings is an important aspect of the reliability and validity of case findings. Case researchers could effectively use tables to summarise	A description of the data sources has been provided. Tables of participant profiles are provided in later chapters. Information about the data collection process has been provided by a combination of tables, text descriptions and graphics

Guideline	How this guideline was addressed in this study
information about the data collection process	
Multiple data collection methods and mix of qualitative and quantitative data Case study offers the opportunity to use many different sources of evidence and should be seized	Data for this research was collected by participant observation, semi structured interviews and document/artifact review. Both qualitative and quantitative data have been collected.
Data Triangulation Data triangulation must be more widely used in positivist case research to increase internal validity of the findings	Where ever possible, data triangulation was aimed for e.g. details on funding received were checked against published documents, claims on number of participants and transaction levels on portals were checked against statistics on the web sites
Case study protocol and case study database Increase reliability of the findings	These were used in this study
Elucidation of data analysis process This allows the reader to better understand the findings and judge the extent to which they are the fruit of a systematic and rigorous process	This has been provided in the preceding section
Field notes, coding, data displays and flexible processes Greater use of these tools enable greater rigour in analysis which is a major factor in the validity of the findings	These tools were incorporated in the design of this study
Logical chain of evidence Sufficient relevant evidence must be provided to external observers so they can follow the derivation of any evidence from initial questions to ultimate conclusions and vice versa. This increases reliability and internal validity of findings	In the N*Vivo data base, the chain of evidence is done by means of hyperlinks. Thick description will be used in the chapters on findings
Empirical testing, explanation building and time series analysis Positivist case researchers must be more explicit about how data is analysed. The adoption of an explicit and appropriate mode of analysis is likely to increase the validity of the findings	The data analysis process has been described. The use of N*Vivo allowed a systematic way of analysing the documents but at the same time allowed flexibility by allowing the coding of new themes from search results
Cross case patterns Researchers should continue to go beyond initial impressions through the use of structured and diverse lenses on the data to enhance the probability of capturing novel findings and internal validity of findings per se	The iterative processes of data collection, analysis and reflection has been used to achieve this
Quotes Sufficient quotes must be presented in case reports so that the external observer can reach independent judgment regarding the merits of the analysis	This will be done in the chapters on findings
Project reviews This should be done whether in the form of formal presentation to key actors or a review of the case report itself must be used to corroborate the evidence presented in the case report	Reviews of interim findings and comparisons to extant literature were presented to NFPO of TwinTowns.com
Comparison with extant literature Comparison of findings with both conflicting and similar literature increases the confidence in the case findings (generalisability and internal validity).	This is one of the core activities in the structured case methodology and the findings in later chapters will be compared to the extant literature

As illustrated in tables 4.5 and 4.6, there is considerable overlap in the positivist and interpretivist guidelines to conducting rigorous case or field research. The term validity is not used in the Klein and Myers (1999) principles as interpretivists are concerned with defensible claims about the knowledge they have acquired through their research. Thus readers should be able to examine the evidence collected by the researcher, the rigour of the research process used, and the contexts of the research and determine that the researcher's claims are valid. Criteria used by interpretivists for evaluating knowledge claims are credibility, transferability, dependability and confirmability (Weber, 2004). Perhaps the juxtaposition of the principles/guidelines of interpretivism versus positivism in the examination of reliability, validity (or credibility), generalisability, triangulation, relevance and rigour in this study demonstrates that there is credence to Weber's (2004) belief that the differences in the two paradigms are merely rhetoric.

The above analysis indicates that the criteria suggested in both approaches have been addressed in this research.

4.5.4 The Role of the Researcher

Walsham (1995) speaks of the importance of interpretive researchers having a view of their own role in the research. He speaks of two roles, as outside observer or as involved researcher in participant observation. The role of outside observer has merits in that the researcher is not seen to have a personal stake in interpretations and outcomes, which could mean that participants may be more open in their responses. The disadvantage is that the researcher may not get to understand the 'inner context' of the organisation and would have limited access to documents. On the other hand while participant observation would remove some of the barriers to access to inside information, the role could cause participants in the organisations to be guarded in their comments. In this research, both roles were played by the researcher in the case of TwinTowns.com and a more detailed discussion of this dual role and the problems encountered will be presented in the next chapter.

For the general research design though, the researcher needs to have a good understanding of the research area and an acknowledgement of the biases brought to the study (Trauth, 1997; Walsham, 1995). Although researchers give voice to their own interpretations, the iterations of reflection that occur in structured case together with the thick description and chain of evidence provided should help audiences determine the effect of researcher's role on the research.

4.6 SUMMARY AND REVIEW OF RESEARCH QUESTIONS

This chapter set the institutional context of the research from the perspective of the effect of funding on the research objective and approach. While the research approach is predominantly interpretivist, the opportunity arose for introducing positivist and critical nuances into the study in a supportive way. The research was viewed not just from an IS perspective but from an intervention policy perspective as well. The approach selected thus sought to evaluate government-supported regional Internet trading platforms for SMEs by using reliable data in the cases to measure quantifiable effects and interpret and describe other effects, to arrive not at a precise arithmetical comparison of costs and benefit, but mid-level theoretical propositions about what affects them.

With the underlying philosophy determined, the structured case methodology was found to be suitable for the research as it aligned with the research problem, objective, philosophical stance, theoretical perspectives and conditions of funding. It was flexible and allowed the opportunity to respond to changes in circumstances or new opportunities that arose in the research. A discussion of the local context of the research showed how it would impact on the research design and a combined participant observation/in-depth longitudinal case study and multiple-case analysis of two mini cases using embedded levels of analysis at the different stakeholder levels was selected for the research design. Participant observation, document review and semi-structured interviews were deemed appropriate data collection techniques and qualitative content analysis of text documents using N*Vivo was the data analysis technique.

Using the principles and guidelines of both the positivist and interpretivist approaches to field and case studies, it was demonstrated that the research approach and design met the criteria (or would address it in further chapters) for rigorous research. Thus the research design aligns methodology, data collection and analysis with objectives, institutional contexts of the research and epistemology.

It is also in alignment with the research questions as evidenced below:

> **Research Question 1 - What are the factors that facilitate and inhibit the successful implementation of government-sponsored regional Internet trading platforms for SMEs?**

Subsidiary Questions:

> RQ1iii. How do existing theoretical frameworks explain these facilitators and inhibitors?

> RQ1iv. Why are these factors significant?

> **Research Question 2 – How and where can existing theories of IT adoption be used to explain the adoption and use of Internet trading platforms by**

governments in promoting SME uptake of e-commerce and regional economic development?

Subsidiary Questions:

RQ2iii. What are the strengths of existing IT adoption theories?

RQ2iv. What are the limitations of these theories?

These questions were partially answered by the synthesis of existing theories into the Integrated Theoretical Framework of Factors Affecting Success or Failure of Government-Supported Regional Internet Trading Platforms for SMEs (table 3.2). The use of the constructs as nodes to code and analyse data collected will allow the findings of the study to determine which constructs are more significant and why.

Research Question 3 - What are the costs and the benefits (for SME participants, government sponsors and the region) of government-sponsored regional Internet trading platforms for SMEs?

Subsidiary Questions:

RQ3iii. How can these costs and benefits be measured?

RQ3iv. How can this type of platform be effectively evaluated?

Research Question 3 was partially answered with the development of the Trading Success Platform Success Model (Figure 3.3) and its accompanying tables of costs (table 3.3) and success metrics (table 3.4). In this chapter, it was demonstrated how the metrics and relationships in this model were used to design data collection and analysis instruments. The findings of the analysis will add to the answer for this question.

The application of the Integrated Theoretical Framework of Factors Affecting Success or Failure of Government-Supported Regional Internet Trading Platforms for SMEs and the Trading Platform Success Model within the overarching content-context-process (CCP) to evaluation will answer fully the research questions posed above and this will be demonstrated in the chapters to come.

CHAPTER 5

TWINTOWNS.COM: FINDINGS AND ANALYSIS

5.1   INTRODUCTION

This chapter deals with an analysis of the findings from the action research and in-depth case study of TwinTowns.com. The findings from the participant observation were used as insights in the development of the conceptual frameworks for the study. The conceptual frameworks were used to guide the development of the case protocol and interview schedules that were used in the interview of 9 owner representatives of TwinTowns.com and 7 SME participants between February and April of 2004. The portal unofficially ceased operations in April 2004 and a further 2 SME participants were interviewed in August 2004.

The findings from the study of TwinTowns.com are presented and discussed according to four major contexts, viz. the owner, organisational (SME participants), technology and environmental contexts (the discussion on the owner context includes findings from the participant observation). The findings are then discussed in the light of the extant literature, themes that emerged from the analysis and how they affect the conceptual frameworks of the study. The chapter concludes with a discussion of success and benefits in the case of TwinTowns.com.

5.2   OWNER CONTEXT

5.2.1   The View of the Researcher

The interpretive researcher's prior assumptions, beliefs, values and interests always intervene to shape their investigations (Orlikowski & Baroudi, 1991, p. 15). When the interpretive role is combined with one of participant observation in action research within the same study, it becomes even more important for these biases to be acknowledged.

Although the researcher had no formal IS qualifications while working in industry, the last IS-related position held was in the late 1980s and early 1990s as project manager of three user-driven computerisation projects in a large bank in Kuala Lumpur. Some of the responsibilities undertaken in that role were cost-benefit analysis, budgeting, staffing, contract negotiations with vendors, package evaluation, software and hardware acquisition, testing, user-training, and writing parts of the user documentation for the systems. The researcher was also a resident/rate-payer in one of the towns in the TwinTowns.com project and was involved in various community groups in that town but had not heard of the portal prior to the advertisement for the scholarship nor had any experience of government-funded collaborative projects.

In previous chapters, the background to the study of TwinTowns.com and significant events in the project to February 2003 were discussed. Additional details of the TwinTowns.com project viewed from the researcher's perspective were:

- There were on-going problems with the technology preventing the official launch of the product.

- The development of the portal and trading platform were outsourced. Nevertheless, there did not appear to be any IT people from the stakeholders involved in the planning and development stages of the project.

- The procurement departments of the local governments were not directly involved, even though the REM was supposed to be also for B2G business

(Note: The chains of evidence to support these views are provided in interviewee's comments in later sections).

The project thus appeared to be severely under-resourced and lacking good management practices. There also appeared to be undercurrents in the relationships between the project partners and this was reflected in the minutes of the Board meetings.

> *"Lack of action and cooperation from [Town 2]. They doubt capacity of the REM to deliver....Part of problem is that [Town 2] want their staff to have a 'one stop shop' system for purchasing, and are not keen to add another system. They have also raised the issue of possible confidentiality breaches"* (Minutes of NFPO Board meeting dated 27 March 2003).

In March and April 2003, the researcher attended NFPO Board meetings, had discussions with the project manager about administration and solicited free use of labs for training of REM users from one of the local schools (an application to the federal government for a training grant was declined in April 2003). Procedures and manuals were reviewed and suggestions made to both the project manager and the board about the need for extra resources and obtaining community involvement in the project. These suggestions were not acted on.

In April 2003, a mail out was made to existing suppliers of LG 1, LG 2 and ECU inviting them to a free trial on the REM. Only 30 responded. As at May, 2003, there were *"97 businesses currently on the REM. 52 have registered as a paying business and 45 are on a free trial. Of the 52, 30 have paid and 22 are non-financial"* (Minutes of NFPO board meeting dated 8 May 2003).

The project was plunged into crisis again as its viability hinged on REM sales which were not forthcoming. Everything was put on hold until the board of NFPO decided on the fate of the project. Three scenarios were proposed:

1. The local governments would absorb the project under their economic development plans (but the councils had to approve this first and if approved, ownership of TwinTowns.com had to be transferred to them). This option was favoured by the local governments and ECU.

2. The entire REM would be offered up for sale to any interested commercial buyers.

3. Trim costs further, and concentrate on building sales.

The latter two options were preferred by the business associations.

> *"If management is taken internally to the Councils, it becomes a bureaucratic exercise and both the business associations would step aside. There may be difficulty with transparency should the portal be run internally by the Councils"* (Business Association representative cited in minutes of NFPO board meeting dated 8 May 2003).

By July 2003, there was no prospect of the REM being sold for any commercial value and the mayors of the cities did not agree to invest any more funds into the project. The business associations argued that sale of the product (REM participation) had not been truly tested in the market. They felt that by trimming costs further, with a targeted sales plan, in-kind resource support from the local governments and having the purchasing departments of the local governments 'embrace' the REM, the project should be able to continue for a few more months. ECU was not in favour and abstained from voting on the continuation plan. The project manager cum business development manager returned to LG 1 but ran the project by proxy. In October 2003 a marketing manager was appointed and was to begin her sales campaign to the public after the Christmas period. In the interim, she spent time at LG 1, marketing the REM to their purchasing staff via seminars and competitions to encourage use. Between October 2003 and January 2004, requests from the researcher to both the former project manager and the marketing manager for sales and project progress reports and to be present at the seminars did not receive any response. It appeared that the problems between the partners in the project now extended to ECU and to the research position as well.

According to Johnsen & Normann (2004), regional development coalitions are complex environments which are a particular challenge for action research due to the many stakeholders who are representatives but not end users. Conflict is likely to evolve and stakeholders do not have as much legitimacy as in an intra-organisational project. Trust and openness are therefore required among participants. Collaboration in these types of coalitions is easier to achieve when all stakeholders feel that they will personally benefit from the project. However, benefits are more difficult (though not impossible) to identify, as the stakeholders originate from different formal organisations and as such "do not have a sense of shared destiny that involves them personally prior to the project" (Johnsen & Normann, 2004). A central role of the action researcher in such a context (and indeed in Guba and Lincoln's (1989) Fourth Generation Evaluation) is to use a dialogue-based approach to establish shared goals, strategies and understandings which reflect the diversities in the group.

In the case of TwinTowns.com, internal documents like the ITOL and ARC funding applications stated the expected benefits for the local governments and major regional purchasers were expected to be lower procurement costs through the electronic trading system. For SME businesses it was the opportunity to be part of this new electronic trading environment as only regional SMEs would be allowed membership. The region would benefit from increased levels of e-commerce and online activity that would lead to economic development.

ECU was approached to be a financial stakeholder in the TwinTowns.com project as a major purchaser in the region. While the university was willing to support local regional development activities, it also sought to benefit from this participation by using the project for research opportunities. Its participation was on the basis that NFPO would be a research industry partner in the application for an ARC grant. According to Cheek (2000), there could be a number of pitfalls or issues associated with funded qualitative research, among which are those that deal with the question of who controls the research and issues relating to the effect on the relationships among the various players in the research project. It is therefore important to clarify exactly what the deliverables of the research will be. Problems could arise if these are not clearly articulated and understood by all parties concerned.

When the financial crisis occurred and the marketing manager was subsequently appointed, the researcher perceived that there was a deliberate attempt to exclude the research and conserve limited funds (the researcher was not invited to attend further NFPO Board meetings after October 2003). This perception was confirmed when the ECU representative on the NFPO Board was questioned about the contribution of research to the project thus far. An extract from the minutes of the NFPO board meeting dated 29 January 2004 reads:

"What could research help with?" (Representative of Business Association Town 1).

"Paid to evaluate the [TwinTowns.com] REM" (ECU representative).

"Could [the researcher] be used to evaluate the feedback from the users?" (Representative from Business Association Town 2).

"To check with [the researcher]/supervisor to see what else [the researcher] can do to assist" (ECU representative).

The researcher felt that the lack of openness was detrimental to both the research and the project and circulated a memo to members of the NFPO Board (and the former project manager, the economic development manager of LG 1 and the marketing manager of TwinTowns.com) reminding them of the following:

a) The presentation made in March 2003 on the role of the researcher as per the ARC application (see section 3.1) to which no objections were raised.

b) That no formal interviews of users could commence until the University's Ethics Committee had approved the application. This was submitted only in November 2003 as it was contingent upon knowing whether the project was on-going.

c) That the researcher had reviewed user manuals, procedures, made recommendations about resources and community involvement (which were not acted upon) but that everything had been put on hold since June 2003 when the NFPO had been deciding the fate of the project.

d) That despite repeated requests since October 2003 to the former project manager and the marketing manager for the researcher to be involved in the marketing/local government user meetings, no further communication was received from them.

e) That the Ethics Committee approval had been received in January 2004 to commence data collection by way of user interviews and this was scheduled for February 2004.

After this communication, the researcher was invited to attend the Board meetings once again. By then, the community part of the portal and the B2C, B2B aspects of the trading platform were momentarily side-lined. The purchasing departments of the local governments were to be the impetus to gain the critical mass of participants on the REM. These problems, the tensions in the relationships between the partners in the consortium and the continued threat to the existence of TwinTowns.com justified the multiple case study approach (see Chapter 4) as the most suitable way forward to conduct research that was rigorous yet relevant. The following sections will deal with the results of the analysis of the findings from the interviews and the participant observation in TwinTowns.com.

Based on the action research, certain constructs of trading platform owners were considered to be important to the success of the platform and were incorporated into the conceptual frameworks of the study. These will be discussed in the sections after a description of the owner representatives interviewed.

5.2.2 Description of Owner Representatives Interviewed

Table 5.1 below provides a list of the owner representatives of TwinTowns.com who were interviewed and gives their position in the organisations they represented.

Table 5.1 Profile of the 'Owner' Interview Participants in TwinTowns.com

Position	Organisation
Economic Development Manager	LG 1
Business development cum project manager	Seconded from LG 1
Chief Executive Officer (Chairman of NFPO)	LG 1
Chairman (Board Member of NFPO)	Business Association, Town 2
Strategic Development Manager (proxy for CEO of LG2)	LG 2
Strategic Development Officer	LG 2
Executive (Board Member of NFPO)	Business Association, Town 1
Purchasing Team Leader	LG 1
Purchasing Manager	LG 2

Note: In the interview with the current CEO of the Chamber of Commerce of the largest town which originally owned RegWa.net (he was the original business development cum project manager of TwinTowns.com), some clarifications were sought on the TwinTowns.com project and are included in this chapter.

5.2.3 Motivation and Focus

The motivation or focus of the market-maker affects the choice of exchange mechanism for the trading platform, the type and level of services offered, the benefits to be gained and the time taken to achieve these benefits. The creation of TwinTowns.com was driven by a hybrid of community and economic motives and the trading platform was designed to be a horizontal REM catering for B2B, B2G and B2C e-business. Most of the owner representatives interviewed agreed that the trading platform arm of the portal resulted from the need to ensure that SMEs in the region were not left behind in the dot.com revolution and was a way to leverage the Internet to promote regional economic development. However, the owner representatives of LG 2 also alluded to other motives as follows:

> "A couple of people....were also looking after themselves in that this project would give them a name, a presence and would give them work" (Strategic Development manager, LG 2)

> "The then Department of Commerce & Trade of the State department was quite instrumental in sponsoring a number of regional portals....but I think they were created with a view that they would be a community resource....those people who were part of [Towns 1 & 2] aspired to emulate those portal developments but in order to successfully get funding I presume there was an onus to sell the package on the grounds that it would actually make a profit". (Strategic Development officer, LG 2).

From the internal documents of TwinTowns.com and the interviews, there also appears to be some confusion about which part of the portal was to be the initial focus, the community side, the e-commerce side or both simultaneously.

A document dated August 2001 by the then business development cum project manager states the project goals to be a) develop a Community Web b) establish a sustainable model and c) economic development. However, his response in the interview was:

> "I think in [TwinTowns.com] we got it the other way around....The original plan was to get right down in the community....But I think because there was that pressure to generate income to make it sustainable, they concentrated at the top so they were feeding businesses in but there was no one to feed the businesses".

The business associations saw the REM and the e-commerce side of the portal as the driving force of the project. According to the Representative of the Business Association of Town 1, the motive behind the project was "improving business opportunities to gain work from the councils and other government departments". When questioned about the B2C and community aspects of the portal, his reply was "The ideas were pie in the sky ideas....right the way through I've basically seen this as a business tool. The community is a secondary thing".

Although there appeared to be pre-project consensus about the motivation behind the creation of the portal and trading platform, the interviews revealed that there were variations in what stakeholder groups eventually believed the motive was, resulting in a lack of focus of the trading platform. According to Brunn et al. (2002), an e-marketplace without a clear focus "runs the risk of trying to sell everything to everybody....[and is]....likely to result in selling nothing to anybody". In TwinTowns.com, the project expected to impact on four distinct types of local relationships, B2B, B2C, B2G and C2C.

Although B2G business was supposed to spearhead transaction liquidity on the REM, lack of funding meant that streamlining the REM technology with that of major purchasers (LG 1, LG 2 and ECU) was too expensive. There were insufficient funds for a marketing campaign that would promote the REM to the general public and effectively B2C participants were left without a market. The initiative also appeared to have a long payback period due to the underlying motives of improving SME uptake of e-commerce and regional economic development. There was thus a fundamental flaw in basing an initiative with such a broad scope on a business model that was to be self-sustainable in a short time. When queried about why this was so, the following response was obtained:

> "The problem is going to council or going to the state & saying 'I want you to fund this wonderful idea but you're going to have to fund that for at least 10 to 15 years'. The answer they are going to give is almost always No. So what you end up doing is asking for $50K, $100K upfront once off & we say 'we've done our business plan, we will be viable, cash flow positive within a couple of years & you won't have to do any more. It will be self-funding', knowing in your heart that it is certainly a difficult thing to achieve. So then you're hoping that the thing will become so energised, so attractive to the political masters that they will say 'OK, here's some more money'...." (Chairman TwinTowns.com and CEO of LG 1)

In the light of the interview responses, constructs of institutional theory were used to understand the motivations behind the consortium's involvement in the TwinTowns.com project, their dogged continuation with it even in the face of the internal problems and why the local governments and ECU were not prepared to contribute a greater level of funding or have their IT/purchasing departments more involved in the project.

Institutional theory (DiMaggio & Powell, 1983; Haveman, 1993) posits that organisations mimic the behaviour of other structurally equivalent organisations to increase legitimacy in an effort to improve their reputation, image and prestige or to conform to institutional norms. The bandwagon effect causes organisations to adopt an innovation or carry out an activity regardless of its technical value in an effort to 'keep up' with its peers in a particular economic or political network. Rahim, Shanks and Johnston (2002) use constructs of institutional theory to investigate type and source of motivation for adopting IOISs. Based on their analogy, market-makers may be motivated by socio-political reasons of legitimacy and image enhancement, status and influence or by the pursuit of economic value. Socio-politically motivated market-makers may create REMs for reasons other than efficiency gains, may be willing to invest only limited resources into the IOIS to build a positive image and may not be willing to integrate the IOIS into their own systems or processes. Organisations adopting IOIS for socio-political reasons are also unlikely to conduct systematic evaluations of the benefits and downsides of the IOIS.

The undertaking of such a wide-scoped initiative with inadequate resources in the case of TwinTowns.com can be attributed to the 'bandwagon effect' of mimetic pressure and legitimacy as LG 1 and LG 2 sought to become a part of the government-funded collaborative e-commerce projects that were being initiated around Australia at that time. Spencer (2002, p. 29) is of the opinion that where states compete for economic advantage, the competitive bandwagon effect of policy diffusion can be significant; it is characterised by rapid adoption of policies with long term payback yet are adopted in a relatively short time and offers a "theoretical basis for subsequent abandonment of innovation". The bandwagon effect of policy diffusion is an analogy that can be used to describe the outcome of the TwinTowns.com initiative.

> *"It was a progressive thing for council to consider taking on a project like this....it was a bit of a punt....so they didn't want to put too much into it....but the understanding from council of what the actual benefits would be & how it will actually benefit in reality probably wasn't there"* (Last Project-manager of TwinTowns.com and Economic Development officer in LG 1)

As a construct or factor that can affect the success of government-sponsored regional Internet trading platforms for SMEs, the following need to be considered as far as motive/focus is concerned: developers of such platforms need to carefully examine the motive behind the endeavour; all owners need to have a shared vision about the motive and focus of the platform; there is a need to match the focus or scope of the platform (and thus its exchange mechanism) to the available resources and a need to match the model chosen to the motive.

5.2.4 *Ownership Structure and Governance*

Would single or multiple owners have a better outcome on the success of the trading platform? While the latter has potential for collaboration and a larger funding base, it can also lead to conflict. In the case of TwinTowns.com, there was tension among the various stakeholder groups and a lack of candidness about what exactly was expected from each stakeholder in the consortium.

In viewing ownership structure and governance as a factor that could affect the success of a trading platform, there was a need to examine if indeed the owners had a clear vision of their role in the project and if the roles of the various owners were complementary. In the content analysis of published case studies on REMs/trading platforms (the Lonxanet (Dans & Freire, 2002), RETFC (Wilkins et al., 2003a; 2003b) and gatetrade.net (Brunn et al., 2002; Hunter & Doz, 2002)), besides the increased amount of funding provided by the wide stakeholder base, each stakeholder had specific expertise to offer and these were leveraged to contribute to the initial success of the projects. Questions that surfaced during the participant observation of TwinTowns.com were: what were the underlying institutional factors that prompted the formation of the consortium and how did they impact on its lack of success to date? There was also a need to determine the effect of the governance process on the success of the platform from both the owners' and participants' views.

A combined lens of resource dependence and institutional theories was used to understand the formation of the consortium. According to Oliver's (1990) inter-organisational relationship types and critical contingencies of relationship formation, the ownership structure of TwinTowns.com is closest to the 'Joint Programme' relationship. This type of relationship "may improve the agencies' abilities to convince government sources to provide funding, particularly if the programme is a new initiative in the social service domain" (Oliver, 1990, p. 255). This is indeed one of the reasons for TwinTowns.com's wide ownership base:

> *"If it [ownership base] had been smaller, we wouldn't have got the support &*
> *the resources"* (Economic Development Manager, LG 1).

However, contrary to Oliver's (1990) typology of Joint Programme relationships, LG 1 and LG 2 had high domain similarity (similarity of their services, clients and outputs) which theoretically could introduce the potential for competition leading to impeded interaction. Thus the actual alliance between owners could be unstable from the start. There was some history of tension when Town 1 was carved up and Town 2 became the satellite town for the region. There was tension between the LG 1 and LG 2 representatives on the project.

Table 5.2 Evidence to Support Tension between Owners in TwinTowns.com

Position	Comment
Strategic Development manager, LG 2	I'm talking about politics & culture now and I don't think the politics and culture was ever that well aligned. I don't think we built a team in the first place, I don't think we had team spirit
Officer, Strategic Development, LG 2	To the frustration of certain people at [LG2]....because [TwinTowns.com] is designated as a regional portal, they cannot do anything with the [LG2] name or leverage the local business, so they're hamstrung in that sense as well
SME participant from Town 1	There's always going to be this friction between the two towns & to mix the two of them together in a business association type of relationship is never going to work
SME participant from Town 1	We've got a situation where we've got Town 2 & Town 1 & they sometimes appear to be at loggerheads. They don't seem to be working together & you get the 'them & us' type of thing

While the decision to include the business associations as owners (albeit non financial ones) could have been motivated by the need to have the interests of regional business represented, it can also be interpreted as a public show of the local governments' commitment to SMEs in the region. It is questionable whether the SMEs were adequately represented, as membership of the business associations numbered less than 20 percent of regional businesses. Nevertheless, many of the initial participants who signed up with the TwinTowns.com REM were members of the business associations and had been recruited through them. While LG 1 and LG 2 viewed the REM as a stimulant for B2B e-commerce in the region, the business associations viewed it as largely a B2G instrument that would provide opportunities for local businesses to get a slice of the local government trade and bring some transparency to the procurement process. The motive of the business associations in being party to the project could well have been to legitimise their role as a lobby group for the regional SMEs in relation to obtaining a share of the local government spending.

> *"What I see the use of the REM for is discretionary purchasing of the councils where without hesitation they pluck 1 or 2 out of the REM & give them the chance to quote....I know for a fact that there are excuses that can be used for not allowing the best quote to win....The culture thing has got to be broken down as well...what this* [the REM] *should do, is that it should be transparent & give the opportunity to the other people. I'd be interested to find out from the council who were the people that used it, how many did they put out, who they put it out to & how many of the quotes did they accept"* (Representative, Business Association Town 1).

The LG 2 representative was candid on this issue:

"If [LG 2] was to go & deliberately facilitate small business, it will cost a lot more & who will fork out the much higher rates? To some extent I think that's what the local Business Associations want....but they do it in nowhere near the volumes. In time they might".

However, despite complaining that the local governments purchased from outside the region to obtain bulk discounts, the business association representative was scathing of the idea of SMEs collaborating to provide the volumes that would enable bulk discounts:

"Aggregation, its pie in the sky stuff. I think that would be so complex I wouldn't enter into it....So I would say business (I'm thinking of business from the business association point), very few of them would want to enter into it because they would be going into an unknown area, with unknown people & they wouldn't feel comfortable" (Representative, Business Association of Town 1).

The wide ownership base of TwinTowns.com, the bandwagon effect behind its creation and the lack of openness could have also contributed to the project dragging on despite the numerous problems encountered.

"So the two CEOs attend committee meetings, maintaining face, making sure they don't upset the local business associations but at the same time they know that if they were to start throwing their weight around it will also be detrimental to their own positions in their own organisations. So there is that façade that they maintain" (Strategic Development officer, LG 2).

The comments were in stark contrast to the business associations' view of how the CEOs of the local governments would get their purchasing departments to support the REM:

"All you have to do is talk to the CEO & say it's not working & these are the reasons. I know that [CEO, LG 2] went back & banged heads & I know that [CEO, LG 1] would as well. If they issue a directive & then their staff don't work to it, then their staff are in trouble". (Representative, Business Association Town 1). (Note: The CEO of LG 2 was subsequently 'paid out' for the premature termination of his contract due to disagreements with the mayor and some members of the council).

The lack of openness among the owners was detrimental to the project and this spilled over to the role of research in the project. The 'undercurrents' perceived by the researcher about the role of research in the project were subsequently explained when the full set of NFPO board minutes became available after the project ceased.

Table 5.3 Evidence to Support Researcher's Perceptions of Undercurrents about the Role of Research in the TwinTowns.com Project

Date of Minutes of NFPO Board Meeting	Excerpt of Minutes
17 April 2002	The [ARC] grant application describes the role as purely research. The position will need to include a strong business management focus (CEO of LG 1). The application had an emphasis placed on research, to allow the best possible evaluation. In reality the role would have a management focus. (ECU Representative)
10 October 2002	4.1 Australian Research Council Grant. ECU grant successful. A PhD student will be appointed next year. The grant total is $120,000. $69,000 cash component and $51,000 in-kind. [TwinTowns.com] is committed to a cash component of $8,000 per year for the three year term of the project. A panel will be appointed to select the person for the role of which [TwinTowns.com] has the option to be apart of. [TwinTowns.com] will have ownership of half the person's time - 20 hours per week. This time may be used on training, sales, administration etc
31 October 2002	2. MINUTES OF PREVIOUS MEETING. [The ECU representative] request [sic] to remove the last point made on 4.1. The PhD student job role and hours may become flexible and varied

While on the one hand projects with wide stakeholder bases can have positive implications in terms of resources, they need to be examined carefully to determine that all owners/sponsors are fully committed to the common objectives of the initiative. There needs to be a clear understanding of the stakeholders' expectations, of how each stakeholder's resources can be used to complement the others' and above all collaborative projects of this type need openness, trust and a willingness to learn from each other (Johnsen & Normann, 2004), something which was not present in TwinTowns.com as evidenced below:

> *"I get very frustrated at these meetings. When I'm in the real world & I'm the only real world person there....sorry....but I'm not an academic, I'm not a government employee, I'm actually there at the coal face, spending my dollars, paying people to do things....I don't sit behind a desk...."* (Representative of Business Association Town 1).

> *"It all comes down to people, those who want to make it happen. We can make it happen. You need champions. In the Board as well....you also need trust, respect."* (Chairman of NFPO and CEO of LG1).

Thus the empirical data indicates that in the owner context, ownership structure and governance are issues that can have a significant effect on the success of a regional Internet trading platform for SMEs.

5.2.5 Financial Resources

In TwinTowns.com, AU$360,000 had been expended on the project and that amount did not appear to be sufficient to achieve the objectives behind the wide scope planned for it. In comparison, although the RETFC was more focused, there were still hidden costs as the software vendors *"invested in development of the interface software without real cost to the recipients. Neither local councils nor growers would have been able to make this investment prior to the entry of [the ASP]"* (Wilkins et al., 2003a; 2003b). For relevance, there was a need to give practitioners an idea of all the different costs that a project like TwinTowns.com would entail. The evidence from the literature indicates that even where projects are more focused, they involve substantial financial investments. The projects to provide Internet trading platforms for SMEs under the e-Europe Go Digital programme (E-Business Policy Group, 2002) were either better funded, narrower in scope or both when compared to TwinTowns.com and other similar government-funded projects in Australia.

Despite the ubiquitousness of the Internet, substantial financial resources are required to establish and maintain Internet-based trading platforms on a commercial basis (see for example Brunn et al., 2002; Dans & Freire, 2002; Hunter & Doz, 2002; Ming Zeng, 2001). The mere provision of the technology and the touted benefits of lower transactions costs alone may not be sufficient to guarantee success. E-marketplaces need to be able to offer participants value added services from which they can improve their competitive positions (Ordanini, 2003). Where these platforms are used to improve regional development by engaging the SME community in e-commerce, there may be a need for one-on-one training or consultancy for the SMEs, not only in the use of the platform but also to help them determine how best their businesses can prepare to compete in this new environment.

Financial resources for REMs and trading platforms for SMEs thus need to be considered for maintenance and on-going support, not just for initial platform development and this was not the case in TwinTowns.com:

> *"in reality these things take a long time to get established and become sustainable....I think it comes back to the initial comment I made about commitment by stakeholders to fund the platform but not the ongoing operations."* (Last business development cum project manager of TwinTowns.com and Economic Development Officer, LG 1).

From the TwinTowns.com case it may be concluded that properly costed (i.e. there are no hidden costs), AU$360,000 is not sufficient to create a community portal launched simultaneously with a horizontal trading platform for SMEs that caters for B2B, B2G and B2C business and which would be self sustainable in the short term (less than 3 years). Such an initiative needs to be viewed as a longer term investment if the owners believe that there will be benefits in the longer term.

> *"But the reality may be that if there is a total benefit, a total good from the project, then we should be honest enough upfront to say that this will require an ongoing subsidy".* (Chairman of NFPO and CEO of LG 1).

To a large extent, some of the blame for the lack of success in TwinTowns.com was placed on the inability to get external funding.

> *"From the murmurings of the State & Federal governments we expected a lot more funding to come in but that wasn't happening. I don't even know where the State government's gone. They're just gone...."* (Economic Development manager, LG 1)

That the TwinTowns.com business model was based on mainly external funding and a quick payback, had wide socio-political objectives (e-inclusion via the community side of the portal and the REM) but yet was 'rushed' into production, lends credence to the bandwagon effect of information policy diffusion (Spencer, 2002). It can also be explained by Rahim et al.'s (2002) view that organisations that adopt IOS for socio-political reasons of legitimacy and image enhancement, status and influence may be willing to invest only limited resources into the IOS.

5.2.6 Competencies (IS/project management skills)

Although the TwinTowns.com project and others like it were regional development projects, the underlying IT artefact still demanded a good project manager to drive the project, especially given the wide scope and stakeholder base. This need corroborates the preliminary findings of the McGrath and More (2002) study of the first 67 projects funded under the ITOL programme. While the funding of such projects may not allow the hiring of top-notch professional IT project managers, based on the researcher's past experience, user-driven IT projects can be successful with the following (among others): project champions among senior management, a good understanding of the business, commitment of owners, good vendor management (where outsourced), ensuring that users who will be affected by the project have an input into the specifications and an open consultative atmosphere between project members and owners who work together for the common good of the project. In TwinTowns.com there appeared to be a lack of commitment from the owners in so far as supporting the business development cum project manager in terms of level of resources and expertise needed.

While local governments may be best placed to know the needs of their local communities, they are normally resource-poor (Spencer, 2002). Thus, while it may have been innovative for LG 1 and LG 2 to take a leading role in a project like TwinTowns.com, it still begged the question of why their IT and purchasing departments were not better represented on NFPO especially during the planning and development stages. Prior to 2004, ethics considerations prevented the researcher from interviewing IT and purchasing personnel from LG 1 and LG 2 who were not directly involved with TwinTowns.com. According to the business development cum project manager and economic development manager of LG 1 these people were consulted very early on in the project.

However, the result of the face-to-face interviews drew the following responses:

> *"I think in theory it would make a good e-procurement tool but unfortunately the technology and the development of it isn't as advanced as the in-house systems that we've got here....I know that has caused problems particularly for our people in the purchasing area who see [the REM] as another process that's going to be layered on top of existing processes....they've always felt that it was an imposition on them....Our IT department are vehement....it's like no way, we don't want a bar of it"* (Strategic Development manager LG 2).

The responses from the interviews with the purchasing staff of LG 1 and LG 2 corroborate the view that there was poor management of the project in terms of determining local government user requirements.

> *"We've been kept at arm's length....I think obviously at an earlier stage there could have been a bit more input from procurement or IT or probably both....I know the IT guys have had little or no involvement."* (Purchasing Manager, LG 2).

> *"For us integration was & still is vital for it to work....I'll be honest, I'm not keen on a 2 system approach because unfortunately what that effectively means for me as the person who administers out the internal system at the moment, is 2 sets of passwords, 2 sets of problems & interfaces between them both, that sort of thing"* (Purchasing Manager, LG 2).

LG 1 representatives blamed the lack of better project management on inadequate funding.

"It's a part time board, we spent a couple of hours a month at meetings and we had no expertise on the Board....We did not have the dedicated staff & we did not have the money to do that. We try & do this on a shoestring...." (Chairman NFPO and CEO of LG 1)

"We expected a lot more funding to come in but that wasn't happening.... in 1999 the first base plan was for a project manager, 2 admin people, a sales & marketing person etc....5 or six people minimum". (Economic development manager, LG 1).

This finding supports the findings of the McGrath and More (2002) report on the projects under the first five rounds of ITOL funding wherein one of the major causes of project delays was the lack of funding and resources for project management.

Funding constraints were also blamed for the lack of integration of REM technology with that of major purchasers'.

"I know that the successful tender was for $90K. My recollection was that the other tenders that actually had those interfaces were up around the $400K to $500K mark, a quantum leap in costs". (Original business development cum project manager, TwinTowns.com).

While the lack of external funding could have been due to the downturn in the dot.com boom, the lack of greater levels of internal funding could be attributed to the socio-political bandwagon effect of policy adoption. The project was owned by a separate entity and there was no real ownership by the individual owners who may have only wanted to commit limited resources to the initiative. By keeping the technical and purchasing people at arm's length, when it was decided that the towns would be the primary purchasers on the REM, their IT and purchasing people had misgivings about the REM and portal systems. Poor project management was also cited as a factor in the failed government-supported B2B portal for SMEs in Victoria studied by Fisher and Craig (2004; 2005).

5.3   THE ORGANISATIONAL (SME PARTICIPANTS') CONTEXT

This section deals with the discussion and analysis of the findings from the organisational or SME context. The research sought to uncover if there were particular characteristics of SMEs that made them more amenable to adoption of online trading on platforms like TwinTowns.com. The section starts with a brief description of the SME interview participants and then goes on to describe in further detail some of their characteristics. Their views on the costs incurred, the benefits that the REM had to offer and its ultimate success will be discussed in the final sections of the chapter.

5.3.1 Description of Interview Participants

The characteristics of SME participants from TwinTowns.com who were interviewed are provided in table 5.4 below:

Table 5.4 Profile of the SME Interview Participants inTwinTowns.com

SME #	Position of Interviewee	Number of Employees	Turnover AU$'000 (Annual)	Buy (B) Sell (S) on 'Net?	Whose decision to join and when?	Business Description
P1R1	Co-directors	2 (plus specific associate resources)	New Company	B-No S-No (has own website)	Interviewees Joined Feb 2004	Delivery of specific IT products & IT Management Services (B2B)
P2R1	Director	2	50-100	B-No S-Yes (through own website)	Directors. Joined in Dec 2002	Garden Supply Products (Organic) (B2C)
P3R1	Director	3	1,500 (in operation for 13 years)	B-No S-No (wants to via portal)	Interviewee. Joined in Dec 2002	Supplier of specialist materials for construction & marine adhesives sealants waterproofing (B2B)
P4R1	Franchise Owner	5	450	B-No S-Yes (through own website)	Interviewee. Joined in Dec 2002	Full Service Sign & Design Co (B2B)
P5R1	Proprietor	6 part -time	100 (in 3rd year of operation)	B-No S-No	Interviewee. Joined 1 year ago	Functional rehabilitation services (B2B. B2C)
P6R1	Owner	1	480	B-Yes if necessary S-Advertising only	Interviewee. Joined in Dec 2002	Printing (B2B, B2C)
P7R1	Manager	7	1,000 – 1,500 (Operating since 1984)	B-No S-Yes (through own website)	Directors. Joined in Dec 2002	Printing (B2B mainly)
P8R1	Franchise Owner	5	<1,000 (National Franchise operating for 20 years)	B-Seldom S-Yes (through own website)	Interviewee. Joined in Dec 2002	Printing, Graphic Design, colour copying (B2B mainly)
P9R1	Part Owner /Director	2	N.A (operating for 10 years)	B-Yes S-Advertising only	Interviewee. Joined in 2002	Printing & Graphic design (B2B. B2C)

The selection of interview participants was skewed towards SMEs in the printing and design business as this was the area in which the few RFQs in TwinTowns.com were issued. SMEs from both the goods and services sectors were represented as were SMEs who catered for B2C and B2B e-commerce.

5.3.2 SME Owner Innovativeness

A number of studies point to factors like owner innovativeness, managerial enthusiasm and top management attitude as positively affecting SME adoption of IT (Cragg & King, 1993; Thong, 2001; Thong & Yap, 1995). In TwinTowns.com, the decision of SMEs to participate in the REM was made by the owners or directors of the companies. Of the nine SMEs interviewed, four did not have their own web pages and were satisfied with just a listing on the REM that had their contact details and an e-mail address (but no flyer pages). However, these businesses did have computer-based systems for their back-office operations. Of the five SMEs which had their own websites, two were part of national franchises which had common integrated back office systems throughout the franchise. Only one SME had the ability to accept online payments, and this SME catered mainly for the B2C market. The others who reported selling via their website took orders and RFQs via their websites but did not offer the facility to take online payments.

In the case of TwinTowns.com, it is difficult to make any inference about the relationship between SME owner-innovativeness and the decision to participate in the REM. Six of the nine SMEs interviewed were mainly interested in getting business from the local governments and there were no changes expected to be made to their internal IT systems as they could receive RFQs by e-mail, fax or SMS (short messaging system). The wide scope of the trading platform and the lack of resources meant that there were no opportunities for clustering, competence building or knowledge sharing. There were also no opportunities for feedback or suggestions from SME participants as all but one of the SMEs (which was owned by the board member of NFPO), had not been contacted by anyone from TwinTowns.com since they had signed up as participants. Four SMEs participated without paying fees as they were part of the pilot group (the rest paid no more than AU$200 each) and none of the SMEs interviewed participated in any other e-marketplace or Internet trading platform. Therefore while the SMEs interviewed may have had innovative owners/directors in so far as their own IT-driven internal operations were concerned, most of them were cautious about e-marketplace trading and appeared to be willing to invest only minimal amounts to be listed on TwinTowns.com.

5.3.3 E-Commerce Readiness

Chau (2001) and Iacovou et al. (1995) examined SME adoption of EDI, while Mehrtens, Cragg, and Mills (2001) investigated adoption of the Internet by SMEs. In these studies, organisational readiness was found to significantly affect adoption. In an Internet trading platform, having participants who are e-commerce ready (or experts) can lead to quicker liquidity (as they may not need to be trained and would already have the basic IT infrastructure in place). According to Grewal et al. (2001), having 'experts' as participants in e-marketplaces can even be the impetus for others to join due to the bandwagon effect.

Internal documents from TwinTowns.com showed that a survey done prior to the project indicated that SMEs *"in this region are at least as well advanced as average Australian businesses, and possibly more advanced in the areas of web page and online transactions"*. There was a perception by the owners of TwinTwins.com that this meant SMEs in the region were e-commerce ready and this would facilitate their adoption of REM trading. This group of SMEs was targeted first due to the need for the project to be self-sustaining or even profitable in the short term. The selected business model meant that any mentoring or advice on e-business uptake for SMEs had to be deferred until a critical mass of paying participants could be achieved on the REM.

Targeting e-commerce ready SMEs would mean that the trading platform has to provide the SMEs with advantages that they cannot obtain by their own online endeavours. In TwinTowns.com, the 'carrot' for SMEs looking to break into the local government and major regional purchasers' market was the promise that local governments and major regional buyers would use the trading platform to procure. For SMEs who were ready to tap the B2C e-commerce market, the community portal of TwinTowns.com held the promise of driving regional consumers to the site, giving added exposure to the participants of the REM. However, these promised advantages never materialised as the purchasing departments of the local governments were not sufficiently involved in the development of the trading platform, and were thus not sufficiently motivated to alter their existing procurement approach. This was exacerbated by technology which was not fully functional. The lack of focus on the community side of the portal meant that B2C e-commerce was also not being promoted by the project.

In a government-supported regional Internet trading platform for SMEs which is designed to promote adoption of e-commerce and regional development, the targeting of e-commerce ready SMEs may not be sufficient to guarantee participation if immediate and continuing benefits cannot be demonstrated. With limited resources, targeting this group of SMEs could mean having to provide more sophisticated offerings with few resources left over for building competencies of less e-commerce ready SMEs.

5.3.4 Size of Firm

One of the reasons why SMEs lag behind larger companies in innovation adoption is their lack of slack resources (Thong, 1999; 2001). The Internet with its open standards and ubiquitousness has been viewed as a way to lower size and distance barriers faced by SMEs. Nevertheless, Internet trading platforms with proprietary software could be a barrier to participation by smaller SMEs who may not have the capacity to invest in the software or may not have the slack resources to buffer any negative effects of participation.

As such, the technology used in trading platforms like the TwinTowns.com REM was designed such that SMEs without web pages could also be listed on the REM to receive quotes from purchasers. It was hoped that the REM would demonstrate to SMEs the wider benefits of moving to the online environment and that the project would provide technical and advisory support for those SMEs making the move. Thus government-supported trading platforms like the one in TwinTowns.com would be viewed by SMEs as a low cost introduction to e-marketplace trading in a nurturing and trusted environment.

All nine SMEs interviewed in the TwinTowns.com case were either small or micro businesses and none of them spent more than AU$200 to participate in the REM. All had not experienced e-marketplace trading previously. In a study of e-commerce adoption by SMEs in Australia, Chong (2004) found that perceived level of governmental support had a strong negative relationship with the state or level of adoption. SMEs already having a high level of e-commerce adoption perceived governmental assistance to be less helpful than those who were not self-starters or innovators. Chong (2004) suggests that since firms in Australia are more independent in terms of experimenting and venturing into new technology, the role of the government "is best suited to supporting the laggards in adoption rather than encouraging the leaders". This is precisely what projects like TwinTowns.com have as their objective and their target group of adopters would then signal the need for longer term support to build the necessary competencies that would enable SMEs to adequately compete in the online environment. However, the need for TwinTowns.com to be self sustainable in the short term appears to have been at odds with the long term implications of the project.

5.4 THE TECHNOLOGY (TRADING PLATFORM) CONTEXT

Past conceptual and empirical research on adoption of IT, EDI, e-commerce and e-marketplace trading was used to identify constructs or characteristics of the technological context that could promote participation in government-supported regional Internet trading platforms for SMEs. After synthesising the constructs from the literature, those selected for this study were: perceived benefits (perceived relative advantage), value added services/strategic partnering, training and technical support, trust, compatibility with participants' systems, perceived ease of use, development process, marketing plan and critical mass or liquidity,.

5.4.1 *Perceived Benefits*

Perceived benefits or perceived relative advantage has been found to be an important motivator of SME adoption of IT (Cragg & King, 1993), EDI (Iacovou et al., 1995) and the Internet (Mehrtens et al., 2001; Poon & Swatman, 1997). To obtain a holistic view of the perceived relative advantage or perceived benefits of regional Internet trading platforms for SMEs, it was necessary to examine both the owners' and SME participants' views.

5.4.1.1 Owners' View of Perceived Benefits

The owners were asked what they perceived the benefits of the trading platform to be for themselves, SMEs in the region, and the region itself.

Owners' Perceived Benefits

For the benefits to themselves, the local government representatives of LG 1 saw the trading platform mainly as a tool that would bring convenience and time savings to the procurement process for small (or discretionary) purchases that were not being done through their existing e-procurement systems. The process for such purchases was to call up three suppliers by phone, record their quotes and award the tender to one. However, the purchasing staff interviewed indicated that this involved only a very small portion of the discretionary spend of the local governments, would not sustain a critical mass of transactions on the REM and tenders received via the REM would need to be treated competitively as with other tenders.

> *"There will be opportunities to quote but they have to be competitive & offer value for money & it's only on a proportion of the discretionary purchasing that aren't already unique...a proportion of a proportion"* (Purchasing Team leader, LG 1).

However, there were no baseline figures collected on a) the existing volume of the local governments' discretionary spend being channelled to SMEs in the two towns and b) the actual costs of the current way of awarding the tenders for the discretionary spend. The REM system was also perceived by some of the LG 1 and LG 2 representatives as being a good tool to monitor the RFQ process for discretionary spending (by an audit trail) as *"[i]f we had someone saying 'OK, I got 3 quotes', it would be nice to be able to look & see if they actually did request for the 3 quotes. We wouldn't do it in every situation, but once in a while we'd look & see what people are doing"*

(Purchasing manager, LG 2). The question arises as to whether the resistance to the use of the REM by the purchasing staff of the local governments could be due to the fact that the RFQ process could now be closely monitored. In a study of an energy e-marketplace, Koch (2004b) found that when the e-marketplace use mandate was passed to the procurement department, they resented it. They would do anything to undermine the e-marketplace as they felt that the management had joined the e-marketplace because purchasing staff were not getting the best price form vendors. Koch (2004b) is of the opinion that "operational involvement facilitates e-marketplace use", something which was lacking in TwinTowns.com.

One business association saw the trading platform as a way of helping it bring together businesses in the area. The REM would also get people to spend their money within the region rather than out of it. The other business association saw the REM as a way for local businesses to get requests for quotes (RFQs) from the towns and major purchasers in the region and as a secondary purpose, to put out RFQs for their own businesses if they required something as well.

Perceived Benefits to SMEs

The representatives of LG 1 were of the opinion that the trading platform would benefit SMEs in the region by giving them exposure to a new market (the government one) which they never had access to; would help build business networks; create ease of access and efficiency in quoting and would help in developing a regional identity. The strategic development manager of LG 2 felt that the TwinTowns.com REM would provide SMEs the skills and the capability to manage their products, particularly the marketing and promotion, and to grow their demand instead of just pushing from a supply perspective. *"Of course there's also the training, the skills development that they would get because a lot of them weren't terribly IT literate & are still running paper-based offices not realising there's a whole new mechanism or vehicle for businesses these days".*

The opinions of the purchasing staff of both the local governments were that the benefits for SMEs were not automatically tied to the opportunity to quote for local government discretionary spending but more to allow SMEs to identify each other and get a foot in the door to e-business. They felt that the REM could show SMEs some benefits from e-business like operating more cost-effectively. One business association representative felt that the REM would make SME businesses more sustainable, while the other felt that there was no value for SMEs other than getting requests from the local governments and other major purchasers in the region.

It appears that while LG 1 management and the business associations took a very short-term economic view of the benefits that could accrue to SMEs (the ability to get a share of the local government discretionary spend), the very people themselves who were being counted upon to stimulate critical mass of transactions (the purchasing departments of the local governments) thought otherwise. They, together with the LG 2 representative, saw longer term benefits like community and competence building. This once again demonstrates the divided perceptions of the owners about the role of the portal and trading platform in the TwinTowns.com project.

Perceived Regional Benefits

The majority of TwinTowns.com owners perceived that the trading platform would benefit the region by making it attractive to investment thereby strengthening the local economy and creating more employment opportunities. Management of LG 1 and the business associations expected the REM to be viewed by businesses as the 'key' to preferred trading arrangements between local SMEs and major regional purchasers (because membership was restricted to local SMEs) and hoped that it would cause an influx of businesses who would 'set up shop' in the region because they wanted to be suppliers to the local buyers.

However, there does not appear to have been proper consideration of a number of issues in the planning stage of the project that would support these perceived benefits. Some of the issues that needed to be considered are: what were the characteristics of existing trading relationships of the major buyers in the region? Were they locked into long term contractual trading relationships which would impose significant switching costs if they were to use the REM to procure? Could the benefits from procuring via the REM outweigh these switching costs? Could local SMEs supply in the kinds of volumes that the local purchasers needed? What proportions of the local spend could be catered for by the REM and would this be enough to create a critical mass on the trading platform? What were the online purchasing habits of local consumers and how would SMEs registered on the trading platform be able to attract these consumers. Was the presence of the REM alone enough to change existing purchasing patterns or would SMEs require hybrid online/off-line arrangements and advice on the best e-commerce strategies to take advantage of the Internet and the REM?

The purchasing personnel of LG 1 and LG 2 did not see local government purchasing as the impetus that would lead to regional benefits from the trading platform. They viewed regional benefits in terms of increased levels of B2B and B2C e-commerce among SMEs by giving local purchasers easily accessible knowledge to what was available locally online. The strategic manager of LG 2 saw regional economic development as a longer term outcome, with the portal and REM being used for upgrading of skills and building network externalities of local SMEs. The other LG 2 representative did not see any benefits from the project as *"It's not just the merit of the actual portal itself. This is in the context of the politics surrounding this region"*.

5.4.1.2 Participants' (SMEs') Perceived Benefits

Participants' perceived benefits are related to their motives for joining the REM. Of the nine SMEs interviewed in TwinTowns.com, six were motivated to join because of the lure of becoming suppliers to the local governments. Of these six, two companies were associated with the business association representatives who were members of NFPO. The remaining three SMEs not drawn by the promise of business from the local governments thought it *"sounded like a good idea"* because of the way it was marketed and it seemed like an inexpensive way to get exposure to an e-marketplace. These three SMEs were attracted to what they perceived to be the targeted exposure of their businesses to the local region because of the purported involvement of the many levels of the community that would drive traffic to the portal and REM.

Two of the SMEs were also motivated to join the REM as they were new companies and felt it would be good exposure for them in terms of *"playing with the local boys"*. Only one out of the nine SMEs interviewed had been recruited in 2004, and one of the main reasons this company signed up was because they were told that *"the councils were forced to go through the REM in order to get quotes for every technical and non technical requirement"*. However, from the minutes of the NFPO Board meetings and the interviews with the purchasing staff of LG 1 and LG 2, the reality was that such a directive was not issued. Due to the ethical dilemma faced, the researcher felt that it was prudent to avoid interviews with newly recruited participants until such a directive actually materialised as participants appeared to be willing to talk to the researcher only if they could get some idea about how the REM was progressing.

All nine SMEs felt that if the REM worked according to the plans that were originally presented, there could be benefits in the form of increased business and cost savings at least in terms of advertising costs. One SME (P7R1) perceived that while there could be benefits for buyers and the community, the REM would have the effect of driving already low margins further downwards for SME suppliers. In this SME, it was the directors' decision to participate in the TwinTowns.com REM and not the interviewee's.

Prior research by ECU on the businesses in Town 1 found that home-based micro-businesses had only a little over 10 percent of their customer base within the town (and nearly 40 percent in other locations throughout the metropolitan area), while few of the 1000 businesses in the Town 1 industrial park did business with LG 1. According to the study done by the economic development manager of LG 1 for his professional doctorate (a case study of TwinTowns.com to determine if B2G portals could be used to stimulate business in SMEs), there was overwhelming verbal support (from the 40 SMEs in the region interviewed and the 12 SMEs participating in the focus groups) for the use of local supply networks. His study revealed that portal membership was one method to reverse the effect of poor local supply networks. Interestingly only one of the nine SMEs in this study perceived that the REM could be beneficial by making it easier to source locally thereby saving time and transport costs. The other eight SMEs commented that they had ongoing long term relationships with their own suppliers or in the case of franchises, supplier arrangements were made by the national office. One SME even went as far as saying that

> *"Again, being blunt, only penny pinchers call for quotes...You build up a relationship, you've been dealing with a company for 10 years, it knows your terms of trade, your funny little idiosyncrasies, about how you want things delivered and when. Not many businesses would be in a quoting situation. Government departments yes, but to me not general business".* (P6R1 who was also the Town 1 business association representative on the NFPO Board).

Thus while there may have been overwhelming support for the 'buy local online' idea behind the REM and portal, in reality the majority of the SMEs were waiting for someone on the REM to buy from them and were not looking to be purchasers on the REM themselves. Fairchild, Ribbers and Nooteboom (2004) in their study of four e-marketplaces concluded that "it is questionable whether electronic markets will change long-term existing close relationships between buyers and suppliers".

5.4.2 *Value Added Services/Strategic Partnering*

In TwinTowns.com, because the wide ranging motives behind portal and trading platform creation gave way to basic survival in 2003/2004, the value-added services like logistics, financing, internal operational support that some researchers have come to view as an important part of e-marketplace success (Ordanini, 2003) were not present. However, the importance of value added services to the success of e-marketplaces has been questioned by Fairchild et al. (2004) who found that services like multiple transaction mechanisms and credit/logistic services were not sufficient to contribute to critical mass (which they viewed as a critical success factor). Fairchild et al. suggest that provision of 'real value' to e-marketplace traders was more important.

According to the owner representatives of TwinTowns.com, the project needed to provide a basic working transactional model first and the non-technical value-added pieces could come later. The local government representatives opined that if the platform worked properly, there could be value in services like bundling hosting services with REM offerings, data mining on the REM to provide advice to SMEs on where opportunities could be found and aggregation services. However, the business association representatives were sceptical of the value that such services would offer to SMEs.

SME participants interviewed were asked for their opinions on whether provision of value-added services would be attractive to them. One SME responded that it would only make sense if there was clustering of like businesses which could aggregate so that services like logistics could be offered at discounts to individual players. Another felt that the more sophisticated SMEs could require more than mere transaction opportunities in order for the REM to be attractive to them. When asked what would keep them satisfied in the short-term when transactions or RFQs were not forthcoming, all the SMEs replied that that would like to see feedback on what was happening with the project, data on successful transactions on the REM, success stories of SME participants and would be happy with information about upcoming activities in the region so that they could plan for opportunities that could arise.

In a government-sponsored regional Internet trading portal for SMEs, especially where the model is a horizontal one and is not industry or function-specific, it appears that value-added services like logistics and financing would not be a success factor in the short term. Consequently, partnering with providers of these services may not be strategic. In TwinTowns.com while partnering with the business associations and ECU could be viewed as strategic, the conflicting motives of the owner and stakeholder groups and the lack of trust and respect between them negated any benefits of complementary resources and expertise. The owners of TwinTowns.com should have also examined the opportunities of partnering with major community groups to leverage volunteer resources (as demonstrated by one of the local school's willingness to allow the use of its training facilities without any costs).

5.4.3   Training and Technical Support

The process of requesting for (and responding to) tenders in TwinTowns.com is as follows: a requester goes to the business directory of TwinTowns.com and selects the relevant business category. A list of suppliers appears and those who are enabled to receive RFQs will have a check box next to their listing. The requester checks the boxes of the selected suppliers, types out the request (or cuts and pastes, or attaches it) and clicks the send button. Each of the selected suppliers will receive notification by the method they have previously agreed upon (e-mail, fax or SMS) that there is a RFQ in their inbox on the REM. To respond to the RFQ, the supplier has to log on to the REM system, retrieve the RFQ, and respond to it by typing in the relevant information (or attaching it) and sending it off to the requester. The requester is advised of receipt of tenders, selects the most suitable and issues accept/reject notices to the suppliers via the REM.

In TwinTowns.com, there was not much SME user-training provided to participants due to the following: the owners of TwinTowns.com felt that the REM systems was relatively easy to use; a demonstration model was available on the REM page and the marketing manager used a lap top computer to demonstrate the procedure during marketing calls (beginning 2004); there were limited resources (after the soft launch) for one-on-one training. Consequently, the majority of SMEs interviewed reported little or no training but agreed that they had managed to use the REM using the documentation provided.

Koch (2004a) found that support (defined as helping e-marketplace members identify situations in which marketplace use can provide benefits and training members to use the marketplace) drives perceived relative advantage and e-marketplace use. This supports the findings of Khalifa et al. (2003) that e-markets need to support participation and adoption through IT consultancy and support for learning during the early stages of deployment especially in the case of SMEs.

While the SMEs did not view the lack of training as a factor preventing them from using the TwinTowns.com REM, they were disparaging of the level of technical support provided by the owners of the REM:

> *"Support was offered but again it's the marketing officer who did that....the problem is that one person is trying to do all the things. Specifically, what should have been set up was some form of help desk that is equally business related as it is technical. That doesn't appear to be there"* (P1R1).

> *"We couldn't get through & I think he might have come once but his answer was 'Well, its working here.....mine's OK'; but I said 'I'm a customer & mine's not. I got to the point where I just thought forget it, just go to the local paper-based directory & it was quicker...."* (P8R1).

In TwinTowns.com, launching the REM before technical problems were fully addressed and not having adequate technical support for participants did great damage to the image of the portal and REM. In examining a failed government-supported B2B portal for SMEs in Victoria, Fisher and Craig (2004) found that the technology did not have the promised functionality when it was launched, which was detrimental to the management of SME participants' expectations and led to their eventual mistrust of the technology and portal.

5.4.4   Trust

Trust-building between buyers and sellers in an e-commerce environment is a much researched topic especially where SMEs are involved. SMEs receiving online RFQs could be unsure of the authenticity of the requester. Online buyers of SME products could be wary of the authenticity of the SME supplier. In TwinTowns.com, there were some initial attempts at system-induced trust measures with buyers required to be authenticated before they were allowed to issue RFQs (the owners felt that the registering of SME suppliers and the regional nature of the trading platform would to some extent reduce buyer mistrust). The proposal was to sight some form of identification (e.g. business registration for companies, drivers' licences for individuals) before registering buyers. Due to the lack of resources needed to practice this authentication process and in an effort to "break down the barriers to public usage of the REM" (TwinTowns.com internal document), the need to authenticate buyers on the REM was abandoned in mid 2003. In his study of the ability of TwinTowns.com (as a B2G portal) to stimulate SME business, the economic development manager of LG 1 found that 10 percent of SME interview respondents were sceptical about the value of online RFQs. They felt that they could be wasting time responding to people who were just shopping around for quotes and that online RFQs could become similar to SPAM. As none of the SMEs interviewed from TwinTowns.com had received a RFQ from anyone other than a local government department, trust in the requester was not an issue for them.

In TwinTowns.com the issues of mistrust of the REM system by SME participants stemmed not from cultural issues (as in the case of the REM in Singapore investigated by Hsiao (2003)), but from flaws with the system, lack of adequate technical support and lack of feedback on project progress. Having the local business associations involved in the development of the trading platform and listing community groups on the portal could have leveraged the trust embedded in the local social networks of the region (Steinfield & Whitten, 1999) for the project. However, the lack of trust and openness between the portal owners, the lack of focus of the REM and the local governments' involvement in the project made it appear a 'top-down' project, forced on the SME participants. To them, the governance of the REM was not satisfactory.

> *"It did smell of local government. People knew they were dealing with the local government & it wasn't a player in the commercial world & didn't have credibility....if [LG1] decided to help every business in its area advertise, then by all means set it up, but make sure you're using people with outside expertise to actually run it"* (P8R1).

5.4.5   Compatibility with Systems and Practice

Among the main technological barriers to SME participation in e-marketplaces (especially in regional areas) are the lack of common standards, the differing technology platforms adopted by market makers and connectivity problems (Standing & Stockdale, 2003, p. 25). In TwinTowns.com, the horizontal and non function-specific nature of the trading platform required technology that would be simple enough to use, such that SMEs would only need their existing Internet connections and a bit of training. Thus compatibility of the REM technology with that of participants' systems was not important. Six of the nine SMEs interviewed felt that there could be some benefits if the system could allow some form of integration. However, as they viewed the REM more as a quoting tool, they saw limited potential benefits of integration, mainly to their potential customer database (i.e. downloading and saving information from requesters of tenders). To the purchasing staff of the local governments, not having the REM technology integrated with their purchasing systems meant that the potential business that they could channel through the REM was marginal, leading to problems in creating a critical mass of transactions.

Participation in TwinTowns.com did not require any additional technological investments on the part of SMEs. However, the design of the platform (REM users needed to access the main portal site first, then log onto the REM) and the slow connectivity rates combined to create technology issues which were damaging to the image of the project in its first year of operation. This was because many areas (especially the business or industrial areas) within the region serviced by TwinTowns.com were in 'urban broadband black spots', a problem which was only partially addressed in 2004. Thus although SMEs received notification of RFQs easily enough, they had problems logging on to the REM to retrieve and reply to the RFQs because of the graphics-laden portal site and slow connections.

Of more importance than compatibility of technology in initiatives like TwinTowns.com is the compatibility of the system with existing business practices. Koch (2004a) found higher usage rates in e-marketplaces that changed their focus from free open marketplaces to customised offerings to accommodate the relationships inherent in existing business practices. The initial success reported in e-marketplaces like the Lonxanet (Dans & Freire, 2002) and RETFC (Wilkins et al., 2003a; 2003b), where SMEs were part of the target participants, came from the ability to improve practices among existing business relationships within specific industry sectors. All participants and stakeholder groups could perceive immediate benefits from the initiatives. In TwinTowns.com, the wide scope of the trading platform meant that there were no immediate benefits for existing business relationships (which were not examined in any case) and any benefit of using TwinTowns.com as a regional online directory were negated from a lack of marketing and publicity

155

and because there were insufficient resources to maintain current information. This implies that initiatives like TwinTowns.com that face resource constraints need to be more focused if they are required to be self sustainable in the short term.

5.4.6 Perceived Ease of Use

While the majority of the SMEs interviewed in TwinTowns.com perceived that the trading platform system was easy to use, three had not used it for some time. Those who actually went in to try and retrieve RFQs, viewed the system as non user-friendly because of the technical problems and the slow connections.

> *"It was so complicated in the way that it was set up....Look at what hard-nosed free enterprise businesses are doing out there & take a page out of their books & keep it simple, because if Mum at home can't go in there & use it simply, she won't use it"* (P8R1)

> *"I never really got to learn how it worked exactly even in spite of it appearing to be simple, the way they showed us the demo when we went for the evening. I don't know whether they changed the system subsequent to that but it was incredibly difficult to use both from the point of view of trying to log on & get the info about the quotes that had supposedly been sent to you....I never actually managed to do that, and also in terms of finding your way around it"* (P9R1).

Both these SMEs were interviewed after TwinTowns.com had been officially terminated and this may have allowed them to be more forthcoming with their views. P4R1 who had actually got some business out of participation, at first claimed the system was easy to use but on further probing revealed that the RFQ was replied to outside the system after problems trying to attach a file to the reply.

5.4.7 Development Process

Based on the researcher's experience with implementing large novel computer systems, it was surprising that the TwinTowns.com project although wide in scope and under-resourced, was not implemented in smaller manageable stages. The motivation behind the creation of TwinTowns.com was to increase adoption of e-commerce by SMEs in the region and stimulate regional economic development. The target participants of these types of REMs are SMEs that are traditionally further along the innovation adoption curve. These factors indicate that such initiatives are long term ones that require proper evaluations of costs, benefits, inhibitors and facilitators. From a systems analysis perspective, the recommended way to develop and implement such systems is an evolutionary or staged/phased approach, learning as development progresses and being able to modify plans if there are unexpected outcomes at each stage (Kendal & Kendall, 2005).

In TwinTowns.com the decision was made to launch all functions of the portal simultaneously even though parts of it were not working properly and there were scarce resources to maintain its currency. To some extent this could be reflective of poor project management, but the conflict between the owners, their lack of a cohesive vision for the portal, the need for self-sustainability and the socio-political motives behind the development could have contributed to the decision.

One SME participant had this comment about the development process in TwinTowns.com: *"obviously someone thought they could put this together fairly quickly & it's well beyond your average website of expertise that's needed to set it up. That's where I think it falls short"* (P9R1). An incremental stage approach to development could also have meant that a functioning community portal and online business directory could have been offered first while options of further functionality were explored and evaluated more extensively against available resources. One SME participated in the TwinTwons.com REM because she was attracted to the idea of getting up-to-date online information on local suppliers:

> *"a local directory type thing that works across for everybody....& it's got to be cost-effective. You can't have something that's too expensive because as small businesses we're not making that much money & we can't be funding you to set up a web-type thing or print out a separate directory"* (P9R1).

Since the closure of TwinTowns.com, LG 1 has collaborated with the provider of the Yellowpages Online directory to allow businesses in Town 1 to be listed for free in a regional business directory which has a link from the LG 1 homepage. The directory provides basic contact details of companies and *"costs [LG 1] AU$3,000 a year"* (economic development officer of LG 1).

5.4.8 Marketing Plan

Most of the academic literature on commercial e-marketplaces does not mention marketing or promotion per se as a critical success factor. At most it is subsumed under the heading of the need to build liquidity or critical mass. This is due to the implicit assumption that marketing/promotion is part and parcel of the normal business strategy of commercial entities. In government-supported regional Internet trading platforms for SMEs the need for a good marketing plan is equally important, especially where the platform is part of a community portal catering for all types of business across various industry sectors. Dans and Freire (2002) reported that in the Lonxanet, online visits to the e-marketplace increased after heavy promotion. Fisher and Craig (2004) who studied a failed government-supported regional B2B Internet trading platform for SMEs in Victoria found that "a major problem and one of the issues raised by many of those interviewed was the lack of promotion for the portal".

According to internal documents of TwinTowns.com, potential strategies for promotion of the REM were the of use media, direct mail and follow-up calls to businesses, business after hours gatherings and attendance of REM personnel at business association events, incorporating REM membership into relevant business association membership and targeting dominant sectors for REM membership (professional services, trades and services, automotive). A marketing budget of AU$20,000 was originally proposed for the REM based on receipt of external government funding as initially envisaged (there does not appear to have been any amounts budgeted for the promotion of the community side of the portal). Internal documents pointed to plans for sales staff to be recruited at the end of 2002 but the shortfall in funding and the problems with the technology forced a postponement. Although the full extent of external funding did not materialise, some marketing strategies were employed but it was left to the business development cum project manager to single-handedly manage the promotion in addition to the whole project. His opinion of the funds available for promotion of TwinTowns.com was:

> "Comparatively low marketing budget [compared to] $90,000 for [RegWa.net] which has 350 REM listings costing $149" (TwinTowns.com Business Case Analysis document dated May, 2003).

The business associations felt that concerted sales efforts were required and a marketing manager was hired in late 2003. She had to sell 2 REM participations a day to guarantee the ongoing viability of the project. This was in addition to running promotional campaigns at local shopping centres, arranging 'sundowners' for existing and prospective REM participants, training internal purchasing staff of the two towns, running competitions to get these staff to use the REM, as well as taking on the role of project manager. The researcher's suggestion that the marketing of the REM to internal staff of LG 1 and LG 2 should be handled internally by the local governments was not heeded. Only after interviews with the purchasing staff of LG 1 and LG 2 did it emerge that they did not support the REM as the driving force behind critical mass and top management in the local governments did not appear to want to mandate the use of the REM by their staff.

There were disagreements among the board members of NFPO as to how the marketing needed to be done and there was not much in-kind support offered by the owners for the marketing manager. The business associations felt that it would not be difficult to get the 2 sales per day (based on 60

158

calls a week) despite the additional project management function that was hoisted on the marketing manager and despite thinking that the REM system was flawed, unstable and unreliable.

Even the SMEs interviewed from TwinTowns.com felt that the REM and portal were not sufficiently promoted.

Table 5.5 SMEs' Comments on Promotion of TwinTowns.com REM

Participant	Comment
P1R1	That poor girl has not got a chance on her own, she's completely overloaded with different responsibilities & that's not a criticism of her but a criticism of the processes that they have in place....it's marketing....you need a marketing section, to have e-commerce seminars, get sponsors, build interest....
P2R1	If it was promoted and run properly, and obviously this hasn't happened, it could have had an effect. It hasn't been sold to people properly.
P6R1	There's been no follow up.... it [has to be] marketed properly and used as the way to promote a 'buy local' policy
P7R1	I've never seen any promotion

In TwinTowns.com, the better part of 2003 could not be spent on aggressively marketing the REM as there were insufficient resources and also because of the technical shortcomings with the system. Thus while marketing and promotion are vital to build critical mass and bring visitors to the portal, the system needs to first be working properly so that participants can perceive some benefits.

One important aspect overlooked in TwinTowns.com in its marketing efforts was customer relationship management of its existing participants. Apart form the participant who had signed up in 2004 and those who had received RFQs, others were not aware that the REM and portal were still operational. All participants commented on the lack of communication from the project sponsors, which they felt was detrimental to their trust in the project and the sponsors. Most SMEs felt that even if they did not receive any business via the REM or even if there were problems with the technology, they should have been kept informed of progress through newsletters or e-mails. The absence of communication was also viewed as a shortcoming of the failed B2B portal for SMEs in the Fisher and Craig study (2004; 2005).

5.4.9 Critical Mass

Where there is a short term economic motive behind the creation of a government-supported regional Internet trading platform for SMEs (i.e. self-sustainability or profitability of the platform or portal), achieving a critical mass of transactions or paying participants on the platform becomes critical to the success of the platform. In TwinTowns.com, because the ultimate financial sponsors (the councils of the local governments) were not convinced about the longer term regional benefits of the portal and REM (like building e-commerce capabilities in SMEs or becoming a knowledge region), they were not willing to provide the level of funding that would be required to produce these benefits.

The original business plan for the TwinTowns.com REM (based on an ITOL application dated August 2001) was to involve total project costs of approximately AU$448,500 which would be met by an ITOL grant of AU$174,500; state government grants of AU$174,000; cash contribution from the two towns of AU$30,000 and the balance to be met by 'in-kind' contributions from the owners. The portal was expected to be self sustainable in the third year of operations based on "a conservative estimate of business take up" beginning March 2002, as per table 5.6 below:

Table 5.6 Estimated Business Take Up for TwinTowns.com REM (Source: TwinTowns.com ITOL application)

	Members Growth	Monthly Transactions/member	Business Listings Growth
Year 1	10 – 65	16	25 – 300
Year 2	70 – 125	16	324 – 600
Year 3 – 5	20%	16	20%
Pricing	AU$500/annum	AU$0.50/transaction	AU$60/annum

The operating costs of the REM were projected to be AU$28,500 and AU$22,800 in the first two years respectively and AU$79,000 annually in the years to follow.

However the ITOL funding did not materialise, total external grants (from the RAP programme and the state-owned Small Business Development Corporation) received eventually amounted to approximately AU$203,000 and the two towns and ECU made cash contributions totalling AU$158,000. While this meant a shortfall of only AU$17,500 in the cash contributions, the cash and in-kind support had now to be spent on the entire project (both the REM and portal). Technical problems caused a nine month delay in the 'live date' of the REM and portal. Continuing technical problems meant that only a 'soft launch' was possible in December 2002 with many SME participants recruited as non-fee paying pilot customers and those who were charged paid only AU$199 to have a REM link (the ability to receive RFQs). There were no transaction fees imposed and after concerted marketing efforts by the marketing manager during the first quarter of 2004, TwinTowns.com had only 157 paying participants many of whom had signed up originally and had not paid anything more since they joined.

In the absence of additional cash (or in-kind) injections by the owners, by April 2004, the viability of the portal hinged on obtaining 2 new paying participants per day or alternatively, sponsorship income (advertising fees) from large companies in the region. It was difficult to obtain sponsorship based on the poor promotion that the portal had received and further funds were not available for media advertising.

The absence of feedback to the participants on REM activity and technical problems with the REM software led them to believe that the REM was not actually functioning and this was detrimental to further sales. The one SME interviewed who had got any business from the REM subsequently conducted further transactions off-REM and believed he would have "*got the business anyway, even without the REM*" (P4R1). The purchasing staff of the local governments had the excuse that there were too few suppliers listed on the REM to make requesting for tenders through it a cost-effective alternative even for small discretionary purchases (according to the interview responses, discretionary purchases not requiring written quotes were capped at AU$300 for LG 1 and AU$1000 for LG 2 per transaction). The use of the REM at the local government level could thus not be mandated. The business association representatives on NFPO were of the opinion that the marketing manager was not being pushed hard enough to make sales but at the same time one of them interviewed in his capacity as participating SME felt that the REM system was "*flawed, it's unstable, it's unreliable. I believe the reliability of it is still a problem*" (P6R1).

Building a critical mass of participants or transactions on an Internet trading platform will be dependent on the perceived benefits that participants believe the platform will deliver. According to Koch (2004a), support and investor commitment drive perceived relative advantage. In TwinTowns.com these were seen to be absent and subsequently had a negative effect on SMEs' perceived benefits.

Critical mass can also be achieved if existing off-line relationships are migrated to the platform and participants view trading via the platform as "being better than the idea that it supersedes" (perceived relative advantage as defined by Rogers' (1995) diffusion of innovation theory). However, existing relationships between the local governments, major buyers and their suppliers were not investigated to see if they could be migrated to the REM. As the REM technology could not be integrated with the purchasing systems of the major buyers, according to the purchasing staff of the local governments, only a very small portion of the discretionary spend could be channelled through the REM and in their opinion this was not sufficient to generate a critical mass of REM transactions.

As such, TwinTowns.com was never able to build critical mass on the platform, leading to its ultimate demise. However, had the REM been perceived by the owners as a development tool to be used for building e-commerce competencies in regional SMEs and were the owners willing to fund it as such, there would not have been the pressure to launch an incomplete product in order to generate paying participants. By using a short-term business model to implement a long-term economic development strategy, public funds of approximately AU$360,000 were spent without enhancing uptake of e-commerce by SMEs in the region or building their competencies.

5.5   THE ENVIRONMENTAL CONTEXT

The environmental or external context in a government-supported regional Internet trading platform for SMEs has to be examined form two aspects. First, the actual profile of the region needs to be considered in terms of demographics (size of area to be served, location, business activity etc.) and how these affect the success of the platform in promoting increased use of e-commerce by SMEs in the region. Next, consideration needs to be given to the institutional context within which the SMEs are embedded i.e. the influence from competitors, customers, trading partners, business associations and chambers of commerce (normative, mimetic and coercive pressures).

5.5.1   Regional Profile

Steinfield, Mahler and Bauer (1999a) concluded that there is a mismatch between much of the electronic commerce rhetoric and the capabilities of many local businesses, and policymakers may need to take a more local approach to e-commerce to prevent it from becoming a threat to local economies. The move to focus on regional e-commerce in initiatives like TwinTowns.com can be regarded as a step in the right direction, as the region is not renowned for global exports or major tourism activities.

However, in developing regional Internet trading platforms for SMEs, there is a need to first determine if the profile of the SMEs and the region are suitable for this type of initiative and can be leveraged to achieve adoption of Internet trading. The profile of the SMEs and the region should thus determine the focus of the platform (will it be vertical, horizontal, part of a community portal?) and the motivation for its development (to raise e-commerce uptake by SMEs, to introduce cost effectiveness in strategic regional industries where SMEs are involved, to raise the general level of Internet use in the region?).

In a region where the SMEs are predominantly in manufacturing, the market mechanism of an Internet trading platform may be a procurement tool to cater for B2B e-commerce, while the e-marketplace model in a region with SMEs predominantly in the retail industry could take the form of an e-mall to cater mainly for B2C e-commerce. A region already having strong off-line SME networks or alliances may provide impetus for early online collaboration in SME regional trading platforms. The attitude of SMEs in the region towards growth will also have a bearing on the structure of the market, its features offered and ultimately the benefits to be gained. If the majority of SMEs are lifestyle SMEs (Jeffcoate, Chappell & Feindt, 2000), the owners of the platform may choose to consider an e-marketplace model that reflects the SME owners' strategy for business growth (Levy & Powell, 2003). The geographical location of the region to be served by the trading platform also needs to be considered (Steinfield & Whitten, 1999).

TwinTowns.com was developed to serve Towns 1 and 2 which are located in metropolitan Western Australia and cover 900 km^2, have about 220,000 residents and 7000 SMEs. Major industries include manufacturing, agriculture, retail trade, services and tourism but none stand out significantly. In the geographical area served by TwinTowns.com, as with many suburban areas, the community ties between inhabitants (and businesses) in the region are relatively weak, given the larger population, the very close proximity to vendors of competing goods and services outside the region (in some areas competitors outside the region were actually physically nearer to the buyers of Towns 1 and 2) and the fact that some residents do not even work or study within the physical regional boundaries. As such, it is doubtful whether any 'buy local' campaign would have had much success even in an off-line mode unless the goods or services offered regionally were cheaper, of a higher quality or the benefits perceived from buying local were enough to convince businesses and consumers to alter buying patterns. Although the survey done by ECU prior to the project showed that SMEs in the region were as good as or better than the national average in terms of buying and selling online, there were no detailed studies of what was actually being bought and sold and who the buyers/suppliers were. While household connections to the Internet in the region were relatively high, this did not automatically guarantee a ready market for local online B2C sales as no data was available about consumer online purchasing behaviour at the regional level.

As indicated from the interviews of SMEs participating in the TwinTowns.com REM, only one considered using the REM to look for local suppliers. The majority of SMEs were small and micro businesses which reported that they were locked into relationships with their existing suppliers and did business mostly on a face-to-face basis. They were thus looking to become suppliers to the major local buyers who, however, were also locked into existing relationships with their own suppliers and would only be able to channel RFQs for small infrequent discretionary purchases via the REM. Thus a horizontal regional Internet trading platform for SMEs catering for B2B, B2C and B2G e-commerce (and developed with limited resources as part of a community portal) should not have been viewed as a short term self-sustainable or profitable proposition without more detailed information about the patterns of online behaviour in the region. The lack of a full understanding by the portal sponsors of the diversity of backgrounds, cultures and business sizes of the SMEs was reflected in the failed B2B regional portal in Victoria (Fisher & Craig, 2004).

5.5.2 Normative, Coercive and Mimetic Pressure

External or environmental factors in the form of government intervention can also affect the implementation of a REM. Khalifa et al. (2003) who studied 8848.net, a leading e-marketplace in China serving state-owned enterprises, are of the opinion that government intervention may force these enterprises to adopt the e-marketplace for trading, causing a knock-on effect of participation by their smaller trading partners, if its use by government purchasers is mandated. In TwinTowns.com, many of the participants joined the REM because it was supposed to be one of the sources through which the governments of the two towns would procure but the use of the REM was not mandated by the local governments. In GEM, the WA state government-owned procurement REM, one of the recommendations for building critical mass is to mandate the use of the REM wherever technically possible (AOT, 2003).

E-marketplace operators may need to consider the effect that coercive, normative and mimetic pressures and trust/embeddedness can have on early liquidity. In a number of studies on SME adoption of e-commerce (Al-Qirim & Corbitt, 2004; Chong, 2004; Scupola, 2003, 2004), external pressure from buyers, competitors and suppliers were strong predictors of the decision to adopt. In TwinTowns.com although the local governments had the 'power' to get SMEs to participate on the REM by procuring through it, they could not exercise this power as their purchasing staff were not behind the decision to adopt the REM for their purchasing needs. As the REM did not take off, the effect of mimetic pressure could not be tested. Although some of the leading figures in the local SME community were participants and the embedded relationships in the business associations were viewed as a way to garner support and trust in the initiative, launching a product that was flawed and charging SMEs for it destroyed any such trust. In fact this worked against the project in the later stages due to the mistrust between the business associations and the other owner representatives on the REM. In the failed B2B portal for SMEs in Victoria (Fisher & Craig, 2004, 2005), although many of the initial participants were not clear about the benefits of the portal, they joined to support the local initiative. However, the trust embedded in the desire to contribute to the development of the region was not leveraged as there was no consultation or communication with participants after they had signed up.

In TwinTowns.com, the profile of the region did not support a widely scoped Internet trading platform that was supposed to build new business relationships between various existing groups in the region while yet being self sustainable or profitable in the short term. Although relationships embedded in the local institutional networks in the region could have been leveraged to build liquidity on the REM and portal, the lack of focus and lack of commitment of the owners in financing the project as a long-term development initiative resulted in no benefits to SMEs in the region.

5.6 EMERGENT THEMES AND EXTANT LITERATURE

Trust, Motive and Institutional Pressure

The initial conceptual framework of the study posited trust as a critical success factor on two levels, viz. trust between participants and the platform owners and trust in the technology.

The empirical data showed that the lack of trust in the technology (due to the technical shortcomings of the REM system) was one of the factors that prevented some existing participants from responding to RFQs and caused others to circumvent the REM system for subsequent dealings. SMEs had no perceived issues with trust of the technology if it worked as it should have (in terms of security, fraudulent RFQs etc.) for a number of reasons. They did not view it as something that would be integrated with their back office systems; they accepted that having the local governments involved would mean that the owners were not out to make a quick profit from them; they just wanted some activity from the REM and therefore had not thought very deeply about the issue. To a large extent, trust between participants and the owners was established in the beginning by having the business associations as collaborators in the project. The business associations saw themselves as representatives of SMEs in the region. They sold the REM to their members as a way to break into the local government market and to bring transparency to the existing purchasing policies/processes of the local governments (which they believed were not in favour of local SMEs). While the SMEs in the TwinTowns.com project felt that having the local governments as owners meant they would be protected from opportunism, they did not trust the way the REM was managed as they felt the local governments did not have the requisite expertise. Although trust continued to attract significant interest in the extant e-marketplace literature (McKnight, Kacmar & Choudhury, 2004; Pavlou & Gefen, 2004) the aspects of trust mainly discussed (building buyer trust) were not tested in Twin Towns.com as the REM did not progress that far.

One area of trust that did not receive much attention in the conceptual frameworks but emerged from the empirical data as highly critical in the case of TwinTowns.com was the trust and respect between the owners themselves. In the academic literature, this was discussed in terms of the need to engage potential participants as partners in the development process to gain commitment (Fisher & Craig, 2005). In TwinTowns.com, the lack of trust between the owners stemmed from a lack of consensus and openness about the motives of each owner group. In using 'convergence in the motives of stakeholders' as a critical success factor for e-marketplaces, Fairchild et al. (2004) found that in cases where the motives of all stakeholders were not met the e-marketplace was likely to fail.

In the literature on e-commerce, IOISs and e-marketplaces, the role of institutional constructs (like mimetic pressure and legitimacy) were discussed in terms of how they could be leveraged to promote adoption and build critical mass. For example, one of the lessons learnt from the eEurope Go Digital Programme to increase SME uptake of e-commerce was that networking is the most successful marketing strategy to reach SMEs (Commission of the European Communities, 2004). In the study of TwinTowns.com, however, the theme of legitimacy or mimetic pressure also emerged on a more fundamental level i.e. in the owner context. Mimetic pressure or legitimacy underlying the creation of the TwinTowns.com portal and REM can account for the mismatch between the long term objective (and benefits) of the project and the short term business model of sustainability or profitability, the over-dependence on external funding and the view of the purchasing staff of the local governments' that the REM system was an 'external' system.

Matching the Scope of the Initiative and Development Process to Resource Constraints and the Profile of the Region

The empirical findings from TwinTowns.com revealed that the regional profile (in terms of geographical location, demographics, major business activities, culture, communications infrastructure etc.) is an important consideration in determining the scope of the initiative and the type of regional Internet trading platform to be used (or even if indeed a trading platform is the answer to the perceived digital divide). These characteristics also need to be assessed against the resources available to the consortium undertaking the initiative. InTwinTowns.com, the support of the general community for the portal and REM was not tested. It was therefore inconclusive as to whether the urban culture of the region (characterised by the lack of strong community and business ties within the region) and the proximity of competitors outside the regional boundaries would have been an impediment to the buy-local online campaign that the REM set out to promote. It was however, an issue worth investigating in the two trading platforms to be studied in regional WA.

While it was certainly not expected that the communications infrastructure would be an impediment in a metropolitan area, it appeared that many parts of Towns 1 and 2 (especially the industrial areas and business parks) were in urban broadband black spots and that fact should have been considered when the design of the REM and portal were planned.

> "It's very slow although we've got broadband here & this was right up to last week. I don't know if it's the sheer amount of information on it" (P7R1).

Another finding from the TwinTowns.com study was that development of a government-supported collaborative regional Internet trading platform for SMEs is a complex phenomenon and when combined with a regional portal, should be developed in phases. This finding is supported by a study of the collaborative development of a regional portal for the tourism industry in Victoria (Braun, 2004), which although more focused, still encountered a number of problems. In TwinTowns.com, the launching of the community portal with the business directory could have been the first offering to test the market and plans could have been altered if the response was not as expected or the environment changed.

> *"In my opinion the REM should only have been a method of people advertising their business. We should be able to go in there, check on their name & go to them directly to get a quote. Not go through this middleman who grabs it then on-sends it. That was causing the problem"* (P8R1).

Although TwinTowns.com was planned at the height of the dot.com boom, the 'digital shakeout' occurred in mid 2001, which was not too late for project plans to be altered, especially if the project had progressed in phases.

Many of TwinTowns.com's problems can be ascribed to poor project management. However, one of the underlying causes that led to poor management decisions was the need to generate income and make the portal/REM self sustainable in the short term. In TwinTowns.com this was due to the original expectations of external funding. There appears to be a fundamental conflict between the motives behind government-funded SME e-commerce collaborative projects like TwinTowns.com and the public funding paradigm of short-term self sustainability of the project/initiative/innovation under programmes like ITOL. One would argue that the self sustainability should not be of the initiative or innovation or technology but of the experience and knowledge gained by regional SMEs (and general community if the trading platform is part of a community portal) that would sustain them in the e-environment. In TwinTowns.com, there was no new knowledge or experience that SMEs and the community had gained from the project. Its lack of focus and endeavours towards a self sustainable income generating trading platform led to the demise of the entire project before any e-commerce training, consulting or competence building could be engendered. There was however, some knowledge gained by the LG 1 economic development staff.

Communication, Feedback and Promotion

The findings from the empirical data from TwinTowns.com also revealed the importance of communication with and feedback to the existing participants as well as the promotion of the REM and portal within and outside the region. SMEs which had not received any RFQs would have been pacified with regular feedback about the progress of the trading platform or statistics like number of RFQs issued, which industries or business types received RFQs, hits to TwinTowns.com or those redirected from the portal to their own websites. Some SMEs indicated they would have been interested about upcoming events in the region that could have an impact on the business community (like new local government developments) and others felt that even news of problems and delays would have been *"better than this dumb silence"* (P2R1).

Thus although projects like TwinTowns.com are government-funded initiatives that involve smaller businesses and relatively lower financial outlays by participants, customer relationship management and making the portal or REM 'sticky' still remains an important issue. It is not enough to attract participants; they need to be kept interested so that they return to the portal/REM.

Action Research and Stakeholder Conflict in Public Funded Collaborative Regional Development Initiatives

A final theme that emerged from the study of TwinTowns.com concerns the role of the action researcher when working in complex collaborative regional development initiatives. Johnsen and Normann (2004) conclude that in such a context, the role of the action researcher is set to be a collaborator in a context of power play and the ultimate stakeholders must be defined as the citizens in that region. They opine that strategic power play by stakeholders represents a clear threat to the 'soft approach' of collaboration, reflectivity and democratic dialogue that action research represents. As such, in order to produce reliable and socially robust knowledge, the action researcher must sometimes be able to withdraw from the practice field and be 'protected' by the academic community to be able to be a critical voice in the public deliberation.

In cases like TwinTowns.com, the ability of the researcher to adopt a non-partisan approach is hampered when the funding of the research is dependent on the consortium of stakeholders themselves and the academic institution of the researcher is interested in maintaining an on-going collaborative partnership with the stakeholder groups in other projects. There is therefore a need for a clear understanding upfront by all parties about the role of the researcher. However, given the public funding paradigm of this type of research and the pressure on Australian universities to obtain industry-linkage grants, there may be temptation to a) succumb to stakeholder-controlled research b) be deliberately nebulous about the role of research when applying for the grant and c) suppress a non-partisan voice even in times of conflict. This implies the need for fully government-funded research of public-funded collaborative regional development initiatives. Action research could be conducted in such projects if the research is made part of the condition of funding for the initiative. Although it may not guarantee absence of conflict, the action researcher in such a case would be able to maintain a non-partisan voice in the interest of the citizens of the region who are the ultimate beneficiaries of the initiative.

5.7 SUMMARY - SUCCESS AND BENEFITS OF THE TRADING PLATFORM IN TWINTOWNS.COM

The preceding sections examined and analysed the results of the participant observation and in-depth case study of TwinTowns.com from the owner, participant, technology and environmental (or external) contexts. The constructs from each of these contexts were examined empirically to determine the effect they had on the success or failure of TwinTowns.com. The results support and provide an understanding of the outcome of the application of the metrics in the Trading Platform Success Model (figure 3.3 and tables 3.3 and 3.4) to the TwinTowns.com trading platform and portal which are reported in the next section, i.e. the content in the CCP evaluation approach adopted in this research. Given that TwinTowns.com did not progress into a full working model, it was only possible to apply some of the metrics in this case.

5.7.1 Owners' Costs

Apart from the underestimations of the costs of funding TwinTowns.com, no data was available on existing costs of purchasing within LG 1, LG 2 and ECU and no effort was made to collect this data. Although the success of TwinTowns.com eventually hinged on B2G commerce, there appears to have been no consideration by the towns of their own internal costs and benefits of procuring through the REM. For example, by not integrating the REM system with the e-procurement systems of the towns, they were running two separate systems for their procurement needs, which could have impacted on efficiency. Although the REM was to be used for the discretionary purchasing of the local governments, any efficiency savings to them were not factored into the return on investment of the REM, despite claiming that one of the benefits was the "time and efficiency savings in the process of discretionary purchasing". There was thus no base line data against which to measure the purported perceived gains if they eventuated. As at April 2004, operating costs for twinTowns.com stood at AU$4000 per month (by this time there was only one staff and only the REM was focused on).

Studies on initiatives to encourage SME uptake of e-commerce point to training and consultancy as key issues (Commission of the European Communities, 2004). In Finland, which has a 90 percent web access rate for SMEs, the eASKEL programme (E-Business Policy Group, 2002) involves private consultants analysing and developing appropriate tailor-made action e-business plans for each of the participating SMEs. In Singapore, the LETAS scheme provides assistance to SMEs for up to 50 percent of the costs of engaging external experts for short-term assignments to assist them on their e-commerce journey (http://www.spring.gov.sg/portal/products/assist/edf/letas.html). These moves derive from the belief that SMEs are not homogenous and require one-on-one advice to best leverage the new systems for their businesses. In TwinTowns.com, although training costs were factored into the financial plan, they were for training on REM use, thus a purely techno-centric view. Authors like Taylor and Murphy (2004) conclude that the take up of e-business by SMEs needs to be viewed as a means to an end and not an end in itself and governments need a realistic view of how SMEs operate. Therefore costs have to be included for provision of help/consultancy to enable SMEs to understand how each of their businesses can benefit from the online environment.

In TwinTowns.com, evaluation of costs and benefits was not thought through properly. The Trading Platform Success Model (figure 3.3) and the accompanying tables of costs and success metrics (tables 3.3 and 3.4) could help identify possible costs and benefits for all stakeholders in such initiatives. In the case of TwinTowns.com, this lack of proper evaluation could be symptomatic of socio-politically motivated adopters of IOIS who are unlikely to perform systematic evaluations of the IOIS (Rahim et al., 2002) or of "the public funding paradigm that favours relatively quick results and easily measured outputs" in Australia (Otis & Johanson, 2004). However, the lack of proper cost-benefit analyses in projects like TwinTowns.com is not surprising given that even major public e-procurement initiatives in Australia (and in Europe) are "implemented in the absence of adequate baseline information for assessing their associated cost/benefit movements" (Tonkin, 2003).

5.7.2 SME Participants' Costs

Five SMEs interviewed in the TwinsTown.com case had paid participation fees of between AU$149 and AU$199 (the lower fees were discounted in 2004 to attract more participants), while four participated without any joining fees. No other costs were associated with participating in the REM as the SMEs interviewed already had Internet connections and some, their own web pages. The SMEs felt that the cost of participation was not prohibitive "*as long as there was some benefit, even if it was just another form of advertising*". However, because the portal and REM were not marketed and publicised and as there was no feedback from the REM/portal owners about how the project was progressing, those that paid felt it was a waste of money. One SME stated "*It's not sour grapes, but if I've paid and not received a quote....Right now you can't even tell if there are any quotes being issued at all. It's OK if the thing is running and I'm paying for a presence even if I don't get any business in the short term, but I need to know that it's running*" (P1R1).

One SME who declined to participate in the interview but agreed to allow his comments over the telephone to be used in the study commented *"I've paid AU$700 for two of my companies to be listed* [this SME paid for flyer pages as well] *but have not seen anything advertising [TwinTowns.com]. It's been a waste of time and my money. It may not seem like much but to a small business this could be the whole of the year's advertising budget"* (SME in the furnishing business).

Thus the SMEs in TwinTowns.com were willing to pay up to AU$200 each even if they did not get any immediate economic benefits (in the form of quotes or business) provided they knew that the project was progressing. However, a few commented that even if the REM was running properly, they would need to review their participation if they did not receive any quotes or business within a year of joining.

5.7.3 Content Quality, Trading Platform System Quality and Service/Value Added Quality

The quality of content, system, value-added and service offerings were determined based on the researcher's own observations and the interview responses of owners and SMEs.

Content Quality

Given the simplicity of the system, content quality was only assessed using the following metrics: currency, accuracy, relevance, timeliness and security.

In a purely online environment, content quality is important because it is the first encounter of a user with the owner of the website. In TwinTowns.com, because the thin resources were used to maintain both the content on the general portal and trading platform, the information was out of date, not accurate, comprehensive, complete or totally relevant. The researcher tried e-mailing some of the REM participants with the e-mail address provided on the REM listing but the e-mail address was wrong. This was also a problem encountered by researchers in the Fisher and Craig (2004) study. In TwinTowns.com, there were test companies on the live system and these shortcomings were not lost on the SMEs. The following comments were responses from SMEs on their view of content quality.

Table 5.7 Interviewees' Opinions of Content Quality in TwinTowns.com

Interviewee	Comment
P1R1	You go to wineries & there's nothing there except every page you're bringing up is telling you how much it will cost you to join...they're not doing themselves any justice because users will be switched off....It's fairly obvious to me that it's not finished & appears unprofessional....
P2R1	Well, it doesn't really work at the moment so you can't really comment can you?
P3R1	Don't know
P6R1	No one appears to have maintained the data
Economic Development manager, LG 1	Not enough content. Not enough businesses listed. Need to be more....a way of showing its full, Needs to be more detailed
Project manager, TwinTowns.com	It would be good to have other content but it's cost again, the resources....who's going to generate the content? What's going to be the source for it? Who's going to pay for it

Of the owners interviewed, most of the NFPO board members commented that they were not the best people to comment as they did not have hands-on interaction with the website. According to the SMEs who had used the system to retrieve RFQs, the quality of the content presentation was also less than satisfactory, given the issues they had with the design vis-à-vis the connection speeds. Security, privacy and authenticity of content were not fully tested but most of the SMEs took it for granted that these would be addressed by the owners. One SME involved in the provision of IT services had this comment:

"There were some security issues there that we identified....you've registered & you don't know what stage you're at; you come out & you're still logged in" (P1R1).

However, it is pertinent to note that this SME was trying to push its IT consultancy services which included auditing existing IT implementations and contracts.

Trading Platform System Quality

Metrics used to determine the system quality are: reliability of software/network; ease of use; online response time and page loading speed; visual appearance; convenience of accessibility and market reach.

Although the researcher was provided with two passwords to test the technical aspects of the system and view website statistics, the passwords were not used to test the REM or portal as the testing domain was on the live system (not a separate domain but a few test customers listed together with normal participants). The researcher's suggestion that there should be three separate versions of the system (development, testing and live) was not acted upon because of lack of resources.

In TwinTowns.com, although some SMEs perceived that the system was easy to use, those who had actually accessed the REM to retrieve or respond to RFQs encountered technical problems, to the extent that two ignored any further RFQs issued to them and did not visit the portal anymore. Again, the owner representatives did not have much knowledge about the system and assumed in late 2003 that it was sound enough to be aggressively marketed. Some were surprised when informed during the interviews that there were still issues with the technology and that there were test companies on the live system. When told that the SME in IT services had commented about this, the response was that it would perhaps be better not to target such sophisticated users in future. Of the owner representatives who had an intimate knowledge of the system, the following responses were elicited about system quality:

"Supposed to be business grade, supposed to be working, reliable but people are having problems with certain things....things not displayed, server errors....whatever....that can't be good" (Economic Development manager, LG 1).

"But the service delivery of the thing.....the availability due to server being down, internet connection not being the right type, browser not being the right type, impact on the ability to provide the end user with a quality service...." (Project manager TwinTowns.com)

Flexibility/adaptability of the system and the ability to integrate it with the systems of SMEs was not an issue for the SMEs. Some SMEs felt that it would be good if the details of issuers of RFQs could be saved in a file of prospective customers but they did not see any advantage of integrating it with their back office systems. Two SMEs thought it should have been only an online local directory with the ability to access participants' websites to view their offerings and perhaps send them an e-mail, lending credence to a phased or staged development and also to the findings of Fong et al. (1998) that successful early e-marketplaces in the agricultural sector were successful because they "fulfilled a strong genuine existing need regardless of any new facilities proffered". The inability to integrate the REM system with that of the purchasing systems of the local governments was however, one of the stumbling blocks to their greater usage of the REM.

Market reach of the REM was something that all participants agreed was not satisfactory because of the almost non-existent promotion or advertising. One SME and one owner representative felt that there was an actual flaw in the regional concept itself given the locality of the region and existing intra-area buyer/supplier relationships of the SMEs. They maintained that the concept would have had a better chance of success if the entire Perth metropolitan region was considered the marketplace.

Service/Value Added Quality

Although there were no value-added facilities like logistics and financing for participants of TwinTowns.com, service quality can still be measured in terms of the effort to provide trust; site intelligence; feedback mechanisms; relevant search facilities; calculators; tracking capabilities; helpdesk, set-up help, advice (listings of frequently asked questions [FAQs]); account maintenance and training (in conversion to e-business and for system use). None of these were available to the participants in TwinTowns.com and the absence of technical support and feedback was a common grouse of SMEs interviewed.

Thus in TwinTowns.com, the quality of content, the trading platform system and value-added services was unsatisfactory.

5.7.4 Use, User Satisfaction and Net Benefits

The SME participants interviewed in TwinTowns.com were not at all satisfied with the REM system. In order to assess the use the net benefits of the TwinTowns.com REM (and portal as that would indicate the potential for B2C commerce and for advertising value), the following statistics were obtained in addition to participants' views.

Table 5.8 Selected Statistics for TwinTowns.com as at April 2004

Item	Statistics
Businesses listed on Portal	Approx. 1000 of which 219 had REM links but only 157 were paying participants
Community groups listed	Total not available but 35 had web pages
Government Listings	Not Available
Hits to the portal	Monthly Average 500
Requests for Quotes via REM	Monthly Average of 11 (based on 2 months activity before operations ceased)
Operating costs	AU$4000 per month (by this time there was only one staff and only the REM was focused on).
Direct Income	AU$600 per month from participation fees
Evidence of online networks and participation in them	NIL

These statistics show that the 157 paying participants each paying AU$199 fell short of the initial projections. The monthly direct income of AU$600 was insufficient to cover monthly operating costs (comprising only salaries at this stage) and the mere 500 visits to the portal per month were unable to convince potential advertisers of the value of sponsoring advertising banners on the website. There was no evidence of online networks on the portal which could have facilitated knowledge building and sharing among SMEs or the general community.

All the 11 RFQs had been issued by LG 1 staff at the coaxing of the economic development manager of LG 1 and the former project manger of twinTowns.com. In the interview with the economic development manager, he indicated that 4 to 6 requests had been put through his department (each request generated individual RFQs to 3 suppliers). The purchasing team leader of LG 1 indicated that all but one of the RFQs sent via the REM were eventually unsuccessful in winning the tender. Some RFQs did not receive any response from participants and some responses did not comply with either the closing date or the specifications. The majority of SMEs had no intentions of using the REM to purchase as they had existing supplier-relationships. None of them accessed the portal any more except to prepare for the interview.

According to Bakos (1991), e-marketplaces are socially desirable when net welfare gains are greater than development and operating costs. This means that each stakeholder's view of welfare gains or benefits would have to be determined in order to arrive at the net welfare gains or benefits. None of the SMEs interviewed saw any benefit from their participation in TwinTowns.com even though half of them had paid nothing to participate. The only SME which had any business from the project was confident that he would have got it even without the presence of the REM. Of the owners interviewed only the CEO of LG 1 felt that there were any actual benefits but these were in the form of the knowledge that his staff had gained (the economic development manager and officer involved in the development of TwinTowns.com). However at a cost of AU$360,000, that gain may not be considered greater than the development and operating costs, especially as there was no gain to the intended targets of the initiative, the SMEs.

5.7.5 Success of TwinTowns.com

Application of the Trading Success Platform Model (figure 3.3) to the empirical data collected from TwinTowns.com indicates that the initiative was not a success. Owners and SME participants were also asked for their opinion on the success of TwinTowns.com (all research participants except two SMEs were interviewed before the decision was made to cease operations).

Owners' View of Success.

The owner representatives were asked if they thought the TwinTowns.com REM was successful.

Table 5.9 Owners' Opinions on the Success of the TwinTowns.com REM

Position	Comment
Chairman of Business Association Town 2 and NFPO Board Member	No it hasn't, because it hasn't achieved its primary objective
Purchasing Team leader LG 1	No. It's lagging....Relying on the [town] for it is not necessarily the way to go because the vast majority of our spend is on contracts and our discretionary purchases make up a very small portion of our spend
CEO of LG 1 and Chairman, NFPO	The jury is out on that. We need to get some more money to adequately market, adequately support the technology.... If we had $100K to $200K, we could adequately do it. The training, the education, a lot of things we need to do. Community engagement would help make it more successful but....My backers/shareholders [the local governments] won't put any more money into it unless it is proven over the next 2 months
Representative of Business Association Town 1 and NFPO Board member	Well, it's never been used by the main players & when it gets used by them you can judge whether it is successful

These responses were obtained from interviews in February and March 2004. By April 2004 the marketing manager reported that it was not possible to obtain 2 sales per day given that she was expected to handle administration and maintenance of the REM and portal as well. The Board resolved to change her terms of employment from a salaried to a commission-only basis and she resigned. A move was then made to suspend operations of TwinTowns.com and it was officially wound up in October, 2004.

Owners were asked how they thought the TwinTowns.com REM could have been more successful and the LG 1 representatives felt that better funding would have helped. The former project manager felt that a strong board was needed with people who had the ability to drive the project operationally. The LG 2 representatives were sceptical that more funding would guarantee success as they felt that there were fundamental flaws with the project. The purchasing staff of the local governments felt it could be more successful if a critical mass of suppliers were recruited and they purchased from each other on the REM. The business association representatives felt that it would be more successful if the major purchasers (the local governments) used it to procure.

SME Participants' Views of Success

Of the nine SME participants interviewed in TwinTowns.com, only one had any business via the trading platform (P4R1). This SME had one RFQ from one of the local government departments. The SME eventually became a supplier to the department concerned but all subsequent dealings were conducted outside the REM. None of the SMEs saw any real benefits in terms of cost savings. Four SMEs felt that the networking via the sundowners arranged by the marketing manager in early 2004 was a benefit as it gave them exposure to other businesses in the region but one (P5R1) felt that it would be beneficial only if it was targeted to the group of people in his industry. However, these SMEs felt that online networks would not be of interest to them as they did not have the time and were physically close enough for telephone or face-to-face contact to be a more viable option of communication after initial contact.

In response to the question of whether the TwinTowns.com REM was successful, SME participants' comments were as follows:

Table 5.10 SME Participants' Views of the Success of the TwinTowns.com REM

Participant	Comments	Date of Interview
P1R1	Success? No, I wouldn't say so.	23/02/2004
P2R1	No, not at all	25/02/2004
P3R1	No.	04/03/2004
P4R1	No, I don't think so	15/03/2004
P5R1	Currently, no. I'm not negative but I think currently no.	17/03/2004
P6R1	No.	18/03/2004
P7R1	No	05/04/2004
P8R1	It speaks for itself	11/08/2004
P9R1	No	11/08/2004

The SMEs felt that the REM could be improved with a technically sound product, better marketing and promotion, feedback and bulletin boards, communications from the owners, mandated use by the purchasing departments of the local governments, success stories and statistics of RFQs issued via the REM and successful tenders won.

Conclusion

The empirical evidence from both trading platform statistics and interview responses indicate that according to the Trading Platform Success Model (figure 3.3) the TwinTowns.com REM was not successful. There was no net welfare gain or net benefits when all perspectives or contexts were considered. There were however, small pockets of strategic or community gains. The CEO of LG 1 claimed that although the project failed, the actual benefits from the project were the knowledge that his staff obtained (the economic development manager and officer) and it was the first time that local stakeholders had attempted to collaborate.

Although at first glance many of the issues that led to the failure of the platform involved inadequate resources, a closer analysis revealed that the institutional factors that influenced the decision to undertake the initiative, form the consortium and run the project were not conducive to success. In addition, the culture and profile of the region were not properly considered and the lack of openness within the consortium itself was detrimental to the project.

The results from TwinTowns.com revise the conceptual framework of the study, as follows:

Table 5.11 Significance of the Constructs in the Conceptual Framework of the Study in Terms of TwinTowns.com

Context	Construct	Importance
Market-Maker (Owner)	Ownership structure and Governance	Critical
	Motivation/focus	High
	Competencies (IS/project management skills)	High
	Financial resources	High
	Trust	Critical
	Strategic partnering	High
Technology (Trading Platform)	Perceived benefits, relative advantage and Usefulness	High
	Critical mass/liquidity	High
	Value-added services/Strategic partnering (e.g. logistics, financial)	Low
	REM training and technical support	High
	Compatibility (with users' systems)	Low
	Trust	Critical
	REM development and timing of features offered	High
	Perceived ease of use	High
	Good marketing plan	High
Organisational (SME participant)	Top management commitment/innovativeness	Inconclusive
	Internal IT/IS/e-business (readiness).	Context dependent
	Size of firm	Context dependent
Environmental (External)	Regional SME profile. Local consumer needs and behaviour. Regional profile	Critical
	Government support and incentives	High
	Normative, coercive and mimetic pressure/existing trading relationships	High

Although there may also be relationships and dependencies between the constructs from the various contexts, these could not be explored in the case of TwinTowns.com given its early demise.

It is evident from the TwinTowns.com case that AU$360,000 is not sufficient to guarantee success of a horizontal non function specific government-sponsored regional Internet community cum trading platform for SMEs in the short term. This is especially so if success is measured in terms of self sustainability of the platform itself and in terms of increasing SME uptake of e-commerce. It would thus be more meaningful for such initiatives to be viewed as long term regional economic development initiatives and to be planned and funded as such.

CHAPTER 6

REGWA.NET: FINDINGS AND ANALYSIS

6.1 INTRODUCTION

This chapter deals with an analysis of the findings from the mini case study of RegWa.net. The chapter begins with a discussion of the findings from the owner context. Secondary data collected from the portal website and from published sources was first used to gain as much background knowledge as possible about RegWa.net prior to the face-to-face interviews with owner representatives. In 2003 it was observed on the Internet that the RegWa.net portal was a regional community portal that incorporated a regional e-marketplace (REM) through which RFQs could be issued to local sellers, much like TwinTowns.com, but better populated and organised. Access to the REM page was via a link on the regional portal. In 2004, any reference (and link) to a REM was removed from the portal page. To send RFQs via the portal, one had to click on the category of business and a list of businesses would appear. Businesses which were 'authorised' to receive RFQs had an identifying icon and check-box next to their listing. The removal of the REM page and reference to it was noted as an item of interest to be discussed with the RegWa.net owners.

The questions in the owner interviews in RegWa.net were similar to that posed to the owners of TwinTowns.com. However, the new themes (and variations to existing themes in the conceptual frameworks) that emerged from the study of TwinTowns.com and specific observations from the Internet and published sources were explored in the study of RegWa.net. This approach was also used for the SME interviews with RegWa.net participants. New themes (or variations to existing themes) that emerged from any of the interviews during the study of RegWa.net were also incorporated into subsequent interviews (and explored) in the study. They were also used to revisit and re-examine data collected from TwinTowns.com in line with the structured case methodology (Carroll & Swatman, 2000).

Interviews with owner representatives of RegWa.net were conducted in August 2004. During the interviews it transpired that the portal was undergoing a change of platform design with a new look and more offerings planned for November that year. As such, the interviews with SMEs in RegWa.net were conducted in two phases; 6 face-to-face interviews were conducted in November 2004, while 14 telephone interviews were conducted in May/June 2005. This was to enable a reasonable time to elapse after the introduction of the new services/portal upgrade so that their impact could also be assessed during the interviews. Follow up with the owner representatives of RegWa.net was conducted by telephone and e-mail.

For purposes of consistency and comparison, the format used to present and discuss the findings from the interviews in TwinTowns.com will be maintained in this chapter.

6.2   OWNER CONTEXT

RegWa.net was originally owned by the Chamber of Commerce (CoC) of the largest town in the region. It was successful in obtaining state and federal government funding totalling AU$242,000 for the project. The CoC had gathered together a group of about 60 people from the region who were interested in technology and in using it as a regional development tool. These people comprised software developers, ISPs, representatives from the business centres and members of the general community. From that, a small management committee was formed to manage the portal. In 2000, the region (which was a marginal electorate held by the then governing state Liberal party) was promised AU$5.5 million for regional 'e-development' if the opposition was elected. The state Labour party subsequently came into power and made good on its pre-election promises to the region. Of the AU$5.5 million, AU$2.2 million was to be used for e-commerce training and a regional Internet portal. The funds were to be administered by the regional development corporation. RegWa.net was identified as the ideal vehicle through which to use the AU$2.2 million. Ownership of the RegWa.net portal was subsequently transferred in June 2003 to a non-profit organisation (Connect RegWa) owned by the regional development corporation.

6.2.1   Description of Interview Participants

Table 6.1 below provides a list of the owner representatives of RegWa.net who were interviewed and gives their position in the organisations they represented.

Table 6.1 Profile of the 'Owner' Interview Participants in RegWa.net

Position	Organisation
E-Commerce Manager	Connect RegWa
Portal Administrator	Connect RegWa
Advisory Board Member (Also original project manager of TwinTowns.com)	Connect RegWa & CEO of CoC of largest town (Previous owners).
E-Business Advisor	Connect RegWa

The owner representatives were interviewed at their premises, which was located just off the main street in the largest town in the region (RegWa.net had previously operated from the offices of the CoC). At the time of the interviews, Connect RegWa had 6 staff and its premises, although not ostentatious, had a more professional look than the TwinTowns.com office. Brochures were available advertising the services offered by Connect RegWa and the features of RegWa.net. The back office was not in view of visitors and staff were able to immediately provide portal statistics and other information.

6.2.2 Motivation

According to the interview responses, RegWa.net started out with a purely business focus. There was fear that income from the region was being lost 'outside' to e-tailers like Amazon.com because local businesses were not equipped to compete online. The group of interested local parties spearheaded by the local CoC came together to propose solutions and one idea was to create a web site with an online local directory so that people in the region could shop online locally. A small grant of AU$6,000 was obtained from the regional development corporation and the current portal administrator of RegWa.net (who is a marketing graduate) was employed 3 days a week to conduct a market study of the viability of the idea. Local governments, chambers of commerce, business enterprise centres, tourist bureaus, large buyers etc. in the region (that would be the mainstay of the site) were approached and supported the idea in principle. Further funding of AU$20,000 was obtained from the WA state government (Office of Information and Communications through the Department of Commerce and Trade) to determine site and user specifications and market the idea.

There were no software development cots of the initial portal and business directory as it was developed by a local developer who contributed to the project by licensing the software to RegWa.net for AU$1. The first version of the web site was a simple business/community/government directory which nevertheless had a lot of community input and therefore support. In the opinion of the e-commerce manager of Connect RegWa, the community part of the portal was included to attract greater funding, which subsequently came from ITOL and state government grants. The additional funding enabled the website to be upgraded to a regional community portal cum regional e-marketplace and allowed the employment of a part-time project coordinator, a full-time trainee for data input and administration, and a sales coordinator. The additional funding was also used for marketing and promotion, the purchase of a server and partly for further IT training of local TAFE (Technical and Further Education) college students. Essentially, the motives in RegWa.net and TwinTowns.com were similar.

However, the difference between RegWa.net and TwinTowns.com in terms of motive was that all stakeholders/owners had a common vision for the portal and how it would progress throughout the life of the project. Despite this however, it became obvious after four years of operation that the 'buy local' focus and REM were not going to sustain the portal. According to the e-commerce manager of Connect RegWa:

"[According to purchasing officers of regional major buyers] 99% of their purchases are locked in to contracts, so they don't issue quotes. They all agree in principle with the concept & they all support the buy local idea...but most of them don't have small purchasing power any more".

When Connect RegWa assumed ownership of RegWa.net, the focus shifted to include using the portal to sell the region online to buyers outside the region, a move supported by all stakeholders. RegWa.net now regards its target market as those who will be purchasing from the region via the portal, not those who will be selling on the portal. The portal now caters for both virtual and hybrid 'click and mortar' (Steinfield, Bouwman & Adelaar, 2002; Steinfield et al., 1999a) sales approaches. The community and local content on the portal has increased with competitions for visitors to the site and specials offered in niche areas like accommodation, tourism and agriculture, for which the area is renowned. In addition, each town in the region has its own version or 'view' of the portal under the name of the town. Visitors can go to the main portal (RegWa.net) or into a town version of the portal (MyTown1, MyTown2 etc.). The reason for this move was that research undertaken by the e-Commerce manager of Connect RegWa showed that the smaller the 'catchment area' of a community portal, the greater the usage of the portal.

By increasing buyer traffic and stickiness of the portal, the owners of RegWa.net hope to make it an attractive place for sellers to list and be able to sell online. In order to facilitate smaller SMEs to sell online, shopping cart facilities are being offered by RegWa.net to suppliers for a flat fee of AU$250 per annum (this has been waived for the first year for smaller SMEs) and a transaction fee that is only a very small percentage of each online sale. Through the stronger buyer-focus now, the e-commerce uptake by SMEs is also being fostered. The e-commerce and community sides of RegWa.net are now being inextricably inter-twined with B2C business being the driving force for e-commerce on the portal. This is why the separate REM page was removed and replaced in late 2004 with a 'shopping' page (with shopping carts) organised by categories of goods or services (although the ability to search the directory and issue RFQs has been retained).

6.2.3 Ownership Structure and Governance

According to Standing et al. (2005) shared ownership structures may be seen as more neutral and hence fairer compared with a solely owned or private e-marketplace. While RegWa.net was owned by the CoC of the largest town, because of the wide regional stakeholder input into the planning, design and management of the project, it was seen as a 'grass-roots' or 'bottom-up' project, developed and managed by the people themselves. Although RegWa.net had received less funding than TwinTowns.com at the time the REM was launched, the broad consultative approach and management style produced technology champions within the community.

> *"Because of the people that were involved, quite high profile, local key people, a lot of people really supported the initiative really thinking about how it was going to help their businesses"* (E-Commerce Manager, Connect RegWa).

Moreover, the CoC was viewed as a truly neutral body as it was not expected to be a major buyer or seller on the portal. Nevertheless, when RegWa.net was identified as the vehicle through which the additional AU$2.2 million funding would be expended, it was perceived that the ownership of RegWa.net was more suitably held by a party that was not associated with any particular town in the region. In June 2003, RegWa.net was purchased by Connect RegWa from the CoC. Despite the change in ownership, the CoC maintains its interest in RegWa.net by having its representatives on the Connect RegWa advisory board. The owner representatives interviewed were of the opinion that SMEs were happy with the governance of RegWa.net and general community users were also satisfied due to the shift in focus to B2C.

While neutrality of e-marketplaces may preclude or reduce bias, there are downsides to this form of ownership structure in terms of revenue generation. In order to survive the e-marketplace shakeout early this century, third party neutral B2B exchanges have had to become niche service operators, whose exchanges deal only marginally with pure transactions and who now act as technology outsourcers and consultants for supply chain activities within specific vertical industries. Nevertheless, these neutrally-owned hubs do not perform as well as large privately-owned exchanges in generating turnover (Ordanini, Micelli & Di Maria, 2004). This has serious implications for government-sponsored horizontal regional Internet trading platforms for SMEs like RegWa.net. It is expected to be a self sustaining model in the short term and is dependent on limited public funds to carry out what is essentially a socio-economic function. Until the socio-economic motives of improving SME uptake of e-commerce and raising e-commerce awareness in the region are met, there is a need for governments to continue to be financial partners or financial owners of such projects.

6.2.4 Financial Resources

Ordanini et al. (2004) found that compared to large privately-owned e-marketplaces, neutral niche operators of commercial e-marketplaces exhibit a more fragile financial structure, which is largely based on funds by venture capitalists and the management itself. Alibaba.com a large many-to-many commercial multi-industry horizontal e-marketplace for SMEs which is perceived to be 'successful' (Markus et al., 2002; Ming Zeng, 2001), has not only required huge venture capital financing but needs to constantly look for new sources of revenue in order to survive (Wharton School of the University of Pennsylvania, 2005). While reports of the success of Alibaba.com (in both academic and business sources) are based on the number of participants and transactions, there is little evidence of actual revenue or profit of the e-marketplace. Neither is there evidence of the financial performance of government-supported regional e-marketplaces for SMEs like emb.net, the Korean Marketplace, Nextr@de of Japan, Taiwantrade and Thailand.com.

In RegWa.net, although it appeared that the funding of AU$242,000 from external sources, plus membership fees, listing fees and advertising revenue prior to 2003 enabled the portal and REM to survive, there were a lot of hidden costs involved in the project.

Table 6.2 Evidence of Hidden Costs in RegWa.net

Participant	Comments
Representative of the technical developer of RegWa.net who was also interviewed as a SME participant	Yes [the REM] was paid for....it definitely wasn't enough in the end for what [the portal] is because there were plenty of 'extra hours' and stuff put into it and it got rather painful
Portal Administrator	So I was getting paid for 15 hours but was doing 40 with the baby in the office....put it this way, if I hadn't done what I did, we wouldn't be here....it would have fallen because the portal was very much a volunteer-based thing and without that we wouldn't be here
E-commerce manager	It really wasn't sustainable. We were in borrowed offices, we weren't paying any rent, there were no overheads, and the chamber gave stationery to us....It also suffered trying to be all things to all people

It was only with the additional AU$2.2 million funding, that RegWa.net was able to really address the building of e-competencies of both SMEs and the general public, the *raison d'être* behind government-supported regional Internet community cum business portals like the ones in this study. The portal is now able to offer free one-on-one e-business advice for SMEs, seniors' IT training and web pages for community groups.

The findings from the study of RegWa.net (as with that from TwinTowns.com) show that financial resources in these projects are not just required for the development of the technology and marketing/promotion. Funding is also necessary for the ongoing maintenance and provision of services to not only retain the interest of both the business and general public but to also provide them with the competencies that will help sustain them in the digital world. This confirms the findings of the McGrath and More study (2002).

6.2.5   Technical Resources

In RegWA.net, the portal and REM software were developed by a third party (as in TwinTowns.com). However, the owners of the software development company (which also hosted the RegWa.net portal on its server without any cost for two years), were also on the management committee of RegWa.net when it was first established. The company worked closely with the other members of the committee which included the current portal administrator and e-business advisor who were either alternately employed part-time on RegWa.net or volunteered their services for free between 2000 and 2003. The e-business advisor started in television, had done website and graphic design and had lectured at TAFE in these subjects. The portal administrator was a marketing graduate who had done web programming and had created an intranet for a new business. Together they managed the project prior to 2003 and as there were commission-only sales people to do the marketing, and a trainee to do data entry and administration during the time the REM was being developed and marketed, they were able to devote their time exclusively to technical issues and project management.

Given the level of stakeholder involvement, the support of influential technology champions from the community, the general support and volunteerism from the region's citizens and the close working relationships between all parties, the project was satisfactorily managed within the constraints of the limited financial resources. This finding supports the findings of the McGrath and More study (2002) that one of the critical success factors of such collaborative projects is the importance of managing people, relationships and business processes rather than concentrating only on managing the technology. In short, good holistic project management is needed.

Nevertheless, despite managing the project satisfactorily, additional funds of AU$200,000 were still needed to update to the current version of software. At the time of the interviews there were still problems with integrating the portal database with the back office systems of RegWa.net.

6.3   THE ORGANISATIONAL (SME PARTICIPANTS') CONTEXT

This section deals with the discussion and analysis of the findings from the organisational or SME context. As in the chapter on TwinTowns.com, this section starts with a description of the SME interview participants. It then goes on to discuss some of the constructs in the SME or participant context and how they impacted on the project. SMEs' views on the costs incurred, the benefits that the REM had to offer and its ultimate success will be discussed in the final sections of the chapter.

6.3.1 Description of Interview Participants

The characteristics of SME participants from RegWa.net who were interviewed are provided in table 6.3 below. SMEs P1R2 to P6R2 were interviewed face-to-face in November 2004. The other 14 SMEs were interviewed by telephone in May/June 2005.

Table 6.3 Profile of the SME Interview Participants in RegWa.net

SME #	Position of Interviewee	Number of Employees	Turnover AU$'000 (Annual)	Buy (B) Sell (S) on 'Net?	Whose decision to join and when?	Business Description
P1R2	Owner /Director	2	150-200	B-Yes S-No	Interviewee. 2002	Computer services
P2R2	Web Developer & Marketing manager	7 staff, 4 directors	Not Available	B-seldom S-Yes*	Previous Owner. 2002	Internet Services (RegWa.net portal developer)
P3R2	Regional Manager	4	Not Available	B-No S-Yes*	Interviewee. 2004	Provision of industrial labour/personnel
P4R2	Partner, Share-holder	2	650	B-Yes S-Hybrid	Partners. 2002	Media services (including online)
P5R2	Manager	2 f/t 3 casual	Not Available	B-No S-Yes*	State marketing manager. 2004	Car & truck hire
P6R2	Owner	18 f/t	Several 000	B-Yes S-No	Interviewee. 2002	Machine Hire, Digital Copy Centre
P7R2	Owner/ Partner	2 f/t 4 p/t	Not Available	B-No S-Yes	Partners. 2004	Giftware, soap, oils
P8R2	Owner/ Partner	2	<100	B-No S-Yes	Interviewee. 2003	Lavender Farm & Lavender Products-soaps, giftware
P9R2	Owner/ Director	5	400	B-Yes S-Yes	Interviewee. 2005	Natural products, Soaps, oils
P10R2	Partner	3	400	B-Seldom S-Yes* (via own website)	Partners. 2002	Patterns, Fabrics, Threads etc. supplier
P11R2	Owner/ Partner	1	54	B-Yes S-Yes	Interviewee. 2005	Apparel/Batik Goods
P12R2	Owner/ Partner	2	<50	B-No S-Not yet	Partners. 2005	Alpaca Park, Apparel
P13R2	Owner/ Partner	12	1,500-2,000	B-Yes S-Yes (own website)	Partners. A few years ago	Lavender gardens, café, Lavender products
P14R2	Owner/ Partner	2	70	B-Yes S-No	Partners. Only a listing for a few years	Wines
P15R2	Owner/ Partner	18	Not Available	B-No S-Yes	Partners. < 1 year	Café, Hampers
P16R2	Owner/ Partner	<5	>1,000	B-Yes S-Yes*	Partners. 2004	Diving Instructors & tours
P17R2	Owner	10 (casual)	>800	B-Yes S-Yes*	Interviewee. 2001	Local Tours
P18R2	Owner	5	Not Available	B-Yes S-Yes	Interviewee. 2002	Adult Entertainment
P19R2	Partner	4	250	B-No S-Yes	Interviewee. 2005	Cheese Factory
P20R2	Owner/ Partner	9	700-1,000	B-No S-Yes*	Interviewee. 2002	Coach Charters & Tours

* Not enabled to accept online payments.

186

6.3.2 SME Owner Innovativeness

In the majority of SMEs interviewed, the owners' managed the business and it was their decision to participate on the portal. Some had provided input into the project and others were willing to provide feedback to the portal owners about improvements. Targeting these SMEs first enabled early liquidity to be built in terms of number of participants which then provided the impetus for others to join via the 'bandwagon' effect (Grewal et al., 2001).

However, now that the additional AU$2.2 million has taken the pressure off from having to make sales to survive, RegWa.net can target smaller SMEs who may not have the resources to embark on the e-commerce journey on their own.

6.3.3 E-Commerce Readiness

In RegWa.net, 18 of the SMEs interviewed already had their own web pages before joining the portal. Some were already purchasing online and a few could accept online payments. Those who did not have the ability to accept payments via their web sites accepted orders and bookings online and communicated with clients and prospective clients via e-mail. While targeting the e-commerce ready SMEs in the region to participate on RegWa.net has enabled it to build listings and liquidity, the difficulty lies in keeping them interested or improving their existing e-business skills. Horizontal and non function specific government-supported Internet trading platforms like RegWa.net have no major buyers, are under-resourced and exist to grow e-commerce capabilities for smaller SMEs and the region. Yet at the same time, they need to be self sustainable and compete with commercial portals and e-marketplaces for paying members. Thus they either need to provide superior services or find a niche to fulfil.

The one thing that RegWa.net has in its favour is the community support common in rural or regional areas for 'home-grown' efforts and the fact that the online regional directory is comprehensive. However, the directory is only one advertising avenue and in economic downturns, advertising budgets are one of the first items to be scrutinised. For the smaller SMEs especially, it may be difficult to continue paying for listings or member fees if there are no visible economic or strategic benefits or growth in competencies.

As such there is a need to revisit the whole 'self-sustainability' issue of public-funded projects like RegWa.net to determine if it obscures the ultimate objective of growing the online capabilities of the region. Such an objective would mean targeting SMEs who are not already e-commerce ready. It may well be that models like RegWa.net and TwinTowns.com are not suitable vehicles to meet such objectives under the existing funding paradigms.

6.3.4 Size of Firm

The conceptual frameworks of this study posit firm size as a construct that could have an effect on the adoption of trading by SMEs on a government-supported regional Internet platform. Research has shown that larger businesses may have the slack resources to experiment and these firms need to be targeted if there is a need to build liquidity quickly. All SMEs interviewed in RegWa.net had fewer than 20 employees and were thus small or micro businesses. The most any of them had paid to participate was AU$250 p.a. (for the e-commerce solution in 2005) and on average most had paid AU$149 for preferential listing (with e-mail and web-link) on the REM. Seven of them were small businesses of which five joined the REM of RegWa.net when it was first introduced in 2002 and continued to participate despite not seeing commensurate financial returns from their participation. However, they had no plans to cancel their participation in the near future.

With the exception of SMEs in IT (P1R2 and P4R2 who need to maintain a presence and be seen to be associated with all things IT in the region), the micro businesses were more discerning about the returns from their participation. The more they paid to participate, the greater attention they gave to monitoring the returns from participation.

> "It wouldn't pay for our cost to stay with them. From what we've been led to believe it will be about $300 to $400 per year and the turnover that we're getting through them at the moment, it wouldn't even warrant us to pay $50" (P12R2 which received free participation for the first year).

> "I guess my only concern is that I wonder if it will be there in 2 to 3 years if things change and hope that we're not left high and dry....Things like these if it does become too costly then people won't use it and it will die" (P14R2).

While the larger SMEs were more ready to respond to external or institutional pressure to participate and were willing to settle for community or strategic benefits in the shorter term, the smaller businesses needed to see quicker results for their investment. Therefore, if trading portals like RegWa.net need a longer gestation period before they can start to show economic benefits for smaller SMEs, there may be a need for these SMEs to be subsidised for longer periods.

6.4 THE TECHNOLOGY (TRADING PLATFORM) CONTEXT

The technology context in RegWa.net is examined in the light of the evolution of the portal and its offerings as follows:

- 2000 to November 2002: community portal and regional business directory (listed by categories). Businesses can have a free listing with the business name, address, telephone number, fax number and they can upload a photo/logo and have about a 300-word text for their listing; businesses pay AU$22 p.a. for live e-mail link and AU$66 p.a. for web link. (Buy local seller-focused).

- December 2002 to October 2004: The above plus REM included and AU$149 p.a. for ability to receive RFQs or for a preferred listing (shuffled up the directory when a search is done). RFQs can be received by e-mail, fax or SMS (note: the RFQ is received together with the notification). RFQ enabled business identified by checkbox against which requester can tick to select a business to send a RFQ to. (Buy local seller-focused).

- November 2004 to present: The above plus AU$250 p.a. for an e-commerce solution (Shopping cart facility) and a small percentage per transaction for use of the platform's credit card facilities. REM link/page removed and replaced with shopping page displaying the goods of businesses with the e-commerce solution. To send RFQs, visitors to the portal will now have to click on the category of business on the homepage, and if there are any REQ enabled businesses in that category, a 'form' will appear. (Buy local buyer-focused).

6.4.1 Perceived Benefits

The perceived benefits of the trading platform in RegWa.net are examined in terms of both the owners' and SME participants' views (as in TwinTowns.com.).

6.4.1.1 Owners' View of Perceived Benefits

The owners were asked what they perceived the benefits of the trading platform to be for themselves, SMEs in the region, and the region itself.

Owners' Perceived Benefits

The owners of RegWa.net perceived their benefits from the portal as the income that would sustain them financially. This would enable them to continue to move forward with their services to the less 'e-enabled' in both the business and general communities. On a personal level, it guaranteed them their jobs.

> *"It's given me a job....the way the business enterprise centre came in to the funding was that it was required of [RegWa.net] to actually use [the e-business advisor's] services.*

So we used [RegWa.net] as a basis to get that funding to support his role" (Portal Administrator).

Perceived Benefits to SMEs

For the SMEs of the region, RegWa.net owners saw the free listing on the portal as providing a web presence even for those who were not on the Internet.

"For Ma & Pa B&Bs [bed and breakfast's] where they've got the 1 room, that's often all they need. A photo of the cabin in tranquil settings & that can be enough" (E-commerce manager, Connect RegWa).

The owners felt that fee-paying SMEs would benefit in two ways. Firstly from communicating more efficiently with local customers as the level of online activity in the area increased (due to the community training and e-business advisory services offered by Connect RegWa) i.e. a new way of maintaining existing relationships. SMEs would also benefit from the new online buyer-focus marketing by RegWa.net as the current target market includes national and international buyers. For RegWa.net this would mean designing strategies to drive visitors to the portal and making sure they return (the attraction and contagion stages of Damsgaard's (2002) portal life cycle model and Zott et al.'s (2000) 'stickiness').

Perceived Regional Benefits

The regional benefits that RegWa.net owners perceived from the project were economic development and the positioning of local businesses commercially to respond to the next wave of IT or e-commerce development. Thus, the project would allow the building of sustainable knowledge and experiences in local SMEs that would enable them to successfully compete in the online environment.

However, they recognised the need for an integrated approach by *"providing information and training, the provision of the portal structure & finally helping drive infrastructure development. They need to be done together because if any of them are not then it won't work"* (Advisory Board member of Connect RegWa and CEO of the CoC).

In the case of RegWa.net, although some of the actual perceived benefits have yet to materialise, the additional funding of AU$2.2 million and the support of all the stakeholders has enabled the owners to move forward with a new focus as the 'buy local' did not deliver the promised benefits. In contrast, the continuing power struggle between the business associations and the local governments in TwinTowns.com did not allow them to move beyond the flawed 'buy local online' policy.

6.4.1.2 Participants' (SMEs') Perceived Benefits

Perceived benefits from participation in platforms like RegWa.net are linked to the motive for joining. Nearly half the SMEs interviewed in RegWa.net indicated that they initially joined the portal (and REM) to support the local initiative, as they thought it would be good for the region. They joined the REM when it was first launched (2002) and were not motivated by immediate strategic or economic gain. In contrast, the SMEs who had other motives for joining signed up in 2003 or later, when a more targeted sales approach was adopted. Three SMEs joined in 2005 when the shopping cart facilities were offered to them without the need for a participation fee (they only had to pay a small commission on each transaction). These were SMEs who offered niche products (SMEs P11R2, P12R2 and P19R2) and were considered good targets for tourism purposes. The joined because it was an opportunity to experiment with e-commerce in a supportive environment.

> *"It's a case of being a free trial and what a perfect example to actually have a go to see what happens....it's giving you the experience to know whether or not you would want to pay for something like that"* (P12R2).

Four SMEs paid for the shopping cart facility even though three (P7R2, P9R2 and P13R2) had their own shopping-cart enabled web sites and the other (P8R2) was already listed on a local 'e-bay' enabled e-marketplace. They claimed to have been impressed with the plans that were being discussed for advertising the portal and joined to determine if they were missing out on a segment of the market. They were thus motivated by perceived strategic benefits initially. Two SMEs (P14R2 and P15R2) joined the REM after having their web sites built by RegWa.net staff (one previously had just a directory listing), while SMEs P3R2 and P5R2 which were part of state and national franchises joined to raise their profile locally. SME P16R2, a business offering diving classes wanted to be part of the tourist trade generated from outside the region.

RegWa.net was therefore able to give two SMEs their first taste of an Internet presence and three the ability to accept online payments.16 SMEs indicated that they did not use the portal for purchases and three said they would if they could find things relevant to their business. Only one had issued RFQs and this was the company who had originally developed the portal. It appears to be timely that RegWa.net has shifted away from its 'buy local online' focus.

SME participants in RegWa.net which joined to support the local initiative could not perceive any immediate economic benefits from participation. However, they saw benefits in being associated with the project due to its high profile and the networking opportunities from involvement.

> "There were other people going there & I wanted to have my name there as well, as an option because of all the buzz" (P1R2).

> "Lifting our profile & networking. I lived next to [the E-commerce manager] for a while. She's fairly prominent in the community" (P3R2).

> "We wanted to be out there, to be known in the community" (P10R2).

Other SME participants in RegWa.net perceived that there would be better market reach than they could achieve on their own and signed up for the shopping cart facility even though they already had their own payment-enabled websites. The three SMEs which received the shopping cart facility free for the first year (P11R2, P12R2 and P19R2) perceived that it would be a good opportunity to experiment with e-commerce without having to commit financially to something that may not have been suitable for them. For the smaller SMEs, one-on-one consultation was needed to demonstrate how they could benefit from participation. Regardless of the type of benefit, all SMEs perceived that they would benefit somehow and this drove them to participate.

6.4.2 Value Added Services/Strategic Partnering

Unlike TwinTowns.com, the owners of RegWa.net were not constrained by major technology problems. This meant that they could invest some of their time in providing value-added services. They were however constrained by financial resources and the design of the portal/platform. The wide horizontal nature of the platform meant that it was difficult to target services like logistics and aggregation. However, one value-added service within their means was feedback. There was a monthly newsletter to participants about developments and occasional e-mails from the owners to the participants. More importantly, the wide stakeholder group meant that the relationships embedded in the local institutional networks in the region were leveraged to keep everyone abreast of project developments.

Nevertheless, it was only with the additional funding of AU$2.2 million, that the owners of RegWa.net were able to incorporate further valuable value-added services into their offerings.

> "We had stagnated. So by encompassing ourselves with [Connect RegWa], we are able to provide value-added services like the one-on-one training, training money, assisting people to get ADSL connections with the broadband ADSL register, giving community

groups free web sites, by providing community-type things like seniors' training, IT
coaching by [the e-business advisor]. If we didn't have all those outside our core
services, it wouldn't be successful" (Portal Administrator).

These value-added services (and accepting online credit card payments on behalf of smaller SMEs)
were important to the SME participants interviewed. Some SMEs also thought it would be useful if
they could be provided with data mined from the portal and platform about the demographics of
visitors and also the hits to their individual sites via the portal. According to the owners of
RegWa.net, these offerings are being considered.

In RegWa.net (as in the RETFC (Wilkins et al., 2003a; 2003b)), strategic partnering with a
technology provider meant that limited project resources could be conserved. The wide consultative
approach taken in RegWa.net meant that the ultimate stakeholders were also partners in the
initiative leading to its wide acceptance. At the time of the interviews, the owners of RegWa.net
were also in discussions with Australia Post on the possibilities of *"aggregating the spend to reduce*
distribution costs for everyone who will be involved in the portal" (E-commerce manager, Connect
RegWa).

The need for strategic partnering thus supports the findings from the e-marketplace literature
(Fairchild et al., 2004; Le, 2002; Lenz et al., 2002). Findings on the importance of value-added
services to success of e-marketplaces are mixed. Fairchild et al. (2004) did not find any support for
the importance of value-added services in creating critical mass of transactions in e-marketplaces.
However, some studies show that value-added services do have a role to play in e-marketplace
success (Ordanini, 2003). Where the e-marketplaces are targeted at SMEs, services like
personalised consultancy are important (Khalifa et al., 2003).

6.4.3   Training and Technical Support

All SMEs interviewed were satisfied with the level of training in portal use provided by the owners
of RegWa.net, although they felt it was a simple enough system. SME P14R2 which had a website
built by RegWa.net, was full of praise for the free one-on-one IT advice and coaching provided by
the e-business advisor who *"has been up here a few times working with us to help us get an Internet*
presence".

The level of technical support provided by RegWa.net was also viewed favourably by SME
participants. There appeared to be a lot of two-way communication between RegWa.net staff and
SMEs especially when problems occurred or even when the SMEs had suggestions for
improvements.

"When I buy a button or banner, it's there the next day. It looks good and I know it's going to work" (P6R2).

"I'm very pleased with the people" (P9R2).

The importance of support and training in driving perceived benefits and e-marketplace use has been discussed by Koch (2004a). Ongoing access to support services has also been identified as imperative for longer-term sustainability and ongoing improvement of government-funded online regional service initiatives (Thompson, 2005). Fisher and Craig (2005) found in their study of the failed Victorian B2B portal for SMEs that although training was provided for those who joined early, only 14 percent of businesses surveyed had availed themselves of the training. The findings supported Vidgen's (cited in Fisher & Craig, 2005) argument that it is unrealistic to expect users to attend training. However, if the system is simple to use and user instructions are clear and easy to follow, then SMEs can be asked to try it on their own first and revert back to the owners if the need arises, where upon personalised training can be conducted. This is the approach adopted in RegWa.net.

6.4.4 Trust

Trust in the system and the governance of RegWa.net was rated positively by 16 SMEs with comments ranging from *"absolutely"* to *"no issues with that"*, while one SME replied that it was not tested. Given that the RegWa.net system was simple and didn't require any integration with back office systems of SMEs, there were no issues relating to trust in the integrity or security of data. Issues with trust and governance raised by the three SMEs which did not give a positive rating were:

Table 6.4 Negative Comments by SMEs on Trust and Governance in RegWa.net

Participant	Comments
P1R2	Currently it's an ISP who's hosting it & it is a competitor that does the same thing & they have control of the information....Perhaps they can scan quotes etc...It's free hosting for the portal but if you look at it, it's not squeaky clean either
P4R2	Where we found they fell down was when a customer wanted a website, they went to see the REM people, who then referred them to another ISP who was not [local]. To me it defeats the purpose of having the REM then. The fact that he had to come and find us himself, that was a let down by the REM
P8R2	The only thing that concerns us is that they've been fairly open with some of the things and really our only concern is that just in conversation when they're talking to the 2 competitors and they might say "Oh Gee they're selling a lot of X" not meaning to; but we just have the concern because I've been quite open on a friendly level. We just have to make sure our trade secrets don't get out.

Unlike TwinTowns.com, there were no issues of trust between the owners/stakeholders or partners of RegWa.net as participants and users were considered partners and their input was used in the initial and ongoing development of the portal. The owners of RegWa.net used the trust embedded in the local business and community relationships (Steinfield & Whitten, 1999) to foster trust and therefore participation in the initiative. In the outlying towns, the local tele-centres were used to identify potential micro SMEs which would benefit from one-on-one IT advice and coaching. The researcher was also able to observe the close working relationship between Connect RegWa, the CoC, the software developer and the advisory board members during visits to the region. The importance of partner-trust and stakeholder input has been highlighted in the literature on portals (Fisher & Craig, 2005) and regional online community initiatives (Thompson, 2005).

RegWa.net had for four years been locally focused and trust between buyers and local SME sellers was not considered an issue. Although the portal is now outward looking for its buyers, buyer-seller trust issues have not yet surfaced to warrant facilities like trust certificates for SME sellers. On the sellers' side though, the risk of accepting financial payments by credit card over the Internet has been absorbed by RegWa.net for a small fee.

6.4.5 Compatibility with Systems and Practice

The system in RegWa.net was similar to that of TwinTowns.com and compatibility of the REM technology with that of participants' systems was not considered important. Most SMEs felt that there was no need for integration of systems at this stage.

Table 6.5 SMEs' Opinions on Integration of RegWa.net REM Technology with their Systems

Participant	Comments
P1R2	No integration with the REM....I'd lose control & people still want control
P3R2	Small business, they want to be seen but they don't want to be committed
P4R2	At this point it's too early for that. It's still in the first steps of getting people online. Integration is a long way away
P6R2	In a more stable environment perhaps it could. It would be better in verticals like Office National, more in stationery where there is small income and high turnover

As there were no major purchasers on the system, integration with buyers' systems was not needed then and especially not now with the change in focus from B2B to B2C.

While the simple and ubiquitous nature of the RegWa.net system meant that there were no compatibility issues with participants' systems, a more serious problem in regional areas like the one served by RegWa.net is the quality of the communications and power supply systems. A regional portal catering for both the business and general communities needs to have content that can attract and retain users from both communities. This means a web site that is typically graphics-laden and it is only recently with the help of Connect RegWa that users in the region have been able to get access to broadband. Prior to this however, the design of the RFQ part of the system was such that the notification of RFQs had the actual RFQ attached to it and suppliers did not have to go into the system to retrieve it. However, it was not just the issues with the telecommunications infrastructure that needed to be addressed but the power supply as well. Spikes in the power supply meant that prospective participants in certain areas did not want ADSL (asymmetrical digital subscriber line) connections that had to be continuously open because *"there's no way our computers are always on because of the spikes we get everyday. We've already done 5 hard drives"* (SME in RegWa.net cited by the E-commerce manager, Connect RegWa).

In RegWa.net (as in TwinTowns.com), although major regional buyers supported the buy local online principle in theory, they were locked into buyer-supplier relationships which accounted for most of their purchasing needs and did not need to tender. Hence the system was not compatible with their business practices. For local B2C business, most SMEs agreed that face-to-face interaction was the preferred way of doing things in the country. The incompatibility of the system with existing business and consumer purchasing practices has forced the change of focus in RegWa.net. While it is now targeting purchasers outside the region with its accent on tourism and niche products for which it is renowned, the use of competitions and special offers on the portal are being used as a hybrid online/off-line strategy for the local B2C business (Adelaar, Bouwman & Steinfield, 2004; Steinfield et al., 1999a).

6.4.6   Perceived Ease of Use

The owners of RegWa.net conceded that while most participants find the system easy to use some do have problems with the search function as they compare it to other popular search engines like Google. There was also some confusion (in the pre-November 2004 system) with the listings as the REM, e-mail and free listings were all mixed. However, the owners were quick to point out that *"we have listened to people's feedback along the way & we have tried to work with that & use that feedback constructively. If people criticise, it's a good thing if they're telling you what they find is wrong; you can try & come up with a better solution"* (Portal Administrator).

15 of the 20 SMEs interviewed perceived that the RegWa.net system was easy to use and that it was especially important for SMEs that it was so. The other five felt that it could be cumbersome if a user didn't know what they were looking for (referring to the missing REM link) and that it could be improved further. These were participants who had joined the trading platform in 2002.

6.4.7   Development Process

In RegWa.net, although the project had received less funding compared to TwinTowns.com prior to 2003, more was achieved because of the wide stakeholder input, the spirit of volunteerism, the open consultative governance style and the support of technology champions in the community. One other factor that contributed to RegWa.net's perceived early success (in the sense that it was still operating while other portals which were better funded had folded) was the development process employed by the owners. The owners worked for two years to build listings on its business directory and community content before introducing the REM. It took another two years (and an additional AU$2.2 million) for RegWa.net to move on to the next stage (the shopping cart and change in business focus). This staged or phased approach allowed time to build participants' confidence with the system and owners, and also allowed the owners the ability to respond to changing business conditions.

According to the E-commerce manager of Connect RegWa, given the nature of the region, the participants involved and the novelty of the application, it was the best way to proceed.

> *"It would have been too much for people to get their heads around if it was not staged"*
> (E-commerce manager, Connect RegWa).

One of the advantages of a stage approach to regional Internet trading platforms like RegWa.net is the opportunity for the kind of evaluation proposed by Farbey et al. (1999, p. 190) i.e. "[a] process, or group of parallel processes, which take place at different points in time or continuously, for searching and for making explicit, quantitatively or qualitatively, all the impacts of an IT project and the programme and strategy of which it is a part". Given that Internet trading platforms are novel systems especially for SMEs, the owners of such systems should also adopt a theory-based evaluation approach, using theory to advise the ex ante evaluation of every stage of development.

The owners of RegWa.net were shown the Trading Platform Success Model (figure 3.3) and the accompanying tables of costs and success metrics (tables 3.3 and 3.4 respectively) to elicit their response on its applicability to the evaluation of RegWa.net. Their comments were as follows:

Table 6.6 RegWa.net Owners' Opinions on the Trading Platform Success Model as an Evaluation Tool

Participant	Comments
E-commerce manager	The model is spot on but the challenge with it....the motivation of the owner & sponsor can be quite conflicting...In our case, I don't think there was a clear idea of what it was they were wanting to get out of it...It's interesting the outcomes you say we should be looking at. I agree whole-heartedly. We've actually spent 18 months debating what it is we want to measure with my Board & it becomes very difficult when you have the conflict between measuring activity & measuring outcomes....it's vastly different
Advisory board member	Looking at the initial data that we have, that model makes sense & as far as the REM is concerned, we assumed benefits would accrue without really evaluating from the outset....So we drove it in anticipation of what the REM would do without identifying what business needed

6.4.8 Marketing Plan

RegWa.net had (and still has) promotion of its services via local television, radio and in the print media, as well as outdoor advertising. The E-commerce manager maintains a high profile in the community addressing meetings at the chambers of commerce and attending local and national conferences. Brochures were available on RegWa.net's services and Connect RegWa uses the region's tele-centres to advertise its services.

When the trading portal of RegWa.net first started in 2002, about AU$25,000 of the ITOL funding was used for marketing (not AU$90,000 as reported by the TwinTowns.com project manager) and this was used for advertising and a sales person on a 50 percent commission basis. While the sales person did a good job of selling participation, in hindsight the owners of RegWa.net believe that it may have done more harm than good. Because of the commission basis, the sales person tried to sell to anyone who would buy regardless of whether participation would benefit them. Consequently, people who were happy to pay for an e-mail or web-link on RegWa.net for the first two years subsequently ended their subscriptions to the portal altogether when they didn't get any return for their AU$149 REM link after a year.

According to the owners of RegWa.net, the additional funding of AU$2.2 million has allowed them to be more targeted in their marketing of shopping cart and RFQ link sales. The approach is now to understand the business of the SME first and only recommend shopping cart or RFQ links if the business is suitable.

With the change in focus of RegWa.net now, the advertising is to people outside the region and there were promises to prospective sellers about targeted marketing of the region on the Internet. However, at the time of the interviews with the SMEs in May/June 2005, that had not yet materialised. When asked how they felt the portal could be improved, a good number of SMEs felt it should be better promoted in the tourism and travel magazines and programmes outside the region.

6.4.9 Critical Mass

The owners of RegWa.net used a variety of approaches to obtain a critical mass of participants on the portal as its sources of revenue were participation fees and advertising revenue. First all businesses were offered free listings of static company data. Then a graduated fee structure was used for the different types of links, depending on the sellers' needs. By the time the REM was introduced, the business directory of RegWa.net was well-populated and well supported because of the 'ownership' by the community. *"95% of the people in [this town] will know [RegWa.net] &*

would have been at least once on the [RegWa.net] website" (P2R1). The critical mass and high profile of the project made advertising on the portal an attractive option and the portal was able to sustain itself but did not have the resources needed to encourage and mentor smaller SMEs in the e-environment.

With the change in focus in November 2004, the financial model of RegWa.net has also evolved to include revenue from transactions. The upgrade to the portal has included a statistics package which should in future be able to also give individual sellers data about hits to their sites. The owners hope that this will convince sellers about the advertising benefit of participation while waiting for sales to eventuate.

6.5   THE ENVIRONMENTAL CONTEXT

In examining the environmental context of RegWa.net, particular attention was paid to the culture, economic activities and institutional relationships of the region to compare and contrast this initiative to TwinTowns.com.

6.5.1 Regional Profile

The region served by RegWa.net is considered regional or country and is about 25 times the size of the region serviced by TwinTowns.com. The nearest competitors to businesses in the region are located 2 hours away by road and it has almost half the population of Towns 1 and 2 in the TwinTowns.com case. According to Steinfield and Whitten (1999) the location of a region's nearest competitors by road can affect the uptake of e-commerce in the region. This effect can work in two ways. If a local merchant only deals online and the nearest competitor is too far away for a user to drive to, the user may be forced to buy online from the local merchant. Conversely, if the local merchant does not have the goods a buyer wants and the nearest physical competitor is too far away to be conveniently reached by road, the user may be forced to shop online outside the region. In the case of RegWa.net, local people still preferred dealing face-to-face with suppliers within the region. *"We're definitely more countrified here. People like the face-to-face interaction"* (P4R2).

While the trading platform of RegWa.net was built on the same mistaken premise (as TwinTowns.com) that local major buyers would provide the impetus for a critical mass of transactions, the region had other redeeming characteristics that could still be leveraged to push the initiative. It was renowned for its tourism and agricultural products which are being used to sell the region online to the outside world. Given the size of the region and the distances involved, there may be opportunities for the portal to be used as a vehicle to aggregate supplies from small sellers or to encourage collaboration between them.

One other characteristic that the SMEs in the region covered by regWa.net have is that *"a large proportion of them are lifestyle SMEs....they come down here to get their little business & say to you "I don't want to be or get bigger"* (E-commerce manager, Connect RegWa). While this argument can be countered by showing these SMEs how e-commerce can be used to reduce the time spent on the business (Simpson & Docherty, 2004) so that they can have an even better lifestyle, a one-on-one approach will be needed.

6.5.2 *Normative, Coercive and Mimetic Pressure*

In regional or country areas like the one served by RegWa.net, community ties are strong and people have a strong sense of belonging and pride in the region. Membership in local not-for-profit organisations is common, networking is important and business associations like the CoC are strong lobby groups for local businesses. The RegWa.net project was initiated by the CoC (of the largest town) which used its influence to garner support for the initiative. By getting high profile and respected members of ultimate stakeholder groups in the community to be on the management committee of RegWa.net, the trust embedded in the local institutional structures in the region were transferred over to the project. Thus many businesses joined RegWa.net because they were demonstrating their support for the initiative, as it was the norm. This later led to mimetic or competitive pressure as some businesses felt pressure to join or remain participants even though there were no immediate significant returns.

> *"The last thing you want to do is to go to a place like [RegWa.net] & have a list of all your competitors & you're not on the list. That's really plain silly"* (P2R1).

> *"Maybe cheese off a few competitors by having a link there & there's one link that had my logo & someone wanted it & I said No, I still want to keep it. It cheesed them off but I'm glad I did"* (P1R2).

As there were no major buyers on RegWa.net, there was no coercive pressure for suppliers to participate. External or environmental factors in the form of the additional AU$2.2 million funding has allowed facilities and IT advice to be offered free of charge to smaller (micro) businesses, encouraging them to participate.

Thus the profiles of the region and the SMEs within the region will have an enormous effect on the uptake of initiatives like RegWa.net and TwinTowns.com. More attention needs to be paid to theory-based ex-ante evaluation of the impact of these contexts on such initiatives.

6.6   EMERGENT THEMES AND EXTANT LITERATURE

Trust, Motive and Institutional Pressure

The empirical data from RegWa.net shows that trust surfaced as a critical success factor on many levels (trust between partners, trust in the technology, trust built by the phased development, leveraging embedded trust). By successfully addressing the need to build or engender trust at these many levels, the portal has managed to survive where others like it have had to close.

In terms of motive, the data from RegWa.net showed that there was a convergence or understanding of the motives of all stakeholders (Fairchild et al., 2004) in the initiative leading to its continued existence. Many businesses joined the portal on the understanding that it would be the leading online directory for the region and it would get wide coverage because it drew the community as well. This is how it was originally sold and this is what it currently is. The group of businesses that joined for this purpose still make up the highest percentage of paying participants on the portal. For businesses that were prepared to experiment further, additional features like the RFQ and shopping cart were offered. Albeit, the RFQ facility did not achieve its intended purpose of fostering local online B2B business, to its credit, the management of RegWa.net has been able to change the focus of the portal to now align it better with the profile and strengths of the region.

RegWa.net is a good example of the positive effect of institutional pressure in promoting participation. Mimetic pressure, legitimacy and networking were leveraged well to build support of the portal and the initiative. This may even have had a stronger influence than participant and technology contexts in building early critical mass.

Matching the Scope of the Initiative and Development Process to Resource Constraints and the Profile of the Region

The empirical data from RegWa.net supports the findings from the TwinTowns.com data that the regional profile (in terms of geographical location, demographics, major business activities, culture, communications infrastructure etc.) is an important consideration in determining the scope of the initiative and the type of regional Internet trading platform to be used. While the culture of the region (the strong business and community ties) enabled strong support to be built for the initiative, the support was also due to the consultative and inclusive governance style of the RegWa.net management. The effect of isolation of the region's businesses from nearby outside physical competition did not work in favour of local B2B online business because of the preferred face-to-face way of dealing. A number of the SMEs (particularly in the IT industry) report the need to obtain their supplies online from outside the region because they cannot source it locally, Perth (the capital city of WA) is too far away to drive to, some of their suppliers will not trade with them any other way and some of the items are only available overseas. Thus industry characteristics also appear to have an effect on SME uptake of e-commerce. There may be a need to take a more targeted or personalised approach (as is currently done in RegWa.net, albeit on a limited basis) instead of treating all SMEs as a single homogenous group with similar needs.

As expected, telecommunications infrastructure was an issue that had to be addressed in trying to achieve successful adoption of participation in the RegWa.net portal. This issue was resolved to some extent by Connect RegWa coordinating the move to pressure the telecommunications carriers into providing better bandwidth to the region. One finding that was not expected was that the power supply also had an effect on the type of system that would work well and these issues need to be considered in the planning stage of the project. Thus an integrated approach is needed.

To a large extent RegWa.net's continued existence and its ability to change its focus can be attributed to the alignment of the development process with the resources available. Prior to 2003, the project had received less funding than TwinTowns.com (although there were hidden costs) but because the portal was already receiving advertising and membership revenue from directory listings, the lukewarm response to the introduction of the REM did not cause the portal's demise. The stage approach also provided the flexibility to respond to changing market conditions.

The management of the RegWa.net project was in many ways better than that of TwinTowns.com. However, the fact remains that it was only after the additional injection of AU$2.2.million in 2003 that Connect RegWa has been able to get down to fulfilling the true objective behind its funding i.e. of increasing e-commerce uptake among SMEs and increasing uptake of IT in the region (the purpose behind the ITOL and state government funding received prior to 2002). This once again displays the incongruence of the long term socio-economic objectives behind projects like RegWa.net and the short term business model of self sustainability imposed by funding conditions and constraints. There is a need to match funding to scope or breadth of the objectives and in cases where the target population is a non homogenous group of SMEs, the need to understand individual SME needs. It may well be that the government could get more for its dollar if it targeted its funds into one-on-one consultancy for targeted SMEs.

Communication, Feedback and Promotion

Communication, feedback and promotion in RegWa.net have had a positive impact on the implementation of the portal/trading platform and participation in it. While participants have been happy thus far with the level of communication, they are now looking for more positive evidence of benefits from participation. SMEs that have not been getting any RFQs or e-mails want statistics to show the traffic directed to their sites via RegWa.net.

While the promotion of RegWa.net has so far been successful in building local awareness and support of the portal, SMEs interviewed feel that advertising the portal outside the region should be increased. This has implications for the need for ongoing funding.

How Should IT Advisory Services for SMEs be Provided?

Studies have shown that print or online e-business advice for SMEs may not be effective (Stansfield & Grant, 2003). The additional funding of AU$2.2 million has given Connect RegWa the much needed funds to offer targeted personalised advice, services and training to the business and general communities. While most participants have welcomed these latest offerings, there have been rumblings of discontent from SMEs providing IT services.

> "I actually run a business where we sell our IT expertise out to people so to have the local REM saying they will go out and do it for nothing, I'd say 'Thanks very much but get out of my back yard'....I don't know what level they're going to go to" (P6R2).

On the other hand, even though the IT advice is offered free, according to the e-business advisor of Connect RegWA, "even if we had more money for more people, it's just that SMEs just don't seem to want it at this time....people are only rolling up to that doorstep on a casual manner". It could well be the case that the IT advisory services may be better received if provided by a panel of approved commercial local providers who are financed in this role by the government as proposed by Beckinsale and Levy (2004). This may also have the effect of growing the local IT industry as evidenced in research by Evans (2002).

Visitor's Centres – Competition, the Next Step for SME Participants or Collaborators?

The Western Australian Tourist Commission in conjunction with tourism associations in certain tourist 'hot-spots' in WA, have set up online 'Visitor Centres' to complement physical offices in these areas. The online Visitor Centres allow secure online booking for accommodation and tours and while they have a standard main page, in some regions or towns, they are actually a link to a regional portal offering the same kind of functions as RegWa.net (web pages for businesses, IT training and advice etc). This is happening in the more renowned tourist districts where local tourism associations feel they can leverage their reputations to give better exposure to the businesses in their areas than the RegWa.net regional portal can.

The rates charged on these Visitor Centre and tourism association portals are higher than that in RegWa.net. The question now is whether they are viewed as competition or the next stage that smaller SMEs can take after getting their first experience on RegWa.net. Some towns are collaborating with RegWa.net in the sense that the booking form is all they offer. However, if portals and trading platforms like RegWa.net are viewed as development tools and are funded as such without the pressing need to be self sustainable, they do not need to compete with Visitor Centres and can concentrate on providing consultancy, training and an inexpensive 'dipping of toes in the water of e-commerce' for small SMEs who are not able to do it on their own or are not prepared to risk it at the higher costs on the other portals.

6.7 SUMMARY - SUCCESS AND BENEFITS OF THE TRADING PLATFORM IN REGWA.NET

The Trading Platform Success Model (Figure 3.3) and the accompanying tables of costs (table 3.3) and success metrics (table 3.4) have been used to determine the success of the initiative based on the data collected from the interviews with owners and SME participants of RegWa.net.

6.7.1 Owners' Costs

Although funds of AU$242,000 over four years appeared at first glace to be sufficient for the development and running of RegWa.net, in reality there were many hidden costs that need to be considered. These include the free software development and hosting, the hours which were volunteered and the overheads absorbed by the CoC prior to 2003. These costs would have pushed the actual total project costs much higher.

The additional AU$2.2.million has enabled an upgrade in the platform technology, a shift in focus that is more aligned with the profile of the region and targeted training and consultancy. It has also enabled funding for another extremely important activity, evaluation.

> "One of the things that we're just in the middle of doing is the idea of doing business take-up surveys....because the whole idea is that adoption of e-business strategies will be taken up at a greater rate[here] than Australia on average" (E-commerce manager, Connect RegWa).

Nevertheless, the need to keep generating revenue (and look for new revenue sources) detracts from more detailed (and effective) evaluation. Studies have shown that B2C Internet portal business models are constantly changing in an effort to generate revenue (Ortelbach, 2005). Given the current focus of RegWa.net, the self-sustainable model means that there is a need to keep up with commercial portals to achieve visitor loyalty, which could come at the cost of building the e-competencies of regional SMEs.

6.7.2 SME Participants' Costs

Most of the SMEs interviewed in RegWa.net were already on the Internet and their additional costs were just participation fees. SMEs that had paid for only web links (AU$66) or RFQ facilities ($149) appeared not to view these costs as prohibitive, as long as the business directory continues to be comprehensive and they get the odd RFQ every now and then. SMEs which have paid more (AU$150 shopping cart or additional fees for advertisement banners or listings) but already have their own e-commerce enabled web sites and smaller SMEs which are currently enjoying free membership appear to be more concerned with their economic returns. These SMEs appear to be willing to give the portal only a year within which to provide them with positive returns.

6.7.3 Content Quality, Trading Platform System Quality and Service/Value Added Quality

The quality of content, system, value-added and service offerings were determined based on the researcher's own observations and the interview responses of owners and SMEs.

Content Quality

The metrics used in this case for determining content quality are: currency, accuracy, relevance, timeliness and security.

As far as the researcher could ascertain from the portal web site, the content on the Regwa.net business directory and shopping page was current, accurate and relevant. Links worked but the pages with the shopping carts appeared to be sparsely populated (less than 20 merchants). The organisation of the content was a bit confusing especially the listing of businesses under certain categories (i.e. a very wide business/finance category).

The owners felt that one of the greatest challenges had been keeping the listings accurate and current, given the lack of resources in the past. According to the portal administrator since the receipt of the additional funding, cleaning up the data base has been ongoing and it was currently about *"80% there"*. Apart from a few navigation and classification issues which they felt will be addressed with the portal upgrade, the owners felt that other areas of content quality were satisfactory.

SME participants' were asked their opinion of content quality. Responses were categorised as per table 6.7 Responses considered positive were *"good"*, *"OK"*, *"No problems with that"*, *"its fine"* and *"satisfactory"*.

Table 6.7 SMEs' Opinions of Content Quality in RegWa.net

Metric	Positive (Number of Responses)	Negative (Number of Responses)	Other (Number of Responses)
Currency	13		7
Accuracy	12		8
Relevance	14	1	5
Timeliness	15	1	4
Security	16	1	3

The responses in the column rated 'other' for currency, accuracy, timeliness and security ranged mostly from *"average"* to *"I can't answer that"* to *"I don't know"*. One SME rated timeliness negatively because of delays between RegWa.net processing the shopping cart requests and e-mailing the order on to them. The delays occur as the SME does not have the computer on all the time because of power spikes.

Those that did not rate relevance either positively or negatively said it was *"average"*, *"I haven't really used it much"*, *"it's nice but not substantial"* and *"the problem is the navigation"*. The SME which rated relevance negatively had signed up for the shopping cart on being told that it was going to be widely promoted (which had not yet eventuated), felt that it was not hitting the relevant market. One SME had concerns about the security of the content because of inside knowledge about the storage and hosting arrangements of RegWa.net.

On the whole, the quality of content on RegWa.net had a positive rating.

Trading Platform System Quality

The metrics used to determine the system quality in RegWa.net are: reliability of software/network; ease of use; online response time and page loading speed; visual appearance; convenience of accessibility and market reach.

Table 6.8 SMEs' Opinions of Trading Platform System Quality of RegWa.net

Metric	Positive (Number of Responses)	Negative (Number of Responses)	Other (Number of Responses)
Reliability	18	1	1
Ease of use	16		4
Response time & page loading speed	16		4
Visual appearance	16		4
Convenience of Accessibility	15		5
Market reach	16	1	3

The responses from SMEs on the quality of the trading platform were categorised in the same manner as for content quality. Responses categorised under 'Other', were *"could be better"*, *"a bit cumbersome"*, *"looks a bit busy"*, *"visibility of the REM can be improved"*, *"it can take a bit of time but I guess that depends on the line speed"*, *"I don't know"* and *"I can't answer that"*. The SME which had a negative response for reliability of the system commented that he knew from inside knowledge that there were problems with the way it was hosted. SMEs whose opinions of market reach were categorised under 'Other' felt that more could be done to market the portal outside the region. The negative opinion of the market reach of the platform was made by the same SME who was disappointed with the marketing of the shopping cart facilities. The response was *"They are not getting enough traffic I don't think"*.

The portal administrator of RegWa.net felt that while reliability of the front end was good, there were still problems linking the back office systems together. The AU$30,000 paid for the REM technology in 2002 had involved a reconfiguration of the entire system including integration with the back office systems and that was still unfinished (this could be why the software developer [P2R1] mentioned hidden costs and extra free hours put into the job). The owners felt that problems with response time and page loading speed of the system had more to do with lack of broadband in many areas in the region, while convenience of access and visual appearance would improve when the upgrade was fully operational. As for market reach, the owners commented that they were still working on it, trying to determine the best strategies.

On the whole, the trading platform system quality was also rated positively.

Service/Value Added Quality

In terms of service and value added quality, metrics used were: site intelligence; feedback mechanisms; relevant search facilities; tracking capabilities; helpdesk/set-up help/advice (listings of frequently asked questions [FAQs]); account maintenance and training (in conversion to e-business and for system use).

While all SMEs rated training, advice, technical support, account maintenance and feedback (in terms of communication with RegWa.net owners) positively, site intelligence and tracking capabilities were absent. For SMEs that did not yet get any business from the platform or were not pressured to remain listed by competitors, these functions were beginning to increase in importance especially if they were paying more than the standard rates. Only 2 SMEs had their own tracking counters which could tell whether hits were being routed to their websites via RegWa.net.

According to RegWa.net owners, with the full implementation of the new system these features will be incorporated. Overall, service/value added quality was viewed positively.

6.7.4   Use, User Satisfaction and Net Benefits

17 SMEs felt that on the whole they were satisfied with the portal and its offerings while three were not because they perceived that there were no returns from participation. Two of the three had not used the portal for some time. In order to assess the use the net benefits of RegWa.net, the following statistics were obtained in addition to participants' views.

Table 6.9 Selected Statistics for RegWa.net as at August 2004

Item	Statistics
Businesses listed on Portal	9800 (95% of businesses in the area). 1790 paying participants; 273 full REM links
Community groups listed	1770 of which 1155 had Web/e-mail links.
Government Listings	142 of which 69 had Web/e-mail links.
Hits to the portal	Monthly Average 7000 (In 2005: 30,000)
Requests for Quotes via REM	Monthly Average 33
Operating costs	AU$28000 (for the whole portal including training costs etc.)
Direct Income	AU$7000 per month from participation fees only (other income breakdown not available)
Evidence of online networks and participation in them	NIL

These statistics show that although RegWa.net was generating direct income of about AU$7,000 a month, this was still insufficient to sustain the level of training, consultancy, free services offered, marketing and maintenance that was being undertaken with the receipt of the extra AU$2.2 million in funding. There was no evidence of online networks but the owners did mention that it was trialled in the early days of the portal but *"that's been an outstanding failure. Again it's going back to people wanting a sense of true community not an artificial community through an electronic medium"*. However, with the change in focus of the trading platform, it will be interesting to see whether the response to online networks will change in the future or alternatively, if the portal can be used for knowledge networking and collaboration among SMEs.

While regional economic benefits like increasing the attractiveness of the region for business and skilled labour, reduced communication costs and increased productivity are not evident yet, RegWa.net is managing to achieve an efficient show-casing of regional offerings. Also, according to the e-commerce manager of Connect RegWa, the take up rate for e-business strategies by SMEs in the region was higher than the Australian average. *"The early statistical data looks like that is the case. Because of all these incentives, that is the data to prove that the investment is worthwhile before getting businesses to take that next step"*.

The owners are also of the opinion that the greatest regional benefits at the moment are at the community and strategic levels. This is based on the increased levels of collaboration, partnerships and cooperation between regional stakeholders and an increased level of online participation of both the business and general communities of the region. If the statistics are anything to go by, the business uptake of e-commerce strategies in the region indicates that the digital divide between the region's SMEs and the rest of Australia has closed. With additional funding and continuing support from the government, the region has a good chance of becoming a knowledge region and forging relationships with other markets.

SMEs opinions of the actual benefits from participation in RegWa.net are categorised and summarised in table 6.10 below:

Table 6.10 SMEs' Opinions of Actual Benefits from Participation in RegWa.net

Metric	Yes (Number of Responses)	No (Number of Responses)	Other (Number of Responses)
RFQs & Orders Received?	12	6	2
Increased Business?	10	8	2
Cost Savings?	3	14	3

The 2 SMEs whose responses were categorised under 'Other' in terms of RFQs and orders received via the portal said that they received some hits to their websites via the portal. Although 12 SMEs had received RFQs and orders, for only 10 this translated into actual increases in business volume. However, most SMEs reported that the increases were marginal. The responses that were categorised as 'Other' for increased business reported that they *"couldn't tell because the redirected hits from the portal may have well turned into orders"*. In terms of cost savings, only three responses were positive; one SME was participating without any fees and two others considered the cost savings in terms of advertising costs. The responses that were categorised under 'Other' for cost savings were: *"It's an opportunity to add to what we have"*; *"I don't know, it's still too early to tell"* and *"The jury is still out on that"*.

6.7.5   Success of RegWa.net

Application of the Trading Success Platform Model (figure 3.3) to the empirical data collected from RegWa.net indicates a mixed result. If viewed from a purely commercial economic basis (self sustainability or profitability) and the value of strategic and community benefits is weighted much less than economic benefits, then one may be tempted to conclude that RegWa.net is not a success. RegWa.net may be considered a success, however, if community and strategic benefits are considered more important than short-term economic benefits (as should be the case in regional economic development initiatives like this one).

Owners and SME participants were also asked for their opinion on the success of RegWa.net and their view are presented in the next sections.

Owners' View of Success.

Table 6.11 Owners' Opinions on the Success of RegWa.net

Participant	Comments
E-commerce manager	I would say its success is limited. I'm hoping for more, but I think the site overall has been
Portal Administrator	In some cases yes....It's really hard to judge because there's no stats package. That will change in November. So unless people say so or you've used it yourself & you know you've benefited....it's hard to quantify. So for me yes, it has been successful, it's done its job, but there are downfalls
Advisory board member	No, not yet. It is still a work-in-progress & certainly I think its worthwhile continuing with it & making it work in the longer term but I don't think it will generate income to support the portal in the longer term....I think it needs almost a visionary approach, a nebulous economic development concept
E-business advisor	It's not a short-term thing. I think it will start to plateau out but it does need a longer incubation period & an integrated approach

SME Participants' Views of Success

In response to the question of whether RegWa.net was successful, 11 SME participants said yes, 5 said no and 4 said it was still a work-in-progress. Those that said it was not a success qualified their answers by saying that it was because they did not get any business from it or had not been told if traffic was actually being directed to their websites from RegWa.net

Conclusion

The empirical evidence from both trading platform statistics and interview responses indicate that the success of RegWa.net varies according to the perspective taken. As an economic development strategy, it has achieved some of its objectives of increasing uptake of e-commerce by SMEs, lifting online awareness in the region and bridging the digital divide. However, it must be remembered that it was at a cost of AU$2.442 million. The impact on the success of RegWa.net of factors like the profile of the region and the SMEs, the trust created by the open, inclusive governance style of the owners and the staged development process, and the simplicity of the technology which worked well also cannot be underestimated. From a participant perspective, some SMEs have had economic gains (albeit small ones) from participation in RegWa.net, some strategic gains like legitimacy, while others did not gain at all. Nevertheless, from a purely economic perspective of self sustainability or profitability, RegWa.net has yet to prove itself.

One of the difficulties for RegWa.net owners in evaluating achievements against objectives is the absence of measurable (and where ever possible quantifiable) targets. The objective was to raise e-commerce uptake in the region but there were no predetermined targets about what percentage of up-take the project was supposed to achieve or the timeframe in which to do it. This supports the findings of Tonkin about the lack of proper evaluation of costs and benefits in government and government funded projects (2003). While targets like percentage increase in SME uptake of e-commerce might be too ambitious for collaborative projects like RegWa.net, the example of the European Union's efforts to set quantifiable and measurable targets for such projects against which to measure outcomes should be followed (Commission of the European Communities, 2003a). Targets such as 'number of SMEs to be trained by a certain period' or 'number of community groups to be online' etc. are more specific and meaningful targets which are easier to quantify and cost. It also encourages owners to conduct evaluations and benchmarking throughout the initiative, which is a hallmark of good evaluation practice.

Finally, as per table 6.12, the empirical data from RegWa.net has further refined the integrated theoretical framework of factors affecting success or failure of government-supported regional Internet trading platforms for SMEs.

Table 6.12 Results from the Findings of RegWa.net in terms of Integrated Theoretical Framework of Factors Affecting Success or Failure of Government-Supported Regional Internet Trading Platforms for SMEs

Context	Construct	RegWa.net
Market-Maker (Owner)	Ownership structure and Governance	Critical
	Motivation/focus	High
	Competencies (IS/project management skills)	High
	Financial resources	High
	Trust	Critical
	Strategic partnering	Partners with participants
Technology (Trading Platform)	Perceived benefits, relative advantage and Usefulness	High
	Critical mass/liquidity	High
	Value-added services/Strategic partnering (e.g. logistics, financial)	Low
	REM training and technical support	High but consultancy should not compete with commercial providers
	Compatibility (with users' systems)	Low
	Trust	Critical
	REM development and timing of features offered	Critical
	Perceived ease of use	High
	Good marketing plan	High
Organisational (SME participant)	Top management commitment/innovativeness	High in the beginning (under self-sustainability model)
	Internal IT/IS/e-business (readiness).	High in the beginning (under self-sustainability model)
	Size of firm	Low. Small firms were willing to join if they can see the benefits and costs are not prohibitive.
Environmental (External)	Regional SME profile. Local consumer needs and behaviour. Regional profile	Critical
	Government support and incentives	Critical. Just 'building it will not guarantee that they will come'.
	Normative, coercive and mimetic pressure/existing trading relationships	High. Tied in to regional/SME profile

The new themes that emerged, the variations to existing themes and the refined theoretical conceptual framework that arose from the study of RegWa.net were used to plan, collect and analyse data form CountryWa.com, the final case in this multiple-case study research design. The findings from CountryWa.com will be discussed in the next chapter.

CHAPTER 7

COUNTRYWA.COM: FINDINGS AND ANALYSIS

7.1 INTRODUCTION

In this chapter the findings from the mini case study of CountryWa.com will be presented and analysed. The owner context is first discussed according to the constructs used in the TwinTowns.com and RegWa.net cases. Collection of secondary data on CountryWa.com began in 2003 from the portal website and published data. The original project manager used the project as the subject of her PhD thesis. It forms part of the secondary data collected in this study.

In 2003 the CountryWa.com website appeared to be a regional community Internet portal incorporating community content, forums, member and business listings and a link to a 'Shopping Mall' page. The shopping mall page was a clustering of merchants who were grouped according to categories (e.g. gifts, office goods etc.) and each merchant had shopping cart facilities. A few statistics were available on the website to indicate the most visited pages, the number of hits to the portal, the number of members etc. When the secondary data collection for CountryWa.com began (late 2003), the community part of the portal appeared to be vibrant. However, it was observed that there were only 4 merchants on the shopping mall page. Although the number of merchants listed did not change, in 2004 the link to the shopping mall page was removed from the portal homepage. No other evidence of e-commerce activity was visible except for individual participants' websites.

Interviews with 4 owner representatives of CountryWa.com were conducted by telephone in May/June 2005 and follow up was done via telephone and e-mail. This was at the suggestion of the former project manager (currently a board member of the owners of CountryWa.com) as the owner representatives were geographically dispersed. Telephone interviews with 20 SME participants were also conducted during the same period. The questionnaires for the owner and SME interviews in CountryWa.com remained broadly similar to the ones in TwinTowns.com and RegWa.net. However, variations were introduced to cater for the themes that had emerged in the previous two studies.

The findings and analysis from the interviews in CountryWa.com will be presented in a similar manner to that of TwinTowns.com and RegWa.net for consistency (i.e. according to the four major contexts identified, viz. the owner, organisational, technology and environmental contexts). The findings are then discussed in the light of the extant literature, themes that emerged from the

213

analysis and their effect on the conceptual frameworks of the study. The chapter concludes with a discussion of success and benefits in the case of CountryWa.com.

7.2 OWNER CONTEXT

The idea behind the CountryWa.com regional community portal was formulated in 1999 by two major Perth-based IT companies which were working on projects in the region. The Office of Information and Communication of the State Government (OIC), which had worked on a business development website for business enterprise centres in the region, was invited to become part of the advisory committee as was ECU. This committee is henceforth referred to as the Perth Consortia. At the local level, representatives from the regional development commission and business enterprise centre of the largest town, and two prominent people from local industry made up the 'Steering Committee'. The Perth Consortia was considered the instigator group assisting the Steering Committee with professional expertise. CountryWa.com was to be a way to bring together the non-commercial IT projects that were being developed in the region under one portal.

The two committees held a workshop for about 40 interested community stakeholders and the idea for CountryWa.com was accepted. An application was submitted to ITOL for funding and the committees were informed that the application was short-listed but needed more local community and management. A further workshop was held where a local developer demonstrated his website 'CountryWa Online' which he had used to bring a few tourism businesses online. This was used as a prototype to sell the idea further to local SMEs and interest was expressed by the local business community in the concept of online trading and enabling people to buy local online. The committees then decided that e-commerce enabling would be a key driver of CountryWa.com and this was incorporated into the reworked ITOL submission.

In March 1999, a local resident of the region was appointed as project manager and began gathering user-requirements for the community part of the portal. Funding of AU$75,000 was received under ITOL and the portal development was outsourced in the middle of the year to a Perth-based IT company while hosting was to be done by a local provider. The Perth Consortia pushed for e-commerce offerings and an E-commerce Incubator Project (EIP) was proposed. The project involved providing 15 SMEs from the region 3 one-day intensive workshop sessions (over 18 weeks) on e-commerce. The objectives of the EIP were to assist participating businesses in laying the foundations for e-commerce planning and strategy and provide them with on going support through the incubation stage. At the conclusion of the workshops, the businesses were expected to become regional e-commerce champions and to offer mentoring services to other businesses operating in a similar sector.

Unfortunately, the response from local businesses was not encouraging. Although a discussion board had been set up to mentor SMEs between workshops and mentors appointed (albeit, it was mostly online), the boards were not utilised and the Perth-based mentors were not approached between workshops. At the end of the 18 week period, the number of businesses participating in the EIP had dwindled to 6, and of these, only one had implemented their web site. However, the community part of the portal progressed well and the CountryWa.com portal was launched in May 2000. The general community aspect of CountryWa.com continued to grow, but by then the interest of the Perth Consortia had dwindled due to the lack of progress in the e-commerce side of the portal.

In 2001, the portal received AU$100,000 funding under the Networking the Nation programme. Funds were used to purchase a server, upgrade the portal by building back-end applications and enabled CountryWa.com to offer participants shopping cart-enabled web pages with order forms. It was also in March 2001 that ownership of the portal changed. A cooperative was formed under the West Australian Cooperatives Board with locals owning shares (AU$1 per share but each shareholder has only 1 vote, irrespective of number of shares held) and it became the owner of CountryWa.com. The CountryWa Cooperative is overseen by a Board of community representatives. This ownership structure of the portal is still maintained to date.

7.2.1 Description of Interview Participants

Table 7.1 below provides a list of the owner representatives of CountryWa.com who were interviewed and gives their position in the organisations they represented.

Table 7.1 Profile of the 'Owner' Interview Participants in CountryWa.com

Position	Organisation
Original Project manager & currently ex-officio member	CountryWa Cooperative
Part-Time Portal Manager	CountryWa Cooperative
Board Member (& part-time marketing/sales person)	CountryWa Cooperative
Board Member	CountryWa Cooperative

At the time of the interviews, the original project manager had not been the running the portal for two years but remained an ex-officio of the CountryWa Cooperative board. The portal manager had been appointed three months earlier as had the part-time sales person. The other board member had been involved in the portal since its inception.

7.2.2 Motivation

In essence, the motive behind the creation of CountryWa.com was similar to that of TwinTowns.com and RegWa.net viz. *"to build awareness of the benefits and opportunities of the*

Internet; to encourage engagement in the Information Age and to provide access to the online environment and the region" (excerpt from the thesis of the original project manager).

These motives were confirmed by responses of the other owner representatives.

"To bring the region online" (Board Member and part-time marketing/sales person).

"To give the region an identity because it contains many small country towns and because it was the early days of Internet usage, it was a process of educating people in remote areas" (Board Member).

However, although the Perth Consortia saw e-commerce as being the driver of the project, early feedback from the community suggested to the project manager and other local representatives that to attract traffic to the site, it was the community side of the portal that needed to be focused on first. This became a bone of contention between the Perth Consortia and the local representatives as the former tried to push the e-commerce agenda despite the lack of resources needed to get the necessary participation of local SMEs, while trying to build a regional community portal as well.

Table 7.2 Evidence to Support Non-Convergence of Owners' Motives in CountryWa.com

Position	Comment
Original Project manager & current ex-officio member	It was asking far too much too quickly of the Project to attempt this component in the region. Businesses were barely adopting e-mail and web sites as a functionality of their businesses, let alone having the idea or ability to become 'e-commerced up'. Members of the Perth consortia, who tended to come down here in their advisory capacity with theory and postulation, pushed this....The local businesses were interested but definitely NOT ready (*excerpt from her thesis*).
ECU representative, cited in original project manager's thesis	The Perth consortia were frustrated with the lack of awareness in the region and even though this sounds arrogant, but there was a lack of leadership, appreciation and understanding of what went into the project from a number of sides which supported the project from the outset. I still believe that [CountryWa.com] needed to have a strong commercial strategy to become sustainable.
Original Project manager & current ex-officio member	In the first meeting with the Perth consortia I had suggested a survey of the region to specifically identify computer and Internet use, skills levels etc., but I had been dissuaded. The Perth consortia wanted the project to quickly get underway, to produce something to show as a model in community online development for government funding bodies, as soon as possible (*excerpt from her thesis*).

There was thus a rush to push through the e-commerce agenda in CountryWa.com regardless of the adequacy of resources and despite not having fully researched the alignment of the initiative with the local environment. This mirrors the socio-political 'band-wagon' motive of IT policy adoption (Spencer, 2002) behind the creation of TwinTowns.com. While there was initial consensus that the driving force behind CountryWa.com would be e-commerce, the local representatives changed their views after early results showed that the SMEs needed more than just three one-hour workshops to set them on their e-commerce journey. However, the Perth Consortia did not budge from its position, creating difficulties with the governance and administration of the project. Although the lack of convergence in the motives of owners/stakeholders (Fairchild et al., 2004) could have caused CountryWa.com to collapse (as in the case of TwinTowns.com), it was salvaged by the project manager who went ahead with the community side of the portal on her own, with the help of the local community.

According to interview responses form owner representatives, the original motives behind the creation of CountryWa.com have not changed. However, the owners have not been able to move ahead with their targeted plans for e-commerce due to lack of funding.

7.2.3 Ownership Structure and Governance

In theory the loose ownership structure of CountryWa.com prior to 2001 allowed access to the expertise of the Perth Consortia while still having the administration of the portal in the hands of the local steering committee. The reality, however, was that having the dual committee and loose ownership structure in some ways hindered the development of the portal. Scarce resources were stretched in an effort to meet the differing agendas of the committees.

> *"The two committees' structure, in the early stages of the [CountryWa.com] process, was doomed from the beginning despite the best of intentions of those concerned. Conflicting ideas and management styles....put [CountryWa.com's] first steps at risk....I would strongly recommend any such project to be headed up by only one, cohesive body, working locally with the project Manager and local community and businesses"* (excerpt from the original project manager's thesis).

Although the Perth Consortia was supposed to provide expertise, in some cases the lack of hands-on administration was detrimental to the project in the early stages. The first workshop for the E-Commerce Incubator (EIP) was to be conducted by a representative of the OIC (supported by ECU representatives and the project manager). This presenter did not turn up on the day and it was left to the remaining representatives to attempt to salvage the workshop, leaving an indelible poor impression on the SMEs concerned.

> *"The failure to deliver a presenter and resources for the first e-commerce workshop was an early indicator that this administrative structure was dysfunctional....I feel drained as it took quite a bit of liaison, encouraging and educating to get the 15 businesses to attend and commit"* (excerpt from the original project manager's thesis).

This again reflects the parallels between CountryWa.com and TwinTowns.com. The difference however, in terms of the effect of ownership structure and governance style, was that in CountryWa.com the structure was more loosely arranged and the project manager was passionate about what the region needed. The loose ownership structure enabled her to carry on with the community side of the portal despite the misgivings of the Perth Consortia and by eventually creating a cooperative to own CountryWa.com, the ownership of the portal was vested in the ultimate stakeholders, the inhabitants of the region.

> *"But if anything I found the conflicts between those people who were chest-bumping over positioning held me up more than anything so I would just go ahead with what ever it was they thought I should be doing but I must admit I went ahead with what intuitively felt right"* (Interview response from original project manager).

The following comments (excerpts from the original project manager's thesis) are pertinent about the governance of the portal and project in initiatives such as those studied in this research.

> *"What I really needed was a team to work with on a daily basis, not just reports from a monthly meeting, which often progressed without my involvement....Anyone being asked to manage a community portal must be kept in the loop at all times, given solid support on ground level tasks and allowed a certain amount of autonomy for creative decision-making and strategy implementation".*

Interview responses from the owner representatives on their perception of participants' satisfaction with the current governance of CountryWa.com were as follows:

Table 7.3 Owners' Perception of SME satisfaction with the Governance of CountryWa.com

Position	Comment
Original Project manager	We haven't had anything to the contrary that I know of.
Portal manager	They're absolutely ecstatic.
Part time sales person/ CountryWa Cooperative board member	In my experience they are.

7.2.4 Financial Resources

The initial ITOL funding of CountryWa.com of AU$75,000 was to pay for a project manager, develop a community cum business portal and directory, get SMEs and the general community online and make the portal self sustainable. As with TwinTowns.com, given the wide scope of the project, this amount was not sufficient to achieve all the objectives satisfactorily. The project manager's salary was incommensurate with the level of responsibilities and the volume of work involved.

> *"As with so many community projects, [CountryWa.com] was to become a work of passion, not a work for pocket!....The initial $75,000 NOIE/ITOL funding barely paid for the first year of operation....The premature push to progress e-commerce throughout the region, by government and service provider representatives along with inadequate maintenance funding within the first two years of operation, imposed pressure to become self sustaining before practically or physically possible...."* (Excerpts from original project manager's thesis).

As in the cases of TwinTowns.com and RegWa.net, the objectives of encouraging SME uptake of e-commerce and improving regional uptake of ICT (and hence improving regional development in general) were not congruent with the short-term self sustainable economic model imposed by the owners and the funding paradigm. In the case of CountryWa.com, it took AU$243,500 to get a working community portal cum business directory up and running and offer SMEs shopping carts and order forms but much of the content had been generated and maintained by users themselves. The funding to date has not been sufficient to mentor SMEs or the general public as is being done in RegWa.net. A further application for funding of AU$50,000 from ITOL to finance 90 SMEs on CountryWa.com and provide them one-on-one training and consultancy in e-commerce has thus far not been successful. In RegWa.net, there was a political agenda behind the additional funds that the project was able to procure. CountryWa.com is not in any position to 'flex political muscles'.

These findings confirm the fears of the interview respondents in the McGrath and More (2002) study that funding constraints could limit the full realisation of future plans for their projects which included provision of full online e-commerce capabilities at a later date. It is timely here to reiterate the call for the evaluation of such projects and initiatives to be based on the self sustainability of the knowledge and experience gained by all parties in the project (that will enable them to compete in an online environment), and not on the self sustainability of the projects, technology or systems that are developed.

The responses from owner interview participants with regards to financial resources are as follows:

Table 7.4 Owners' View of the adequacy of Financial Resources in CountryWa.com

Position	Comment
Board member, CountryWa Cooperatve	If we were more successful in applying for grants and getting more funding then we could enhance the site further....It's had actually a pittance in comparison to other things and I think it's relied on the benevolence of the people who have been involved.
Part time sales person/ CountryWa Cooperative board member	We have a part-time sales person and a part-time manager and for a long time we didn't have an active manager....We don't have the money to train and I would love to do some more training. I think that's a huge area that would really benefit small business in the area. Training and how to bring your business online, e-commerce-wise and everything

7.2.5 Technical Resources

Two success factors that emerged from the McGrath and More (2002) study were the choice of project manager and the need for the project to be driven hard. The conceptual frameworks of this study posit IS project management skills as critical to the success of the implementation of a regional Internet trading platform for SMEs.

The project manager of CountryWa.com, a local resident, had a background in community, media communications, Internet/IT/ICT development and had for six years been running an education, software and IT consultancy business. As with projects like TwinTowns.com and RegWa.net, the incumbent was expected to do more than normal IT project managers would with even fewer resources. Promised technical help from the Perth Consortia was not forthcoming.

> *"Despite a lot of theory and rhetoric from government and business development organisations, no one was able to provide a workable e-commerce application or model from which to work. I felt we were being asked to do what hadn't as yet been done in the community web portal world....There was supposed to be an experienced, e-commerce project coordinator employed, to work alongside and under the direction of the [CountryWa.com] Project Manager on a part-time basis. This did not eventuate."*
> (excerpts from the original project manager's thesis).

However, even these shortcomings can be overcome if the project manager has good management skills and vision for the project. In the case of CountryWa.com, the project manager built a close working relationship with the software developer although they had to interact mostly online. A partnership was also forged with the region's inhabitants via community champions who became editors of their own content on the portal.

Thus in projects like those in this study, it is critical to adopt a holistic MIS (management information systems) view of managing information, the system, the people involved in the project and the ultimate users of the system. There needs to be alignment between the technology and the culture, politics, economic and social constructs of the region (Steinfield & Klein, 1999).

7.3   THE ORGANISATIONAL (SME PARTICIPANTS') CONTEXT

This section discusses and analyses the findings from the organisational or SME context of CountryWa.com. The section starts with a description of the SME interview participants and goes on to discuss some of the constructs in the SME context and their effect on the project. SMEs' views on the costs incurred, the benefits that the REM had to offer and its ultimate success will be discussed in the final sections of the chapter.

7.3.1   Description of Interview Participants

The characteristics of SME interview participants from CountryWa.com are provided below:

Table 7.5 Profile of the SME Interview Participants in CountryWa.com

SME #	Position of Interviewee	Number Of Employees	Turnover AU$'000 (Annual)	Buy (B) Sell (S) on 'Net?	Whose decision to join/when	Business Description
P1R3	Owner/ Partner	1 plus casual when needed	<50	B-Yes S-Yes*	Interviewee. 2003	Motorcycle Tours
P2R3	Owner/ Partner	2	New company	B-Yes S-Not yet	Interviewee June 2005	Gourmet Food Supplier
P3R3	Owner/ Partner	2	Just started. 2	B-Yes S-Yes via portal*	Interviewee. 2003 (previously had listing)	Holiday Accommodation / Farm Stay
P4R3	Owner	6	>1,000	B-Yes S-Yes	Interviewee. 2000	Office Machinery, Printers etc
P5R3	Owner/ Partner	2 f/t 6 p/t	>300	B-No S-Yes*	Joint decision. 2003	Diving Supplies and instruction
P6R3	Proprietor	1	Not Available	B-No S-No	Interviewee. 2005	Supply of Wheelchairs etc for disabled
P7R3	Agent	N/A	Not Available	B-No S-No	Partners. 2003	Real Estate Agent
P8R3	Partner	3	180	B-Yes S-No	Joint decision 2002	TV, Video, Digital Media Productions
P9R3	-	N/A	Not Available	B-No S-Yes * (own website)	Interviewee. 2001	Artist
P10R3	Proprietor	9	900	B-Yes S-Yes*	Interviewee. 2002	Cabinet makers
P11R3	Owner/ Partner	2	75	B-Yes S-Yes*	Interviewee. 2000	Holiday Accommodation
P12R3	Cellar Door manager	8 f/t 5 p/t	3,000	B-rarely S-yes (own website)	Owners. 2003	Winery

SME #	Position of Interviewee	Number Of Employees	Turnover AUS'000 (Annual)	Buy (B) Sell (S) on 'Net?	Whose decision to join/when	Business Description
P13R3	Owner	5	400	B-No S-No	Interviewee. 2000	Cushions, Beanbags, gifts
P14R3	Owner	2	70	B-No S-Yes*	Interviewee. 2001	West Australian Art & Craft
P15R3	Owner/ Manager	6	Not Available	B-Yes Sell-Yes*	Group Decision. Chamber of Commerce. No idea	Servicing Computers, New peripherals
P16R3	Owner/ Partner	-	Not Available	B-No S-Yes*	Partners. 2003	Holiday Accommodation
P17R3	Partner	35	Not Available	B-No S-No	Previous Owners. No Idea	Building Contractors
P18R3	Owner	1	Not Available	B--yes S-No	Interviewee. 2002	Ballroom Dancing Classes
P19R3	Owner/ Partner	1	<100	B-No S-Yes*	Interviewee. 2001	Wooden Puzzles and Winery
P20R3	Franchise Owner	4	160	B-Yes S-Yes*	Interviewee. 2005	Termite Control

* Not enabled to accept online payments.

The sample of participants was mixed in terms of industry sector, B2B and B2C type of business targeted, type of listing and length of membership on the portal. There were businesses that targeted the local market, those that looked beyond the region for their business and those who served both markets.

7.3.2   SME Owner Innovativeness

As with the SMEs in TwinTowns.com and RegWa.net, the majority of SMEs interviewed in CountryWa.com were managed by the owners, and it was their decision to participate in the portal. Most had their own web pages but only two had the ability to accept payments online. The majority had been listed on the portal for two years or more. On one hand, the owners may be considered to have been innovative in choosing to participate despite no clear idea of the gains. However, 12 still do not have any listings on (or links to or from) any other sites and their business processes have not changed significantly. Owner-innovativeness needs to be kept in perspective in terms of which SMEs this sort of initiative hopes to impact upon. It is often the smaller and less able SMEs who need help on their e-commerce journey and properly funded, projects like CountryWa.com and RegWa.net should not need to target SMEs with innovative owners just to build liquidity quickly.

7.3.3   E-Commerce Readiness

Similar to the case of RegWa.net, while targeting e-commerce ready SMEs in CountryWa.com may have led to early liquidity, the question is whether or not the trading platform or portal can provide them with benefits that they cannot obtain by their own endeavours or from other providers. Given the limited funding, the wide scope and non-industry or function specificity, it is unlikely projects like CountryWa.com can adequately compete with commercial e-marketplaces, portals and service providers to provide the levels of services that e-commerce ready SMEs need or want. Even if it is only for the advertising value that the portal may hold for the more e-commerce ready SMEs, the regional online directory needs to be maintained, kept updated and traffic needs to be driven to the portal to make it a worthwhile advertising alternative.

One of the major problems with the projects in this study is that SMEs are treated as a homogenous group with similar needs and wants in terms of e-commerce. Taylor and Murphy (2004) surmise that given the diversity of SMEs, a better understanding is needed of how these businesses recognise and develop business opportunities in general and not just with a given set of technologies. By doing so, it may be possible to determine how best (or if at all) e-commerce can improve the competitive position of each SME (or groups of like SMEs). This implies the need for one-on-one dealings with SMEs to determine their particular needs (as is being done in RegWa.net). The lack of funding for projects like CountryWa.net and the need for them to be self sustainable may exclude the very group that these initiatives are meant to reach i.e. the less e-commerce ready SMEs. With the latest request for ITOL funding of AU$50,000 for their proposed E-Business Programme 2005 - 'Dipping the Small Business Toe into E-business', CountryWa.com had already identified 90 businesses from the region for which a one page shopping-cart and order form would have been provided on the portal at a cost of only AU$220 each (training and mentoring were to be provided via the local telecentres). However, to date the request for funding has not been successful.

7.3.4   Size of Firm

In CountryWa.net, only one SME interviewed was a medium sized business; six were small businesses and the rest micro businesses. The micro businesses (especially those in tourism and accommodation) appeared to be enthusiastic about their experience on the portal even though some of them had not yet obtained any economic returns from participation.

Table 7.6 Comments of Micro Businesses on Their Participation in CountryWa.com

Participant	Comments
P1R3	I know there are other portals around and some private ones, but I think the [CountryWa.com] is the best around here
P3R3	[It's given me] credibility in the business. I mean if you run an accommodation place and you don't have a web site that sort of indicates that you're not sort of professional
P6R3	Yes it's [services/features/offerings] pretty good
P11R3	We have a link to [CountryWa.com] from our own web page
P14R3	At one stage they were looking at setting up e-commerce and I was quite interested in that. They had a couple of examples that went up online at one stage, but to the best of my knowledge and I might be wrong now, it never got off the ground but it was a good idea and I think it just faltered from lack of funding
P16R3	I'm 100% satisfied
P18R3	It's a good way to advertise
P19R3	Well I'm satisfied with them, I just feel I'm not doing my part
P20R3	Yes I'm satisfied [with the services/offerings/features]

The larger SMEs appeared less satisfied.

Table 7.7 Comments of Larger SMEs on Their Participation in CountryWa.com

Participant	Comments
P4R3	Yes, my money is better spent elsewhere
P5R3	I don't know anybody who uses it. I have not heard of it being spoken outside of this conversation or the conversations I've had with [the CountryWa.com salesperson] or with the Visitor's Centre (I was on the Board of the Visitor's Centre for a few years).
P12R3	We are not going to renew our listing because it's just not providing the service that we wanted. The information was basically incorrect.
P15R3	It was government funded and you can't compete with it. You can run it at a loss without the same level of service or profit required of a commercial entity therefore there is no requirement to make it 'work at all costs'....Currently it's run by volunteers and it'll never pay off.

The owner of SME P4R3 had been one of the participants to have a shopping cart facility on the CountryWa.com 'Shopping page'. He had paid *about AU$1000 for it'*. The representative of SME P15R3 had many negative comments and was affronted that the portal was developed by a company outside the region. He also felt that there were existing available models locally that CountryWa.com could have gone with in the beginning.

7.4   THE TECHNOLOGY (TRADING PLATFORM) CONTEXT

The CountryWa.com community portal (with listings of local businesses, community groups, towns, discussion boards and topic pages) was officially launched in May 2000. The portal used a distributed publishing system which enabled much of the content to be user-managed. Volunteers managed the topic pages and discussion boards. Business listings on the CountryWa.com portal were originally static listings, listings with links to e-mail addresses and web sites and listings of businesses that had their web page on the portal (the pages were created and maintained by the businesses themselves using templates). Subsequently, with the AU$100,000 funding under the NTN (Networking The Nation) programme, the portal was able to offer shopping cart enabled web pages with order forms. Businesses now pay between AU$77 and AU$1,650 for a listing depending on the package chosen (from simple listings to 10 fully editable web pages with shopping cart and order forms) with discounts for members of the Cooperative. However, some businesses can also be listed for free on CountryWa.com via the support of the chamber of commerce of the largest town in the region, which has linked its online business directory to the portal. This has effectively increased the number of businesses listed on CountryWa.com. There are no RFQ facilities available and although a Shopping Mall page was trialled in 2003, this was discontinued in 2004. Apart form being listed on the portal, businesses manage their own e-commerce endeavours.

7.4.1   Perceived Benefits

The perceived benefits of the trading platform in CountryWa.com are examined in terms of both the owners' and SME participants' views.

7.4.1.1 Owners' View of Perceived Benefits

The owners were asked what they perceived the benefits of the trading platform to be for themselves, SMEs in the region, and the region itself.

Owners' Perceived Benefits

To the owners of CountryWa.com the perceived benefits to themselves were tied to the perceived benefits of the region. Most of them were volunteers and it was their passion for the region and the need to see it develop in tandem with the rest of the nation that drove their involvement in ConuntryWa.com. To the original project manager, it also enabled her to gain a PhD out of it.

> *"I was passionate about this because this is my country, this is my homeland, and also like you what I got out of it was a PhD; it cost me a lot of money to do myself but it became the platform for my thesis and my hypothesis"* (Original project manager).

Perceived Benefits to SMEs

The owners of CountryWa.com perceived that the portal would give SMEs exposure both locally and outside the region for a small cost.

Table 7.8 Benefits for SMEs in CountryWa.com as perceived by Portal Owners

Participant	Comments
Part-time sales person and CountryWa Cooperative Board member	It's a web portal link that gives them a place to be linked on that Internet that relates to their geographical location...it's a huge benefit but it's really an online directory as well for business to be associated with other businesses
CountryWa Cooperative Board member	If I'm a business and I need to advertise, that is very cheap exposure for a year....just continuous exposure and of course it reaches a world audience

The additional AU$50,000 ITOL funding for e-commerce (if approved) was perceived to able to provide a secure, affordable and functional e-commerce solution for SMEs to compete with other e-commerce enabled businesses. It was also expected to *"foster a creative and competitive local e-market by showcasing local businesses, particularly early adopters, and by offering special 'beginner's packages' to selected local businesses"* (ITOL application of CountryWa Cooperative and other local bodies).

Perceived Regional Benefits

Owners of CountryWa.com perceived the regional benefits from the portal to be exposure to the rest of the world by *"providing access to the new technologies, training, introducing marketing and e-commerce solutions to move local goods and services, encouraging on-line engagement and building community awareness....sustainable regional community web portals have a greater chance at succeeding if they become "knowledge connected" i.e. the sharing and use of different ideas and methods to maximise communication and productivity"* (Excerpt from the thesis of the original project manager).

While community benefits and ICT awareness have materialised, without additional funding, CountryWa.com will not be able to move forward with its e-commerce agenda and bring about the additional benefits perceived for SMEs.

7.4.1.2 Participants' (SMEs') Perceived Benefits

As in the other two cases studied, benefits perceived by SMEs from participation in CountryWa.com are linked to their motives for joining.

226

Table 7.9 SMEs' Motives for joining CountryWa.com

Motive for Joining	Number of Participants	Examples of Comments
To support the local initiative	9	We're strong members of the community. I wanted to support something that was local. We wanted to be part of a community based organisation. I like seeing these community initiatives and I like to support them.
An experiment; to advertise; to get more traffic	4	To target people who were actually looking for this town. We had a product that I thought we could sell on CountryWa.com. I though it was a very good way of advertising.
To be known locally	2	I think because it is the regional web site for this area. To get our name around in this new venture.
Knew the owners	3	She's a very motivational lady. Someone I was dealing with at the time was involved.
Unknown	2	It was before my time. It was not my decision.

Of the SMEs interviewed, only a small number perceived that there would be any immediate personal economic benefits from participation. Pliaskin and Tatnall (2005, p. 344) in studying Bizewest, a B2B portal in Melbourne that closed in 2003 (2 years after being launched), found that businesses that joined had no clear idea of benefits and "few had looked objectively at the characteristics of portal technology or business-to-business e-commerce".

7.4.2 Value Added Services/Strategic Partnering

As the e-commerce side of CountryWa.com did not progress as far as that of RegWa.net, the question of value-added services was not raised with the SMEs. Given the failure of the EIP scheme and the short e-commerce workshops for SMEs, the owners felt that the portal could provide personalised e-commerce training and consultancy services to SMEs as part of the value-add, but only if further funding was received. This finding concurs with the view of Khalifa et al. (2003) that SMEs need personalised consultancy services to help them become active e-marketplace participants.

In terms of strategic partnering, CountryWa.com has managed to come as far as it did as a regional community portal because of partnering with the ultimate stakeholders, the regional inhabitants. The importance of strategic partnering with ultimate owners mirrors the findings of Fisher and Craig (2005) and Thompson (2005). The close working relationship with the software developer was also deemed to be a strategic partnership. The chamber of commerce of the largest town lists its online directory on CountryWa.com and the local government provides sponsorship. The owners of CountryWa.com partnered with local newspapers and the local television station for successful 'cross-media' advertising where each would promote the other on the different media and this helped overcome lack of funds for promotion.

7.4.3 Training and Technical Support

As the business section of the CountryWa.com portal is still basically an online directory, most users did not need any training. Those that created their own web pages via the portal were given training in the distributed publishing system by the project manager in the early days, and other volunteers later on. Training for the editors of the community and topic pages and bulletin boards was comprehensive to the extent that a major portion of the content is today user-managed. None of the SMEs had anything negative to say about technical support and one of the SMEs commented that *"I did ring up a few times with questions but they do have a very good manual that I downloaded"* (P1R3).

The findings from the CountryWa.com case indicate any general collective-type training or workshops in e-commerce for SMEs, while increasing awareness, will be unlikely to be translated into any major positive changes in the businesses themselves. The one-on-one approach is needed (as in RegWa.net) with consultants having to spend time with the owners (preferably at the business premises) to understand specific e-commerce needs.

7.4.4 Trust

Trust in CountryWa.net was rated positively by 18 SMEs with comments like *"it's all right"*; *"It is good considering a lot of it is voluntary"*; *"Very good, for a portal with no money they do extremely well"*; *it's OK so far"* and *"Because I wasn't doing any financial transactions, no problems"*. The 2 SMEs who did not rate trust in the portal positively commented that *"It's just the politics of it"* (P13R2) and *"I have some concerns about it"* (P15R2). 14 SMEs had no issues with the governance of CountryWa.com, while the remaining 6 SMEs had the following comments:

Table 7.10 SMEs that did not rate the Governance of CountryWa.com positively

Participant	Comments
P4R3	I don't know how much these questions are relevant to me now because I've been disassociated with the whole thing for so long that it has no relevance for me at all.
P5R3	It sort of fell in a hole for a while. We've only recently had contact again back with [the part-time sales person].
P8R3	I think it was run really well for a while there then went through a flat phase; then I thought the new Board would crank it up but there hasn't been a lot there.
P12R3	No, not really I'm not satisfied.
P13R3	Actually I'm not very happy.
P15R3	I think there is a conflict of interest. It can be very hard to get information about how it's being run or to have some say about how to run it. The way the model has been set up, you can have any number of shares but you don't have the voting rights about who ran it. I know people who are willing to invest in it but they want to be able to have a say in how it's run, not have just one vote for any amount of shareholding

In CountryWa.com, trust was fostered between the portal owners and the ultimate stakeholders because of the wide consultative process employed in the development of the portal and the governance process. As with RegWa.com trust embedded in the local relationships (Steinfield & Whitten, 1999) was used to promote participation in CountryWa.com. In attempting to account for the some of the negative responses about trust and governance, the researcher perceived the following:

- P4R3 had paid about AU$1000 (presumably it was for a few web pages with shopping cart and order form) and was listed on the 'Shopping Mall' page which was eventually taken down.

- P13R3 felt that it was time for CountryWa.com to take a quantum leap as it could be a powerful tool if *"someone wants to use it to get involved in politics....a lot more businesses would be online if it took on a more professional business-like attitude"*.

- P15R3 is a local developer/IT provider and could have been affronted at not being chosen to develop the portal software. *"Make it a self sustaining system or make a decision to shut it down. I think the community in general is not using it. There was no effort to amalgamate what was already available in the area before [CountryWa.com] and I think the other ones before didn't get costed the same way....If we talk of economic sustainability, why didn't they get a local company to do it? [CountryWa.com] hired a Perth company to handle the technical design of the portal"*.

7.4.5 Compatibility with Systems and Practice

The question of compatibility of the Countrywa.com system with that of SMEs was not raised as in essence it was an online directory for businesses. Compatibility was however an issue in terms of power supplies, connectivity and the telecommunications infrastructure, as in the case of RegWa.net *"The system itself is OK, it's sometimes the communications lines and electricity supply in the country that's a problem"* (original project manager). Some SMEs could not afford to invest in the multi web page option because of slow dial-up speeds and the erratic power supply. This finding supports that of the RegWa.net case that an integrated approach is needed in terms of the technology, the telecommunications infrastructure, power supplies and the training/mentoring of SMEs.

7.4.6 Perceived Ease of Use

The owners of CountryWa.com felt that the system was easy to use especially since the distributed publishing system did not require any knowledge of HTML (hypertext mark-up language) coding for users to be able to use them. 10 SMEs agreed with the views of the owners while some of those who did not rate ease of use positively had the following comments:

Table 7.11 SMEs that did not rate 'Ease of Use' of CountryWa.com positively.

Participant	Comments
P5R3	What I hate about websites is the scrolling down stuff to find the information. I think it'd be better off to have a direct link to something.
P9R3	I don't have very much to do with it.
P12R3	No I think it's a little bit difficult to navigate.
P15R3	It can be cumbersome to find something. It's not consistently organised. Not topics within towns; accommodations are not geographically coded; there does not seem to be any relation in the way the listings are made.
P17R3	I can't really say.
P19R3	Not bad, it's fairly limited when you go in and edit your pages.

7.4.7 Development Process

The development process of Countrywa.com was almost similar to that of RegWa.net except that the former did not have the requisite funds to take the e-commerce side of the portal to the next level (personalised consultancy for SMEs). The stage or phased development used in CountryWa.com meant that the lack of e-commerce activity has not forced the closure of the portal as the existing traffic still makes it an attractive and cost-effective advertising alternative for some SMEs. This is especially true of SMEs in tourism and accommodation as in the case of RegWa.net. This would indicate that the value of the portal in terms of e-commerce in the short-term lies in the B2C market for specific business types (tourism, accommodation, agriculture) with the market being outside the region.

7.4.8 Marketing Plan

The marketing and promotion plans for CountryWa.com were comprehensive and innovative, designed to capitalise on community ties to conserve limited project funds and to engender trust and inclusiveness of the general community. A logo competition was held to launch the [CountryWa.com] concept and promotion. A 13 year old resident from one of the towns was the winner and the logo is still used.

> "The young computer fanatic in a way symbolises the future of [CountryWa.com]. We must include and encourage young people in [CountryWa.com's] development if we are to succeed" (Excerpt from original project manager's thesis).

Flyers for the portal were distributed to every town through newspaper advertisements, inserts in local magazines, schools, TAFE colleges, libraries, main street shops and other commercial outlets. Local printers and graphics firms were used for the production of the promotional material. There were also interviews on local radio stations and news coverage in local newspapers and on the regional television network. Most important was the constant networking with local industry, media and community groups.

The current part-time portal manager of CountryWa.com has his own media consultancy and his view is that in terms of e-commerce it is not the number of hits to the portal that is important, but the number of completed transactions. *"Having a web site from an e-commerce perspective is not just being able to get people to see your products. You want them to buy your products and the way you get them to buy your product is by finding people who want to buy your product"*. His emphasis now is on bringing in advertising revenue for the portal and one of the ways to do this is by driving traffic to the portal through free online 'classifieds' started late in 2005.

7.4.9 Critical Mass

CountryWa.com was able to achieve a critical mass of participants on CountryWa.com by drawing on the support of the community for the local initiative. As in RegWa.net, graduated fee structures were used depending on the needs of the businesses. The stage approach used in the development of the portal helped build trust and support. Ownership of the portal by the community further engendered trust and use of the portal.

Nevertheless, while hits to the portal are relatively high and bookings and enquiries are being received via the portal (especially for the businesses in tourism and accommodation). CountryWa.com is not able to capitalise on these strengths to advance the e-commerce side of the portal due to a lack of funds.

7.5 THE ENVIRONMENTAL CONTEXT

This section looks at the effect of the environmental or external context on the CountryWa.com project.

7.5.1 Regional Profile

CountryWa.com serves a regional or rural area about a 4½ hour drive from Perth, the capital of WA. The area serviced by CountryWa.com is almost double the size of the area covered by RegWa.net but with slightly less than half the population and number of SMEs of the region served by RegWa.net.

From the thesis of the original project manager, it appears that CountryWa.com was also based on the same mistaken premise (as TwinTowns.com and RegWa.net) that local online trade would be the impetus for e-commerce even though the businesses in the regional areas had a preference for dealing face-to-face with established partners. Like RegWa.net, the region served by

CountryWa.net is renowned for tourism and agricultural products and it is the SMEs in accommodation and tourism that appear to be benefiting most from participation. However unlike RegWa.net, the lack of additional funding for promotion of the portal outside the region and to bring other SMEs in accommodation and tourism online is curtailing the further development of its e-commerce endeavours.

7.5.2 *Normative, Coercive and Mimetic Pressure*

The origins of CountryWa.com lie in the mimetic pressure on government agents and IT providers involved in the region to become part of the federal government-funded e-initiatives at that time. The push by the Perth Consortia for e-commerce despite inadequate resources and (apart from ECU) without committing their own resources to the project; the subsequent abandonment of interest by the Consortia in the project when there were no quick demonstrable returns are traits of the legitimacy motive behind adoption of both policy (Spencer, 2002) and IOIS (Rahim et al., 2002). In this case it was not even the consortia members which were to be the adopters of the actual technology.

However, the value of the CountryWa.com portal in increasing awareness and use of IT and simple e-commerce applications in the region has been achieved through leveraging the normative pressures that exist in a rural or regional society such as the one serviced by the portal. Community ties are strong in the region and people feel the need to belong to the community by supporting local initiatives. Three of the SMEs which joined the portal were either new to the area or in a new venture and saw participation as underscoring their positions as part of the community. Some participants joined because of social links with the members of the community who were championing the initiative. There was no indication of either coercive pressure from customers or buyers or mimetic pressure of competition that motivated participation.

7.6   EMERGENT THEMES AND EXTANT LITERATURE

Trust, Motive and Institutional Pressure

As with the case of RegWa.net, the empirical evidence from CountryWa.com shows that a 'bottom-up' grassroots approach to the development and management of regional community portals has positive outcomes for participation and use of the portal. Engaging the community of end-users in the development and management of the portal has engendered trust in the governance process and in the initiative as a whole. In CountryWa.com, vesting the ownership of the portal in the community itself has allowed continued support for it even though economic gains have not yet been realised. Leveraging the strength of the normative pressure inherent in the social networks of the region to garner support for the initiative ensured that the portal survived despite non convergence in the motives of the original owners. The phased development process of the portal that moved in tandem with the sophistication of regional users also allowed the building of trust in the initiative and the opportunity for the portal owners to experiment with other e-commerce offerings without jeopardising the existence of the portal.

In CountryWa.com, there has not yet been an opportunity to determine if the relationships embedded in the institutional business networks of the region can be enhanced by the portal. While such portals may not be able to compete with supply chain type e-marketplaces or vortals (and given their underlying objectives, should not), there may be an opportunity to utilise the existing technology of Countrywa.com to enhance SME communities of practice for sustainable regional development (Mason, Castleman & Parker, 2005). There should thus be a stronger emphasis on the community motive of such portals in terms of the business community and the portal should be viewed as an enabler of regional development and not as an end in itself.

Matching the Scope of the Initiative and Development Process to Resource Constraints and the Profile of the Region

Data from CountryWa.com supports the findings from both the cases of RegWa.net and TwinTowns.com that the environmental or external context of the initiative has a strong effect on its outcome. A techno-centric view of the initiative without proper consideration of the existing culture, business practices, consumption patterns and socio-economic nuances of the region could result in technology that although theoretically useful, has no practical application in improving existing business practices of SMEs in the region.

In CountryWa.com, the push to try and provide both e-commerce offerings and the community side of the portal simultaneously with the limited resources could have impacted negatively on the project (as in TwinTowns.com). The decision to allow the community side of the portal to be the focus of the initial offerings after the poor initial response by regional SMEs to e-commerce efforts by the owners of the portal has enabled it to survive this far. This is because the project capitalised on the culture of the region in supporting 'home-grown' projects and the trust embedded in the social networks that provided volunteers and user-driven content for the community side of the portal. By realising that they could not be everything to everybody, the local owners of the portal narrowed their focus to fit the available resources and the needs of the region. Given the profile of SME activities in the region, any effort expected to significantly affect uptake of e-commerce by SMEs would have had to be a targeted, personalised approach, one which the project could not afford either financially or in terms of the expertise needed at that time.

Findings from research have also shown that not all SME businesses are suitable for more advanced e-commerce options and that simple applications such as e-mail may suffice for the time being for some businesses (Commission of the European Communities, 2004; Taylor & Murphy, 2004). SMEs are thus not homogenous and they have differing e-commerce needs depending on a number of factors like business type, resources and attitude to growth. There is therefore a critical need for ex-ante theoretical evaluation of government-funded ICT programmes like the ones in this study to determine which SMEs need to be targeted and how best the programmes can fulfil their needs. In the participant context, one important construct that has emerged from the empirical data is the suitability of the business to Internet trading.

Communication, Feedback and Promotion

As with RegWa.net, communication, feedback and promotion in CountryWa.com have helped build traffic on the portal. Nevertheless, while there are site statistics about hits to the site, the top ten pages visited and so on, business participants are looking for evidence of statistics related to their own participation. Similar to the SMEs on RegWa.net which have not yet seen any business from participation, CountryWa.com SME participants want feedback on the amount of traffic directed to their sites via the portal.

Although some studies indicate that discussion forums are the most popular tool used in virtual communities (Lee et al., 2003), after six years of operation, the community online discussion boards on CountryWa.com appear to be waning in popularity. One of the reasons for this is that people in the region have become more familiar with the use of e-mail, MSN type chat facilities and online conferencing. It may be that the portal could be of more use for online collaboration in certain clusters of SMEs or groups of citizens (although it has not proved successful in RegWa.net) and this is one avenue that needs to be investigated. Another option is for feedback and communication to be personalised so that users get only very targeted information. However, both these options carry connotations of the need for further funding.

Self Sustainability versus the Public Funding paradigm

According to a study by Galloway, Mochrie and Deakins (2004) Internet forums have the potential for rural economic development but face problems of sustainability. This is especially so because of the limited number of businesses in the region and revenue streams are "diminished further in the long term if the forum provides ICT training, as the add-on market (site maintenance, hosting, etc.) will decrease as ICT skills among the population increase". As such, they argue for assistance in the form of developing strategic direction for individual forums and subsidies to perpetuate them.

In Australia, Internet forums like community portals are more often than not seed-funded by the government or collaboratively by industry partners but are expected to be self sustainable after some time. In the United Kingdom, a number of these portals are managed by local governments but problems abound in areas like interoperability and service delivery and few are capable of supporting interactive citizen services with local government departments (Musgrave, 2005). Nevertheless, it could be that one way in which community portals can become sustainable in Australia is for them to be financed by the federal government, owned by local governments but managed jointly with the citizens. This would mean incorporating the content of existing community portals with that of the local governments and could be one way of actually creating a 'one-stop shop' for all community related information and services. Federal government funding for local e-commerce projects could then also be coordinated by the local governments who although they may be best placed to know the specific needs of their communities, are not financially or technically able enough to fulfil these needs.

7.7   SUMMARY - SUCCESS AND BENEFITS OF THE TRADING PLATFORM IN COUNTRYWA.COM

This section deals with the application of the data collected from CountryWa.com the Trading Platform Success Model (figure 3.3) and the accompanying tables of costs (table 3.3) and success metrics (table 3.4) to determine the success of the initiative.

7.7.1   Owners' Costs

In CountryWa.com, AU$243,500 enabled the building and management of a community portal incorporating community content, a business directory and the availability of shopping-cart and order enabled web pages for participants. However, as in the case of RegWa.net, there were hidden costs in the form of help from volunteers and user-generated content. The funding was not sufficient for the kind of personalised training or consultancy that SMEs would need to enable them to make e-commerce part of their business plans, nor was it sufficient to adequately promote the portal outside the region to attract visitors for tourism.

CountryWa.com did not have a 'hands-on' portal manager for two years till the second quarter of 2005. At the moment, only a part-time manager can be employed and although he is actively trying to find ways to make the portal sustainable, he will have to make it compete with commercial models in order to generate new revenue streams. There are also insufficient funds for the kind of statistics package that would enable tracking of hits for each SME participant to convince them of the advertising value of participation. As content is user-managed, some of it is outdated and there are insufficient funds to employ anyone to ensure currency of the information on the portal. Once again it appears that the funding paradigm has provided only for the technology but not the ongoing maintenance and enhancement of the portal.

7.7.2 SME Participants' Costs

SMEs interviewed in CountryWa.com already had Internet connections and some had their own web pages before joining the portal. Most paid between AU$66 to $300 dollars to participate depending on the listing options chosen and two were listed for free via the chamber of commerce link. One SME paid AU$1000 for the shopping cart and order page option but has not continued to pay (although he is still listed as a member). Most SMEs did not think the participation fees were prohibitive.

7.7.3 Content Quality, Trading Platform System Quality and Service/Value Added Quality

The quality of content, system, value-added and service offerings were determined based on the researcher's own observations and the interview responses of owners and SMEs.

Content Quality

The metrics used for determining content quality in this case are similar to those used in RegWa.net i.e. currency, accuracy, relevance, timeliness and security.

From the website of CountryWa.com, it appeared that most of the information managed by portal staff was current, accurate and relevant (e.g. calendar of events, classifieds, newsletter, and site statistics), although there were occasions of more than one listing for a business within the same category. The organisation of the content could be confusing especially as there were listings for members (anyone who paid to be on the portal), a listing for trades and services (which included CountryWa.com members and members of the chamber of commerce) and the chamber of commerce directory itself. The information managed by users varied in terms of currency and accuracy and owners agreed that because so much of the content was user-managed, it was hard to keep track of it. The owners felt that the business information would be current and accurate whereas some of the community content may not.

The owners also felt that the information was relevant as it was posted by the owners themselves (businesses) and interested community groups and that because the pages were capable of being dynamically updated, it was timely. In terms of security of the content, the owners felt that each member had control of its own information although there are now controls in place to prevent misuse of open discussion boards and 'unsuitable material'. This was due to a breach of security in the early days of the portal where one of the volunteers attempted sabotage by linking member sites (like the local primary school) to sites containing pornography and posting abuse on the bulletin boards.

SME participants' opinions of content quality are categorised as per table 7.12. Responses considered positive were *"very accurate"*, *"no problems"*, *"usually pretty good"*, *"it is, for what they're trying to do"* and *"Yes, For sure"*.

Table 7.12 SMEs' Opinions of Content Quality in CountryWa.com

Metric	Positive (Number of Responses)	Negative (Number of Responses)	Other (Number of Responses)
Currency	5	4	11
Accuracy	6	4	10
Relevance	10	2	8
Timeliness	10	2	8
Security	17	3	

Some of the responses in the column rated 'other' for currency, accuracy, timeliness and security were *"I can't answer that"*, *"I don't know"*; *"haven't looked lately"*; *"it's 80%"*; *"there's not enough information"* and *"I think it's better off since I last looked"*. In terms of security, the remaining 3 SMEs that rated security of the content negatively had the following comments:

Table 7.13 Negative Comments by SMEs on Security of CountryWa.com

Participant	Comments
P4R3	I did get one order and it was a fake order that someone did specifically to test it out, some smart aleck...about a million dollars worth of an order for about 500 photocopiers and he did it deliberately to prove a point that it was not secure and you couldn't tell who you were getting your orders from
P13R3	I do have some issues. The people who do the technical work for [CountryWa.com], they interfered with my site and I was not happy with that.
P15R3	Failures happen

On the whole, the quality of content on RegWa.net had a mixed rating.

Trading Platform System Quality

The metrics used to determine the system quality in CountryWa.com are: reliability of software/network; ease of use; online response time and page loading speed; visual appearance and convenience of accessibility (unlike RegWa.net, the question of market reach was not broached as there has been no active promotion of the portal outside of the region, nor has there been any communication about any intentions to do so).

Table 7.14 SMEs' Opinions of the Trading Platform System Quality of CountryWa.com

Metric	Positive (Number of Responses)	Negative (Number of Responses)	Other (Number of Responses)
Reliability	15	1	4
Ease of use	10	5	4
Response time & page loading speed	14	2	4
Visual appearance	14	2	4
Convenience of Accessibility	12	4	4

Examples of responses categorised under 'Other', were *"I can't answer that"*; *"I haven't been in there for a while"*; *"not sure"* and *"not qualified to say"*. The SME which had a negative response for reliability (P14R3) is a software developer and commented that *"There was a time when it was down for several weeks because of a hardware failure and there was no backup copy. We could provide that type of service but the spin offs don't seem to be reaching far from this"*.

The owners of CountryWa.com felt that reliability was an issue only because of the shortcomings in the telecommunications infrastructure and the power supply. The newly appointed part-time portal manager was of the opinion that some of the features could be better but again the portal was faced with funding constraints.

On the whole, the trading platform system quality was rated better than content quality and on balance responses were more positive.

Service/Value Added Quality

Metrics used to ascertain service and value added quality were: site intelligence; feedback mechanisms; relevant search facilities; tracking capabilities; helpdesk/set-up help/advice (listings of frequently asked questions [FAQs]); account maintenance and training (in conversion to e-business and for system use).

While on the whole SMEs in CountryWa.com did not have any grievances with training, advice, technical support, account maintenance and feedback (in terms of communication with owners), as with RegWa.net, site intelligence and tracking capabilities for individual participants were absent. This is an important point as SMEs that have not yet obtained any business from the portal are not sure of even the advertising value of being listed.

According to the portal manager of CountryWa.com, this issue was being considered but funding constraints limit further enhancements.

7.7.4 Use, User Satisfaction and Net Benefits

13 SMEs felt that on the whole they were satisfied with the portal and its offerings while 5 were not because there were no returns from participation and had grievances with the governance process. The remaining 2 SMEs said they didn't know. The following statistics were obtained in addition to participants' views.

Table 7.15 Selected Statistics for CountryWa.com as at May 2005

Item	Statistics
Businesses listed on Portal	Approximately 1500 (Figure yet to be obtained for the current number of paying participants). In 2001, 165 paying businesses and organisations listed on the portal. In May, 2005 230 members listed.
Community groups listed	Approximately 100 of which 4 are members.
Government Listings	Approximately 15 of which 9 are members. 28 towns and 15 schools listed
Hits to the portal	Monthly Average 1.2 million
Operating costs	Approximately AU$5000
Direct Income	Slightly less than AU$5000 per month from all sources
Evidence of online networks and participation in them	Inactive

According to the statistics, CountryWa.com can barely sustain its existence. There is no money for the kind of activities that would enhance the e-commerce side of the portal and provide individualised feedback to SMEs on the economic returns for their participation. While it is encouraging that SMEs in the accommodation and tourism sector are beginning to realise some benefits, funds are insufficient to bring other non participants on Board. The portal also faces a threat from the more targeted 'Visitor's Centre' which is funded by the state tourism development commission because of the wider promotion opportunities available to the latter.

The owners of CountryWa.com are of the opinion that the greatest benefits at the moment are at the community level. The general public's awareness of ICT and e-commerce has grown because of the project and some citizens have gone on to seek careers in the ICT industry. One local micro IT company that was employed to do work for the project has now become a medium sized business and small holiday accommodation vendors have embraced Internet advertising via the portal. It is only in certain areas that some SMEs are beginning to see small economic returns from participation.

SMEs' opinions of the actual benefits from participation in CountryWa.net are categorised and summarised in table 7.16:

Table 7.16 SMEs' Opinions of Actual Benefits from Participation in CountryWa.com

Metric	Yes (Number of Responses)	No (Number of Responses)	Other (Number of Responses)
Increased Business?	7	8	5
Cost Savings?	6	12	2
Other benefits?	5	15	

Most SMEs that experienced an increase in business reported that it was only marginal while responses classified under 'Other' involved SMEs which could not comment because there was no statistics package to let them know if business was channelled to them via the portal. In terms of other benefits, positive responses were *"No direct benefits but indirectly it has increased awareness of the Internet and e-commerce and I've learned lots"*; *"we've got to know them in that time and built a good relationship there"*; *"it's given us a presence in the community"* and *"it gives us credibility"*.

7.7.5 Success of CountryWa.com

Although CountryWa.com has received the most hits of the three portals in the study, application of the Trading Success Platform Model (figure 3.3) to the empirical data indicates a mixed result. As in the case of RegWa.net, viewed from a purely commercial economic basis (self sustainability or profitability) CountryWa.com has not been a success. If viewed from the perspective of raising awareness of the Internet, ICT and e-commerce in the region, then CountryWa.com has been a success.

Owners and SME participants' opinions on the success of CountryWa.com are presented in the next sections.

Owners' View of Success

Table 7.17 Owners' Views of the Success of CountryWa.com

Position	Comment
Original project manager	Yes. If it folded tomorrow, it was a success and therefore one can put that up academically, socially and economically as a viable model....to me, now that I see it growing well beyond what it was 3 years ago, I think that that could be seen as a success and financially we might not be turning over a lot of money but if there's enough to keep [the portal manager] there, [the part-time sales person] who is the new marketing person, who only wants to work part time, then eventually I hope that we can train some young people up to take over, that's my dream.
Portal manager	It has been successful and the thing that points to the success is that it's been established for 6 years and I think it's probably a record and it will stay around.
Part time sales person/ CountryWa Cooperative board member	Yes given the limited resources we've had to work with.
CountryWa Cooperative board member	Yes I think it has.

240

The owners felt that improvements especially on the e-commerce side and marketing side could be achieved if there was funding support form the state or federal government.

SME Participants' Views of Success

8 SME participants felt that CountyWa.com was a success and 4 did not. Of the four that did not, two qualified their responses by saying it may well have been a success for others. Examples of the 8 responses classified as 'Other' are: *"too soon to say"*; *"I haven't thought about it"*; *"I can't comment on that"*; *"still a work-in-progress"* and *"for new businesses perhaps"*. SMEs felt that the portal could be improved with more promotion and with statistics and targeted feedback on traffic directed to their sites.

Conclusion

As the motive of CountryWa.com was more focused on bringing the regional community online rather than on e-commerce, the general consensus is that for what it tried to achieve it is a success. If measured in terms of increased uptake of e-commerce activities by SMEs then there is no evidence that SMEs have actually been moved to grow their e-commerce activities by participating on the portal. Nevertheless, most SMEs were reticent about calling the initiative a failure even if they had no returns from participation. This could be due to the community culture of being supportive of the local effort. As an example, the following is an excerpt from the interview with P4R3 (this SME had spent AU$1,000 for shopping cart and order page options) when asked if CountryWa.com could be considered a success:

> *"I couldn't tell you. I haven't been associated with it for so long that I'd be making stuff up"* (P4R3).

> *"Well that's fine because even a negative response tells us something"* (Researcher).

> *"It's neither negative nor positive"* (P4R3).

> *"Well, what I mean by negative in this sense is that you've tried it and found that it's not for you and what that can tell us is that perhaps it doesn't work for businesses like yours in the short term"* (Researcher).

> *"It was an experiment; I didn't really know what I was doing when I did it. I fully understand it now and I won't be entering into e-commerce again until I am totally set up and ready to go....Well it's been nice and I've learnt from it"* (P4R3).

Although the owners feel that the portal is now ready to move to the next stage of e-commerce activities, they are unable to make that move due to insufficient funds.

The findings from CountryWa.com have further refined the conceptual frameworks of the study as per table 7.18.

Table 7.18 Results from the Findings of CountryWa.com in terms of Integrated Theoretical Framework of Factors Affecting Success or Failure of Government-Supported Regional Internet Trading Platforms for SMEs

Context	Construct	RegWa.net
Market-Maker (Owner)	Ownership structure and Governance	Critical
	Motivation/focus	High
	Competencies (IS/project management skills)	Critical
	Financial resources	Critical
	Trust	Critical
	Strategic partnering	Partners with participants
Technology (Trading Platform)	Perceived benefits, relative advantage and Usefulness	High
	Critical mass/liquidity	High
	Value-added services/Strategic partnering (e.g. logistics, financial)	Low
	REM training and technical support	High but there may be a need to involve more local providers to grow the local IT industry.
	Compatibility (with users' systems)	Low
	Trust	Critical
	REM development and timing of features offered	Critical
	Perceived ease of use	High
	Good marketing plan	High
Organisational (SME participant)	Top management commitment/innovativeness	Not conclusive.
	Internal IT/IS/e-business (readiness).	Not conclusive
	Size of firm	Low. Small firms were willing to join if they can see the benefits and costs are not prohibitive.
Environmental (External)	Regional SME profile. Local consumer needs and behaviour. Regional profile	Critical
	Government support and incentives	Critical. Just 'building it will not guarantee that they will come'.
	Normative, coercive and mimetic pressure/existing trading relationships	Critical. Tied to regional/SME profile

Results indicate that constructs from the environmental and trading platform owner perspectives appear to have the greatest effect on the success or failure of Government-Supported Regional Internet Trading Platforms for SMEs.

CHAPTER 8

DISCUSSION AND CONCLUSIONS

8.1   INTRODUCTION

This chapter discusses some of the more salient findings across the three cases and their impact on the conceptual frameworks formulated at the beginning of the study. A refined framework is then presented of the facilitators and inhibitors to successful implementation of government-sponsored regional Internet trading platforms for SMEs.

The discussion then turns to the evaluation of the initiatives in this study. The efficacy of the Trading Platform Success Model (figure 3.3) and its accompanying cost and success metrics (tables 3.3 and 3.4) within the overarching content-context-process (CCP) evaluation approach (Symons, 1991) are assessed in the light of the findings. The research questions are revisited and an integrated model is proposed for the staged evaluation and implementation of government-supported regional trading platforms for SMEs that are part of community portals. At the end of the chapter, the conclusions that can be drawn from this study are summarised.

8.2   THE MISMATCH BETWEEN MOTIVATION AND BUSINESS MODEL

The original motive behind the creation of the three portals in this study was the provision of Internet trading platforms to encourage adoption of e-commerce among the regional SME business community. Increased e-commerce uptake was viewed as a way to foster regional economic development. The trading platforms were to provide SMEs with an inexpensive introduction to e-marketplace trading in a trusted environment. It was an intervention against unmet needs of the regional SME sector by regular market forces and one that would enable them to compete in the e-environment.

According to Stockdale and Standing (2004), one of the barriers to SME participation in e-marketplaces is market makers' lack of perception of the difficulties of smaller companies and their differing needs. High membership fees and complicated technology compliance issues preclude SME participation in many e-marketplaces and leave them uncertain of the benefits that they can obtain from e-marketplace trading. Any intervention to provide SMEs a platform to experiment with Internet trading would then have to incorporate the following features: a) low entry fees b) minimal outlays by SMEs on technology compliance c) training and mentoring to demonstrate how Internet trading can benefit each SME involved. Given their *raison d'être,* it is reasonable to expect that such government-supported trading platforms would be viewed as longer-term economic development tools. However, the three trading platforms in this study were funded on the basis that they would become self sustainable (or even profitable) in the short term. The mismatch between motive and business model was not only based on the mistaken premise that 'if you build it they will come' (a sentiment which prevailed during the dot.com boom), but also on the public funding paradigm for initiatives like the ones in the study.

8.2.1 Funding

The business plans for all three trading platforms were prepared and submitted for funding under the ITOL programme. Apart from funding up to 50 percent of the cost of the project subject to a maximum of AU$200,000, other conditions of ITOL funding are that projects need to be completed in 12 months and there is the need to demonstrate how the application meets the market criteria of sustaining or commercialising the project when grant funding ceases. The TwinTowns.com application for ITOL funding was declined while RegWa.net and CountryWa.com were successful in obtaining funding of AU$90,000 and AU$75,000 respectively. As some of the owners' contributions to the project were 'in-kind' and not 'in-cash', effectively Regwa.net and CountryWa.com had less than AU$180,000 and AU$150,000 to pay for software development, training, promotion and maintenance of the trading platforms and portals. Although the owners of the three portals in this study were not prevented from seeking other sources of external funding (from other government funding schemes or even applying again under ITOL but for a different purpose), it is not reflective of good project or economic development planning to have such a fragmented method of financing.

In contrast, some of the more successful public-funded Internet trading platform projects for SMEs in Europe appear to be either better funded or more targeted or both (E-Business Policy Group, 2002). The European Commission acknowledges the need for such projects to be adequately resourced not only for development but also for monitoring and evaluation of project results against pre-defined targets. There does not appear to be any standard timeframe for completion of projects, nor is there a pre-determined maximum amount available for funding. For example, the West Midlands Collaborative Commerce Marketplace (or WMCCM, which can be found at http://www.wmccm.co.uk/WMCCM) was already a functioning regional portal catering for engineering SMEs in the core West Midlands region of the United Kingdom, when additional funding of £1.2 Million was invested into the project in 2003. At that time, it was reported that a total cost of the project was £3.1 million (Government Office for The West Midlands, 2002). The WMCCM aims to increase sales and lower costs through providing easy access to the core competencies and capabilities of SMEs by providing tools such as projects, clusters, catalogues, auctions, bazaars and marketplace tenders. The project is spearheaded by the Warwick Manufacturing Group of the University of Warwick.

Funding for e-commerce projects for SMEs in Europe are also viewed as having only limited lifetime as publicly supported initiatives and "once they reach an end, they should, where possible and appropriate, be turned into self-sustainable solutions, building upon the content and experience acquired during the lifetime of the projects" (E-Business Policy Group, 2002, p. 35). However, the funding appears to be rooted in a more realistic view of the necessary resources required to get SMEs to take their first steps in Internet trading. The incremental and techno-centric public funding paradigm in Australia under programmes like ITOL can result in wasted public funds and scepticism. In the case of TwinTowns.com, a number of SME participants stated that they would look askance at any such initiatives in the future. The techno-centric funding policy can also result in the actual objectives of the initiative not being realised. In RegWa.net, it was only with the additional funding of AU$2.2 million from the WA state government that the smaller SMEs in niche product areas have been given free consultation on their e-business needs and free shopping cart facilities on the portal. In CountryWa.com, this has not been possible despite it having the highest amount of traffic among the three portals.

8.2.2 Development Process

Although TwinTowns.com was not successful in obtaining ITOL funding, it was still financed to the extent of AU$360,000 from internal and other government funding. Despite receiving the most funding of the three portals prior to 2003, TwinTowns.com did not manage to achieve a working portal. To a large extent this was due to the attempt to launch all features of the portal simultaneously even before the REM portion was technically ready. In comparison, RegWa.net and CountryWa.com launched the business directories first, together with the community portal. The response and support from the local community for the portal and from the business community for the directory made it an effective advertising alternative for local businesses. It was only when this support was demonstrated that the e-commerce functions of the portal were introduced. This development process also appears to be one that the WMCCM has taken, first gaining support of local SMEs and other businesses for the regional business portal and directory and only later developing the collaborative e-marketplace.

The staged or phased development process in RegWa.net, CountryWa.com and the WMCCM offers two distinct advantages. Firstly, the sophistication of the portal or offerings can grow in tandem with the competencies of the SME participants. Secondly, the staged approach enables proper evaluation of the initiative. This allows owners to determine if project objectives are being met and to alter plans if they are not, and to also determine if the underlying factors that would facilitate a successful transition to the next stage of offerings are in place.

TwinTowns.com, RegWa.net and CountryWa.com are communities that have been brought online, not communities that had their foundations built in cyber space. They should therefore be viewed as part of a hybrid online/off-line strategy to build uptake of e-commerce that can lead to economic development in a region. Market makers need to understand how best the online initiative can be deployed so as to complement local off line strategies and leverage local strengths and relationships. The stages discussed in the literature on portal (Clarke & Flaherty, 2003; Damsgaard, 2002) and e-marketplace (Raisch, 2001) development may well be appropriate for an integrated and IT active community with high levels of motivation to interact. In regional Internet trading platforms for SMEs, the stages need to be preceded by additional steps when small businesses are involved and the 'village' concept embraced. These include: developing real understanding of benefits from e-communities; stimulating and nurturing motivation to actively participate; education and training on IT and e-business for all users; gaining commitment from all stakeholders and realistic budgeting and hands on project management.

Fisher and Craig (2005) demonstrated the need for proper planning and evaluation in designing B2B portals for SMEs, while Braun (2003) demonstrated the steps necessary in building virtual communities of collaboration involving SMEs. Based on the research and the findings from this study, a staged or phased approach to the development and management of government-supported community portal regional trading platforms for SMEs like those in this study is recommended as per figure 8.1:

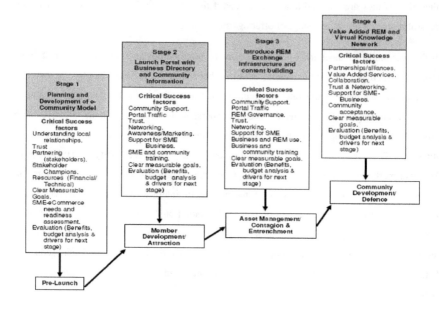

Figure 8.1 Model for Staged Development of Government-Supported Community Portal Regional Internet Trading Platforms for SMEs.

In Stage 1, it is important that market makers understand the regional profile and how it can be leveraged to promote trust and support of the initiative. This will determine the ownership structure and governance of the portal. For example, are there strong community or local business ties? Are businesses in the region largely B2C, B2B or a mix? Would the prevailing type of regional trading relationships favour a vertical REM? An assessment needs to be conducted to determine if the SMEs in the region are ready for such an initiative; if not, resources may need to be dedicated to training them. There is also a need to set clear and measurable goals and to balance this against resources. If there are sufficient drivers, the launch of the portal can proceed with a business directory and general community content; otherwise there may be a need to up-skill SMEs or a need to work on the development of community ties first.

Stage 2 in the development of community portal regional Internet trading platforms will be where critical mass or member development occurs. There should be content to attract the general and business communities as well as training for them to be able to use the features of the portal. At this stage market makers should identify and target players who will create a bandwagon effect of participation. In RegWa.net and CountryWa.com, this was done through leveraging the existing

248

community and business ties to create support of the portal. There is a need to continuously promote the portal to both communities. As with stage 1, there is a need to evaluate if there are benefits to further development, set measurable goals and measure them against resources and decide if the time is right for the next stage. If it is not, then work needs to be done to achieve the critical success factors like critical mass. It is in this stage that the trading platform exchange infrastructure should be developed based on what is most suitable for the region.

The trading platform exchange mechanism can be introduced in Stage 3. While there should be ongoing training, awareness building and membership development of the general community, this stage of development will focus on the e-commerce aspects of the portal. There is a need for one-on-one e-business consultancy for SMEs to demonstrate how participation can benefit them. Market makers need to introduce content that will firstly attract participants and then entrench them in platform usage. The strategies used in this phase could be membership discounts, special offers, business advice and industry information.

In the next stage, the introduction of value added services such as logistics or finance, networking, clustering and data mining would help defend and grow the membership of the portal and the trading platform. As with the case of RegWa.net, there may be a need to form vertical clusters in order to more effectively attract buyers from outside the region by promoting the region's special offerings.

The staged approach of incremental development thus allows platform sophistication to grow alongside evolution of learning in the SME e-business context so that one does not get ahead of the other. It also allows the latest developments in the regular e-marketplace landscape to be incorporated into the planning and development of community portal regional Internet trading platforms for SMEs. This can lead to realistic goal setting and a structured approach to the evaluation of costs and benefits.

8.2.3 The Need for a Shared View of Benefits

Perceived relative advantage or perceived benefits appear to be one of the main drivers in initiatives like the ones in the study. It is vital that SMEs perceive some value or benefit from the portal in order to get them to participate. Findings from RegWa.net and CountryWa.com indicate that even though some SMEs had no clear idea of the economic benefits from participation, they still participated in order to support the local initiative. Although some of them have yet to reap any financial returns, they are still not prepared to label the initiative a failure as they recognise that there are some community benefits for the region and that other SMEs may well have benefited financially. In the two portals in regional WA, the wide consultative governance approach and the staged development resulted in most participants being able to make informed decisions about what they expected to get out of participation. Some SMEs that have not benefited financially view participation as a learning experience at a cost that was not prohibitive.

In contrast, SMEs in TwinTowns.com were led from the outset to believe that there would be increased business (either from the local governments or the major regional buyers) in the B2B scenario and that the community portal would ensure a market for those targeting B2C business. There does not appear to be any effort made by the owners to push through the idea of economic development and competence building to participants. This lack of openness by the owners was compounded by the infighting and power-plays among them.

The findings from the study thus show that it is important for trading platform owners to be candid with SMEs about the benefits that they can expect to receive and the timeframe within which those benefits can be realised. It is also important to keep participants informed about the progress of the portal so that they can review the reasons for their participation. Apart from the community benefits of increased awareness of e-commerce, participants in RegWa.net and CountryWa.com that have not seen any economic returns still see the strategic value of the portal as an alternative advertising avenue; one which is more targeted to the region, has a wider reach than they can obtain by their own endeavours and at a fraction of the cost of other alternatives.

8.3   THE IMPORTANCE OF THE EXTERNAL/ENVIRONMENTAL CONTEXT

One of the major findings from this research is the importance of the external or environmental context in using e-commerce as a regional economic development strategy. The findings support the literature on SME adoption of IS (Scupola, 2003), IOIS (Kumar et al., 1998), regional e-commerce (Steinfield & Whitten, 1999) and e-marketplace participation (Hsiao, 2003) which highlight the importance of considering external factors like culture, normative, coercive and mimetic pressures, institutional structures and actual regional needs and geographical location on the decision to adopt a particular ICT.

8.3.1   Community Networking and Trust Embeddedness

The cases of RegWa.net and CountryWa.com illustrate how the trust embedded in the existing social and business networks of the region can be leveraged to draw support for the initiative. In RegWa.net, one SME equated participation with being a member of an online Chamber of Commerce. In addition, the initial involvement of the chamber of commerce, the local ISPs and other local businesses in RegWa.net created strong institutional pressures for businesses to join the portal. In CountryWa.com some SMEs joined because they wanted to show their support of the community initiative and because some personally knew the people who were involved in the project. The areas serviced by RegWa.net and CountryWa.com are regional areas where such community and business networks are strong to the extent that a lot of voluntary work went into the projects. The ownership structure of both RegWa.net and CountryWa.com capitalised on the culture and institutional ties within the region.

In the case of TwinTowns.com, the portal was set up to service two towns within a metropolitan area, where community and business ties are not as strong as that of country areas. A number of people living in the two towns do not exclusively work, study, shop or visit entertainment venues within the region. They belong to smaller fragmented communities (for example the school, the business and neighbourhood communities) which may not converge and they may thus not feel any 'ownership' of local initiatives like TwinTowns.com. This can have a negative effect on a 'buy local online' campaign like the one that was supposed to drive business on the portal.

It is therefore important for proper evaluation to determine how the existing culture and networking in the region can impact on the initiative.

8.3.2 Alignment of Platform Model with Regional/SME Profile

It is crucial that ICT driven regional economic development initiatives like trading platforms for SMEs are aligned with the needs and characteristics of not only the SMEs targeted but the region as well. Theory-based programme evaluation (Shadish Jr. et al., 1991; Torvatn, 1999; W.K. Kellogg Foundation, 1998) involves assessing the suitability of the intervention against the needs and assets of the community and the influential factors (the theory) that can impact on the programme. The results of this study indicate that it is difficult to build short term transactional liquidity on a B2B/B2C portal based on local regional buying and selling. This is especially so where major buyers are already in existing buyer-seller relationships that cannot be migrated to the platform and local consumers prefer face-to-face dealings. In the cases studied, SMEs which had goods or services that were suitable for Internet trading (tourism, accommodation and niche products) and that were attractive to buyers outside the region appear to have benefited more from participation. A regional Internet trading platform like TwinTowns.com that is part of a community portal may also not be suitable for a diverse group of SMEs in a metropolitan area especially if funding is limited and the region is not renowned for any particular economic activity that can attract buyers from outside the region. This is because in this type of initiative SMEs are treated as a homogenous group when in fact they have differing needs and resources and require different levels and types of assistance to help them on their e-commerce journeys.

251

8.4   SUMMARY OF RESEARCH QUESTIONS

This section will revisit the questions that this research sought to answer and discuss how they have been addressed.

Research Question 1 - What are the factors that facilitate and inhibit the successful implementation of government-sponsored regional Internet trading platforms for SMEs?

Subsidiary Questions:

RQ1i.   How do existing theoretical frameworks explain these facilitators and inhibitors?

RQ1ii.   Why are these factors significant?

Research Question 2 – How and where can existing theories of IT adoption be used to explain the adoption and use of Internet trading platforms by governments in promoting SME uptake of e-commerce and regional economic development?

Subsidiary Questions:

RQ2i. What are the strengths of existing IT adoption theories?

RQ2ii. What are the limitations of these theories?

The building of the conceptual framework of factors affecting success or failure of the implementation of government-supported regional Internet trading platforms for SMEs began with the examination of existing theoretical frameworks from the IS field that have been applied to study the areas of e-marketplaces, portals and virtual communities. Critical success factors and development issues from these frameworks were significant in providing the scaffolding to create the market maker (or owner) and technology contexts of the initiatives to be studied.   However, while some important constructs of the existing frameworks could be used to explain the facilitators and inhibitors, no one framework could be used in its entirety and on its own given the complex nature of the phenomenon to be studied. The existing theoretical frameworks on e-marketplaces, portals and virtual communities did not consider trading platforms with non profit or economic development motives, nor did they consider SMEs as their specific targets. There was therefore a need to determine if this target population had specific characteristics that could impact on the implementation of the trading platform (and how they impacted implementation). Existing theories of SME adoption of IT/e-commerce/IOIS were examined to provide this view.

The adoption theories were used to provide the participant context in determining the facilitators and inhibitors of successful implementation of government-supported Internet trading platforms for SMEs. The theories were examined and relevant constructs identified. The strength of the existing theories lay in the fact that they were the accumulation of theoretical and empirical research in the IS and organisational disciplines and provided tested and tried constructs with which to form the conceptual framework of this study. However, once again, the complex nature of the initiatives in this study limited the use of any single adoption theory to adequately explain the effect of the participant context. Moreover, there appeared to be overlapping constructs between the theories. It was necessary to synthesise the various adoption theories by eliminating duplicate constructs. Having identified some constructs from existing theories and models, the missing link was the particular nature of the trading platforms to be studied (the wide scope, ownership/governance structure and the economic development motive) and the only way to address this gap was by using the findings from the participant observation in TwinTowns.com. A conceptual integrated theoretical framework of factors affecting success or failure of the implementation of government-supported regional Internet trading platforms for SMEs was thus derived (table 3.2) and was refined by empirical findings from the three cases using the structured case study method (Carroll & Swatman, 2000). The findings are reproduced in table 8.1., indicating that some factors are more critical than others, especially those in the environmental and market-maker (or owner) contexts.

Table 8.1 Results from the Findings of the Three cases in terms of Integrated Theoretical Framework of Factors Affecting Success or Failure of Government-Supported Regional Internet Trading Platforms for SMEs

Context	Construct	TwinTowns.com	RegWa.net	CountryWa.com
Market-Maker (Owner)	Ownership structure and Governance	Critical	Critical	Critical
	Motivation/focus	High	High	High
	Competencies IS/project management skills)	High	High	Critical
	Financial resources	High	High	Critical
	Trust	Critical	Critical	Critical
	Strategic partnering	High	Partners with participants	Partners with participants
Technology (Trading Platform)	Perceived benefits, relative advantage and Usefulness	High	High	High
	Critical mass/liquidity	High	High	High
	Value-added services/Strategic partnering (e.g. logistics, financial)	Low	Low	Low

Context	Construct	TwinTowns.com	RegWa.net	CountryWa.com
	REM training and technical support	High	High but consultancy should not compete with commercial providers	High but there may be a need to involve more local providers to grow the local IT industry.
	Compatibility (with users' systems)	Low	Low	Low
	Trust	Critical	Critical	Critical
	REM development and timing of features offered	High	Critical	Critical
	Perceived ease of use	High	High	High
	Good marketing plan	High	High	High
Organisational (SME participant)	Top management commitment, innovativeness	Inconclusive	High in the beginning (under self-sustainability model)	Not conclusive.
	Internal IT/IS/e-business (readiness).	Context dependent	High in the beginning (under self-sustainability model)	Not conclusive
	Size of firm	Context dependent	Low. Small firms were willing to join if they can see the benefits and costs are not prohibitive.	Low. Small firms were willing to join if they can see the benefits and costs are not prohibitive.
Environmental (External)	Regional SME profile. Local consumer needs and behaviour. Regional profile	Critical	Critical	Critical
	Government support and incentives	High	Critical. Just 'building it will not guarantee that they will come'.	Critical. Just 'building it will not guarantee that they will come'.
	Normative, coercive and mimetic pressure/ existing trading relationships	High	High. Tied in to regional/SME profile	Critical. Tied to regional/SME profile

The refined integrated theoretical framework allowed significant factors (and the relationships between them) to be identified. These are presented in figure 8.2.

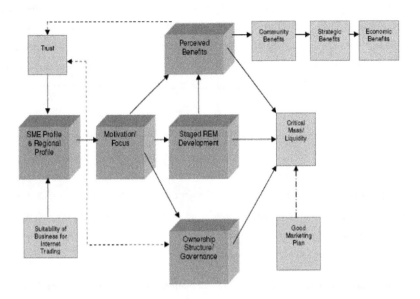

Figure 8.2 Significant Factors affecting Success or Failure of Government-supported Regional Internet Trading Platforms for SMEs.

These factors are significant because they provide a holistic view of the considerations that need to be examined in using such trading platforms as regional development tools. In developing a regional trading platform for SMEs, government authorities should first determine if the profile of the SMEs and the region are suitable for this type of initiative and can be leveraged to achieve success. SMEs with businesses that are suitable for Internet trading need to be identified and their trust and support garnered. SMEs in RegWa.net and CountryWa.com that have appeared to have benefited financially from participation are predominantly small operators in the areas of tourism, accommodation and specialty goods. Participation has given these SMEs exposure to consumers outside the region from which most of their business is generated. SMEs that have not fared so well from participation are those that are dependent on the local area for their business where face-to-face trading is the norm (for example suppliers of office machinery and building contractors who are either too small or too far away to be considered by customers outside the area).

The profile of the SMEs and the region will also determine the effect of normative and mimetic pressure on participation, critical mass and eventually the success of the platform. In RegWa.net and CountryWa.com, the SMEs interviewed joined the portal to support the local initiative because of their 'community spirit' and ties with the chamber of commerce and initiators of the project;

some of them still remain participants despite lack of financial benefits because that is what their competitors are doing. The profile of the SMEs and the region should thus determine the focus of the platform (will it be vertical, horizontal, part of a community portal?) and the motivation for its development (to raise e-commerce uptake by SMEs, to introduce cost effectiveness in strategic regional industries where SMEs are involved, to raise the general level of Internet use in the region?).

The results of the study also indicated that while local major buyers were verbally supportive of the idea of a regional e-marketplace for SMEs, the reality was that most of their purchases were supplied by trading partners with whom they had existing relationships and there was very little discretionary purchasing that could be channelled through the e-marketplace. Market makers thus need to identify strong off-line relationships, which can be migrated to the platform. This may indicate the need for a narrower focused (or vertical) trading platform if it is expected to be self-sustainable or even profitable and not merely a development tool or test bed for SMEs.

The ownership structure and governance of the trading platform will thus depend on the SME and regional profiles and the focus of the platform. If the focus is on a specific industry within the region, then players in that industry need to be part of the platform development process to ensure their specific needs will be catered for. If the focus is wider (as in the three cases in this study) then the ownership structure and governance of the platform and portal will need to reflect the involvement of diverse groups of stakeholders (the general community, the business community, regional development authorities) in order for the initiative to be widely accepted and supported, thus building trust between participants and owners.

The motivation behind the platform creation and its focus will also determine the development process and the timing of the features and benefits offered. In vertical platforms (like RETFC), the adoption of common standards would be one of the first outcomes sought so that reduced communication costs and efficiency gains can be achieved early. In horizontal government-supported platforms (and especially those involving the general community as well), a staged approach to the development of the REM will mean that it progresses incrementally in tandem with the sophistication of the participants and is able to properly consider if conditions are suitable for the next phase or the next offering. For example, in RegWa.net had the portal and business directory not received the support of both the general and business communities, there may not have been good grounds for the introduction of the REM or the shopping cart facility. In TwinTowns.com the simultaneous introduction of the REM and portal strained resources, prevented building of critical mass and led to failure. Whatever forms the platform may take, the technology

256

needs to either be easy to use or proper hands-on training needs to be provided to SMEs to use it effectively. It is also important that adequate technical support is available for SME participants whenever they need it.

The focus of the REM and the development process will also determine the perceived benefits that SMEs hope to gain from participation and this will have an effect on the building of critical mass as well as engendering further trust in the initiative. The growing of critical mass can be moderated by a good marketing or awareness-building plan. In vertical platforms, economic benefits are easy to perceive as common standards reduce costs and improve efficiencies. In government-supported platforms that are horizontal in nature, the wide focus and the community motivation behind creation mean that community benefits are the first to be perceived. In TwinTowns.com, although the initiative failed, one of the positive outcomes was that for the first time various parties in the region attempted to collaborate for the benefit of the community. Where economic benefits may not accrue immediately to participating SMEs, it is important that they are made aware of this. In RegWA.net and CountryWa.com, the first few years of participation on the portal were perceived to offer community benefits like a sense of belonging and a need to demonstrate support in building the image of the region. Once the community benefits are realised, participants begin to look to the platform to deliver perceived strategic benefits. Participants who have currently not received any direct business from the RegWa.net claim to still be there because their competitors are and others from both portals remain listed because the wide community acceptance and use of the portal make it a good advertising channel. However, with time, participants are beginning to view participation in terms of how it is going to affect their bottom line (perceived economic benefits) especially if they are paying for more than just the single directory listing.

Figure 8.2 is thus both a process and causal model. The model is however, one that is aimed at building "theory of the middle range: to discover and discuss relationships between abstract concepts" (Carroll & Swatman, 2000, p. 239). This is because the research is exploratory and there have been no earlier models in the literature of government-supported regional Internet trading platforms for SMEs that have been built as part of community portals.

Research Question 3 - What are the costs and the benefits (for SME participants, government sponsors and the region) of government-sponsored regional Internet trading platforms for SMEs?

Subsidiary Questions:

RQ3i. How can these costs and benefits be measured?

RQ3ii. How can this type of platform be effectively evaluated?

In this study the context in the CCP approach to evaluation (Symons, 1991) was addressed by the integrated theoretical framework of facilitators and inhibitors of success or failure of government-supported regional Internet trading platforms for SMEs (table 3.2). Applying it to the empirical data from the three cases allowed a refined model (figure 8.2) specific to the context of the type of platform in this study, viz a horizontal trading platform that is part of a community portal. The staged approach recommended for the development and evaluation of portals of this nature (figure 8.1) addresses the process of evaluation.

However, in order to evaluate the actual progress of the initiative and the end result, and to use the results of this study to advise both research and practice, it was also necessary to determine the costs and benefits of the initiatives and the metrics that could be used to measure them. In applying the trading platform success model (figure 3.3) and the accompanying tables of costs (table 3.3) and success metrics (table 3.4) to the empirical data in this study, the content of the CCP evaluation approach is addressed.

The results of this study indicate that there are different costs and benefits for the different stakeholders involved. The trading platform success model states that content, system and service/value-added quality can positively affect participant satisfaction and their use of the system (or their intention to use it). By using the platform, benefits accrue to stakeholders, reinforcing their satisfaction and continued use. The success of the platform is determined by comparing the net benefit (of all stakeholders) from the platform against development and operating costs (Bakos, 1991). In initiatives like the ones in this study, stakeholders would be the owners, the SME sellers, buyers, intermediaries and value-added service providers. However, given that the portals still operating (RegWa.net and CountryWa.com) are seller driven locally and it was not possible to identify buyers (apart from RFQs issued by the owners themselves), it was only possible to measure the costs and benefits for owners, SMEs and the region. The portals had also not developed to the stage where commercial intermediaries and value-added service providers were involved.

After considering the costs and benefits from the TwinTowns.com initiative, it can be surmised that net benefits (the experience gained by the economic development manager and officer of LG 1) were not commensurate with the AU$360,000 expended on the project. SMEs did not get to learn from participation as the REM and portal did not take off properly. Some SMEs still think the portal can work as they ascribe the failure to the incompetence of the local governments in handling the project. However, the research has shown that there are other underlying factors (suitability of the business for Internet trading, online consumption patterns of the local inhabitants, inability to migrate existing relationships to the portal, regional profile) that may render this model unsuitable in this context.

In RegWa.net and CountryWa.com, while AU$242,000 and AU$243,500 were sufficient to set up community portals with operating business directories and a few e-commerce transactions, there were a lot of hidden costs involved in the form of voluntary and discounted services. Although e-commerce awareness was raised and Internet use in the region appeared to increase, there were no measurable targets or benchmarks set at the beginning of the projects against which these achievements could be measured. Funds were also not budgeted for the proper evaluation of the outcomes in these projects. In RegWa.net, it is only with the additional AU$2.2 million that the portal can provide the e-business consultancy and free shopping cart facilities necessary to enable target participants to understand how Internet trading can benefit them. The additional funds also allowed the statistics packages necessary to measure transactional and visitor activity of individual SMEs' websites arising from their participation in the portal.

The effect of time on realisable benefits also needs to be considered. Both RegWa.net and CountryWa.com have been in operation for almost 6 years. Although there have been community benefits and perceived strategic benefits it is only a few SMEs in niche areas that appear to be seeing any economic benefits. Others that cater for the local market may only see economic benefits when local online consumption levels rise and this may require further time to eventuate. Some SMEs have come away having learnt that there are no economic benefits for them in the six years of participating and that this type of platform may not fulfil their needs. Nevertheless, they consider the benefit of the experience and the ability to 'test the waters' of Internet trading first hand as outweighing the small costs that they paid for participation on RegWa.net and CountryWa.com.

One common shortcoming across the three cases in the study was the absence of clear and measurable ex-ante goals against which to measure progress and outcomes and to signal the need for necessary changes to project plans viz., the absence of effective evaluation. The literature on programme evaluation stresses the importance of setting project benchmarks and milestones (W.K. Kellogg Foundation, 2004) to determine the effectiveness of a programme. The European Commission in reviewing the outcomes of the initiatives to increase SME uptake of e-commerce has called for measurable goals wherever possible (like number of SMEs trained, number of additional businesses connected to the Internet) to be set for such initiatives (Commission of the European Communities, 2003a). While metrics like number of hits and number of RFQs or number of sales are not difficult to measure, metrics need to be decided upfront for the evaluation and measurement of community and strategic benefits. Plans also have to be made about how the data is to be collected and the evaluation conducted and it is also necessary to properly budget the funds to execute these activities.

The trading platform success model derived from this research can not only provide the method by which government-supported regional Internet trading platforms for SMEs can be evaluated, it can also give market makers or owners guidance about the benchmark data that need to be collected against which to measure future outcomes. The model is thus both descriptive and prescriptive. Findings from the three cases have refined the Trading Platform Success Model to the extent that only the most significant constructs from the organisational, external and owner contexts are now represented in the model. The model is presented in Figure 8.3., and the cost and success metrics (tables 3.3 and 3.4) are reproduced.

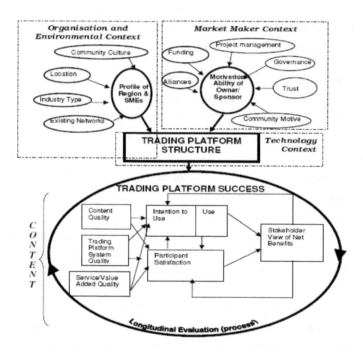

Figure 8.3 Refined Trading Platform Success Model

Table 3.3 Stakeholder Costs

	Owners	Sellers	Buyers	Intermediaries
Direct Costs	Hardware/Software/ Network set-up & maintenance costs User Training & advice costs Marketing & Administration Overheads Provision of value added/ trust/ security services Maintaining parallel systems	Participation fee Transaction fee Flyer fee Hardware/software/ network & maintenance costs Administration costs Integration costs (business processes) Training costs	Hardware/software/ network & maintenance costs Administration costs Integration costs (business processes) Training costs	Advertising Hardware/ software/ network costs Training costs
Indirect Costs	Opportunity cost	Time	Time	Time

Table 3.4 Success Metrics

Content Quality	REM System Quality	Service/Value Added Quality
Quality of content Accuracy & currency of content Security, Privacy, Authenticity Comprehensiveness Timeliness Relevance Completeness *Quality of content presentation* Effective/meaningful organisation of content Navigation techniques Logical structure of content Personalisation	Reliability of software/network Accuracy of system Flexibility/Adaptability Ease of Use Online response time & page loading speed System architecture Visual Appearance Convenience of accessibility Market reach Integration with participants' systems	Trust Neutrality of market-maker Site intelligence (CRM) Feedback mechanisms Relevant search facilities Calculators Tracking capabilities Helpdesk/Set-up help/Advice Account maintenance Training (in conversion to e-business & system use) FAQ's

Use	REM Participant Satisfaction	
Informational Number of Hits/Visits *Transactional* Number of Transactions *Community* Presence of & participation in networks	*Overall satisfaction* Satisfaction with REM Offerings (Repeat visits, repeat transactions, use of networks and use of feedback mechanisms) Satisfaction with governance structure	

Stakeholder Net Benefits		
Industry/Organisational/ Individual Impact	*Transactional Benefits* Lower transaction, staff, communication, search, marketing/advertising, inventory-holding costs Cheaper prices Lower inventory holdings *Productivity gains* Time savings Process efficiencies Wider market reach	*Strategic Benefits* Gains from Network Externalities & Collaboration Image/Legitimacy Improved market share Improved communications with customers (CRM), suppliers & employees Improved decision making process
Regional Impact	*Economic Benefits* Attractive location for business Attractive to skilled labour Efficient show-casing of regional offerings Reduced communication costs Increased productivity	*Community/Strategic Benefits* Collaboration/Partnerships Cooperation Increased level of online participation Become a knowledge region Narrow/Close digital divide Relationships with other markets

Figure 8.3 and tables 3.3 and 3.4 indicate that government and other agencies which may consider developing regional Internet trading platforms for SMEs need first of all to conduct theory-based evaluation of the suitability of the project to the profile of the SMEs and the region. They then need to ensure that the governance and focus of the platform is in alignment with the regional/SME profile and the motivation behind the creation of the platform. The agencies also need to have a realistic view of the resources and capabilities needed to drive the project and deliver the benefits as perceived by stakeholders. In order to do this there needs to be ongoing evaluation of the platform in terms of the costs and benefits. The evaluation can be guided by the metrics in tables 3.3 and 3.4, by collecting data from all stakeholders concerned, as has been demonstrated in this study. In the final analysis, the success of the trading platform will depend on the net benefits of developing and introducing it. This implies that success is contextual and would depend on the weight or importance placed on the various costs and benefits. For example, if at the outset, community and strategic benefits (like increased awareness of e-commerce and collaboration) have been more heavily weighted than economic benefits and the platform is viewed as a development tool, the trading platform may be deemed a success even if it is not breaking even financially. Therefore it will be up to the agencies that develop and implement these types of platforms to determine which metrics are more important.

This research has shown that determining the effectiveness of government-supported regional Internet trading platforms for SMEs as a tool for increasing uptake of e-commerce and for regional development has required synthesising and extending existing models and theories in the research areas of Internet trading platforms; SME adoption of IT and e-commerce and evaluation. It is only by doing so that a holistic picture can be obtained of facilitators and inhibitors to successful implementation and of the costs and benefits to all stakeholders involved.

8.5   CONCLUSIONS AND AN INTEGRATED MODEL

Although regional Internet community portals have much to offer in terms of networking geographically dispersed areas or promoting online participation in remote or regional areas, developing and maintaining such portals can be complex and can require substantial resources. When they are also used as platforms to help SMEs trade on the Internet, there needs to be careful consideration of a number of factors. Some of these factors are: the regional profile, the ownership of the platforms, the timing or development process and the resources required not only to develop the platform but also to train both the general and SME communities and to monitor and evaluate the outcomes of these initiatives.

In an effort to address the lack of specific theoretical and evaluation models to examine the success or failure of government-supported regional Internet trading platforms for SMEs that have been developed as part of community portals, this research produced three models or frameworks. The models and frameworks were based on the wealth of accumulated research in the IS discipline and extended and refined by the empirical data from this study. By combining the models and frameworks, it is possible to derive an integrated model to advise the ex-ante theoretical evaluation of the contextual factors, the process of development and ongoing iterative evaluation during the life of the initiative, and the ex-post evaluation of such platforms.

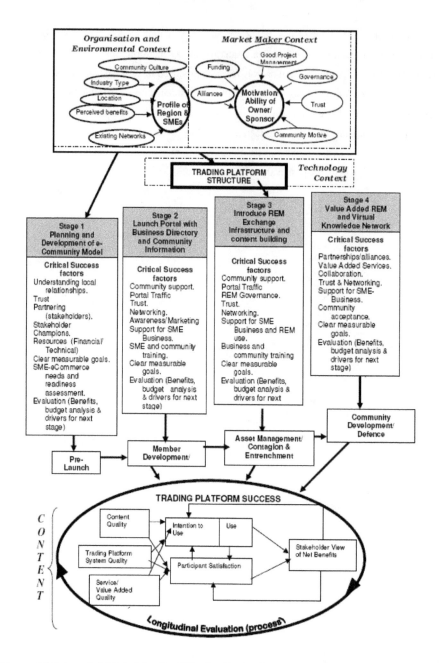

Figure 8.4 Integrated Model for the Effective Evaluation, Development and Management of Community-Portal Regional Internet Trading Platforms for SMEs.

Figure 8.4 is thus an attempt to provide government and other agencies guidelines on a) how to determine the suitability of community-portal trading platforms for the region and the SMEs in it by using theory-based evaluation; b) how to use this theory-based evaluation to advise the process of implementing and managing such platforms (a staged approach) and finally c) how to effectively measure the costs and benefits (and ultimately the success) of the platforms. The model builds on existing frameworks for the development of e-marketplaces and portals by determining the factors that facilitate and inhibit the success of a specific type of trading platform (government-supported community-portal regional Internet trading platforms for SMEs) and by providing metrics on how to measure the said success or lack thereof.

The use of the evaluation framework in this study has shown that while these portals have been successful in raising the online participation of regional communities and the e-commerce awareness of regional SMEs, they have yet to produce economic benefits for some participants. This has been due to the misalignment between the suitability of business type and the trading platform model. The portals have also not produced the kind of economic e-commerce benefits that would make them profitable or even self-sustainable in the short term. As a result, using these portals to promote e-commerce uptake by regional SMEs has required more government funding than was initially envisaged. This research contends that such portals should be viewed as community assets and regional e-commerce development tools and should therefore be funded and planned for as such. Indeed the use of regional portals in WA to promote Internet trading was viewed as a way to provide SMEs with a test bed to experience online trading in an inexpensive and trusted environment. The pressure to make the portals self sustainable in the short term can result in total failure (as in TwinTowns.com) or the non realisation of some of the basic objectives of the initiatives (the lack of e-commerce advice and mentoring for smaller SMEs in CountryWa.com). As such, the success of such platforms should therefore be measured not in terms of viability (Clarke and Flaherty 2003), profitability or self-sustainability (Damsgaard 2002) of the portals themselves, especially in the short term, but in terms of the ability of the community and region to build upon the experience acquired on the portals to adequately compete in the online environment. They should be measured by the sustainability of the community and strategic regional benefits that they can offer or as the scaffolding they provide to promote knowledge sharing and innovation among the participants in the region.

In Australia, the danger of the existing funding paradigm (for innovative projects like those in this study) that favours relatively quick results and easily measured outputs (Otis & Johanson, 2004) is that it results in projects being "implemented in the absence of adequate baseline information for assessing their associated cost/benefit movements" (Tonkin, 2003). The lack of proper evaluation leads to wasted public funds and in some cases may discourage further collaborative efforts to innovate. There is already a wealth of accumulated research in the IS discipline that can be used to advise effective evaluation of such initiatives, if not in specific areas then in related areas as demonstrated in this study. The funding paradigm should therefore be modified to allow for proper theory-based evaluation of government-supported IT initiatives.

The major contribution of this research has thus been to provide insights into a hitherto unexplored model of Internet trading platform viz. government-supported community-portal regional Internet trading platforms for SMEs that are used to promote regional development by encouraging SME uptake of e-commerce. The study contributes to practice (government and other agencies involved in collaborative IT regional development programmes like the ones in this study) by providing three interrelated theory-based and empirically refined frameworks which have been integrated (figure 8.4) to provide a single point of reference to guide the planning, development, management and evaluation of such platforms. For the research community, the models and frameworks produced by this exploratory study provide a frame of reference for further research in this particular area.

CHAPTER 9

LIMITATIONS AND FUTURE DIRECTIONS FOR RESEARCH

9.1   LIMITATIONS

The analysis in the preceding chapters shows that while there are some benefits to be gained from government supported community portals and Internet trading platforms for SMEs, these initiatives may be suitable in only certain situations depending on the profile of the region and the availability of adequate resources to achieve those benefits. However, what the analysis does not do, is determine how long such portals and platforms should be perpetuated. There is evidence to suggest that even community portals designed to promote online participation by networking a geographical region may outlive their purpose after a certain period. They may become less important once members become more proficient with technology and interact with other members directly or join non-geographically defined virtual communities of interest. Alternatively, as costs of access to technology fall, the technology on the portals themselves may be superseded and there may not be a need to perpetuate them. In this study, after six years of operation, the community online discussion boards on CountryWa.com appear to be waning in popularity as people in the region become more familiar with the use of e-mail, MSN type chat facilities and online conferencing.

The research also shows that while government-supported Internet trading platforms may provide SMEs an efficient 'testbed' to experience online trading in an inexpensive and 'trusted' environment, the raison d'être, structure, market-reach and target participants of horizontal community portal Internet trading platforms can combine to preclude them from being self-sustainable or profitable B2B exchanges in the short to medium term. Indeed, the lack of literature on the performance and investment costs of larger government-supported REMs for SMEs (see for example Nextr@de which is the online gateway to trade with SMEs within the whole of Japan) does not shed any light on whether these government-supported trading platforms are profitable or sustainable even in the longer term. Perhaps as suggested by the E-Business Policy Group (2002) such portals and platforms should terminate as publicly funded initiatives once policy objectives are met. In which case, it will be up to each community or project sponsor to decide what those objectives are and in what timeframes they are to be achieved. It is thus difficult to make a definitive recommendation on whether trading platforms like the ones in this study are suitable instruments for increasing e-commerce uptake by SMEs and for regional development purposes without a proper evaluation of the contexts surrounding the initiative.

Another limitation of this study is the small sample of SMEs used from each case and the limited time available for the interviews with the SMEs in regional WA. However, this was not within the control of the researcher, given the voluntary nature of participation in this research and the busy schedules of some subjects. Nevertheless, as the research was exploratory in nature and the cases of the portals in regional WA were mini-cases, every effort was made to try and obtain SMEs across different industry types, of varying sizes and which catered for different markets in order to eliminate bias.

The multiple case study approach is often described as lacking in depth or richness as compared to a single case study. Although multiple case studies provide the benefit of comparative insights, they come at the cost of a deep understanding of a particular social setting (Dyer & Wilkins, 1991). In this study however, as there was little in the literature on government-supported regional Internet trading platforms for SMEs and a multitude of theoretical lenses with which to view the initiatives, there was a need to determine which constructs of which theories were the most pertinent and the way to do this was through structured cross case analysis. To some extent, the embedded design of this multiple case study is an attempt at providing greater depth of understanding of the phenomenon.

Another limitation of this study is the convenience sample of case studies selected, which introduces threats to internal validity. However, this is the result of the limited number of cases available. Nevertheless, cases were selected on the basis of their common purpose viz. a not for profit government-supported regional Internet trading platform designed to encourage SME uptake of e-commerce and the economic development of the region. The embedded design is a way of overcoming this limitation by providing multiple views of trading platform success, both within each case and across cases. Another factor that mitigates the threat of the convenience samples is that there are still variations in independent variables like market mechanisms, ownership-structure, regional SME profile and resources (like funding) to test for theoretical replication (Yin, 2003).

Although the theoretical frameworks developed and refined in this research have been tested across 3 cases, they are by no means definitive given the different context-specific factors that need to be considered in initiatives like the ones in this study. While the frameworks may be suitable instruments to evaluate similar initiatives in Australia, research has shown that theories or frameworks developed in a particular setting may not apply when taken out of that particular context, whether it be country, culture or some other context (Kumar et al., 1998).

Despite the above, every possible step within the control of the researcher has been taken to mitigate the limitations of the research. The study has uncovered valuable insights into government-supported regional Internet trading platforms for SMEs and provided models for their effective evaluation, planning and development where none existed previously for this particular model.

9.2 FURTHER RESEARCH

9.2.1 Following the Progress of RegWa.net and CountryWa.com

Although this study has provided useful insights into government-supported regional Internet trading platforms for SMEs in the Western Australian context, there is a need to follow through with further research on RegWa.net and CountryWa.com. There is a need to determine if the platforms could be used for knowledge networking and online collaboration since the infrastructure is already in place. With the development of other more targeted portals like the Visitor Centres in the regions serviced by RegWa.net and CountryWa.net it would be interesting to investigate if both these portals can maintain their focus on self sustainability or if the government will eventually use them for the purpose that they were intended i.e. to allow SMEs to test the waters of Internet trading at subsidised costs and in a trusted environment.

9.2.2 Research on Different Models of Government-Supported Internet Trading Platforms for SMEs

While this study reports on three cases of horizontal community portal regional Internet trading platforms for SMEs, there are various other government-supported models that offer SMEs the opportunity to engage in Internet trading. Examples of such models are whole-of-country B2B REMs (Nextr@de); government procurement REMs at the country level (MERX of Canada), state level (GEM of Western Australia, Smartbuy of New South Wales) and local/borough/municipality level (Roses Marketplace and London Marketplace in the United Kingdom, RAKAT in Denmark); vertical REMs (Agribazaar in Malaysia); online shopping malls (Wisconsin Common Market). While some of these models may prove to be profitable or at least sustainable in the longer term, others could be only transitory. Recommendations for future research would be an examination of the different models (and different sizes) to determine which is best suited for bridging the digital divide between SMEs and their larger counterparts.

9.2.3 Cross Country Research

One other recommendation for future research is for cross country research on government-supported regional Internet trading platforms for SMEs. This is to determine the importance of issues like culture and type of government on initiatives like the ones in this study. This type of cross country and cross model research could help other authorities contemplating such initiatives to determine which models are best suited for their particular contexts.

REFERENCES

Adelaar, T., Bouwman, H., & Steinfield, C. W. (2004). Enhancing Customer Value Through Click-and-Mortar E-Commerce: Implications for Geographical Market Reach and Customer Type. *Telematics and Informatics, 21*(2), 167-182.

Agarwal, R., & Prasad, J. (1998). A Conceptual and Operational Definition of Personal Innovativeness in the Domain of Information Technology. *Information Systems Research, 9*(2), 204-215.

Al-Qirim, N., & Corbitt, B. J. (2004). Determinants of Electronic Commerce Usage in Small Businesses in New Zealand. *Proceedings of the 12th European Conference on Information Systems (The European IS Profession in the Global Networking Environment)* (CD-ROM). Turku, Finland: Turku School of Economics and Business Administration.

Anderson, P. (2000). Innovation-Online: A Vortal for Supporting Innovative SMEs within a Regional Economy. Retrieved December 23, 2003 from: http://62.73.162.24/ebew/virtualpdf/anderson.pdf

AOT, P. L. (2003). *Review of the GEM Purchasing E-Procurement Business System.* Retrieved July 28, 2004, from http://www.dtf.wa.gov.au/cms/uploadedFiles/Gem_Review_Report_Summary2.pdf

Archer, M. (1995). *Realist Social Theory: The Morphogenic Approach.* Cambridge: Cambridge University Press.

Armstrong, A., & Hagel, J. (May-June 1996). The Real Value of On-Line Communities. *Harvard Business Review, 74*(3), 134-141.

Australian Bureau of Statistics. (1999a). *1997-1998 Small and Medium Enterprises: Business Growth and Performance Survey. Catalogue No. 8141.0.* Canberra: Australian Government Publishing Service.

Australian Bureau of Statistics. (1999b). *1999 Year Book Australia. Catalogue No. 1301.0.* Canberra: Australian Government Publishing Service.

Australian Bureau of Statistics. (2000a). *Business Use of Information Technology 1999-2000. Catalogue No. 8129.0.* Canberra: Australian Government Publishing Service.

Australian Bureau of Statistics. (2000b). *Small Business in Australia 1999. Catalogue No. 1321.0.* Canberra: Australian Government Publishing Service.

Australian Bureau of Statistics. (2002a). *2000-2001 Business Operations and Industry Performance. Catalogue No. 8140.0.* Canberra: Australian Government Publishing Service.

Australian Bureau of Statistics. (2002b). *Small Business in Australia, 2001. Catalogue No. 1321.0.* Canberra: Australian Government Publishing Service.

Australian Bureau of Statistics. (2003). *Business Use of Information Technology 2001-2002. Catalogue No. 8129.0.* Canberra: Australian Government Publishing Service.

Australian Centre for Co-operative Research and Development. (n.d). *Employee Ownership for Small and Medium Enterprises: Three new models.* Retrieved August 10, 2005 from http://www.accord.org.au/social/infobriefs/employee.html

Australian Government Department of Foreign Affairs and Trade. (2005). *A Competitive Economy.* Retrieved August 10, 2005 from http://www.dfat.gov.au/aib/competitive_economy.html

Ba, S., & Pavlou, P. A. (2002). Evidence of the Effect of Trust Building Technology in Electronic Markets: Price Premiums and Buyer Behavior. *MIS Quarterly, 26*(3), 243-268.

Ba, S., Whinston, A. B., & Zhang, H. (2001). Small Digital Business in Electronic Markets: A Blueprint for Survival [Electronic Version]. *Electronic Markets, 11*(1), 59-63.

Bailey, J. E., & Pearson, S. W. (1983). Development of a Tool for Measuring and Analyzing Computer User Satisfaction. *Management Science, 29*(5), 530-545.

Bakos, J. Y., & Brynjolfsson, E. (Dec 1999). Bundling Information Goods: Pricing, Profits and Efficiency. *Management Science, 45*(12), 1613-1630.

Bakos, Y. (1991). A Strategic Analysis of Electronic Marketplaces. *MIS Quarterly, 15*(3), 295-310.

Bakos, Y. (1997). Reducing Buyer Search Costs: Implications for Electronic Marketplaces. *Management Science, 43*(12), 1676-1692.

Bakos, Y. (1998). The Emerging Role of Electronic Marketplaces on the Internet. *Communications of the ACM, 41*(8), 49-55.

Baldi, S., & Borgman, H. P. (2001). Consortium-Based B2B e-Marketplaces - a Case Study in the Automotive Industry. *Proceedings of the 14th Bled Electronic Commerce Conference* (pp. 629-645). Bled, Slovenia: University of Maribor.

Barrett, S., & Konsynski, B. R. (1982). Inter-Organization Information Sharing Systems. *MIS Quarterly, Special Issue*, 93-105.

Baskerville, R. L., & Wood-Harper, A. T. (1996). A Critical Perspective on Action Research as a Method for Information Systems Research. *Journal of Information Technology, 11*(3), 235-246.

Baskerville, R. L., & Wood-Harper, A. T. (1998). Diversity in Information Systems Action Research Methods. *European Journal of Information Systems, 7*(2), 90-107.

Beckinsale, M., & Levy, M. (2004). SMEs and Internet Adoption Strategy: Who do SMEs Listen to? *Proceedings of the 12th European Conference on Information Systems. (The European IS Profession in the Global Networking Environment)* (CD-ROM). Turku, Finland: Turku School of Economics and Business Administration.

Benbasat, I., Dexter, A. S., Drury, D. H., & Goldstein, R. C. (1984). A Critique of the Stage Hypothesis: Theory and Empirical Evidence. *Communications of the ACM, 27*(5), 476-485.

Benbasat, I., Goldstein, D. K., & Mead, M. (1987). The Case Research Strategy in Studies of Information Systems. *MIS Quarterly, 11*(3), 369-386.

Benbasat, I., & Zmud, R. W. (1999). Empirical Research in Information Systems: The Practice of Relevance. *MIS Quarterly, 23*(1), 3-16.

Benjamin, R., & Wigand, R. (Winter 1995). Electronic Markets and Virtual Value Chains on the Information Superhighway. *Sloan Management Review, 36*(2), 62-72.

Blum, F. H. (January, 1955). Action Research - a Scientific Approach. *Philosophy of Science, 22*(1), 1-7.

Bode, S., & Burn, J. M. (2001). Website Design Consultants, Australian SMEs and Electronic Commerce Success Factors. *International Journal of Business Studies, 9*(1), 73-85.

Booker, E. (2000, December 4). Independent Hubs' Fall Prove Pundits Wrong. *B to B, 85*(20), 10. Retrieved June 13, 2003 from ProQuest UMI database.

Boon, O., Wilkin, C., & Corbitt, B. J. (2003). *Towards A Broader Based IS Success Model - Integrating Critical Success Factors and the DeLone and McLean's IS Success Model*. School Working Papers - Series 2003, SWP 2003/10. School of Information Systems,

271

Deakin University, Melbourne, Australia. Retrieved December 28, 2003 from http://www.deakin.edu.au/infosys/docs/workingpapers/papers/2003_10_Boon.pdf

Braun, P. (2002). Digital Knowledge Networks: Linking Communities of Practice with Innovation. *Journal of Business Strategies, 19*(1), 43-54.

Braun, P. (2003). Virtual SME Networks: Pathways towards Online Collaboration. *Journal of New Business Ideas and Trends, 1*(2), 1-19.

Braun, P. (2004). Government-Industry ICT Partnering in Regional Australia: Issues Surrounding Top Down Initiatives. *Proceedings of the Australian Electronic Governance Conference.* Melbourne: Centre for Public Policy, University of Melbourne. Retrieved November 17, 2005 (last accessed) from http://www.public-policy.unimelb.edu.au/egovernance/papers/06_Braun.pdf.

Brown, D., & Lockett, N. J. (2001). Engaging SMEs in E-commerce: The Role of Intermediaries within eClusters [Electronic Version]. *Electronic Markets, 11*(1), 52-58.

Brunelli, M. (2000, March 23). B2B E-Commerce will hit $7.29 trillion by 2004. *Purchasing*, p. S20. Retrieved August 20, 2003 from ProQuest UMI database.

Brunn, P., Jensen, M., & Skovgaard, J. (2002). eMarketplaces: Crafting A Winning Strategy. *European Management Journal, 20*(3), 286-298.

Brynjolfsson, E., & Hitt, L. M. (1998). Beyond the Productivity Paradox. *Communications of the ACM, 41*(8), 49-55.

Bughin, J., & Hagel, J. (2000). The Operational Performance of Virtual Communities - Towards a Successful Business Model? [Electronic Version]. *Electronic Markets, 10*(4), 237-243.

Burns, R. B. (1994). *Introduction to Research Methods* (2nd ed.). London: Longman Cheshire Pty Ltd.

Caldeira, M. M., & Ward, J. M. (2002). Understanding the Successful Adoption and Use of IS/IT in SMEs: An Explanation from Portuguese Manufacturing Industries. *Information Systems Journal, 12*(2), 121-152.

Caldeira, M. M., & Ward, J. M. (2003). Using Resource-Based Theory to Interpret Successful Adoption and Use of Information Systems and Technology in Manufacturing Small and Medium-sized enterprises. *European Journal of Information Systems, 12*(2), 127-141.

Canadian Federation of Independent Business. (2003). *Securities Regulation in Canada: Ensuring Greater Access to capital for Canada's SMEs: Submission to the Provincial and Territorial Ministers Responsible for Securities Regulation.* Retrieved September 22, 2003 from http://www.cfib.ca/legis/national/5176.pdf

Carroll, J. M., & Swatman, P. A. (2000). Structured-case: A Methodological Framework for Building Theory in Information Systems Research. *European Journal of Information Systems, 9*(4), 235-242.

Cavaye, A. L. M. (1996). Case Study Research: a Multi-Faceted Research Approach for IS. *Information Systems Journal, 6*(3), 227-242.

Chaffey, D. (2002). *E-Business and E-Commerce Management: Strategy, Implementation and Practice.* New York: Financial Times/Prentice Hall.

Chau, P. Y. K. (2001). Inhibitors to EDI Adoption in Small Businesses: An Empirical Investigation. *Journal of Electronic Commerce Research, 2*(2), 78-88.

Checkland, P. B. (1981). *Systems Thinking, Systems Practice.* Chichester: J Wiley.

Cheek, J. (2000). An Untold Story? Doing Funded Qualitative Research. In N. K. Denzin & Y. S. Lincoln (Eds.), *Handbook of Qualitative Research* (2nd ed., pp. 401-420). Thousand Oaks, CA: Sage Publications Inc.

Chen, H.-T., & Rossi, P. H. (1987). The Theory-Driven Approach to Validity. *Evaluation and Program Planning, 10*(1), 95-103.

Chen, W., & Hirschheim, R. (2004). A Paradigmatic and Methodological Examination of Information Systems Research from 1991 to 2001. *Information Systems Journal, 14*(3), 197-235.

Chircu, A. M., & Kauffman, R. J. (2000). Limits to Value in Electronic Commerce-Related IT Investments. *Journal of Management Information Systems, 17*(2), 59-80.

Chong, S. (2004). Electronic Commerce Adoption by Small-and-Medium-Sized Enterprises in Australia: An Empirical Study of Influencing Factors. *Proceedings of the 12th European Conference on Information Systems (The European IS Profession in the Global Networking Environment)* (CD-ROM). Turku, Finland: Turku School of Economics and Business Administration.

Choudhury, V., Hartzel, K. S., & Konsynski, B. R. (1998). Uses and Consequences of Electronic markets: an Empirical Investigation in the Aircraft Parts Industry. *MIS Quarterly, 22*(4), 471-507.

Christiaanse, E., & Markus, M. L. (2003). Participation in Collaboration Electronic Marketplaces. *Proceedings of the 36th Hawaii International Conference on Systems Sciences* Big Island, Hawaii: IEEE Computer Society. Retrieved October 7, 2005 (last accessed) from: http://csdl2.computer.org/comp/proceedings/hicss/2003/1874/07/187470178a.pdf

Clarke, A. (1999). *Evaluation Research. An Introduction to Principles, Methods and Practice.* London: Sage Publications.

Clarke, I., & Flaherty, T. B. (2003). Web-Based B2B Portals. *Industrial Marketing Management, 32*(1), 15-23.

Clarke, R., & Jenkins, M. (1993). The Strategic Intent of On-line Trading Systems: a Case Study in National Livestock Marketing. *Journal of Strategic Information Systems, 2*(1), 57-76.

Clemons, E. K., Reddi, S. P., & Row, M. C. (1993). The Impact of Information Technology on the Organization of Economic Activity: The "Move to the Middle" Hypothesis. *Journal of Management Information Systems, 10*(2), 9-35.

Clemons, E. K., & Row, M. C. (1992). Information Technology and Industrial Cooperation: The Changing Economics of Coordination and Ownership. *Journal of Management Information Systems, 9*(2), 9-28.

Cloete, E., Courtney, S., & Fintz, J. (2002). Small Businesses' Acceptance and Adoption of e-Commerce in the Western-cape Province of South-Africa. *The Electronic Journal on Information Systems in Developing Countries, 10* (4), 1-13. Retrieved July 29, 2003 from http://www.ejisdc.org

Coase, R. H. (1937). The Nature of the Firm. *Economica, New Series, 4*(16), 386-405.

Coltman, T., Devinney, T. M., Latukefu, A., & Midgley, D. F. (2001). E-Business: Revolution, Evolution or Hype? *California Management Review, 44*(1), 57-86.

Commission of the European Communities. (2003a). *Adapting E-business Policies in a Changing Environment: The Lessons of the Go Digital Initiative and the Challenges Ahead.* Retrieved May 21, 2003 from http://www.eu.nl/comm/enterprise/ict/policy/doc/com_2003_148_en.pdf

Commission of the European Communities. (2003b). *Report of the Expert Group on B2B Internet trading platforms - Final report*. Retrieved December 27, 2003 from http://europa.eu.int/comm/enterprise/ict/policy/b2b/wshop/fin-report.pdf

Commission of the European Communities. (2004). *The Go-Digital Awareness Campaign 2001-2003: The Main Lessons to be Learnt*. Retrieved October 7, 2004 from : http://europa.eu.int/comm/enterprise/ict/studies/aw_camp_fin_rep.pdf

Cragg, P. B., & King, M. (1993). Small-Firm Computing: Motivators and Inhibitors. *MIS Quarterly, 17*(1), 47-60.

Currie, W. (1989). The Art of Justifying New Technology to Top Management. *Omega, International Journal of Management Science, 17*(5), 409-418.

Curtin, J. (2001). *A Digital Divide in Rural and Regional Australia? Current Issues Brief 1 2001-2002, Department of the Parliamentary Library, Information and Research Services*. Retrieved May 10, 2005 (last accessed) from http://www.aph.gov.au/library/pubs/CIB/2001-02/02cib01.pdf

Dai, Q., & Kauffman, R. J. (2001). Business Models for Internet-Based E-Procurement Systems and B2B Electronic Markets: An Exploratory Assessment. *Proceedings of the 34th IEEE Hawaii International Conference on System Sciences*. Retrieved October 7, 2005 (last accessed) from http://csdl.computer.org/dl/proceedings/hicss/2001/0981/07/09817004.pdf

Dai, Q., & Kauffman, R. J. (Summer 2002). Business Models for Internet-Based Electronic Markets. *International Journal of Electronic Commerce, 6*(4), 41-72.

Damsgaard, J. (2002). Managing an Internet portal. *Communications of the Association for Information Systems (CAIS), 9*, 408-420.

Daniel, E., & Klimis, G. M. (1999). The Impact of Electronic Commerce on Market Structure: An Evaluation of the Electronic Market Hypothesis. *European Management Journal, 17*(3), 318-325.

Daniel, E., Wilson, H., & Myers, A. (2002). Adoption of E-commerce by SMEs in the UK: Towards a Stage Model. *International Small Business Journal, 20*(3), 253-268.

Dans, E., & Freire, J. (2002). IT as an Agent of Social Change: Lonxanet and the Case of the Galician Artisanal Fisheries. *Proceedings of the Twenty-Third International Conference on Information Systems* (pp. 769-777). Barcelona, Spain: Association for Information Systems. Retrieved November 2, 2003 from http://aisel.isworld.org/

Darke, P., Shanks, G., & Broadbent, M. (1998). Successfully Completing Case Study Research: Combining Rigour, Relevance and Pragmatism. *Information Systems Journal, 8*, 273-289.

Davern, F. D., & Kauffman, R. J. (Spring 2000). Discovering Potential and Realizing Value from Information Technology Investments. *Journal of Management Information Systems, 16*(4), 121-143.

Davis, F. D., Bagozzi, R. P., & Warshaw, P. R. (1989). User Acceptance of Computer Technology: A Comparison of Two Theoretical Models. *Management Science, 35*(8), 982-1003.

Davison, A., Burgess, S., & Tatnall, A. (2003). *Internet Technologies and Business*. Melbourne: Data Publishing.

Day, G. S., Fein, A. J., & Ruppersberger, G. (2003). Shakeouts in Digital Markets: Lessons from B2B Exchanges. *California Management Review, 45*(2), 131-150.

DeLone, W. H., & McLean, E. R. (1992). Information Systems Success: The Quest for the Dependent Variable. *Information Systems Research, 3*(1), 60-95.

DeLone, W. H., & McLean, E. R. (2003). The DeLone and McLean Model of Information Systems Success: A Ten-Year Update. *Journal of Management Information Systems, 19*(4), 9-30.

Denison, T., Hardy, G., Johanson, G., Stillman, L., & Schauder, D. (2002). Community Networks: Identities, Taxonomies and Evaluations. *Proceedings of the Electronic Networking 2002 - Building Community Conference.* Melbourne: Centre for Community Networking Research, School of Information Management Systems, Monash University. Retrieved November 17, 2005 (last accessed) from http://webstylus.net/?q=node/44

Department of Industry Tourism and Resources. (2003). *Annual Report 2002–03.* Canberra: Author.

Dickinson Waters, C. (2001, July 9). E-marketplaces Pursue Strategy of Evolution. *Nation's Restaurant News, 35*(28), Start page 51. Retrieved August 24, 2003 from ProQuest UMI database.

Diez, M.-A. (2002). Evaluating New Regional Policies: Reviewing the Theory and Practice. *Evaluation, 8*(3), 285-305.

DiMaggio, P. J., & Powell, W. W. (1983). The Iron Cage Revisited: Institutional Isomorphism and Collective Rationality in Organizational Fields. *American Sociological Review, 48*(2), 147-160.

Dobson, P. J. (2001a). Longitudinal Case Research: A Critical Realist Perspective. *Systemic Practice and Action Research, 13*(3), 283-296.

Dobson, P. J. (2001b). The Philosophy of Critical Realism - an Opportunity for Information Systems Research. *Information Systems Frontiers, 3*(2), 199-210.

Doll, W. J., & Torkzadeh, G. (1988). The Measurement of End-user Computing Satisfaction. *MIS Quarterly, 12*(2), 259-274.

Donegan, M. (February 2000). Contemplating Portal Strategies. *Telecommunications, 34*(2), 48-52.

Downes, L., & Mui, C. (1998). *Unleashing the Killer App: Digital Strategies for Market Dominance.* Boston, MA: Harvard Business School Press.

Doyle, T., & Melanson, J. (2001). B2B Web Exchanges: Easier Hyped than Done. *The Journal Of Business Strategy, 22*(3), 10-13.

Drazin, R., & Kazanjian, R. K. (1990). Research Note and Communications: A Reanalysis of Miller and Friesen's Life Cycle Data. *Strategic Management Journal, 11*(4), 319-325.

Driedonks, C. F., Gregor, S., & Wassenaar, A. (2003). Economic and Social Analysis of the Adoption of B2B Electronic Marketplaces: A Case Study in the Australian Beef Industry. *Proceedings of the 16th Bled eCommerce Conference* (pp. 718-733). Bled, Slovenia: University of Maribor.

DSTI (Directorate for Science Technology and Industry) OECD. (2002, December 4). E-Business and SMEs. Paris: Organisation for Economic Co-operation and Development.

DTI. (2001). *Business in the Information Age. International Benchmarking Report.* London: Department of Trade & Industry. Retrieved May 7, 2003 from http://www.ukonlineforbusiness.gov.uk/main/resources/publication-htm/bench2001.htm

Dubé, L., & Paré, G. (2003). Rigor in Information Systems Positivist Case Research: Current Practices, Trends, and Recommendations. *MIS Quarterly, 27*(4), 597-635.

Duhan, S., Levy, M., & Powell, P. (2001). Information Systems Strategies in Knowledge-Based SMEs: the Role of Core Competencies. *European Journal of Information Systems, 10*(1), 25-40.

Dyer, W. G. J., & Wilkins, A. L. (1991). Better Stories, Not Better Constructs, to Generate Better Theory: A Rejoinder to Eisenhardt. *The Academy of Management Review, 16*(3), 613-619.

E-Business Policy Group. (2002). *eEurope Go Digital: Benchmarking National and Regional e-Business Policies for SMEs.* Retrieved May 7, 2003 from http://europa.eu.int/comm/enterprise/ict/policy/benchmarking/final-report.pdf

Eisenhardt, K. M. (1989). Building Theories from Case Study Research. *The Academy of Management Review, 14*(4), 532-550.

Eisenhardt, K. M. (1991). Better Stories and Better Constructs: The Case for Rigor and Comparative Logic. *The Academy of Management Review, 16*(3), 620-627.

eMarket Services. (2002, July). *Introduction to Emarkets & Why Export Companies Should Care About Them.* Retrieved June 10, 2003 from http://www.emarketservices.com/reports_facts/pdf/eMarketServices_Introduction_to_eMarkets.pdf

European Union. (2003). *Commission Recommendation of 6 May 2003 Concerning the Definition of Micro, Small and Medium-sized Enterprises.* Official Journal of the European Union, Issue L 124 (2003). Retrieved October 10, 2003 from http://www.europa.eu.int/scadplus/leg/en/lvb/n26026.htm

Evans, P. B., & Wurster, T. S. (September-October 1997). Strategy and the New Economics of Information. *Harvard Business Review, 77*(6), 84-94.

Evans, R. (2002). E-commerce, Competitiveness and Local and Regional Governance in Greater Manchester and Merseyside: A Preliminary Assessment. *Urban Studies, 39*(5/6), 947-975.

Fairchild, A. M., Ribbers, P. M. A., & Nooteboom, A. O. (2004). A Success Factor Model for Electronic Markets: Defining Outcomes Based on Stakeholder Context and Business Process. *Business Process Management Journal, 10*(1), 63-79.

Farbey, B., Land, F., & Targett, D. (1999). Moving IS Evaluation Forward: Learning Themes and Research Issues. *Journal of Strategic Information Systems, 8*(2), 189-207.

Feeny, D., & Willcocks, L. (1998). Re-design the IS Function Around Core Capabilities. *Long Range Planning, 31*(3), 354-367.

Fink, D. (1998). Guidelines for the Successful Adoption of Information Technology in Small and Medium Enterprise. *International Journal of Information Management, 18*(4), 243-253.

Fisher, J., & Craig, A. (2004). From Websites to Portals: Success Factors for Business Community Portals. *Proceedings of the 12th European Conference on Information Systems (The European IS Profession in the Global Networking Environment)* (CD-ROM). Turku, Finland: Turku School of Economics and Business Administration.

Fisher, J., & Craig, A. (2005). Developing Business Community Portals for SMEs – Issues of Design, Development and Sustainability [Electronic Version]. *Electronic Markets, 15*(2), 135-145.

Fong, T., Fowler, D., & Swatman, P. M. C. (1998). Success and Failure Factors for Implementing Effective Electronic Markets [Electronic Version]. *Electronic Markets, 8*(1), 45-47.

Gable, G. (1994). Integrating Case Study and Survey Research Methods: an Example in Information Systems. *European Journal of Information Systems, 3*(2), 112-126.

Galliers, R. D. (1992). Choosing Information Systems Research Approaches. In R. Galliers (Ed.), *Information Systems Research: Issues, Methods and Practical Guidelines* (pp. 144-162). London: Blackwell Scientific Publications.

Galloway, L., Mochrie, R., & Deakins, D. (2004). ICT-enabled Collectivity as a Positive Rural Business Strategy. *International Journal of Entrepreneurial Behaviour & Research, 10*(4), 247-259.

Gankema, H. G. J., Snuif, H. R., & Zwart, P. S. (2000). The Internationalization Process of Small and Medium-sized Enterprises: An Evaluation of Stage Theory. *Journal of Small Business Management, 38*(4), Start page 15. Retrieved March 21, 2003 from Expanded Academic ASAP database.

Gefen, D., Karahanna, E., & Straub, D. (2003). Trust and TAM in Online Shopping: An Integrated Model. *MIS Quarterly, 27*(1), 51-82.

Gibson, C. F., & Nolan, R. L. (1974). Managing the Four Stages of EDP Growth. *Harvard Business Review, 52*(1), 76-88.

Gioia, D. A., & Pitre, E. (1990). Multi Paradigm Perspectives on Theory Building. *The Academy of Management Review, 15*(4), 584-602.

Goldsby, T. J., & Eckert, J. A. (2003). Electronic Transportation Marketplaces: A Transaction Cost Perspective. *Industrial Marketing Management, 32*(3), 187-198.

Goles, T., & Hirschheim, R. (2000). The Paradigm is Dead, the Paradigm is Dead. . .Long Live the Paradigm: the Legacy of Burrell and Morgan. *Omega, International Journal of Management Science, 28*(3), 249-268.

Government Office for The West Midlands. (2002, April 23). *£1.2 European Funding Backs University of Warwick's New E-Marketplace for engineering SMEs Project.* Retrieved March 27, 2003 from http://www.go-wm.gov.uk/static/gems/European/DTIWM31702.doc.

Grewal, R., Comer, J. M., & Mehta, R. (2001). An Investigation into the Antecedents of Organizational Participation in Business-to-Business Electronic Markets. *Journal of Marketing, 65*(3), 17-33.

Grieger, M. (2003). Electronic Marketplaces: A Literature Review and a Call for Supply Chain Management Research. *European Journal of Operations Research, 144*(2), 280-294.

Grover, V. (1993). An Empirically Derived Model for the Adoption of Customer-based Interorganizational Systems. *Decision Sciences, 24*(3), 603-640.

Grover, V., & Ramanlal, P. (1999). Six Myths of Information and Markets: Information Technology Networks, Electronic Commerce, and the Battle for Consumer Surplus. *MIS Quarterly, 23*(4), 465-495.

Guba, E. G., & Lincoln, Y. S. (1989). *Fourth Generation Evaluation.* Newbury Park, CA: Sage Publications, Inc.

Gulledge, T. (2001). B2B eMarketplaces and Small and Medium-sized Enterprises (Keynote Address). *Proceedings of the Fourth International Conference on Stimulating Manufacturing Excellence in Small and Medium Enterprises* (pp. 11-17). Aalborg, Denmark: Aalborg University. Retrieved September 19, 2005 (last accessed) from: http://iprod.auc.dk/sme2001/paper/smesme2001.pdf

Gurbaxani, V., & Whang, S. (1991). The Impact of Information Systems on Organizations and Markets. *Communications of the ACM, 34*(1), 59-73.

Hagel, J., & Armstrong, A. (1997). *Net Gain: Expanding Markets Through Virtual Communities.* Boston, MA: Harvard Business School Press.

Harrison, D. A., Mykytyn Jr, P. P., & Riemenschneider, C. K. (1997). Executive Decisions About Adoption of Information Technology in Small Business: Theory and Empirical Tests. *Information Systems Research, 8*(2), 171-195.

Haveman, H. A. (1993). Follow the Leader: Mimetic Isomorphism and Entry into New Markets. *Administrative Science Quarterly, 38*(4), 593-627.

Henderson, D. R. (1984). Electronic Marketing in Principle and Practice. *American Journal of Agricultural Economics, 66*(5), 848-853.

Hess, C. M., & Kemerer, C. F. (1994). Computerized Loan Origination Systems: An Industry Case Study of the Electronic Markets Hypothesis. *MIS Quarterly, 18*(3), 251-275.

Hirschheim, R., & Smithson, S. (1988). A Critical Analysis of Information Systems Evaluation. In N. Bjorn-Anderson & G. B. Davis (Eds.), *Information Systems Assessment: Issues and Challenges* (pp. 17-37). Amsterdam: Elsevier Science.

Ho, D. C. K., Au, K. F., & Newton, E. (2002). Virtual Communities of Trade: The Strategic Fit of Resources Acquisition and Virtual Coordination Mechanisms in Supply Chains. *Proceedings of the Sixth Pacific Asia Conference on Information Systems (PACIS 2002)* (pp. 149-158). Tokyo: The Japan Society for Management Information.

Ho, D. C. K., Au, K. F., & Newton, E. (2003). The Process and Consequences of Supply Chain Virtualization. *Industrial Management & Data Systems, 103*(6), 423-433.

Holland, C. P., & Lockett, G. (1997). Mixed Mode Operation of Electronic Markets and Hierarchies. In M. Ebers (Ed.), *The Formation of Inter-Organizational Networks* (pp. 239-261). New York: Oxford University Press Inc.

Hsiao, R.-L. (2003). Technology Fears: Distrust and Cultural Persistence in Electronic Marketplace Adoption. *Journal of Strategic Information Systems, 12*(3), 169-199.

Hu, P. J., Chau, P. Y. K., Sheng, O. R. L., & Tam, K. Y. (1999). Examining the Technology Acceptance Model Using Physician Acceptance of Telemedicine Technology. *Journal of Management Information Systems, 16*(2), 91-112.

Hunt, S. D. (June 1991). Positivism and Paradigm Dominance in Consumer Research: Toward Critical Pluralism and Rapprochement. *Journal of Consumer Research, 18*(1), 32-44.

Hunter, M., & Doz, Y. (2002). *Opening the Gate on Gatetrade.net.* Fontainebleau, France: INSEAD. Retrieved November 3, 2003 from http://knowledge.insead.fr/

Iacovou, C. L., Benbasat, I., & Dexter, A. S. (1995). Electronic Data Interchange and Small Organisations. *MIS Quarterly, 19*(4), 465-485.

Igabria, M., Zinatelli, N., Cragg, P., & Cavaye, A. L. M. (1997). Personal Computing Acceptance Factors in Small Firms: A Structural Equation Model. *MIS Quarterly, 21*(3), 279-305.

Irani, Z., Ezingeard, J.-N., & Grieve, R. J. (1998). Costing the True Costs of IT/IS Investments in Manufacturing: a Focus during Management Decision Making. *Logistics Information Management, 11*(1), 38-43.

Isaksen, A. (1999). Evaluation of a Regional Innovation Programme: the Innovation and New Technology Programme in Northern Norway. *Evaluation and Program Planning, 22*(1), 83-90.

Jeffcoate, J., Chappell, C., & Feindt, S. (2000). Attitudes Towards Process Improvement Among SMEs Involved in E-commerce. *Knowledge and Process Management, 7*(3), 187-195.

Johnsen, H. C. G., & Normann, R. (June 2004). When Research and Practice Collide: The Role of Action Research when there is a Conflict of Interest with Stakeholders. *Systemic Practice and Action Research, 17*(3), 207-235.

Johnston, R., & Lawrence, P. R. (July-August 1988). Beyond Vertical Integration - The Rise of Value-Adding Partnership. *Harvard Business Review, 66*(4), 94-101.

Kalakota, R., Oliva, R., & Donath, B. (Fall 1999). Move over E-Commerce: Emerging Digital Marketplaces Promise the Next Wave of Business Competition. *Marketing Management, 8*(3), 22-32.

Kambil, A., & Van Heck, E. (1998). Reengineering the Dutch Flower Auctions: A Framework for Analyzing Exchange Organizations. *Information Systems Research, 9*(1), 1-19.

Kaplan, S., & Sawhney, M. (May-June 2000). E-Hubs: The New B2B Marketplaces. *Harvard Business Review, 78*(3), 97-103.

Kendal, K. E., & Kendall, K. E. (2005). *Systems Analysis and Design.* New Jersey: Pearson.

Khalifa, M., Banerjee, P., & Ma, L. (2003). Strategies for Successfully Deploying e-Markets: Lessons from the China Context. *Proceedings of the 36th Hawaii International Conference on Systems Sciences* Big Island, Hawaii: IEEE Computer Society. Retrieved October 7, 2005 (last accessed) from http://csdl2.computer.org/comp/proceedings/hicss/2003/1874/07/187470193b.pdf

King, W. R., & Teo, T. S. H. (1997). Integration between Business Planning and Information Systems Planning: Validating a Stage Hypothesis. *Decision Sciences, 28*(2), 279-308.

Klein, H. K., & Myers, M. D. (1999). A Set of Principles for Conducting and Evaluating Interpretive Field Studies in Information Systems. *MIS Quarterly, 23*(1), 67-94.

Koch, H. (2002). Business-To-Business Electronic Commerce Marketplaces: The Alliance Process [Electronic Version]. *Journal of Electronic Commerce Research, 3*(2), 67-76.

Koch, H. (2004a). Business-to-Business Electronic Marketplace Characteristics Driving Use. *Proceedings of the Tenth Americas Conference on Information Systems (AMCIS)* (pp. 2447-2454). New York: Association for Information Systems.

Koch, H. (2004b). Pegasus: Lessons from a Business-to-Business Electronic Marketplace's Struggle. *Proceedings of the Tenth Americas Conference on Information Systems (AMCIS)* (pp. 2573-2580). New York: Association for Information Systems.

Kollmann, T. (2000). Competitive Strategies for Electronic Marketplaces. A study of German-language trading sites for used cars on the WWW [Electronic Version]. *Electronic Markets, 10*(2), 102-109.

Kozinets, R. V. (1999). E-Tribalized Marketing?: The Strategic Implications of Virtual Communities of Consumption. *European Management Journal, 17*(3), 252-264.

Krammer, M. Y., Browning, J. A., Rozwell, C., & Shu, L. (2001). *The SMB Guide to E-Marketplaces.* Stamford, CT: Gartner Inc. Retrieved September 13, 2005 (last accessed) from http://www.gartner.com/resources/100700/100764/100764.pdf

Krieger, B. L., & Muller, P. S. (Spring 2003). Making Internet Communities Work: Reflections on an unusual Business Model. *Database for Advances in Information Systems, 34*(2), 50-59.

Kumar, K., van Dissel, H. G., & Bielli, P. (1998). The Merchant of Prato - Revisited: Toward a Third Rationality of Information Systems. *MIS Quarterly, 22*(2), 199-226.

Kurnia, S., & Johnston, R. B. (2000). The Need for a Processual View of Inter-organizational Systems Adoption. *The Journal of Strategic Information Systems, 9*(4), 295-319.

Landry, M., & Banville, C. (1992). A Disciplined Methodological Pluralism for MIS Research. *Accounting, Management & Information Technology, 2*(2), 77-97.

Lauren, J. (2003, November). Significant E-marketplaces. *eMarket Services.* Retrieved December 20, 2003 from http://www.emarketservices.com/upload/Reports/SignificanteMarkets.pdf

Le, T. T. (2002). Pathways to Leadership for Business-to-Business Electronic Marketplaces [Electronic Version]. *Electronic Markets, 12*(2), 112-119.

Lechner, U., & Hummel, J. (Spring 2002). Business Models and System Architectures of Virtual Communities: From a Sociological Phenomenon to Peer-to-Peer Architectures. *International Journal of Electronic Commerce, 6*(3), 41-53.

Lee, A. S. (1989). A Scientific Methodology For MIS Case Studies. *MIS Quarterly, 13*(1), 33-50.

Lee, A. S. (1991). Integrating Positivist and Interpretive Approaches to Organizational Research. *Organization Science, 2*(4), 342-365.

Lee, F., Vogel, D., & Limayem, M. (2003). Virtual Community Informatics: A Review and Research Agenda. *JITTA: Journal of Information Technology Theory and Application, 5*(1), 47-63.

Lee, H. G. (1998). Do Electronic Markets Lower the Price of Goods? *Communications of the ACM, 41*(1), 73-80.

Leedy, P. D. (1993). *Practical Research: Planning and Design* (5th ed.). New York: McMillan Publishing Company.

Lenz, M., Zimmerman, H.-D., & Heitman, M. (2002). Strategic Partnerships and Competitiveness of Business-to-Business E-Marketplaces: Preliminary Evidence from Europe [Electronic Version]. *Electronic Markets, 12*(2), 100-111.

Leonard-Barton, D. (1990). A Dual Methodology for Case Studies: Synergistic Use of Longitudinal Single Site with Replicated Multiple Sites. *Organization Science, 1*(3), 248-266.

Levy, M., & Powell, P. (2003). Exploring SME Internet Adoption: Towards a Contingent Model [Electronic Version]. *Electronic Markets, 13*(2), 173-181.

Lin, C. A. (1998). Bridging Positivist and Interpretivist Approaches to Qualitative Methods. *Policy Studies Journal, 26*(1), 162-180.

Lindsey, D., Cheney, P. H., Kasper, G. M., & Ives, B. (1990). TELCOT: An Application of Information Technology for Competitive Advantage in the Cotton Industry. *MIS Quarterly, 14*(4), 347-357.

Löfstedt, U. (2001). Competence Development and Learning Organizations: A Critical Analysis of Practical Guidelines and Methods. *Systems Research and Behavioural Science, 18*(2), 115-125. Retrieved June 11, 2003 from Wiley InterScience database.

Lu, J., Yu, C.-S., Liu, C., & Yao, J. E. (2003). Technology Acceptance Model for Wireless Internet. *Internet Research: Electronic Networking Applications and Policy, 13*(3), 206-222.

Lucking-Reiley, D. (September 2000). Auctions on the Internet: What's being Auctioned and How? *The Journal of Industrial Economics, XLVIII*(3), 227-252.

Malone, T. W., Yates, J., & Benjamin, R. (1987). Electronic Markets and Electronic Hierarchies. *Communications of the ACM, 30*(6), 484-497.

Malone, T. W., Yates, J., & Benjamin, R. (May-June 1989). The Logic of Electronic Markets. *Harvard Business Review, 67*(3), 166-169.

Markus, M. L., Banerjee, P., & Ma, L. (2002). Electronic Marketplaces in Hong Kong's Trading Industry. *Proceedings of the 35th Hawaii International Conference on Systems Sciences* Los Alamitos: IEEE Computer Society. Retrieved October 7, 2005 (last accessed) from : http://csdl2.computer.org/comp/proceedings/hicss/2002/1435/07/14350182.pdf

Marshall, C., & Rossman, G. (1995). *Designing Qualitative Research*. Newbury Park, CA: Sage Publications Inc.

Mason, C., Castleman, T., & Parker, C. (2005). Can Knowledge Management Save Regional Development? *Proceedings of the CRIC Cluster Conference. Beyond Cluster- Current Practices & Future Strategies* [CD-ROM]. Ballarat: University of Ballarat.

Mata, F., Fuerst, W., & Barney, J. (1995). Information Technology and Sustained Competitive Advantage: A Resource-Based Analysis. *MIS Quarterly, 19*(4), 487-505.

Mathieson, K. (1991). Predicting User Intentions: Comparing the Technology Acceptance Model with the Theory of Planned Behaviour. *Information Systems Research, 2*(3), 173-191.

McGrath, G. M., & More, E. (2002). *Forging and Managing Online Collaboration: The ITOL Experience.* Canberra: Department of Communications, Information and the Arts (DCITA). Retrieved August 2, 2005 (last accessed) from http://www.dcita.gov.au/ie/publications/2002/december/forging_and_managing_online_coll aboration_the_itol_experience

McGrath, K. (2005). Doing Critical Research in Information Systems: a Case of Theory and Practice not Informing Each Other. *Information Systems Journal, 15*(2), 85-101.

McKay, J., Prananto, A., & Marshall, P. (2000). E-business maturity: The SOGe model. *Proceedings of the 11th Australasian Conference on Information Systems (ACIS).* Brisbane: Queensland University of Technology.

McKnight, H. D., Kacmar, C. J., & Choudhury, V. (2004). Shifting Factors and the Ineffectiveness of Third party Assurance Seals: A Two-Stage Model of Initial Trust in a Web Business [Electronic Version]. *Electronic Markets, 14*(3), 252-266.

Mehrtens, J., Cragg, P. B., & Mills, A. M. (2001). A Model of Internet Adoption by SMEs. *Information & Management, 39*(3), 165-176.

Mello, A. (2002, June 19). Independent E-markets Struggle for Survival. *ZDNet.* Retrieved July 24, 2003 from http://www.zdnetindia.com/biztech/ebusiness/b2b/stories/60127.html

Miles, M. B., & Huberman, A. M. (1994). *Qualitative Data Analysis* (2nd ed.). CA: Thousand Oaks.

Miles, R., & Snow, C. (1986). Organizations: New Concepts for New Firms. *California Management Review, 28*(3), 62-73.

Miller, J. (2001). Technology Lessons from the E-Marketplace Shakeout. *Biopharm, 14*(5), Start page 70. Retrieved August 24, 2003 from Academic Research Library database.

Ming Zeng. (2001). *Alibaba.com.* Singapore: INSEAD EURO-ASIA CENTRE. Retrieved November 26, 2003 from http://knowledge.insead.fr/.

Mingers, J. (2001). Combining IS Research Methods: Towards a Pluralistic Methodology. *Information Systems Research, 12*(3), 240-259.

Mingers, J. (2002). Real-izing Information Systems: Critical Realism as an Underpinning Philosophy for Information Systems. *Proceedings of the Twenty-Third International Conference on Information Systems.* (pp. 295-303). Association for Information Systems. Retrieved October 17, 2003 from http://aisel.isworld.org/

Mingers, J., & Brocklesby, J. (1997). Multimethodology: Towards a Framework for Mixing Methodologies. *Omega, International Journal of Management Science, 25*(5), 489-509.

Molla, A., & Licker, P. S. (2001). E-Commerce Systems Success: An Attempt to Extend and Respecify the DeLone and MacLean Model of IS Success. *Journal of Electronic Commerce Research, 2*(4), 131-141.

Monge, P. R., Fulk, J., Kalman, M. E., Flanagin, A. J., Parnassa, C., & Suzanne, R. (May-Jun., 1998). Production of Collective Action in Alliance-Based Interorganizational Communication and Information Systems. *Organization Science, 9*(3), 411-433.

Musgrave, S. J. (2005). Community Portals - The UK Experience. A False Dawn over the Field of Dreams? *The Journal of Community Informatics, 1*(2). Retrieved February 28, 2005, from http://ci-journal.net/index.php

Mutch, A. (1999). *Critical Realism and Information Systems: An Exploration.* The Web Site for Critical Realism. Retrieved October 31, 2003 from http://www.reggedclaws.com/criticalrealism/archive/amutch_cris.html

National Office for the Information Economy (NOIE). (2000). *Taking the Plunge 2000: Sink or Swim. Small Business Attitudes to Electronic Commerce.* Canberra: Department of Communications Information Technology and the Arts.

National Office for the Information Economy (NOIE). (2001). *B2B E-Commerce: Capturing Value Online.* Retrieved March 11, 2003 from http://www.noie.gov.au/

National Office for the Information Economy (NOIE). (2002). *E-Business Strategy for Small Business.* Retrieved March 11, 2003 from http://www.noie.gov.au/projects/ebusiness/Advancing/SME/ebusiness_strategy.htm

National Office for the Information Economy (NOIE). (2003). *Wangaratta - NETCo-op: A Cooperative Community Telco.* Retrieved September 4, 2005 (last accessed) from http://www.dcita.gov.au/ie/community_connectivity/communities_online/wangaratta#1

OECD. (2000). *The OECD Small and Medium Enterprise Outlook 2000 Edition.* Paris: Organisation for Economic Co-operation and Development. Retrieved September 22, 2003 from http://www1.oecd.org/publications/e-book/9200021E.PDF

Office of the Advocacy United States Small Business Association. (n.d). *2003 State Small Business Profile: UNITED STATES.* Retrieved August 10, 2005 from http://www.sba.gov/advo/stats/profiles/03us.pdf

Office of the Advocacy United States Small Business Association. (n.d.). *Small Business by the Numbers: Answers to Frequently Asked Questions.* Retrieved August 10, 2005 (last accessed) from http://www.sba.gov/advo/stats/sbfaq.pdf

Ogus, A. I. (1994). *Regulation. Legal Form and Economic Theory.* New York: Oxford University Press Inc.

Oliver, C. (1990). Determinants of Interorganizational Relationships: Integration and Future Directions. *Academy of Management Review, 15*(2), 241-265.

Ordanini, A. (2003). *The Effects of Participation on B-to-B Exchanges: a Resource-Based View.* Irvine: CRITO (Centre for Research on Information Technology and Organizations), University of California. Retrieved January 21, 2004 from http://crito.uci.edu/publications/pdf/ordanini.pdf.

Ordanini, A., Micelli, S., & Di Maria, E. (2004). Failure and Success of B-to-B Exchange Business Models: A Contingent Analysis of their Performance. *European Management Journal, 22*(3), 281-289.

Ordanini, A., & Pol, A. (2001). Infomediation and Competitive Advantage in B2b Digital Marketplaces. *European Management Journal, 19*(3), 276-285.

Orlikowski, W. J., & Baroudi, J. J. (1991). Studying Information Technology in Organizations: Research Approaches and Assumptions. *Information Systems Research, 2*(1), 1-28.

Ortelbach, B. (2005). The Development of Business Models for Internet Portals: An Explorative Investigation of Revenue Streams. *Proceedings of the 2005 Information Resources Management Association (IRMA) International Conference* (pp. 290-293). San Diego: Idea Group.

Otis, N., & Johanson, G. (2004). Community Building and Information and Communications Technologies: Current Knowledge. *Australian Electronic Governance Conference.* Melbourne, Victoria: Centre for Public Policy, University of Melbourne. Retrieved July 7, 2005 from http://www.public-policy.unimelb.edu.au/egovernance/papers/17_OtisJohanson.pdf.

Palvia, S. C., Sharma, R. S., & Conrath, D. W. (2001). A Socio-technical Framework for Quality Assessment of Computer Information Systems. *Industrial Management & Data Systems, 101*(5/6), 237-251.

Pavlou, P. A. (2002). Institution-based Trust in Interorganizational Exchange Relationships: the Role of Online B2B Marketplaces on Trust Formation. *The Journal of Strategic Information Systems, 11*(3-4), 215-243.

Pavlou, P. A., & Gefen, D. (2002). Building Effective Online Exchange Networks with Institutional Trust. *Proceedings of the Twenty Third International Conference on Information Systems* Barcelona, Spain: Association for Information Systems. Retrieved September 26, 2003 from http://aisel.isworld.org/

Pavlou, P. A., & Gefen, D. (2004). Building Effective Online Marketplaces with Institution-Based Trust. *Information Systems Research, 15*(1), 37-59.

Pettigrew, A. M. (1985a). *The Awakening Giant: Continuity and Change in ICI.* Oxford: Blackwell.

Pettigrew, A. M. (1985b). Contextualist Research and the Study of Organisational Change Processes. In E. Mumford, R. Hirschheim, G. Fitzgerald & A. T. Wood-Harper (Eds.), *Research Methods in Information Systems* (pp. 53-78). Amsterdam: Elsevier Science Publishers B.V. (North Holland).

Pettigrew, A. M. (1987). Context and Action in the Transformation of the Firm. *Journal of Management Studies, 24*(6), 649-670.

Pettigrew, A. M. (1990). Longitudinal Field Research on Change: Theory and Practice. *Organization Science, 1*(3), 267-292.

Pfeffer, J., & Salancik, G. (1978). *The External Control of Organizations: A Resource Dependence Perspective.* New York: Harper and Row.

Pliaskin, A., & Tatnall, A. (2005). Developing a Portal to Build a Business Community. In A. Tatnall (Ed.), *Web Portals: The New Gateways to Internet Information and Services* (pp. 335-348). Hershey, PA: Idea Group Publishing.

Poon, S., & Swatman, P. M. C. (1997). Internet-Based Small Business Communication: Seven Australian Cases [Electronic Version]. *Electronic Markets, 7*(2), 15-21.

Popovic, M. (2002). *B2B e-Marketplaces.* Brussels: European Commission. Retrieved May 21, 2003 from http://europa.eu.int/information_society/topics/ebusiness/ecommerce/3information/keyissues/documents/doc/B2Bemarketplaces.doc

Porter, M. E. (March 2001). Strategy and the Internet. *Harvard Business Review, 79*(3), 62-78.

Prananto, A., Marshall, P., & McKay, J. (2002). Stages of Growth of E-business: An Analysis of the Perceived Usability of the Stages of Growth Model in E-business Progression. *Proceedings of the 4th International Conference on Electronic Commerce (ICEC)* Hong Kong SAR, China: City University of Hong Kong.

Prananto, A., Marshall, P., & McKay, J. (2003). A Study of the Progression of E-business Maturity in Australian SMEs: Some Evidence of the Applicability of the Stages of Growth for E-business Model. *Proceedings of the 7th Pacific Asia Conference on Information Systems (PACIS 2003)* (pp. 68-80). Adelaide, South Australia: University of South Australia.

Premkumar, G., Ramamurthy, K., & Nilakanta, S. (1994). Implementation of Electronic Data Interchange: An Innovation Diffusion Perspective. *Journal of Management Information Systems, 11*(2), Start page 157. Retrieved October 1, 2003 from ProQuest UMI database.

PRIME Faraday Technology Watch. (2001). *The Emergence and Impact of the E-marketplace on SME Supply Chain Efficiencies*. Loughborough: PRIME Faraday Partnership. Retrieved December 20, 2003 from http://www.primetechnologywatch.org.uk

Rahim, M. M., Shanks, G., & Johnston, R. (2002). Motivations for Inter-Organisational Systems Adoption: A Tale of Two Organisations. *Proceedings of* The *Adoption and Diffusion of IT in an Environment of Critical Change (IFIP WG8.6)*. (pp. 129-145). Sydney: University of New South Wales.

Raisch, W. D. (2001). *The eMarketplace. Strategies for Success in B2B Ecommerce*. New York: McGraw-Hill.

Rapoport, R. (1970). Three Dilemmas of Action Research. *Human Relations, 23*(6), 499-513.

Remenyi, D., & Sherwood-Smith, M. (1999). Maximise Information Systems Value by Continuous Participative Evaluation. *Logistics Information Management, 12*(1/2), 14-31.

Rheingold, H. (1993). *The Virtual Community: Homesteading on the Electronic Frontier*. New York: Addison-Wesley.

Riemenschneider, C. K., Harrison, D. A., & Mykytyn Jr, P. P. (2003). Understanding IT Adoption Decisions in Small Business: Integrating Current Theories. *Information & Management, 40*(4), 269-285.

Robles, F. (January-February 2002). The Evolution of Global Portal Strategy. *Thunderbird International Business Review, 44*(1), 25-46.

Rogers, E. M. (1995). *Diffusion of Innovations* (4th ed.). New York: The Free Press.

Romm, C., Pliskin, N., & Clarke, R. (1997). Virtual Communities and Society: Toward an Integrative Three Phase Model. *International Journal of Information Management, 17*(4), 261-270.

Rose, J., & Haynes, M. (Dec 1999). A Soft Systems Approach to the Evaluation of Complex Interventions in the Public Sector. *Journal of Applied Management Studies, 8*(2), 199-216.

Rosenthal, D., Shah, S. K., & Xiao, B. (1993). The Impact of Purchasing Policy on Electronic Markets and Electronic Hierarchies. *Information & Management, 25*(2), 105-117.

Rossi, P. H., & Freeman, H. E. (1989). *Evaluation: A Systematic Approach* (4th ed.). Newbury Park, CA: Sage Publications, Inc.

Saha, A. (November 1999). Application Framework for E-Business: Portals. *IBM Software Strategy*. Retrieved November 7, 2005 (last accessed) from http://www-900.ibm.com/developerWorks/cn/web/portal/index.shtml

Sawhney, M. (2002). Putting the Horse First; B2B Exchanges Failed Because They Got Their Business Models Backward. *CIO, 15*(15), 38-40.

Schubert, P. (n.d.). A Framework for the Analysis of Socio-Economic Aspects of Electronic Markets. Retrieved September 13, 2004 (last accessed) from:
http://dwi.fhbb.ch/eb/publications.nsf/dd868c336f5d8971c1256c5600643480/5897b540d77 0f0bbc12569a4003b0676/$FILE/9703BledSubmitted.pdf

Sculley, A. B., & Woods, W. A. (2001). *B2B Exchanges: The Killer Application in the Business-to-Business Internet Revolution*. New York: Harper Collins.

Scupola, A. (2003). The Adoption of Internet Commerce by SMEs in the South of Italy: An Environmental, Technological and Organizational Perspective. *Journal of Global Information Technology Management, 6*(1), 52-71.

Scupola, A. (2004). Adoption of E-Commerce in Small and Medium Enterprises in Australia. *Proceedings of the Tenth Americas Conference on Information Systems (AMCIS)* (pp. 343-352). New York: Association for Information Systems.

Segev, A., Gebauer, J., & Farber, F. (1999). Internet-based Electronic Markets [Electronic Version]. *Electronic Markets, 9*(3), 138-146.

Sensis Pty Ltd. (2003). *2003 Yellow Pages® Business Index E-Business Report: The Online Experience of Small and Medium Enterprises, July 2003*: Telstra Corporation Ltd. Retrieved September 1, 2003 from: http://www.sensis.com.au/Internet/static_files/YellowPages_EBusinessReport_July03.pdf

Serafeimidis, V., & Smithson, S. (1999). Rethinking the Approaches to Information Systems Evaluation. *Logistics Information Management, 12*(1/2), 94-107.

Shadish Jr., W. R., Cook, T. D., & Leviton, L. L. (1991). *Foundations of Program Evaluation: Theories of Practice*. Newbury Park, CA: Sage Publications, Inc.

Sieber, S., & Sabatier, J. V. (Summer 2003). Market Bundling Strategies in the Horizontal Portal Industry. *International Journal of Electronic Commerce, 7*(4), 37-54.

Silverman, D. (1998). Qualitative Research: Meanings or Practices. *Information Systems Journal, 8*(1), 3-20.

Silverman, D. (2001). *Interpreting Qualitative Data: Methods for Analysing Talk, Text and Interaction*. London: Sage Publications Ltd.

Simpson, M., & Docherty, A. J. (2004). E-commerce Adoption Support and Advice for UK SMEs. *Journal of Small Business and Enterprise Development, 11*(3), 315-328.

Skjott-Larsen, T., Kotzab, H., & Grieger, M. (2003). Electronic Marketplaces and Supply Chain Relationships. *Industrial Marketing Management, 32*(3), 199-210.

Smithson, S., & Hirschheim, R. (1998). Analysing Information Systems Evaluation: Another Look at an Old Problem. *European Journal of Information Systems, 7*(3), 158-174.

Soh, C., & Markus, M. L. (2002a). B2B E-Marketplaces - Interconnection Effects, Strategic Positioning, and Performance. [Manuscript Version]. *Systèmes d'Information et Management, 1 (7 Mars)*, 77-103. Retrieved October 1, 2005 (last accessed) from http://web.bentley.edu/empl/m/lmarkus/Markus_Web_Documents_(pdf)/B2B_EMs_Interconnection_Effects.pdf

Soh, C. P. P., & Markus, M. L. (2002b). B2B E-Marketplaces-Strategic Archetypes. *Proceedings of the Twenty Third International Conference on Information Systems*. Barcelona, Spain: Association for Information Systems. Retrieved September 26, 2003 from http://aisel.isworld.org/

Spencer, S. (2002). Diffusion of Information Policy. *Proceedings of The Adoption and Diffusion of IT in an Environment of Critical Change (IFIP WG8.6)* (pp. 23-33). Sydney: University of New South Wales.

Spitzer, T. (February 2000). Vertical Horizon: Surveying the Landscape of Online Industry. *Web Techniques, 5*(2), 50-56.

Stake, R. E. (2000). Case Studies. In N. K. Denzin & Y. S. Lincoln (Eds.), *Handbook of Qualitative Research* (2nd ed., pp. 435-454). Thousand Oaks, CA: Sage Publications Inc.

Standing, C. (2001). The Characteristics of Successful E-marketplaces. *Proceedings of the Fifth Pacific Asia Conference on Information Systems (PACIS 2001)* (pp. 633-640). Seoul: Korea Society of Management Information Systems.

Standing, C., Sims, I., Stockdale, R., Gengatharen, D. E., Standing, S., & Wassenaar, A. (2005). Can E-Marketplaces Bridge the Digital Divide? An Analysis of Two Western Australian Cases. *The Electronic Journal on Information Systems in Developing Countries, 20*(3), 1-14. Retrieved January 14, 2005 from http://www.ejisdc.org

Standing, C., Sims, I., Stockdale, R., & Wassenaar, A. (2003). Can E-Marketplaces Bridge the Digital Divide? *Proceedings of the Organizational Information Systems in the Context of Globalization, IFIP TC8 & TC9 / WG8.2 & WG9.4 Working Conference on Information Systems Perspectives and Challenges in the Context of Globalization* (pp. 340-353). Athens: IFIP.

Standing, C., & Stockdale, R. (2001). Evaluating the Benefits of Electronic Marketplaces. *Proceedings of the 2nd International We-B Conference* (pp. 118-127). Perth, Australia: We-B Centre, School of MIS, Edith Cowan University.

Standing, C., & Stockdale, R. (2003). *Supporting Rural SMEs in the Selection of E-Marketplaces.* Kingston, ACT: Rural Industries Research and Development Corporation.

Stansfield, M., & Grant, K. (2003). An Investigation into the Issues Influencing the Use of the Internet and Electronic Commerce Among Small-Medium Sized Enterprises. *Journal of Electronic Commerce Research, 4*(1), 15-33.

Steele Brown, M. (2001, June 8). E-marketplaces: Promise but Little Business. *The Business Journal, 19*(39), 1. Retrieved July 20, 2003 from ProQuest UMI database.

Steinfield, C., Bouwman, H., & Adelaar, T. (Fall 2002). The Dynamics of Click-and-Mortar Electronic Commerce: Opportunities and Management Strategies. *International Journal of Electronic Commerce, 7*(1), 93-119.

Steinfield, C., & Klein, S. (1999). Preface. Special Section: Local vs Global Issues in Electronic Commerce [Electronic Version]. *Electronic Markets, 9*(1/2), 45-50.

Steinfield, C., Mahler, A., & Bauer, J. (1999a). Electronic Commerce and the Local Merchant: Opportunities for Synergy Between Physical and Web Presence. *Electronic Markets, 9*(1/2), 51-57.

Steinfield, C., & Whitten, P. (1999). *Community Level Socio-Economic Impacts of Electronic Commerce.* White paper presented to the Telecommunications Policy Research Conference, Washington D.C., Sept. 25-27, 1999. Retrieved January 14, 2005 from http://www.tprc.org/ABSTRACTS99/steinwhitepap.PDF

Steinfield, C. W., Mahler, A., & Bauer, J. (1999b). Electronic Commerce and the Local Merchant: Opportunities for Synergy between Physical and Web Presence [Electronic Version]. *Electronic Markets, 9*(1/2), 51-57.

Stockdale, R., & Standing, C. (2002). A Proposed Model for Evaluating the Benefits of Electronic Marketplaces. *Proceedings of the 3rd International We-B Conference.* Perth, Australia: We-B Centre, School of MIS, Edith Cowan University.

Stockdale, R., & Standing, C. (2004). Benefits and Barriers of E-marketplace Participation: an SME Perspective. *Journal of Enterprise Information Management, 17*(4), 301-311.

Straub, D. W., Hoffman, D. L., Weber, B. W., & Steinfield, C. (June 2002a). Measuring e-Commerce in Net-Enabled Organizations: An Introduction to the Special Issue. *Information Systems Research, 13*(2), 115-124.

Straub, D. W., Hoffman, D. L., Weber, B. W., & Steinfield, C. (September 2002b). Toward New Metrics for Net-Enabled Organizations. *Information Systems Research, 13*(3), 227-238.

Subba Rao, S., Metts, G., & Mora Monge, C. A. (2003). Electronic Commerce Development in Small and Medium Sized Enterprises: A Stage Model and its Implications. *Business Process Management, 9*(1), 11-32.

Susman, G. I., & Evered, R. D. (December, 1978). An Assessment of the Scientific Merits of Action Research. *Administrative Science Quarterly, 24*(4), 582-603.

Swatman, P. M. C., Bytheway, A., Cavill, M., Cooper, J., & Wilde, W. D. (1996). Virtual Communities: Linking People and Markets Electronically. *Proceedings of the Seventh Australasian Conference on Information Systems (ACIS)* (Invited panel paper). Hobart: University of Tasmania. Retrieved November 7, 2005 (last accessed) from http://www.uni-koblenz.de/~swatmanp/pdfs/PANEL.acis96.pdf.

Symons, V. J. (1991). A Review of Information Systems Evaluation: Content, Context and Process. *European Journal of Information Systems, 1*(3), 205-212.

Taket, A., & White, L. (1998). Experience in the Practice of One Tradition of Multimethodology. *Systemic Practice and Action Research, 11*(2), 153-167.

Tao, A. L. (2003, April 21). Thriving and Evolving. *Asia Computer Weekly*, p. 1. Retrieved July 23, 2003 from ProQuest UMI database.

Tapscott, D., Ticoll, D., & Lowy, A. (2000). *Digital Capital: Harnessing the Power of Business Webs*. Boston: Harvard Business School Press.

Tatnall, A., & Burgess, S. (2002). Using Actor-Network Theory to Research the Implementation of a B2B Portal for Regional SMEs in Melbourne, Australia. *Proceedings of the 15th Bled Electronic Commerce Conference.* (pp. 179-191) Bled, Slovenia: University of Maribor. Retrieved November 10 (last accessed) from: http://aisel.isworld.org/

Taylor, M., & Murphy, A. (2004). SMEs and e-Business. *Journal of Small Business and Enterprise Development, 11*(3), 280-289.

Teo, H. H., Wei, K. K., & Benbasat, I. (2003). Predicting Intention to Adopt Interorganisational linkages: An Institutional Perspective. *MIS Quarterly, 27*(1), 19-49.

Thompson, H. (2003). Growing Exports via Online Communities and Regional Web-Portals: A case study from the Central Highlands region of Victoria. *Proceedings of the 16th Annual Conference of Small Enterprise Association of Australia and New Zealand* Ballarat: University of Ballarat. Retrieved September 19, 2005 (last accessed) from http://www.cecc.com.au/programs/resource_manager/accounts/seaanz_papers/82Thompson OnlinecommunitieseSME.pdf

Thompson, H. (2005). Using Cluster Theory as the Lens through which the results of Government Funded Online Service Initiatives can be Examined. *Proceedings of the CRIC Cluster Conference. Beyond Cluster- Current Practices & Future Strategies* [CD-ROM]. Ballarat: University of Ballarat.

Thong, J. Y. L. (1999). An Integrated Model of Information Systems Adoption in Small Businesses. *Journal of Management Information Systems, 15*(4), 187-214.

Thong, J. Y. L. (2001). Resource Constraints and Information Systems Implementation in Singaporean Small Businesses. *Omega, International Journal of Management Science, 29*(2), 143-156.

Thong, J. Y. L., & Yap, C. S. (1995). CEO Characteristics, Organizational Characteristics and Information Technology Adoption in Small Businesses. *Omega, International Journal of Management Science, 23*(4), 429-442.

Tonkin, C. (2003). *eProcurement in the Public Sector: Story, Myth and Legend.* Working Paper. The Policy Institute, Trinity College, Dublin. Retrieved January 27, 2004 from http://www.policyinstitute.tcd.ie/working_papers/PIWPO7%20-%20Tonkin.pdf

Torkzadeh, G., & Dhillon, G. (2002). Measuring Factors that Influence the Success of Internet Commerce. *Information Systems Research, 13*(2), 187-204.

Tornatzky, L. G., & Fleischer, M. (1990). *The Process of Technological Innovation.* Lexington, Mass: Lexington Books.

Torvatn, H. (1999). Using Program Theory Models in Evaluation of Industrial Modernization Programs: Three Case Studies. *Evaluation and Program Planning, 22*(1), 73-82.

Trauth, E. M. (1997). Achieving the Research Goal with Qualitative Methods: Lessons Learned Along the Way. In A. S. Lee, J.Liebenau & J. DeGross (Eds.), *Information Systems and Qualitative Research* (pp. 225-245). London: Chapman & Hall.

U. S. Small Business Administration. (2002). *Table of Small Business Size Standards Matched to North American Industry Classification System Codes.* Retrieved August 10, 2005 (last accessed) from http://www.sba.gov/size/sizetable2002.pdf

van Akkeren, J. K., & Cavaye, A. L. M. (1999a). Confusion with Diffusion? Unravelling IS Diffusion and Innovation Literature with a Focus on SMEs. *Australian Journal of Information Systems, 7*(1), 60-67.

van Akkeren, J. K., & Cavaye, A. L. M. (1999b). Factors Affecting Entry-Level Internet Technology Adoption by Small Business in Australia: Evidence from Three Cases. *Journal of Systems and Information Technology, 3*(2), 33-48.

Venkatesh, V., & Davis, F. D. (2000). A Theoretical Extension of the Technology Acceptance Model: Four Longitudinal Field Studies. *Management Science, 46*(2), 186-204. Retrieved October 1, 2003 from ProQuest UMI database.

Venkatesh, V., Morris, M. G., Davis, G. B., & Davis, F. D. (2003). User Acceptance of Information Technology: Toward a Unified View. *MIS Quarterly, 27*(3), 425-478.

W.K. Kellogg Foundation. (1998). *W.K. Kellogg Foundation Evaluation Handbook.* Retrieved August 25, 2003 from http://www.wkkf.org/Pubs/Tools/Evaluation/Pub770.pdf

W.K. Kellogg Foundation. (2004). *Logic Model Development Guide.* Retrieved April 11, 2005, from http://www.wkkf.org/Pubs/Tools/Evaluation/Pub3669.pdf

Walczuch, R., Van Braven, G., & Lundgren, H. (2000). Internet Adoption Barriers for Small Firms in The Netherlands. *European Management Journal, 18*(5), 561-572.

Walczuch, R., Verkiujlen, M., Geus, B., & Ronnen, U. (February 2001). Stickiness of Commercial Virtual Communities. *MERIT, Maastricht Economic Research Institute on Innovation and Technology in its series Research Memoranda with number 021.* Retrieved November 11, 2005 (last accessed) from http://ideas.repec.org/p/dgr/umamer/2001021.html

Walsham, G. (1993). *Interpreting Information Systems.* Chichester: John Wiley & Sons Ltd.

Walsham, G. (1995). Interpretive Case Studies in IS research: Nature and Method. *European Journal of Information Systems, 4*(2), 74-81.

Warkentin, M., Bapna, R., & Sugumaran, V. (2001). E-Knowledge Networks for Inter-Organizational Collaborative E-business. *Logistics Information Management, 14*(1/2), 149-163.

Wassenaar, A., & Gregor, S. (2003). Puzzles and Perspectives in Electronic Market Theory - Reflections on Adoption of a B2B Electronic Market in the Australian Beef Cattle Industry. *Proceedings of the 16th Bled eCommerce Conference* (pp. 734-746). Bled, Slovenia: University of Maribor.

Weber, R. (2004). Editor's Comments - The Rhetoric of Positivism Versus Interpretism: A Personal View. *MIS Quarterly, 28*(1), iii-xii.

Weitzman, E. A. (2000). Software and Qualitative Research. In N. K. Denzin & Y. S. Lincoln (Eds.), *Handbook of Qualitative Research* (pp. 803-820). Thousand Oaks, CA: Sage Publications Inc.

Wharton School of the University of Pennsylvania. (2005). Open Sesame? Or Could the Doors Slam Shut for Alibaba.com? *Knowledge@Wharton*. Retrieved June 16, 2005 from http://knowledge.wharton.upenn.edu/index.cfm?fa=viewArticle&id=1221

Wilkins, L., Swatman, P. A., & Castleman, T. (2003a). Electronic Markets and Service Delivery: Requisite Competencies for Virtual Environments. *Proceedings of the 11th European Conference on Information Systems (ECIS 2003)* [CD-ROM]. Naples: Università di Napoli Federico II.

Wilkins, L., Swatman, P. M. C., & Castleman, T. (2003b). *Electronic Markets and Service Delivery: Governance and Related Competencies in Virtual Environments*. School Working Papers - Series 2003, SWP 2003/02. School of Information Systems, Deakin University, Melbourne, Australia. Retrieved February 9, 2005 (last accessed) from http://www.deakin.edu.au/buslaw/infosys/docs/workingpapers/papers/2003_02_Wilkins.pdf

Willcocks, L. (1994). Introduction: Of Capital Importance. In L. Willcocks (Ed.), *Information Management: The Evaluation of Information Systems Investments* (pp. 1-27). London: Chapman & Hall.

Willcocks, L., & Lester, S. (1999). Introduction. Information Technology: Transformer or Sink Hole? In L. Willcocks & S. Lester (Eds.), *Beyond the IT Productivity Paradox* (pp. 1-36). Chichester: John Wiley & Sons Ltd.

Williams, R. L., & Cothrel, W. J. (Summer 2000). Four-Smart Ways to Run Online Communities. *Sloan Management Review, 41*(4), 81-91.

Williamson, O. E. (1971). The Vertical Integration of Production: Market Failure Considerations. *The American Economic Review, 61*(2), 112-123.

Williamson, O. E. (1975). *Markets and Hierarchies: Analysis and Antitrust Implications*. New York: Free Press.

Williamson, O. E. (1979). Transaction Cost Economics: The Governance of Contractual Relations. *Journal of Law and Economics, 22*(2), 233-261.

Williamson, O. E. (1985). *The Economic Institutions of Capitalism*. New York: The Free Press.

Winkler, R. (2001). Portals – The All-In-One Web Supersites: Features, Functions, Definitions, Taxonomy. *SAP Design Guild, Edition 3*. Retrieved October 7, 2003 from http://www.sapdesignguild.org/editions/edition3/portal_definition.asp

Yin, R. K. (2003). *Case Study Research: Design and Methods* (3rd ed.). Thousand Oaks: Sage Publications, Inc.

Zhu, K., & Kraemer, K. (September 2002). E-Commerce Metrics for Net-Enhanced Organizations: Assessing the Value of e-Commerce to Firm Performance in the Manufacturing Sector. *Information Systems Research, 13*(3), 275-295.

Zhuang, Y., & Lederer, A. L. (2003). An Instrument for Measuring the Business Benefits of E-Commerce Retailing. *International Journal of Electronic Commerce, 7*(3), 65-99.

Zimmerman, H.-D. (1998). Regional Electronic Marketplaces for Electronic Commerce and Beyond. *Proceedings of International Telecommunications Society ITS 1998, Stockholm, June 21-24, 1998.* Retrieved May 23, 2005 (last accessed) from http://www.businessmedia.org/modules/pub/view.php/businessmedia-51

Zott, C., Amit, R., & Donlevy, J. (2000). Strategies for Value Creation in E-Commerce: Best Practice in Europe. *European Management Journal, 18*(5), 463-475.

LIST OF REFEREED PUBLICATIONS ARISING FROM THIS RESEARCH

1. Gengatharen, D. E., & Standing, C. (2003). A Conceptual Framework to Support the Development of Government-Sponsored Community-Portal Regional Electronic Marketplaces for SMEs: A Stage Approach. *Proceedings of the 14th Australasian Conference on Information Systems (ACIS)*. (CD-ROM). Perth, Western Australia: We-B Centre, Edith Cowan University.

2. Gengatharen, D. E., & Standing, C. (2003). A Proposed Model to Evaluate the Benefits of Government-Sponsored Regional Electronic Marketplaces for SMEs: Extending the Updated DeLone & McLean IS Success Model. *Proceedings of the 4th International We-B Conference* (CD-ROM). Perth, Western Australia: We-B Centre, Edith Cowan University

3. Gengatharen, D. E., & Standing, C. (2004). Regional E-marketplaces: Towards a Unified Theoretical Framework for Assessing Facilitators and Inhibitors of Success. *Proceedings of the 12th European Conference on Information Systems. (The European IS Profession in the Global Networking Environment)* (CD-ROM). Turku, Finland: Turku School of Economics and Business Administration.

4. Gengatharen, D. E., & Standing, C. (2004). Evaluating the Benefits of Regional Electronic Marketplaces: Assessing the Quality of the REM Success Model. *Electronic Journal of Information Systems Evaluation, 7*(1), 11-20.

5. Gengatharen, D. E., & Standing, C. (2004). Regional Internet e-Marketplaces and B2B Portals for SMEs: A Review and Research Agenda. *Proceedings of the 5th International We-B (Working for e-Business) Conference: Enterprise Value from e-Business* (CD-ROM). Perth, Western Australia: School of Management Information Systems, Edith Cowan University.

6. Gengatharen, D. E., Standing, C., & Burn, J. (2004). Regional E-Marketplaces and B2B Portals for SMEs: Are Some of Them Failing Because of a Mismatch Between Motivation and Ability? *Proceedings of the 15th Australasian Conference on Information Systems (ACIS)* (CD-ROM). Tasmania: University of Tasmania.

7. Burn, J., & Gengatharen, D. E. (2004). Are Regional Electronic Marketplaces the Answer for SMEs? *Proceedings of the 2004 International Business Information Management Conference* (CD-ROM). Amman, Jordan: International Business Information Management.

8. Burn, J., Gengatharen, D. E., & Standing, C. (2005). Virtual Communities for SMEs: Implementing a Regional Electronic Marketplace. *Proceedings of the 2005 Information Resources Management Association (IRMA) International Conference* (pp. 667-670). San Diego: Idea Group Publishing.

9. Standing, C., Sims, I., Stockdale, R., Gengatharen, D. E., Standing, S., & Wassenaar, A. (2005). Can E-Marketplaces Bridge the Digital Divide? An Analysis of Two Western Australian Cases. *The Electronic Journal on Information Systems in Developing Countries, 20*(3), 1-14. Retrieved January 14, 2005 from http://www.ejisdc.org

10. Gengatharen, D. E., & Standing, C. (2005). Bridging the Digital Divide with Community Portal Regional E-Marketplaces: the Need for an Integrated Approach. *Proceedings of the International Telecommunications Society Africa-Asia-Australasia Regional Conference* (CD-ROM) Perth: Communication Economics and Electronic Markets Research Centre, Curtin University of Technology.

11. Gengatharen, D. E., & Standing, C. (2005). A Framework to Assess the Factors Affecting Success or Failure of the Implementation of Government-Supported Regional eMarketplaces for SMEs. *European Journal of Information Systems, 14*(4), 417-433.

12. Gengatharen, D. E., Standing, C., & Burn, J. (2005). Government-supported Community Portal Regional eMarketplaces for SMEs: Evidence to support a Staged Approach [Electronic Version]. *Electronic Markets, 15*(4), 405-417.

13. Gengatharen, D. E., & Standing, C. (2005). Promoting E-Commerce among SMEs through Community-Based Portals: An Analysis of Three West Australian Cases. *Proceedings of the 16th Australasian Conference on Information Systems (ACIS 2005)* (CD-ROM). Sydney: Australasian Chapter of the Association for Information Systems.

14. Gengatharen, D.E. & Standing, C. (2007). Using a Cultural Lens to Interpret the Success and Failure of Regional Internet Community Portals in Promoting e-Commerce adoption by SMEs. Proceedings of Conference on Information Management and Internet Research 2007. Joondalup: WeB Centre, Edith Cowan University.

15. Gengatharen, D.E. (2008). Interpreting the Success and Failure of Regional Internet Community Portals in Promoting E-Commerce Adoption by SMEs: a Cultural Perspective. Journal of Systems Information and Technology (forthcoming).

APPENDIX 1
LIST OF TERMS AND ABBREVIATIONS

Term	Meaning
ABS	Australian Bureau of Statistics
ARC	Australian Research Council
B2B	Business to Business
B2C	Business to Consumer
B2G	Business to Government
C2C	Consumer to Consumer
CCP	Content-Context-Process: An approach to information systems evaluation
CEO	Chief Executive Officer
CoC	Chamber of Commerce – an independent body representing the interests of member businesses within a town or region
Connect RegWa	The not for profit organisation formed to own RegWa.net
CountryWa Cooperative	The cooperative society formed to own CountryWa.com
CountryWa.com	Pseudonym for one of the portals in this study that served a rural/country region in WA
DOI	Diffusion of Innovation Theory
DTI	Department of Trade and Industry of the United Kingdom Government
ECU	Edith Cowan University
EDI	Electronic Data Interchange
G2C	Government to Consumer

GEM	Government Electronic Marketplace, the procurement e-marketplace of the WA state government
HREC	Human Research Ethics Committee of ECU
ICT	Information Communications Technology
IOIS	Inter-organisational Information System
IOR	Inter-organisational Relationships
IS	Information Systems
ISP	Internet Service Provider
IT	Information Technology
ITOL	Information Technology OnLine Programme, a funding programme of the Australian federal Government to encourage collaborative e-commerce projects especially for SMEs
LG 1	Local Government 1, the local government of Town 1 and one of the owners of TwinTowns.com
LG 2	Local Government 2, the local government of Town 2 and one of the owners of TwinTowns.com
N*Vivo	A code-based theory-building computer programme based on a code-and-retrieve model for analysing text
NFPO	Not for Profit Organisation
NOIE	National Office for the Information Economy
NTN	Net-working The Nation, a funding initiative by the Australian Federal Government for regional/rural projects to encourage uptake of ICT
OECD	Organisation for Economic Co-operation and Development
Regional Internet Trading Platform	A central point on the Internet where a number of sellers are present to provide price and product information to a number of buyers, be they consumers, other businesses or the government, in an effort to secure sales. Sellers usually are from a geographically designated area.
RegWa.net	Pseudonym for one of the portals in this study that served a rural/country region in WA

REM	Regional Electronic Marketplace
Research Industry Partner	The Not for Profit Organisation formed to own TwinTowns.com and the industry funding partner of the ARC research grant
RETFC	Regional Electronic Trade Facilitation Centre – a vertical B2B portal in horticulture in Shepparton, Victoria, Australia
RFQ	Request for Proposal
SME	Small and Medium Enterprises
TAM	Technology Acceptance Model
TPB	Theory of Planned Behaviour
TRA	Theory of Reasoned Action
Trading Platform Success Metrics	Measures of key attributes that are used to determine the success of a trading platform
Trading Platform Success Model	An evaluation framework developed as part of this research to evaluate the success of regional Internet trading platforms
TwinTowns.com	Pseudonym for the portal in this study that served a metropolitan region in WA
UTAUT	Unified Theory of Acceptance and Use of Technology
WA	Western Australia, a state in Australia

APPENDIX 2

INFORMATION LETTER AND INFORMED CONSENT FORM (PORTAL
OWNERS)

Points to Note:

- The documents here were issued to the principal operating officer of TwinTowns.com and involve a list of preliminary questions.

- The letter and consent form for other owners of TwinTowns.com do not make reference to the preliminary questions.

- There was no second round of interviewing due to the closure of the portal

- Letters and consent forms to the owners of RegWa.net and Country.Wa.com have no reference to two rounds of interviews.

Dear

I am undertaking an investigation to assess the success of regional Internet trading platforms and the benefits that they can provide to all parties involved, as part of my studies for a PhD requirement. The title of the study is "Government-Supported Regional Internet Trading Platforms for SMEs: Assessing Success and Evaluating Benefits". For this study, I need to obtain information from the websites of the trading platforms, historical documents and from some of the trading platform participants regarding their experiences, activities and opinions of the success of the platform.

The reason for this letter is to invite you to participate in this study. The study will entail collecting some data from you through a preliminary questionnaire and two face-to-face interviews with you over a six month to one-year period. The data collection procedure is as follows:

1. A preliminary schedule of questions will be sent to you (see schedule of questions attached). This set of questions will be completed and returned to me prior to the first interview and may be discussed during the interview.

2. The face-to-face interview will take a maximum of one hour, during which further questions will be discussed in relation to a) the preliminary schedule of questions, b) other information collected via the Internet or publicly available historical documents and c) your opinions on areas like the services offered by the REM and the benefits from participation. I will take notes during the interview, which will be audiotaped. You may choose not to answer some of the questions and are free to withdraw your participation at any time if you wish. The time and place of the interview is subject to your convenience. I will contact you on this later.

3. Upon transcribing the interview, the audio tape will be erased. You will then be sent the transcript to confirm that it is a true account of the interview.

4. The procedure in 1, 2 and 3 above will be repeated after a period of six months to a year to determine if there has been any change in the nature of your participation and views on the trading platform.

Any information that you give to me whether in writing, by e-mail or verbally, will be kept strictly confidential and will only be used for the purpose of the project. After the study is completed, you will also receive a copy of the published research findings, if you wish, when they become available. Unless otherwise specifically approved by you, at no time will you, any individual or company be identified by name. Please note that should you decide not to participate in this study, your current position will in no way be prejudiced by your refusal to do so.

The potential benefits of the study will be the definition of factors that make Internet trading platforms for SMEs successful, in terms of regional economic development and business community inter-relationships, and the development of a tool to evaluate the benefits of this type of e-marketplace for all types of participants concerned.

Please keep this letter for your information and kindly return the completed Preliminary Schedule of Questions and consent form in the self-addressed envelope provided. Any questions concerning the project entitled "Government-Supported Regional Internet Trading Platforms for SMEs: Assessing Success and Evaluating Benefits", can be directed to:

Mrs Denise E Gengatharen

PhD Candidate

School of Management Information Systems

Faculty of Business and Public Management

Edith Cowan University

Joondalup Drive,

Joondalup, Western Australia 6027.

E-mail: d.gengatharen@ecu.edu.au

Telephone: +61 8 6304 5335

Facsimile: +61 8 6304 5988

If you have any concerns about the project or would like to talk to an independent person, you may contact:

Research Ethics Officer

Edith Cowan University

Joondalup, Western Australia 6027.

E-mail:research.ethics@ecu.edu.au

Telephone: +61 8 6304 2170

Your help in making this study possible is greatly appreciated.

Thank you,

Denise E Gengatharen

Preliminary Questions relating to demographics and statistics

---

Q1.   When was the idea of the REM first conceived?

Q2.   Who are the stakeholders?

Q3.   Do the stakeholders participate in the REM?

Q4.   What was the size of the project team?

Q5.   What were the working backgrounds and experience of the project team?

Q6.   Who was responsible for the development of the REM software?

      If vendors, how were the vendors chosen?

Q7.   Who is responsible for the management of the REM?

Q8.   What was the total cost of funding the REM?

Q9.   What were the sources of funding and individual amounts? (eg. from stakeholders, local government, Federal government grants).

Q10. What are the ongoing operating costs of the REM?

Q11. What is the existing income of the REM (breakdown according to type -eg. membership, sponsorship, transaction fees, etc.)?

Q12. What is the profile of SMEs in the region? (e.g. predominantly manufacturing, retail, etc.)

Q13. How many registered participants does the REM have at the moment?

Q14. What is the volume of transactions created on the REM on a monthly basis?

Q15. What is the number of 'hits' or visits to the REM homepage in a month?

Q16.   What sort of value-added services does the REM provide? (e.g. access to preferred ISPs, arrangements for finance, arrangements for transport, insurance services, training etc.)

Q17.   Are there any networks within the REM (if yes, types)?

Q18.   What sort of marketing plan did the REM have for building liquidity?

PARTICIPANT CONSENT FORM

Project Title: Government-Supported Regional Internet Trading Platforms for SMEs: Assessing Success and Evaluating Benefits

(Please fill in the form below and return it in the self-addressed envelope provided.)

I _____

(The participant's full name)

have been informed about all aspects of the above research project and any questions I have asked have been answered to my satisfaction.

I agree to participate in this activity, realising that I may withdraw at any time. I also understand that at any time I can refrain from answering any question(s) that I feel may jeopardise my (or my company's) position.

I agree that the research data gathered for this study may be published, provided I (and any organisation or employer that I am associated with) am not identifiable by name / understanding that I may be identified (delete whichever is not applicable).

I understand that I will be required to complete a questionnaire and be interviewed twice and that the interviews will be audio recorded. I also understand that the recording will be erased once the interviews are transcribed and I will be asked to confirm that the transcripts are true representations of the interviews. If I wish, the interviews can also be done without the audio recording and be carried on "off-the-record".

I hereby agree to take part in the above-named study.

Participant: _____ Date: _____

Investigator:_____ Date: _____

INTERVIEW SCHEDULE (PORTAL OWNER)

Points to Note:

- Where the principal operating officer was the participant, the interview schedule included the preliminary schedule of questions referred to in Appendix 2, with details filled in either by responses from the officers or by information from other documentation (e.g. government reports and the portal website). These points were raised for discussion during the interview if there was a need for clarification or further discussion.

GOVERNMENT-SUPPORTED REGIONAL INTERNET-TRADING PLATFORMS FOR SMEs: ASSESSING SUCCESS AND EVALUATING BENEFITS

Interview Schedule   Date:

Comments on Setting:

Name of Interviewee:

E-mail address:

Position:

Discussion/ Opinion questions

Q1.   What was the initial motive behind the creation of the trading platform (eg. to encourage SME e-commerce uptake, regional development, to build knowledge community, not-for-profit venture etc.)?

Q2.   Has/have that motive/s changed in any way?

Q3.   What is your opinion of the quality of the content on the trading platform? (e.g. in terms of accuracy, currency, relevance, timeliness, etc.)

Q4.   What is your opinion of the quality of the trading platform system? (Eg. in terms of reliability, response, ease of use, convenience, integration with participants' systems etc.)

Q5.   What is your opinion of the quality of the value-added services provided by the trading platform? (Eg. trust, feedback mechanisms, privacy)

Q6.   In your opinion are users happy with the governance of the trading platform?

Q7.   In your opinion, what are the benefits of the trading platform to:

- Yourselves

- SMEs

- Other stakeholders (advertisers, value-added service providers)

- The Region?

Q8.   Do you think the trading platform has been successful? Why?

Q9.   How do you think the trading platform can be more successful?

Q10. Is there anything else you may wish to mention regarding your experience with the trading platform?

INFORMATION LETTER AND CONSENT FORM (SMES)

Points to note:

- The documents included here are the original information letters and consent forms sent to SMEs participating in TwinTowns.com, hence they make reference to two rounds of interviews. Due to the closure of the portal, only one round of interviews was conducted.

- The documents for SME participants in RegWa.net referred to only one interview.

- For participants interviewed by telephone, the letter was read out to them and their consent recorded

---

INFORMATION LETTER TO SME PARTICIPANTS

Dear

I am undertaking an investigation to assess the success of government-sponsored regional Internet Trading platforms and the benefits that they can provide to all parties involved, as part of my studies for a PhD requirement. The title of the study is "Government-Supported Regional Internet Trading Platforms for SMEs: Assessing Success and Evaluating Benefits". For this study, I need to obtain information from the websites of the trading platforms, historical documents and from some of the participants regarding their experiences, activities and opinions of the success of the platform.

The reason for this letter is to invite you to participate in this study. The study will entail collecting some data from you through a preliminary questionnaire and two face-to-face interviews with you over a six month to one-year period. The data collection procedure is as follows:

1.   A preliminary schedule of questions will be sent to you (see schedule of questions attached). This set of questions will be completed and returned to me prior to the first interview and may be discussed during the interview.

2.   The face-to-face interview will take a maximum of one hour, during which further questions will be discussed in relation to a) the preliminary schedule of questions, b) other information collected via the Internet or publicly available historical documents and c) your opinions on areas like the services offered by the trading platform and the benefits from participation. I will take notes during the interview, which will be audiotaped. You may choose not to answer some of the questions and are free to withdraw your participation at any time if you wish. The time and place of the interview is subject to your convenience. I will contact you on this later.

3.   Upon transcribing the interview, the audio tape will be erased. You will then be sent the transcript to confirm that it is a true account of the interview.

4.   The procedure in 1, 2 and 3 above will be repeated after a period of six months to a year to determine if there has been any change in the nature of your participation on the platform.

Any information that you give to me whether in writing, by e-mail or verbally, will be kept strictly confidential and will only be used for the purpose of the project. After the study is completed, you will also receive a copy of the published research findings, if you wish, when they become available. Unless otherwise specifically approved by you, at no time will you, any individual or company be identified by name. Please note that should you decide not to participate in this study, your current position will in no way be prejudiced by your refusal to do so.

The potential benefits of the study will be the definition of factors that make trading platforms successful, in terms of regional economic development and business community inter-relationships, and the development of a tool to evaluate the benefits of this type of e-marketplace for all types of participants concerned.

Please keep this letter for your information and kindly return the completed Preliminary Schedule of Questions and consent form in the self-addressed envelope provided. Any questions concerning the project entitled "Government-Supported Regional Internet Trading Platforms for SMEs: Assessing Success and Evaluating Benefits", can be directed to:

Mrs Denise E Gengatharen

PhD Candidate

School of Management Information Systems

Faculty of Business and Public Management

Edith Cowan University

Joondalup Drive,

Joondalup, Western Australia 6027.

E-mail:d.gengatharen@ecu.edu.au

Telephone: +61 8 9400 5335

Facsimile: +61 8 6304 5988

If you have any concerns about the project or would like to talk to an independent person, you may contact:

Research Ethics Officer

Edith Cowan University

Joondalup, Western Australia 6027.

E-mail:research.ethics@ecu.edu.au

Telephone: 61 8 6304 2170

Your help in making this study possible is greatly appreciated.

Thank you,

Denise E Gengatharen

Preliminary Schedule of Questions (SME Participants)

(The questions may be discussed during the interview).

1.   What is the nature of business of the company and when was it incorporated?

2.   Who (in the company) is responsible for daily trading on the REM?

       (Were they also involved in the decision to participate)?

3.   What is their technical background?

4.   What is the size of the company?

       Number of employees:

       Annual turnover:

5.   Who was responsible for the decision to participate in the REM and when did you join?

6.   Who in the company was responsible for setting up the technical arrangements to trade on the REM?

7.   What was the total set up cost?

8.   What is the ongoing cost of participating in the REM?

9.   What does your company do (intend to do) on the REM?

           Buy?

Sell?

Look for Information?

Participate in online networks?

10. What is the volume of the company's business going through the REM on a monthly basis?

11. Do you participate in any other e-markets?

12. Does your company currently do any of the following on-line?

Buy/Procure

Sell

Advertise

Look for Information

PARTICIPANT CONSENT FORM

Project Title: Government-Supported Regional Internet Trading Platforms for SMEs: Assessing Success and Evaluating Benefits

(Please fill in the form below and return it in the self-addressed envelope provided.)

I _____

(The participant's full name)

have been informed about all aspects of the above research project and any questions I have asked have been answered to my satisfaction.

I agree to participate in this activity, realising that I may withdraw at any time. I also understand that at any time I can refrain from answering any question(s) that I feel may jeopardise my (or my company's) position.

I agree that the research data gathered for this study may be published, provided I (and any organisation or employer that I am associated with) am not identifiable by name / understanding that I may be identified (delete whichever is not applicable).

I understand that I will be required to complete a questionnaire and be interviewed twice and that the interviews will be audio recorded. I also understand that the recording will be erased once the interviews are transcribed and I will be asked to confirm that the transcripts are true representations of the interviews. If I wish, the interviews can also be done without the audio recording and be carried on "off-the-record".

I hereby agree to take part in the above-named study.

Participant: _____ Date: _____

Investigator:_____ Date: _____

GOVERNMENT-SUPPORTED REGIONAL INTERNET TRADING PLATFORMS
FOR SMES: ASSESSING SUCCESS AND EVALUATING BENEFITS

Interview Schedule

SME/Participant Interview   Date:

Comments on Setting:

Name of Company:

Position in company:

Questions relating to demographics and statistics

(Where possible, these questions will be distributed to participants prior to the interview
and the information collected back. The questions will then be discussed during the
interview if any clarification is necessary).

Q1.   What is the nature of business of the company & when was it incorporated?

Q2.   Who (in the company) is responsible for daily trading on the REM?

        (Were they also involved in the decision to participate)?

Q3.   What is their technical background?

Q4.   What is the size of the company?

Number of employees:

Annual turnover:

Q5. Who was responsible for the decision to participate in the REM & when did you join?

Q6. Who in the company was responsible for setting up the technical arrangements to trade on the REM?

Q7. What was the total set up cost?

Q8. What is the ongoing cost of participating in the REM?

Q9. What does your company do (intend to do) on the REM?

Buy?

Sell?

Look for Information?

Participate in online networks?

Q10. What is the volume of the company's business going through the REM on a monthly basis?

Q11. Do you participate in any other e-markets?

Q12. Does your company currently do any of the following on-line?

. Buy/Procure

. Sell

. Advertise

. Look for Information

Discussion/ Opinion questions

Q13. To what extent is your back office system integrated with your transactions on the REM?

Q14. What are the IT systems currently used in the business?

Q15. What motivated you to participate in the REM?

Q16. How has participation in the REM benefited your company?

Increased business?

Cost savings?

Other benefits?

Q17. What sort of training did you receive before participating in the REM?

Q18. What sort of value-added services does the REM provide? (e.g. access to preferred ISPs, arrangements for finance, arrangements for transport, insurance services, training etc.)

Q19. Does your company utilise any of these services? If yes, which services?

Q20. What is your opinion of the quality of the content on the REM?

Accuracy

Currency

Relevance

Timeliness

Security

Others

Q21. What is your opinion of the quality of the REM system?

Reliability

Response time

Ease of use

Convenience of Accessibility

Market Reach

Other

Q22. How satisfied are you with the REM?

Offerings/Features/Services

Governance

Trust

Q23. In your opinion is the REM a success?

Q24. How do you think the REM can be improved?

Q25 Is there anything else you would like to mention?

LIST OF TABLES

LIST OF FIGURES

www.ingramcontent.com/pod-product-compliance
Lightning Source LLC
Chambersburg PA
CBHW071404050326
40689CB00010B/1753